The President Shall Nominate

The President Shall Nominate

How Congress Trumps Executive Power

Mitchel A. Sollenberger

 University Press of Kansas

© 2008 by the University Press of Kansas
All rights reserved

Published by the University Press of Kansas (Lawrence, Kansas 66045), which was organized by the Kansas Board of Regents and is operated and funded by Emporia State University, Fort Hays State University, Kansas State University, Pittsburg State University, the University of Kansas, and Wichita State University

Library of Congress Cataloging-in-Publication Data

Sollenberger, Mitchel A.
  The president shall nominate : how Congress trumps executive power / Mitchel A. Sollenberger.
     p. cm.
  Includes bibliographical references and index.
  ISBN 978-0-7006-1576-6 (cloth : alk. paper)
  1. Executive power—United States. 2. Nominations for office—United States. 3. United States. Congress. Senate. 4. Legislative power—United States. 5. Civil service reform—United States—History. 6. Presidents—United States—History. 7. United States—Officials and employees—Selection and appointment—History. 8. Representative government and representation—United States. I. Title.
  KF5050.S65 2008
  328.73′07455—dc22   2007041708

British Library Cataloguing-in-Publication Data is available.

Printed in the United States of America

10 9 8 7 6 5 4 3 2 1

The paper used in this publication is recycled and contains 50 percent postconsumer waste. It is acid free and meets the minimum requirements of the American National Standard for Permanence of Paper for Printed Library Materials Z39.48–1992.

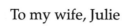
To my wife, Julie

In that sense, the Recommendations Clause is directly analogous to the power to nominate judges and Executive Branch officials. In both cases, a transfer of a proposal to Congress is envisioned, at which point Congress has a constitutionally authorized role. But the process of formulating that proposal is granted exclusively to the President and is beyond Congress's power. Indeed, Congress's ability to address the nominee or recommendation directly renders Congressional intrusion into the pre-nomination or pre-recommendation process unnecessary as well as unconstitutional.

> —Brief for the Department of Justice, *Cheney v. United States District Court for the District of Columbia* (2004)

The actual art of governing under our Constitution does not and cannot conform to judicial definitions of the power of any of its branches based on isolated clauses or even single Articles torn from context. While the Constitution diffuses power the better to secure liberty, it also contemplates that practice will integrate the dispersed powers into a workable government. It enjoins upon its branches separateness but interdependence, autonomy but reciprocity. Presidential powers are not fixed but fluctuate, depending upon their disjunction or conjunction with those of Congress.

> —Supreme Court Associate Justice Robert H. Jackson, *Youngstown Sheet & Tube Co. v. Sawyer* (1952)

Contents

Acknowledgments   xiii

Introduction   1

    The Pre-nomination Process   3

    Additional Concerns of This Study   3

    Existing Research   5

    Organization of This Book   6

Chapter 1. Constitutional Principles   8

    Continental Congress   8

    State Constitutions   12

    Constitutional Convention   13

    State Ratification Conventions   16

    The *Federalist Papers*   19

    Correspondence between John Adams and
    Roger Sherman   20

Chapter 2. Establishing the Pre-nomination Process (1789–1829)   22

    Senatorial Courtesy   23

    The Rejection of Benjamin Fishbourn   24

    James Iredell and the Consent of Senator Benjamin
    Hawkins   30

    William Maclay and Home-State Support   30

    George Washington (1789–1797)   31

    John Adams (1797–1801)   33

    Thomas Jefferson (1801–1809)   35

James Madison (1809–1817)   37

James Monroe (1817–1825)   39

John Quincy Adams (1825–1829)   43

Chapter 3. The Spoils Era I (1829–1845)   47

Andrew Jackson (1829–1837)   47

Martin Van Buren (1837–1841)   55

William Henry Harrison (1841)   59

John Tyler (1841–1845)   62

Chapter 4. The Spoils Era II (1845–1869)   67

James K. Polk (1845–1849)   68

Zachary Taylor (1849–1850)   71

Millard Fillmore (1850–1853)   72

Franklin Pierce (1853–1857)   73

James Buchanan (1857–1861)   76

Abraham Lincoln (1861–1865)   78

Andrew Johnson (1865–1869)   80

Chapter 5. Birth of Civil Service Reform (1869–1881)   86

Ulysses S. Grant (1869–1877)   86

Rutherford B. Hayes (1877–1881)   94

James A. Garfield (1881)   101

Chapter 6. The Pendleton Act: Patchwork Reform (1881–1897)   105

Chester A. Arthur (1881–1885)   105

Grover Cleveland (1885–1889)   111

Benjamin Harrison (1889–1893)   118

Grover Cleveland (1893–1897)   122

Chapter 7. McKinley to Ford: The Tradition Continues (1897–1977)   126

William McKinley (1897–1901), Theodore Roosevelt (1901–1909), and William Howard Taft (1909–1913)   126

Woodrow Wilson (1913–1921)   131

Warren G. Harding (1921–1923), Calvin Coolidge

(1923–1929), and Herbert Hoover (1929–1933)   132

Franklin D. Roosevelt (1933–1945)   135

Harry S Truman (1945–1953)   137

Dwight D. Eisenhower (1953–1961)   138

John F. Kennedy (1961–1963) and Lyndon B. Johnson
(1963–1969)   139

Richard M. Nixon (1969–1974)   142

Gerald R. Ford (1974–1977)   145

Chapter 8. Carter to Bush II: A Lasting Legacy (1977–2007)   147

Jimmy Carter (1977–1981)   147

Ronald Reagan (1981–1989)   150

George H. W. Bush (1989–1993)   153

William J. Clinton (1993–2001)   156

George W. Bush (2001–2007)   160

Chapter 9. Analysis and Conclusions   169

Republicanism and Constitutional Legitimacy   170

The Practical Duty to Consult   171

Institutional and Political Influences   171

Participation in the Pre-nomination Process   173

Failure to Consult: Congressional Responses   174

Congressional Specification of Qualifications   176

Nonstatutory Limits to the President's Appointment
Power   180

Reformers Seeking Nonpolitical Remedies   181

Rise of the Unitary Executive School   182

Interpretive Value of Originalism and Textualism   185

Final Remarks   189

Notes   191

Bibliography   269

Index   293

Acknowledgments

There are a number of people whom I wish to acknowledge for their assistance, both big and small, in the development of this book. I would like first to thank Fairfield University and Catholic University professors Harold Forsythe, Donald Greenberg, Thomas Regan, and Phil Henderson who did much to assist in my intellectual development. Many of the thoughts and ideas expressed in the following pages are a direct result of the education I received from them and others. Much of this book grew out of my doctoral dissertation which would not have been possible without the contributions and encouragement from my committee members Dennis Coyle, Louis Fisher, Mark J. Rozell, and John Kenneth White.

As to the development of my manuscript, I would like to express my appreciation to Eleanor D. Acheson, Michael J. Egan, and David G. Leitch who served in high positions with the Justice Department and the White House and assisted in clarifying aspects of the pre-nomination process for recent administrations. In addition, I am grateful to my former colleagues Kevin Kosar, Walter Oleszek, Harold Relyea, Steve Rutkus, and others at the Congressional Research Service who assisted in varying degrees in this book's development. They are all great public servants who do a wonderful job serving Congress. A special thanks goes to my former colleague, mentor, and friend, Louis Fisher, who helped me develop and shape this book's thesis; offered me many hours of advice, editing support, and thoughtful discussion. My attempt to present fair and balanced judgments on the various issues tackled in this book owes much to the example that he has set. To him I owe a special debt.

I want to also thank my family, especially my parents, who have during my lifetime provided me with the love, joy, and support to enable my dreams. Finally, I would like to give my biggest praise and thanks to my wife, Julie, who has always been helpful and supportive during the development of this book. She has had to sacrifice and put up with many long hours of research and writing. I thank her deeply.

The President Shall Nominate

Introduction

When people come together to organize a community, they must determine how public policy and other decisions are to be exercised. In the United States, the Constitution establishes a federal government centered on express and implied powers. That system, based on republican principles, derives its powers from the consent of the governed and functions through representatives of the people. Although the basic principles of a republican form of government are simple enough, the U.S. Constitution fails to specify with any clarity how various constitutional actors should perform their duties. The question left open is: how does a written constitution work in a republican form of government?

Certainly, the U.S. Constitution provides details about some important concerns. We know that sovereignty rests with the people and that the representative function is placed in the hands of two institutions: Congress and the presidency. Specific powers are given to each branch of government, but the Constitution is silent as to how a number of these powers should operate. Some clauses are rather straightforward. For instance, age requirements are clear and can be followed without difficulty. Structural guidelines calling for the Senate to be composed of "two Senators from each State" are equally direct. Broader, more ambiguous terms can be more trying. The Impeachment Clause is a prime example of the Constitution granting a power without detailing its operation. Should a defendant be given due process rights, and if so, to what extent? What rules of evidence should apply in the Senate? Do all senators have to attend and vote? Such questions were left to Congress to answer.

In addition to affecting how government functions, power relationships influence how the legislative and executive branches work together. In the case of Congress and the president, each usually has its own institutional concerns or goals when it comes to sharing power. At times, this can create conflict. Resolution can occur only if one side defers to the other or if both sides agree on some type of joint exercise of power. This book examines the concept of shared powers and addresses the question of how the nomination process should operate in a republican form of government. For instance, a president may exercise a power that he believes is his alone to control, but republican principles of majority rule and minority rights embodied in the legislative branch influence how he goes about that task. Such principles were important to the founders, who envisioned a government with limited power. Democratic participation by lawmakers is essential because they represent the people and are the people's voice on important policy matters at the national level. This principle was announced in the First Congress by a number of individuals. For instance, Congressman James Jackson declared: "I consider [the president and Congress] as checks upon each other, to prevent the abuse of either; and it is in this way the liberties of the people are secured. I appeal for the truth of this sentiment to the writings of Publius. He has proved that the Senate is a check upon the Executive, for the express purpose of securing the freedom of the people."[1]

Governmental functions must conform to both republican values and constitutional requirements. One of the most important of these functions is the staffing of the government. The Constitution assigns the duty to appoint "principal" officers to the president and the Senate.[2] It states that the president "shall nominate, and by and with the Advice and Consent of the Senate, shall appoint," thus raising the question of power sharing. Although a president may choose to nominate without congressional interference, his power can be restrained by the Senate, an institution that embodies democratic principles and possesses advice-and-consent authority. As the constitutionally mandated and elected representatives of the people, senators (and even representatives) have a right and a sovereign authority to affect various power arrangements and policymaking decisions. That is certainly the case with appointments. Both branches must work together through a process of consultation and compromise.

A republican form of government requires cross-branch, cooperative mechanisms. Collaboration during the appointment process is no different from other power-sharing arrangements. Recent debates center around whether the Senate is obligated to hold floor votes on all judicial nominations.[3] President George W. Bush declared that his nominations of federal judges deserved full Senate votes, but Senate Democrats countered that no such constitutional obligation exists. This controversy highlights the duties of the two branches. How do the constitutional responsibilities of a president influence Congress, and vice versa?

My study analyzes the period before a nomination is officially made, or what I term the pre-nomination process. How does that process operate in a constitutional republic? How should it operate? This early stage is often overlooked in studies of the appointment process, and my analysis offers a look into the various constitutional concerns and their relationship to republican principles.

The Pre-nomination Process

Functionally, the pre-nomination process starts once a person resigns, announces his or her retirement, or dies in office (or when Congress creates a new position). The president and his staff consider and reflect on different factors when making a selection, such as the character or quality of a nominee. A president may be familiar with a potential candidate for office, but it is more likely that the person is an utter stranger. In this case, the president resorts to informal arrangements with outside advisers. Although many people are consulted, members of Congress take the lead in offering advice to a president, based on both branches' interpretation of the Appointments Clause. Benjamin Goodhue noted in the First Congress that this clause was perfectly reasonable and "wise." James Madison agreed and articulated the practical reasons for interbranch cooperation in appointments: "But why, it may be asked, was the Senate joined with the President in appointing to office, if they have no responsibility? I answer, merely for the sake of advising, being supposed, from their nature, better acquainted with the characters of the candidates than an individual." Nearly a month later, Goodhue supported Madison's point, declaring that "it is more probable that the Senate may be better acquainted with the characters of the officers that are nominated than the President himself."[4]

Over time, an unwritten agreement has been instituted whereby presidents consult with senators from their own political party (and sometimes from the opposing party) about appointments in the senators' home states. If the two senators from a state are not in political agreement with the administration, the state's party leader is consulted (usually the most senior House member or the state party chairperson or governor). For appointments that are considered local in nature, the district representative usually has the primary say on who is nominated. Once consultation has occurred and the president has made his decision, the nomination is sent to the Senate. This step concludes the pre-nomination process.

Additional Concerns of This Study

Studying the pre-nomination process is useful from a power-sharing and republican principles perspective, but there are other important issues to address. For instance, I also examine which branch has the last word on the meaning of the Constitution, the operation of express and implied powers, the interpretive value of originalism and textualism, and the scope of presidential authority.

Is the judicial branch the final authority on constitutional disputes? Many people believe that it is. As New York governor Charles Evans

Hughes once declared: "We are under a Constitution, but the Constitution is what the judges say it is."[5] This is a superficial understanding. Congress and the president have a substantial impact on how various constitutional provisions are exercised. A Supreme Court ruling does not necessarily preclude the other two branches from acting. For instance, in *INS v. Chadha*,[6] the Supreme Court held that legislative vetoes were unconstitutional; nevertheless, the executive and legislative branches have continued to abide by committee vetoes with regard to implementing various policy goals.[7] In addition, many key questions of policy and power are never addressed by the judicial branch. Often, Congress and the president make the ultimate decisions on a variety of issues. In the case of the pre-nomination process, the judiciary is excluded because the process preceding a nomination is not the subject of litigation, and it probably never will be. As a consequence, the interpretation of this part of the Constitution comes not from case law but from political practice.

Second, this study examines how government functions under the Constitution. Although many powers of the federal government are well defined by the Constitution, other express and even implied powers often enter the equation. For instance, Article II states that the president "shall nominate," which may lead to the conclusion that this power is solely his to use. Taking a strict separation-of-powers view, that is precisely what it means. However, in a republican form of government, the legislative and executive branches are free to interpret the Appointments Clause in any way they find appropriate. Looking at this issue in a more practical light, if a president unilaterally selected a nominee, the Senate could just as quickly and easily reject (or ignore) his nomination. In that case, neither branch is better off. Through a historical examination of the pre-nomination process and an analysis of the various constitutional and republican principles involved, one can understand that political realities often negate fixed, doctrinaire positions.

Third, I conclude that originalism and textualism are not overriding values in constitutional interpretation, at least in the appointment process.[8] Some presidents have tried to use the plain meaning of the Constitution to ensure little, if any, congressional involvement in the selection of nominees, but they inevitably discover that a broader interpretation that includes Congress in the process is necessary. Supreme Court Justice Felix Frankfurter once articulated this view: "Deeply embedded traditional ways of conducting government cannot supplant the Constitution or legislation, but they give meaning to the words of a text or supply them. It is an inadmissibly narrow conception of American constitutional law to confine it to the words of the Constitution and to disregard the gloss which life has written upon them."[9] That understanding is nowhere more evident than with the Appointments Clause. A president may claim an exclusive authority, but practice will win out.

Guidelines and standards must be devised to carry out the provisions of the Appointments Clause, and republican principles encourage Congress and the president to do just that. Only through repeated use of a power can the branches discover effective ways of implementing the Appointments Clause. As James Madison wrote, "Ambition must be made to counteract ambition."[10] The competing ambitions of Congress and the president produce a political dialogue about procedural and policy issues, resulting in appropriate guidelines for conducting governmental affairs.

My research also reveals the limitations of the unitary executive school. Many scholars believe that all executive powers are centered in the president and subject to his plenary control.[11] At a June 2006 Senate Judiciary Committee hearing on presidential signing statements, Deputy Assistant Attorney General Michelle E. Boardman argued that "Presidents commonly raise a concern when bills seem to restrict the President's ability to appoint officers." She proceeded to explain that Presidents George W. Bush and Bill Clinton had treated any congressional limitations on their nominating power as advisory or suggestive, not dispositive. As such, Boardman claimed, "the Appointments Clause . . . does not permit such restrictions to be imposed upon the President's power of appointment."[12]

Executive-centered control of the pre-nomination process may be of some interest in theory, but it has never worked in practice. Informally, Congress has involved itself in restricting presidential nominations since the founding of the nation (see chapter 2). Even formally, significant limitations have always been placed on the president. Congress eventually created the Civil Service Commission (now the Office of Personnel Management) to formalize some of these accommodations (see chapter 6). More than 200 years of political practice belie the idea that the president is the only recognized actor in the pre-nomination process. The unitary executive school does not take into account the practical accommodations entered into by both branches and how those agreements promote republican government.

Existing Research

Although ample and detailed attention has been paid to the process of making federal appointments, analysis of the pre-nomination process has been lacking. Many studies explain how the Appointments Clause has been implemented at the Senate level but give little scrutiny to the pre-nomination process. This scholarship generally covers only the public record: newspaper coverage of interest-group activity, floor speeches of senators, presidential statements, and congressional hearings. This book explores the private record that precedes a nomination, including informal contacts and letters from lawmakers to presidents.[13] Some of this material can be found in the published papers of presidents and other public figures; however, many letters and other written works are still unpublished and can be discovered only through archival research. The two most useful collections are the National Archives and Records Administration and the Manuscript Reading Room in the Library of Congress.

Despite the lack of detailed accounts of the pre-nomination process, there are several helpful resources for those interested in researching the topic of presidential appointments. A groundbreaking and detailed study of Supreme Court appointments appears in Henry J. Abraham's book *Justices, Presidents, and Senators*.[14] Abraham considers the consultation side of the appointment and confirmation process, and he covers every Supreme Court nomination to the date of publication. His is the most comprehensive examination of how the pre-nomination process functions for Supreme Court appointments.

Although additional studies have addressed other types of appointments, their focus has usually been limited to one or two contemporary presidents.[15] An exception is a 1945 article by Dorothy Ganfield Fowler, who examined the pre-nomination process from George Washington to Franklin D. Roosevelt.[16] Her work offered many insights, but it also skipped over several administrations and presented only a limited review of the presidencies that were covered. Another scholar who has done important research on pre-nomination issues is Sheldon Goldman. His book *Picking Federal Judges* covers every modern president from Franklin D. Roosevelt to Ronald Reagan.[17] Goldman provides detailed accounts of each administration, but his primary focus is on the types of candidates selected (e.g., sex, race, and education of the nominees), not on the pre-nomination interactions between the presidents and members of Congress.

Finally, two classic studies must be credited: a 1938 book, *The Senate of the United States,* by George H. Haynes, and a 1953 work, *The Advice and Consent of the Senate,* by Joseph P. Harris.[18] Both scholars interweave Senate traditions and customs into the larger context of executive-legislative relations. These are foundational studies that ought to be considered before undertaking further research into the Appointments Clause.

Organization of This Book

The first chapter covers the early republic, when state and national governments were moving toward a shared philosophy of making appointments. Through their experience at both the state and national levels, the framers of the Constitution developed practical methods of selecting public officers. Chapter 2 begins with a discussion of the concept of "senatorial courtesy" and its impact on the operation of the pre-nomination process in republican government; it then covers the presidential appointment history from George Washington to John Quincy Adams.

Chapters 3 and 4 examine the shared-power system of making appointments that existed through the 1840s and then go on to recount the beginning of the "spoils era." Chapters 5 and 6 detail the rise and fall of the so-called era of congressional dominance over the appointment power. This period gave way to the civil service reform movement and passage of the 1883 Pendleton Act, which helped bring balance to the pre-nomination process. Chapters 7 and 8 examine the continuing tradition of cooperation between the branches during the twentieth and twenty-first centuries, through the presidency of George W. Bush. In chapter 8, I also discuss the recent controversy over the filibuster "nuclear option" and the Gang of Fourteen compromise that resolved the crisis. A concluding chapter summarizes my findings.

Chapter One

Constitutional Principles

The Constitution is silent about how the pre-nomination process should function. Article II, Section 2, provides that the president "shall nominate, and by and with the Advice and Consent of the Senate, shall appoint Ambassadors, other public Ministers and Consuls, Judges of the supreme Court, and all other Officers of the United States, whose Appointments are not herein otherwise provided for, and which shall be established by Law." Does the Senate's advice and consent role imply any involvement beyond merely voting on presidential appointments?

To better understand the interbranch dynamics between the president and members of Congress when considering appointments, one must look to the history behind the Appointments Clause. The delegates to the Constitutional Convention did not come up with their various proposals out of thin air. Service in the Continental Congress or the state governments gave them the experience necessary to make practical choices when it came to constitution making. This chapter provides a history of governmental experiences at the national and state levels during the Revolutionary period. By examining this period, one can comprehend events that gave shape to the Appointments Clause and started the movement toward a governing system with separate branches sharing the appointment power.

Continental Congress

Once independence was declared, the first national governing body for the thirteen states was the Continental Congress. In terms of structure, there was a president, but he was merely the presiding officer of Congress and had little independent power. For the most part, his duties consisted of looking "after certain official correspondence" and entertaining "Americans and foreigners of distinction."[1] The president was a member of Congress, which was a unicameral legislative body with no distinct executive departments and no independent judiciary. All legislative and executive duties were carried out by Congress unless otherwise provided.[2] Despite this concentration of power, the Continental Congress was not considered the supreme governing body for the entire nation; it was more a tool to bring the colonies together to address one common problem: relations with England. Congress had broad authority over military and foreign affairs, but in domestic matters, the government was nearly powerless. As Julian E. Zelizer notes: "It could not enact statutes binding either individuals or states. Rather, its decisions took the form of resolutions and requisitions, which it conveyed to the states to implement in good faith, and they generally tried to do so. But the fact remained that Congress could not legislate in the ordinary sense of the term."[3] Adding to its inability to govern was the absence of a power to tax or even to enforce measures it passed—those functions rested with the states.[4]

Despite its limited authority, the Continental Congress did possess the ability to make appointments.[5] Although there was no strict separation of powers, whereby an independent executive could nominate with the advice and consent of the legislative branch, the placement of the appointment power in Congress had historical significance. The colonial experience had taught the framers that the power to make appointments should not be given solely to the executive.[6] "Throughout the eighteenth century [royal governors] had continually sought to use their [appointment] authority as the source of honor and privilege in the community to build webs of influence that could match those in effect in England." In addition, "the weeds of tyranny flourished because they were able to sink their roots deep into the community, spreading corruption throughout the entire society by the clever distribution of places and positions."[7] Thus, by the beginning of the Revolutionary War, colonial political leaders believed that sole control over appointments should not be given to an executive authority.[8]

The fear of executive power did not prevent the Continental Congress from instituting some necessary changes in how appointments were made, however. In the summer of 1775, Congress realized that it needed administrative help in disseminating information about the progress of the revolution. As a result, it established the Post Office Department under the direction of a postmaster general. Although he was not a truly independent executive agent, the postmaster general was given the administrative power to conduct postal affairs.[9] From time to time, Congress also gave the postmaster general the power to make certain appointments without formal congressional suspension. In one case, the postmaster general was permitted to appoint a person to the important position of postmaster to the "main army."[10] By October 1782, Congress passed legislation revising and formalizing the haphazard nature of the Post Office Department. The new law gave the postmaster general the power to appoint "as many deputy postmasters as he shall think proper" and to place them where he thought best.[11] This did not mean that his appointment decisions were free from congressional influence, however. For example, in 1775 Postmaster General Benjamin Franklin received a letter of application from Ebenezer Hazard. In his reply to Hazard, Franklin noted that he had "seen a Recommendation of you by your Provincial Congress" and would "pay due Respect by appointing" Hazard to the position of postmaster of New York.[12] In another case, Franklin asked the New Jersey delegation "to nominate Deputy Post-Masters throughout that Colony which [they] did accordingly."[13] These two early examples of congressional input into the pre-nomination process highlight executive deference to Congress.[14]

The Post Office was the only quasi-executive department created before 1781.[15] Until that time, Congress conducted its own affairs by establishing boards or commissions that were given the authority to make appointments to carry out the functions in their policy areas. For instance, the Board of Treasury, the Board of War, and the Committee for Foreign Affairs were all given limited appointment powers.[16] Although these entities were created to retain congressional control over fiscal, war, and foreign policy matters, respectively, they proved to be unworkable.[17] "The strain of discharging both legislative and executive duties, and the inevitable delays associated in carrying this double burden," Louis Fisher notes, "produced strong demands for administrative reform."[18]

Not until the Articles of Confederation were set to be formally ratified did Congress finally move to create executive departments to undertake the day-to-day administrative work.[19] In a span of two months, five executive departments were created where only one had existed before. The departments were Foreign Affairs (January 10, 1781), War, Marine, and Finance (February 7), and the Office of the Attorney General (February 16).[20] Apart from giving them some measure of administrative control, Congress also empowered the department heads to make appointments.[21] A search for capable appointees soon began, with Robert Morris being the overwhelming choice for superintendent of finance. Congress went on to unanimously elect Morris, but the new appointee made certain demands before he would accept the post.[22] The primary issue was the ability to hire and fire any officer or official in the U.S. government "who handled public property."[23] This was a significant increase in the appointment power that Congress had thus far given department heads. In an unprecedented power grab, Morris was attempting to expand his appointment authority to every department of government.[24] Congress formed a committee to consider the matter and, with some reluctance, approved Morris's request.[25]

While carrying out his duties, the new superintendent of finance attempted to settle the accounts of four departments related to the armed services (Commissary, Quartermasters, Hospital, and Marine).[26] In a letter to Congress, Morris proposed the creation of a commission, appointed by him, to investigate claims of fraud in these departments. Although Morris said that he would leave it to the "wisdom" of Congress to do what "shall be most proper," he had the audacity to lecture that body on who should control the appointment power:

> I am far from being desirous of appointment to office, but this is an occasion so important, that I cannot sacrifice my duty to false notions of delicacy. Characters fit for such an intricate and difficult business cannot easily be found, still less can they be known to the several members of Congress, and the debates which sometimes take place when appointments are made, deter the most proper persons from putting themselves in the way of nomination. Besides this, as it is not possible that the several members can be sufficiently acquainted with the talents of the particular persons, it is better that the appointment should be in one, who can be made accountable for an improper choice.[27]

Congress approved the plan and authorized five commissioners, appointed by the superintendent of finance, to audit the various departments. This did not mean, however, that Morris's statement was left unchallenged. In a rebuff, Congress expressed its unwillingness to be dictated to, and it ordered the superintendent to submit said appointments so that its members "may disapprove such appointment if they shall think proper."[28] Despite the need to clean up fraud in government, Congress was unwilling to give executive agents sole appointment power without some measure of legislative control. In this case, Congress created a system of checks and balances whereby the appointment power was shared. This was the first example of a shared appointment power in the federal system.

The Finance Department was also involved in one of the more unusual appointment arrangements devised by the Continental Congress. Several commissioners were appointed for each state "to settle and adjust, and finally to determine the proportions to be borne by the several states of the expences of the [Revolutionary] war." Congress also stipulated that the superintendent of finance would nominate the commissioner for each state, subject to the approval of "the legislatures or the executive of the particular State for which he shall have been nominated."[29] Although these appointments were not subject to congressional approval, members of the Continental Congress quickly involved themselves into the pre-nomination process. For instance, Rhode Island congressman David Howell recommended a candidate for one of the commissioner positions.[30] In considering all recommendations, Morris's only restriction was that he would not name a citizen of the state "to settle the Accounts of that particular State."[31] That policy prevented him from naming North Carolina congressman William Blount's preferred candidate. As Morris explained, "I should have been happy to appoint him, but being a Citizen of the Said State he is not eligible to the Office."[32] Congressional nepotism appears to have been a factor in at least one of these appointments, when the brother of Massachusetts congressman Nathaniel Gorham was appointed and approved as commissioner for New Hampshire.[33] After consultation, Morris submitted the nominations to the several states for final approval.[34]

State Constitutions

As had occurred at the national level, the states experienced a slow progression away from strictly legislative control over appointments toward an arrangement of shared powers. Most state governments began with strong legislative bodies that took the appointment power away from royal governors.[35] Delaware, Pennsylvania, and South Carolina did not even create a governor position; instead, they gave most executive authority to a president appointed by the legislative body. In Virginia, apart from the governor selecting justices of the peace upon the advice of a privy council, the legislative body made all appointments. In Georgia, New Jersey, and North Carolina, the governor had little or no involvement in appointments. Only in Maryland was the governor authorized to appoint a number of officeholders.[36] As William B. Michaelsen noted: "The obvious intent of the constitution-makers was to subordinate the executive office to the legislature. The executive thus became a creature of the legislature and his main function was to do the bidding of that body."[37]

Not until passage of the New York Constitution of 1777 did an independent executive emerge that was on equal footing with the legislative body or the governor's council in making appointments.[38] The constitution gave the governor, with the "advice and consent" of the Council of Appointments, the power to make appointments.[39] This shared appointment power was the first among the pre-1787 state constitutions.[40] Michaelsen explained that New York's advice and consent clause "can be considered the genesis of the involvement of the Senate in the appointing process at the federal level."[41] There was, however, some confusion over who rightly possessed the power to nominate. In the *Federalist Papers*, Alexander Hamilton explained: "the governor claims the right of nomination, upon the strength of some ambiguous expressions in the constitution; but it is not known to what extent, or in what manner he exercises it; nor upon what occasions he is contradicted or opposed."[42] The ambiguity of this arrangement eventually proved to be an unworkable one because of the "lack of clarity . . . over who, exactly, held the power of nomination."[43] For example, on two separate occasions, senators on the Council of Appointments forced their own candidates over the governor's wishes.[44]

By 1801, much of the confusion was clarified in a revision to the New York Constitution.[45]

Two other state constitutions followed New York's model of giving the executive enhanced authority. For instance, under the Massachusetts Constitution of 1780, a number of positions were to be "nominated and appointed by the governor, by and with the advice and consent of the council." To ensure clarity in the division of powers, the clause continued: "every such nomination shall be made by the governor."[46] New York and Massachusetts were the only states to include the phrase "advice and consent" in their constitutions. New Hampshire was the last state to change its constitution before the Constitutional Convention of 1787. The executive officer was given the title of president, and various positions were "nominated and appointed by the President and council."[47] Although it did not adopt the advice and consent language or possess clear lines of authority, New Hampshire, like New York and Massachusetts, moved away from earlier state constitutions and pushed for greater executive authority in appointments.

The Revolutionary experience eventually led to the belief that separation and balance of powers would best serve to protect the people and provide for a limited government. As the early state constitutional experience showed, "vesting the power of appointment to offices . . . in the legislatures destroyed 'all responsibility' and created 'a perpetual source of faction and corruption.'"[48] The states began to correct this problem, but the national government under the Articles of Confederation did not. Although department heads had been given limited appointment power, there was not yet a separate executive branch that shared power with Congress. Not until the Constitutional Convention would the evolution of the appointment power be complete.

Constitutional Convention

Establishing a new system of government with fundamentally different ways of carrying out executive functions was the Constitutional Convention's self-appointed task. Not everyone, however, wanted to give an executive the power to make appointments. For instance, on May 29, 1787, the first proposal (known as the Edmund Randolph Plan or the Virginia Plan) gave "the National Legislature" total control over judicial appointments only, and it was initially rejected by a vote of eight to two. James Wilson of Pennsylvania thought "intrigue, partiality, and concealment were the necessary consequences" of a legislative body making appointments. John Rutledge of South Carolina cautioned against such an idea, reasoning that it might be "leaning too much towards Monarchy." Benjamin

Franklin of Pennsylvania weighed in by proposing that the "Scotch mode" be adopted, whereby lawyers made the selections. James Madison of Virginia thought that appointment by the entire legislature or even an executive was not a good idea; he was more "inclined to give it to the Senatorial branch, as numerous eno' to be confined in—as not so numerous as to be governed by the motives of the other branch; and as being sufficiently stable and independent to follow their deliberate judgments." When Wilson moved for adoption of appointment by the executive, Madison opposed the motion. After further debate, Alexander Hamilton of New York proposed an alternative that involved "the Executive's appointing or nominating the Judges to the Senate which should have the right of rejecting or approving."[49] This was the first suggestion of a shared appointment power between the executive and the Senate.

Although a number of alternatives were suggested, on June 13 the original motion to provide for appointments by the national legislature passed. Again Madison objected, declaring that legislators "were incompetent Judges of the requisite qualifications. They were too much influenced by their partialities." After Madison's plea, the convention adopted appointment by the Senate alone, but the debate was still not settled. Two days after voting in favor of the Senate, William Paterson of New Jersey revived the proposal for the executive to make appointments.[50]

The issue was not taken up again for more than a month, when Nathaniel Gorham of Massachusetts spoke in support of appointment by the Senate. However, he "thought even that branch too numerous, and little personally responsible, to ensure a good choice"; he wanted to divide the authority, giving the executive the power of appointment "with the advice & consent of the 2d branch." Wilson still preferred appointment exclusively by the executive but stated, "if that could not be attained, [I] wd. prefer . . . the mode suggested by" Gorham. Luther Martin of Maryland and Roger Sherman of Connecticut thought the Senate should make appointments because "it would be best informed of characters & most capable of making a fit choice." Gorham still defended executive appointment, noting that "the Executive will be responsible in point of character at least, for a judicious and faithful discharge of his trust, he will be careful to look through all the States for proper characters. The Senators will be as likely to form their attachments at the seat of Govt where they reside, as the Executive."[51]

Madison offered a modification requiring at least one-third of the Senate to concur with executive appointments. The plan, he reasoned, "would unite the advantage of responsibility in the Executive with the security afforded in the [Senate] agst. any incautious or corrupt nomination by the Executive." Both Sherman and Randolph were opposed to having the executive make appointments, and Gunning Bedford Jr. of Delaware agreed, explaining that there were reasons for not giving such power to the executive.

The plan "would put it in [the executive's] power to gain over the larger States, by gratifying them with a preference of their Citizens." Also, the executive "could not be punished for mistakes." Gorham, defending Madison's modified proposal, noted "that the Senate could have no better information than the Executive. They must like him, trust to information from the members belonging to the particular State where the Candidate resided. The Executive would certainly be more answerable for a good appointment, as the whole blame of a bad one would fall on him alone."[52]

Gorham moved to vote on the motion that the executive appoint with the concurrence of the Senate. Gouverneur Morris of New York seconded the motion. Sherman, however, thought that this proposal unnecessarily restrained the Senate. Madison then moved that executive appointments be contingent on the concurrence of two-thirds of the Senate.[53] A vote and further debate were postponed until July 21, when the motion was taken up again. Madison began the debate by expressing no confidence in the Senate's ability to make appointments. That power, he stated, was better secured in "the Executive who would in general be more capable & likely to select fit characters then [sic] the Legislature, or even the 2d. [branch] of it, who might hide their selfish motives under the number concerned in the appointment." Madison also noted that

> concurrence of two authorities, in one of which the people, in the other the states, should be represented. The Executive Magistrate would be considered as a national officer, acting for and equally sympathising with every part of the U. States. If the 2d. branch alone should have this power, the Judges might be appointed by a minority of the people, tho' by a majority, of the States, which could not be justified on any principle as their proceedings were to relate to the people, rather than to the States: and as it would moreover throw the appointments entirely into the hands of ye Nthern States, a perpetual ground of jealousy & discontent would be furnished to the Southern States.[54]

Charles Pinckney of South Carolina was not convinced. "The Executive," he reasoned, "will possess neither the requisite knowledge of characters, nor confidence of the people for so high a trust." Randolph agreed with Madison in thinking that "appointments by the Legislatures have generally resulted from cabal, from personal regard, or some other consideration than a title derived from the proper qualifications." Oliver Ellsworth of Connecticut disagreed. The people, he stated, would regard the executive "with a jealous eye." In addition, "every power for augmenting unnecessarily his influence will be disliked. As he will be stationary it was not to be supposed he could have a better knowledge of characters. He will be more open to caresses & intrigues than the Senate."[55]

Defending Madison's proposal, Morris argued that "the States in their corporate capacity will frequently have an interest staked on the determination of the Judges." In addition, "it had been said the Executive would be uninformed of characters. The reverse was ye truth. The Senate will be so. They must take the character of candidates from the flattering pictures drawn by their friends. The Executive in the necessary intercourse with every part of the U.S. required by the nature of his administration, will or may have the best possible information." Finally, "if the Executive can be safely trusted with the command of the army, there can not surely be any reasonable ground of Jealousy in the present case."[56]

On July 21, 1787, the convention moved to place the appointment power with the executive and give the Senate a negative vote if it so chose ("that the executive should nominate, & such nominations should become appointments unless disagreed to by the Senate").[57] The clause was referred to the Committee of Detail,[58] which changed the draft to represent the current form of the Constitution. When the convention convened to debate and vote on the clause, now extensively rewritten, some delegates expressed a desire for additional changes. Wilson sought to include the House of Representatives in the process, believing that the president and Senate should not be given the power to make decisions that were, in essence, law. For instance, since treaties "have the operation of laws, they ought to have the sanction of laws also." Pinckney wanted to exclude the Senate in appointments altogether and thought that ambassadors should not be appointed by the president. Morris argued in favor of the clause and pointed out that there was a dual protection: first "that as the President was to nominate, there would be responsibility," and second, "as the Senate was to concur, there would be security." On September 7, 1787, the convention voted in favor of the clause without any changes, thus giving the appointment power to the president with the advice and consent of the Senate.[59]

Although there was much debate over the Appointments Clause, once it was settled, the convention never considered how the Article II power would be carried out by the president and the Senate. Many questions were left unanswered. What type of advice should be given, and on what appointments? Is there a give-and-take relationship implied in the word *advice*? Whose advice should the president listen to? Subsequent thoughts were offered at the state ratification conventions and in published statements on the draft Constitution.

State Ratification Conventions

Discussion of the appointment power and the advisory role of Congress at the various state ratification conventions was limited. One of the more thoughtful debates concerned the issue of an executive council as a check on the president's appointment power. The New York Convention went so far as to suggest that "Congress should appoint" an advisory body to make suggestions to the president "in the appointment of officers."[60] The New Yorkers' experience with their own Council of Appointments probably had much to do with this proposal. Most likely they believed that such a body would provide an additional check on the president. Other state conventions, however, were not supportive of the concept. For example, at the North Carolina convention, James Iredell argued against a council system, pointing out that the president already had department heads to offer him advice. Iredell thought the entire enterprise was impractical because "jealousy" would be a natural result "between the different states." If council members "were to be chosen from the Northern, Southern, or Middle States . . . undue preference might be given to those particular states from which they should come." In addition, Iredell reasoned, if a council were created, a president would have no responsibility for his decisions because "you surely would not oblige him to follow [the council's] advice, and punish him for obeying it." If a president's choices caused any harm, he could easily blame his council.[61]

Others thought that the division of powers as they existed would prevent bad appointments. At the Pennsylvania Convention, Wilson reasoned that if a bad appointment was made, "it must be with the approbation of some one of the other branches of government. Thus checked on each side, they can do no one act of themselves." Although Wilson argued in support of the principle of separation of powers in appointments, he did not appear to consider the "advice" component a shared responsibility. A president without a council, he thought, would prevent improper actions because that person could not "hide either his negligence or inattention; he cannot roll upon any other person the weight of his criminality; no appointment can take place without his nomination; and he is responsible for every nomination he makes."[62]

Some feared that the Senate would be too involved in appointments and would eventually overwhelm the president. At the North Carolina Convention, James Taylor recalled: "My experience in life shows me that the friends of the members of the legislature will get the offices. These senators and members of the House of Representatives will appoint their friends to all offices."[63] Another delegate, Samuel Spencer, explained how lawmakers would pressure the president to make their preferred choices:

> The President may nominate, but they have a negative upon his nomination, till he has exhausted the number of those he wishes to be appointed. He will be obliged, finally to acquiesce in the appointment of those whom the Senate shall nominate, or else no appointment will

take place. Hence it is easy to perceive that the President, in order to do any business, or to answer any purpose in this department of his office, and to keep himself out of perpetual hot water, will be under a necessity to form a connection with that powerful body, and be contented to put himself at the head of the leading members who compose it.[64]

Spencer believed that the Senate's "advice" function would naturally turn into dictation. He reasoned that "the powers of the Senate are so great in their legislative and judicial capacities, that, when added to their executive powers, particularly their interference in the appointment of all officers in the continent, they will render their power so enormous as to enable them to destroy our rights and privileges."[65] These remarks strongly anticipate a system of shared appointment power, with senators having a significant role in the pre-nomination process.

Countering Spencer's observation, Iredell thought "the Senate [had] no other influence but a restraint on improper appointments." Going into a detailed account of his interpretation of the Appointments Clause, Iredell remarked:

> If they think him improper, the President must nominate another, whose appointment ultimately again depends upon the Senate. Suppose a man nominated by the President; with what face would any senator object to him without a good reason? There must be some decorum in every public body. He would not say, "I do not choose this man, because a friend of mine wants the office." Were he to object to the nomination of the President, without assigning any reason, his conduct would be reprobated, and still might not answer his purpose. Were an office to be vacant, for which a hundred men on the continent were equally well qualified, there would be a hundred chances to one whether his friend would be nominated to it.[66]

A decorum of sorts was eventually established that would mask the very behavior Iredell thought would be "reprobated." During the First Congress, the Senate would create a custom called "senatorial courtesy," which gave senators the power to block appointments without cause or reason (see chapter 2).

Iredell's view of a well-defined and limited appointment power exercised by the Senate was nice in theory; however, it failed in practice. Out of all the state delegates, only Taylor and Spencer foresaw that the Senate would have a powerful say in who the president nominated. They understood that the natural instinct of any legislative body was to be involved at the initial stage of a nominee's selection. The Appointments Clause could never be practically exercised without giving in to the necessity of sharing information and consulting lawmakers.

The *Federalist Papers*

Although the state ratification conventions provide some insight into the framers' thinking on the Appointments Clause, they do not answer the question whether consultation between the president and members of Congress was a preordained vision. The *Federalist Papers* offer another useful source of information on the perceived function of the pre-nomination process. In *Federalist* No. 66, Alexander Hamilton looked to the president to have the exclusive appointment-making role: "It will be the office of the President to *nominate,* and, with the advice and consent of the Senate, to *appoint.* There will, of course, be no exertion of *choice* on the part of the Senate. They may defeat one choice of the Executive, and oblige him to make another; but they cannot themselves *choose*—they can only ratify or reject the choice he may have made."[67] He believed that the president would have the sole power to nominate; only subsequently would the Senate participate in voting. Hamilton acknowledged that the president's nomination "may be overruled," but any future selection would still be "the object of his preference, though perhaps not in the first degree." This meant that even if a nominee were rejected, any subsequent nominee would still be the choice of the president, not the Senate. The senators probably would not reject many of the president's nominations, Hamilton believed, "because they could not assure themselves that the person they might wish would be brought forward by a second or by any subsequent nomination."[68]

Hamilton pictured little if any Senate involvement in the pre-nomination process, but he assumed that the "possibility of rejection would be a strong motive to [take] care in proposing." A president would think twice if a nomination might ruin his "reputation" and his political future. As a result, he would avoid "favoritism" or the pursuit of a "popularity" contest because of the shame and fear of picking a candidate "who had no other merit than that of coming from the same State [as the president]."[69] For Hamilton, the Senate was vested not with the power to choose but only with the power to reject. In *Federalist* No. 77, he articulated why the Senate would not have a meaningful role in the pre-nomination process:

> In what manner is this influence to be exerted? In relation to what objects? The power of influencing a person, in the sense in which it is here used, must imply a power of conferring a benefit upon him. How could the Senate confer a benefit upon the president by the manner of employing their right of negative upon his nominations? If it be said

they might sometimes gratify him by an acquiescence in a favorite
choice, when public motives might dictate a different conduct; I
answer that the instances in which the president could be personally
interested in the result, would be too few to admit of his being mate-
rially affected by the compliances of the Senate. The POWER which
can *originate* the disposition of honors and emoluments, is more likely
to attract than to be attracted by the POWER which can merely
obstruct their course. If by influencing the president be meant *restrain-
ing* him, this is precisely what must have been intended. And it has
been shown that the restraint would be salutary, at the same time that
it would not be such as to destroy a single advantage to be looked for
from the uncontrouled agency of that magistrate. The right of nomination would produce all the good of that of appointment and would
in a great measure avoid its ills.[70]

Like Iredell, Hamilton's interpretation of the Appointments Clause was
based on his preference for concentrating power and responsibility in the
president. It was a theoretical and reasoned position, but one that did not
square with republican principles or the reality of the legislative branch's
desire to be involved in the pre-nomination process.

Correspondence between John Adams and Roger Sherman

As a strong advocate of the supremacy of the executive branch over
the legislative, Hamilton failed to conceive or anticipate that the Senate
would seek (or possess the ability) to influence selections.[71] No defense for
Senate involvement would be offered by the other authors of the *Federalist
Papers*. However, this did not mean that the debate ended. In correspondence with future president John Adams,[72] Roger Sherman wrote:

[The Senate] is the most important branch in government, for aiding
and supporting the executive, securing the rights of the individual
states, the government of the United States and the liberties of the people. The executive magistrate is to execute the laws. The senate, being
a branch of the legislature, will naturally incline to have them duly
executed, and, therefore, will advise to such appointments as will best
attain that end. From the knowledge of the people in the several states,
they can give the best information as to who are qualified for office;
and though they will . . . in some degree lessen [the president's]
responsibility, yet their advice may enable him to make such judicious
appointments, as to render responsibility less necessary.[73]

In this statement, Sherman became the first to articulate why the Senate and, by implication, the House of Representatives should be involved in the pre-nomination process. The "knowledge of the people" embedded within their representatives would serve to "give the best information as to who are qualified for office"—republican principles stated in a simple proposition. This was groundbreaking not only for its originality but also for how well it resembled actual practice.

With regard to the Appointments Clause, understanding the framers' intent is a difficult task. The early history of the Continental Congress saw the gradual movement away from complete legislative control over all policy areas and the creation of semiautonomous executive departments that had power over appointments. Congress, however, retained control in both formal and informal ways. Although the Post Office and Finance departments selected appointees, they often considered congressional recommendations when doing so. At the state level, the legislative bodies also tended to dominate appointment matters initially, but a gradual change occurred when states such as New York, Massachusetts, and New Hampshire adopted a scheme of shared power between the executive and legislative branches. After much debate about the appointment power, delegates to the Constitutional Convention agreed to a system already in use to varying degrees at the national and state levels. The executive would nominate with the "advice and consent" of the Senate.

Although there was subsequent debate over how the new appointment power would be used, ultimately, no agreement was reached. At the state ratification conventions, the discussions ranged from the idea of creating a "council" to advise the president to the Senate's potential power in the pre-nomination process. Such fears of Senate predominance were countered, and no resolution was made. Next, the *Federalist Papers* argued that the president would have the sole right to make appointments; the Senate's only role was to reject or confirm. Apart from two speakers at the North Carolina Convention, the only person to state practical reasons for Senate involvement in the pre-nomination process was Roger Sherman. He saw the necessity of the two branches of government sharing power, but this view was not yet being articulated with any great frequency. By the end of the ratification process and the start of the new federal government, there was still no uniform understanding of how the Appointments Clause would function.

Chapter 2

Establishing the Pre-nomination Process (1789–1829)

One of the first questions to be addressed after the ratification of the Constitution was how the executive and legislative branches would manage the practical operation of the Appointments Clause. Today, many seek answers to important constitutional questions from the judicial branch.[1] Indeed, over the past fifty years, the courts have provided guidance on such broad-ranging topics as abortion, affirmative action, capital punishment, and legislative vetoes. For better or worse, various policy decisions are made by the courts. However, during no point in our nation's history has the judiciary given direction to how the pre-nomination process should function.[2] That responsibility has been left to the political branches.

The president and Congress must rely on various nonjudicial sources rather than court opinions in determining the proper practice of making a nomination. Looking at the strict letter of the Constitution, there is no clear evidence that lawmakers are meant to be included or excluded in nomination decisions. Article II, Section 2, provides that the president "shall nominate, and by and with the Advice and Consent of the Senate, shall appoint Ambassadors, other public Ministers and Consuls, Judges of the supreme Court, and all other Officers of the United States, whose Appointments are not herein otherwise provided for, and which shall be established by Law." The text points to an executive-centered role in nominating, but does it permit congressional involvement? Professor Michael J. Gerhardt believes that it does. In his study on the appointment process, he argues:

> No one disputes that the president alone has the formal authority to nominate people to confirmable posts—that is, to make the final judgments about whom to nominate; however, it is a far different thing—and not at all inconsistent with the existence of such presidential authority nor with the language of the Appointments Clause—to say that the Senate may be constitutionally permitted to give counsel to the president before he formally announces his choices for confirmable offices.[3]

Gerhardt's remark acknowledges the president's singular authority to nominate yet notes that this does not exclude the Senate from influencing that choice. In other words, the advice and consent phraseology adds a reasonable constitutional justification to the argument that nomination decisions are not the president's alone. Formally, the president makes the final judgment, but the word *advice* opens the door to legislative leverage.

Some of the early members of Congress believed that this was the proper interpretation of the Appointments Clause. For instance, Congressman Benjamin Goodhue noted that "there was a propriety in allowing the Senate to advise the President in the choice of officers; this the constitution had ordained for wise purposes." The reason being, as James Madison declared, that lawmakers "from their nature, [are] better acquainted with the characters of the candidates than an individual."[4] Early on, presidents accepted this conception of how the pre-nomination process would function. However, the Senate also provided insurance that the appointment power would be shared by creating the practice of "senatorial courtesy." This chapter analyzes the origin of this custom and its impact on the pre-nomination process. In addition, it examines how the two branches interacted to make appointments by focusing on the administrations of George Washington through John Quincy Adams.

Senatorial Courtesy

Before filibusters, holds, and blue slips, senatorial courtesy was the traditional basis for individual senators to force presidents to consult them during the pre-nomination process. Traditionally, the custom of senatorial courtesy rested on the assumption that each senator would support a colleague's objection to a nomination for federal office by voting for rejection. That support was based on the condition that the objecting senator was from the same state as the nominee and was also of the same political party as the president.

There are various reasons why a senator would want to be consulted about the selection of federal officials in his home state. Political scientist Harold Chase offered one of the more informative rationales for senators' desire to be involved in the pre-nomination process and for the creation of senatorial courtesy:

Senators, whether chosen by state legislatures, as they were at an earlier time, or by the voters of the state, must continuously nurture their political support back home; that is, if they hope for additional terms in office—and it is a rare senator who does not. In this connection, senators from the First Congress on have recognized that one or two senators have a much greater stake in a particular appointment than others. It is, of course, exceedingly helpful to a senator to be able to reward supporters with good posts in the federal government. Conversely, it is enormously damaging to a senator's prestige if a president of his own party ignores him when it comes to making an appointment from or to the senator's own state. What is even more damaging to a senator's prestige and political power is for the president to appoint to high federal office someone who is known back home as a political opponent to the senator. It was easy for senators to see that if they joined together against the president to protect their individual interests in appointments, they could to a large degree assure that the president could only make such appointments as would be palatable to them as individuals. Out of such considerations grew the custom of senatorial courtesy.[5]

Chase's description shows that senators traditionally viewed their role in the pre-nomination process as a representative function. Political parties also played into the calculus, because the prestige and power of an appointment benefited senators by strengthening their standing with the party faithful back home. Finally, senators, through the collective use of their individual right to reject any appointment, substantially affected constitutional principles.[6]

Providing individual senators with the power to force consultation might appear to be self-evident, but at the start of the First Congress, this was not so apparent. Rather than creating the custom of senatorial courtesy, the Senate could have interpreted "advice and consent" narrowly. Instead, in three early cases, the custom of senatorial courtesy was established, whereby the Senate would rely on individual senator's judgments on home-state nominations to reach a decision about confirmation. The first example of senatorial courtesy concerned the rejection of a naval officer for the Port of Savannah. Less well known, the second and third examples involved the Senate's efforts to seek senators' support for a Supreme Court nominee and other positions. Each case highlights the concept that the Senate, through its own interpretation of the Appointments Clause, would seek the input of home-state senators. Future presidents had to be mindful of this custom, because a senator angered during the pre-nomination process would not be so willing to support, or might even actively work against, a president's selection at the confirmation stage.

The Rejection of Benjamin Fishbourn

The first example of senatorial courtesy began on August 2, 1789, when President George Washington submitted a number of nominations to the Senate, including that of Benjamin Fishbourn to be the naval officer for the Port of Savannah.[7] Three days later, on August 5, the Senate considered Fishbourn's nomination. His was the last nomination to be taken up, the rest having been confirmed over the prior two days. The Senate voted against Fishbourn's confirmation, marking the chamber's first rejection.[8] Although the Senate never provided an official account of its disapproval, the popular story was that Fishbourn had been rejected out of courtesy to the two Georgia senators.[9]

This reason might be true, but the source of senatorial courtesy lacks detail, and there is little evidence to support the basic presumption. Out of every known scholarly account of the incident, only one person cites a document that gives a reason for the Senate's action.[10] George H. Haynes in *The Senate of the United States* refers to a footnote from Thomas Hart Benton's *Abridgment of the Debates of Congress* to confirm that senatorial courtesy was the justification for rejecting Fishbourn. The footnote reads: "a strong instance of the deference of the Senate to the Senators of the State interested in the nomination, Col. Fishbourn having been rejected simply because the Georgia Senators preferred another."[11] Although the Georgia senators, William Few and James Gunn, may have preferred another candidate, this single statement coming from an individual who was not a contemporary of any of the actors in this event is suspect.

The author, Thomas Hart Benton, was a child when the First Congress convened in 1789 and does not appear to have been directly associated with any of its participants. Far from being a significant validation of senatorial courtesy, the Benton footnote offers mere speculation about the cause of Fishbourn's rejection. Scholarly accounts that rely on this citation or fail to cite any evidence for senatorial courtesy provide little in terms of true knowledge or understanding of the reason for the rejection and thus create an unfortunate situation that needs to be fully addressed. After all, if the rejection of Fishbourn is the first instance of senatorial courtesy, one should be able to refer to more useful citations to validate the claim.

I have examined evidence from the primary and secondary actors involved in the event to try to substantiate the claim that senatorial courtesy was the source of Fishbourn's rejection. In various correspondence and letters to newspapers over the course of months, the participants and those associated with the event provided a wealth of information that can be used to fashion a picture of what occurred. The first fact is that the Georgia senators did not agree on a candidate to fill the slot of federal customs collector. Senator Few wanted to select James Seagrove,[12] whereas Senator Gunn supported the incumbent, Reuben Wilkinson.[13] Both candidates had their shortcomings. Wilkinson had been suspended from his post by the governor of Georgia for malpractice.[14] Seagrove had angered Gunn by supporting Anthony Wayne, who had run against the senator in the recent election. Seagrove understood that he was a long shot, acknowledging, "I know [Senator Gunn] will wish to disappoint me."[15]

It is not known whether the Georgia senators eventually agreed on a candidate or whether they understood that the position had been split into three posts—collector, naval officer, and surveyor—under the new federal government and thus could have provided jobs to both Wilkinson and Seagrove.[16] Either way, what can be substantiated is that by August 1789, Washington had decided to select John Habersham as collector, Benjamin Fishbourn as naval officer, and John Berrien as surveyor—none of whom was the preferred candidate of Senator Gunn or Senator Few.[17] However, only Fishbourn's nomination was rejected by the Senate. Both Habersham and Berrien were confirmed.[18]

Most accounts of the event state that both senators opposed Fishbourn, but only Gunn had any reason for this opposition.[19] Four years before, in 1785, Fishbourn had supported Nathanael Greene in an abortive duel with Gunn.[20] Because of this action, Few and other senators may have been willing to support their colleague's rejection of the nominee. Additionally, a letter from "an unidentified 'friend in New York'" points to Gunn as leading the opposition to Fishbourn. The letter, published in the *Georgia Gazette* a week after the Senate action, stated that Senator Robert Morris had supported Fishbourn and had "called upon" Senators Gunn and Few to specify "their reasons" for their objection. In response, Gunn had "urged nothing of any consequence but personal invective and abuse."[21]

Another letter written by Fishbourn's friend Anthony Wayne to President Washington on August 30, 1789, discusses only Senator Gunn's opposition. Wayne explained: "the charge made by Mr Gunn, was groundless—injurous, & malacious, but it had the desired effect." He continued, "I wou'd sooner suffer my right hand to be severed from my body, than recommend to your notice, a Character, such as Mr Gunn represented Colo. Fishbourn to be."[22] Although the letters from the "friend in New York" and Wayne point to the conclusion that Gunn alone was openly opposed to Fishbourn's appointment, only years after the event did strong supporting evidence emerge.

In *Private Affairs of George Washington*, a book based on the accounts of Tobias Lear, the president's personal secretary, author Stephen Decatur Jr. sheds some light on the story. Decatur reports that years after the event, Tobias Lear's son, Benjamin Lincoln Lear, wrote a letter addressed to the *Daily National Intelligencer* concerning an editorial the paper had run on March 11, 1818. In this letter, which he never mailed, Lear recites what occurred after the Senate's rejection of Fishbourn:

> The President immediately repaired to the Senate Chambers & entered, to the astonishment of every one. The Vice-President left his chair & offered it to the President, who accepted it & then told the Sen-

ate that he had come to ask their reasons for rejecting his nomination of Collector &c. After many minutes of embarrassing silence, Gen. Gunn rose and said, that as he had been the person who had first objected to the nomination, & had probably been the cause of its rejection, it was perhaps his office to speak on this occasion. That his personal respect for the personal character of Gen. Washington was such that he would inform him of his grounds for recommending this rejection, (and he did so) but that he would have it distinctly understood to be the sense of the Senate, that no explanation of their motives or proceedings was ever due or would ever be given to any President of the United States. Upon which the President withdrew.[23]

As Benjamin Lear's account explains, Senator Gunn asserted that he had objected to Fishbourn's nomination and that he "had probably been the cause of its rejection." Neither this nor any other account of the event makes reference to Senator Few. The Senate apparently rejected Fishbourn simply because Gunn had a personal objection to the nominee, thus establishing the precedent of senatorial courtesy.

Fishbourn's rejection produced a quick reply by Washington. In a message of withdrawal, he took notice of the Senate's right to "dissent" but suggested that, in the future, "on occasions where the propriety of nominations appear questionable to you, it would . . . be expedient to communicate that circumstance to me, and thereby avail yourselves of the information which led me to make them."[24] This was the first presidential statement concerning the need for consultation, but Washington was not clear as to when this should occur. It appears that he meant after a nomination had been made, but he may have intended the timing to be more open-ended.

The Senate, possibly sensing the divide and confusion, introduced a motion the very day of Fishbourn's rejection that read: "It is the opinion of the Senate, that their advice and consent to the appointment of officers should be given in the presence of the President." A committee consisting of Senators Ralph Izard of South Carolina, Rufus King of New York, and Charles Carroll of Maryland was ordered the next day to "wait on the President of the United States, and confer with him on the mode of communication proper to be pursued between him and the Senate in the formation of treaties, and making appointments to offices."[25] The language expressed in this directive was also vague about the stage at which consultation should be sought. As a result, the committee had room to interpret its mission and compromise with the president in negotiating how the two branches would handle appointments.

The first conference between the Senate committee and the president occurred on August 8. No formal minutes of the meeting exist, but Washington recorded in his diary the points he had expressed:

With respect to Nominations. My present Ideas are that as they point to a single object unconnected in its nature with any other object, they had best be made by written messages. In this case the Acts of the President, and the Acts of the Senate will stand upon clear, distinct and responsible ground. Independent of this consideration, it could be no pleasing thing I conceive, for the President, on the one hand to be present and hear the propriety of his nominations questioned; nor for the Senate on the other hand to be under the smallest restraint from his presence from the fullest and freest inquiry into the Character of the Person nominated. The President in a situation like this would be reduced to one of two things: either to be a silent witness of the decision by Ballot, if there are objections to the nomination; or in justification thereof (if he should think it right) to support it by argument. Neither of which might be agreeable; and the latter improper; for as the President has a right to nominate without assigning his reasons, so has the Senate a right to dissent without giving theirs.[26]

Although Washington expressed a definite preference for written communications, in a letter to James Madison on August 9, he seemed to suggest that there might be room for compromise on the matter. According to the committee, the Senate preferred oral over written communications, and one of the senators implied that doing away with the ballot system and effecting a viva voce vote (voice vote) was the "great object" of his endeavors. Washington, "finding all three [senators] were opposed to the ballotting system," stated, "nothing would sooner induce me to relinquish my mode of nominating by written messages, than to accomplish this end."[27] Although the meeting adjourned with no formal agreement on the communication or ballot issue, the implication was that Washington might be willing to do away with written communications if the Senate would change its consent method from ballot to voice vote. Interestingly, the meeting did not address how the branches would come together in making a nomination.

On August 10, Washington met again with the committee and stated his firm belief that the Senate, in terms of its treaty and appointment power, "is evidently a Council only to the President; however its concurrence may be to his Acts." Therefore, the executive should decide the time, place, and manner of consultation. Although no mention was made of a potential compromise agreement, Washington allowed for some leeway: "The opinions both of President and Senators as to the proper manner may be changed by experience. In some kinds of business it may be found best for the President to make his propositions orally and in person, in others by written message. On some occasions it may be most convenient that the

President should attend the deliberations and decisions on his propositions; on other that he should not; or that he should not attend the whole
of the time."[28]

Washington's willingness to compromise on the issue of written communications may have been a tactical ploy (as his August 9 letter suggests)
to move the Senate's consent method from ballot to voice vote. Washington yielded in the bargaining process by stating that he would accept either
oral or written communications. As such, he suggested that "the Senate
should accommodate their rules to the uncertainty of the particular mode
and place that may be preferred; providing for the reception of either oral
[or] written propositions, and for giving their consent and advice in either
the presence or absence of the President."[29]

By backing down from his earlier views, Washington seemed to give
the committee members enough freedom in the Senate to effect the desired
change in the ballot system. Once their report was given, the Senate passed
a resolution stating (1) "nominations shall be made in writing by the President"; (2) the president can either meet the Senate in the Senate chamber
or convene the Senate at another place; (3) "all questions shall be put by
the President of the Senate, either in the presence or absence of the President"; and (4) "the Senators shall signify their assent or dissent by answering, viva voce, ay or no."[30] The resolution gave Washington the written
communication he sought and the change in the balloting system as well.
The only concession the Senate received from the president was the possibility of Washington attending sessions when a nominee was under consideration. Every subsequent president has followed Washington's
example of submitting nominations in writing,[31] and the Senate has continued its practice of a voice vote.

The compromise, however, did not settle the question of the proper
relationship between the two branches in the pre-nomination process. The
Senate's directive to the committee stated that it wanted a "mode of communication proper to be pursued between [the president] and the Senate
in the formation of treaties, and making appointments to offices." Although
Washington admitted that the Senate would play a "council" role, the final
agreement made no reference to Senate involvement before a nomination
was made. In fact, under the system of communication it established, the
two branches would have almost complete separation when handling
appointments. This formal system of the two bodies operating independently of each other would not last. Already, the Senate had created the
precedent of rejecting a nomination on the basis of a home-state senator's
opposition, and soon, two more examples would support the presumption
that presidents should not make appointments without conferring with
home-state senators.

James Iredell and the Consent of
Senator Benjamin Hawkins

The second example of senatorial courtesy, also occurring in the First Congress, involved the appointment of a justice to the U.S. Supreme Court. On February 9, 1790, President Washington nominated James Iredell of North Carolina to replace Robert H. Harrison on the Supreme Court.[32] According to Iredell's biographer, Willis R. Whichard, "some eastern (northern) senators initially opposed Iredell's appointment, preferring someone from their own region."[33] When the Senate proceeded to consider Iredell's nomination on February 10, his friend, Senator Pierce Butler of South Carolina, gave him high praise. One of the New Hampshire senators, though having "the highest confidence in the gentleman from South Carolina . . . wished to hear the sentiments of the gentleman from the State where Mr. Iredell resided." Senator Benjamin Hawkins of North Carolina satisfied the Senate by largely endorsing the view expressed by Butler.[34] The Senate thus confirmed Iredell to the Supreme Court.[35]

Although this act did not embody the popular conception of senatorial courtesy (i.e., it did not result in a rejection), it showed that this new legislative weapon could take various forms. When asking home-state senators to provide information about local appointments, the implicit assumption is not only that they possess the best knowledge about the candidates in question but also that they rightly represent the interests of the state. The Senate therefore gives great deference to home-state senators in confirmation decisions.

William Maclay and Home-State Support

The final example of senatorial courtesy provides additional support for the principle of Senate deference to home-state senators. In this case, several military appointments were being discussed on the Senate floor when Senator William Maclay rose and objected to "giving my advice and consent to the appointment of men [about] whom I knew nothing." Senator Izard stated that he had similar concerns. The matter was put to rest and the nominations were confirmed when several senators announced their support for their home-state nominees.[36]

These three cases highlight the Senate's early insistence that home-state senators play a major role in the confirmation of nominations. The first case revealed that when a home-state senator objected to a nominee, the Senate would be willing to vote for rejection. In contrast, the other two cases showed that with home-state support, nominees would be confirmed. Such power, though bestowed nowhere in the Constitution or the Senate rules, gives individual senators great control over appointments. Thus, presidents would be wise to respect the role of home-state senators and consult with them during the pre-nomination process so that no objectionable person is nominated. More than any theoretical debate over the Appointments Clause, the precedent of deferring to the advice of home-state senators shaped the concept of senatorial courtesy and would aid in the establishment of congressional consultation with the executive branch.

George Washington (1789–1797)

As the commanding general and leading figure in the country's war of independence, George Washington became the United States' first chief executive. With few precedents to follow, he faced the enormous task of establishing proper presidential conduct for a number of executive duties. Although personally responsible for many appointments, Washington refused to become involved in selecting nominees for departments that were not under his direct authority. For instance, in answering a request for a postal appointment, he wrote: "I can only observe, that I have uniformly avoided interfering with any appointments which do not require my official agency, and the Resolutions and Ordinances establishing the Post Office under the former Congress, and which have been recognized by the present Government, giving power to the Postmaster General to appoint his own Deputies, and making him accountable for their conduct, is an insuperable objection to my taking any part in this manner."[37] Washington saw no reason for his interference in departmental matters, and as a general rule, he always "recognized the full responsibility of the heads of departments and offices." This policy, however, did not prevent him from being consulted as "much departmental business rose from subordinate levels to his desk."[38]

In terms of how his own pre-nomination policy would operate, Washington understood that it would be beneficial to consult with people from a potential nominee's home state. In late 1789, while considering George Wythe for a district court judgeship in Virginia, Washington wrote to Attorney General Edmund Randolph that he had "consulted such Gentlemen from the State of Virginia as I thought most likely to have some knowledge of [Wythe's] inclinations."[39] Throughout his presidency, Washington would continue to rely on home-state advisers to make informed selections. For instance, in New York and Virginia, their respective governors, George Clinton and Henry Lee, were among his confidants. Other notable political figures, such as future secretary of war James McHenry and former Supreme Court justice Thomas Johnson, were consulted about appointments in their states.[40]

Although home-state advisers came from various sources, it was generally presumed that members of Congress would play the primary role in the pre-nomination process. In a letter to Washington, one gentleman explained that he "had determined not to interfere in [local appointment matters], as the Senators and Representatives were generally acquainted with the several Law Characters among us who might be Candidates for offices."[41] Because of the Senate's constitutional advice and consent function, many people assumed that senators would be helpful in securing appointments. One early observer actually thought that senators nominated as well as confirmed appointments: "As the new Government of the United States will soon take place, and of course all appointments be made, it behoves us all to look around and try what we can get. I am advised by all my friends this way to offer for the Collectorship of the Import for Georgia and have little doubt of being *nominated by our Senators to Congress*. But this alone will not do. It will be necessary to have as many friends as possible in the Senate."[42] Others also thought that having friends in the Senate would lead to positions in the new government. For instance, after soliciting an appointment, one office seeker asked Washington to verify his standing with Senators William Paterson, Ralph Izard, Pierce Butler, Robert Morris, and William Johnson, among others.[43] Another person offered a less extensive list of references, naming Senators Robert Morris, William Maclay, John Henry, and Paine Wingate when making his case for office.[44] Most people, however, knew only their home-state senators and either referenced them or received letters of endorsement.[45]

Washington seems to have preferred recommendations from home-state senators. For instance, he openly sought the advice of North Carolina's Samuel Johnston on the possible appointment of James Iredell to the Supreme Court.[16] In another case, Washington wrote to Virginia senator Richard Henry Lee that since he was "perfectly unacquainted . . . with the characters living there, I would thank you for naming a fit person."[47] Senators understood and pandered to the president's preference for home-state advice. Senator William Maclay of Pennsylvania, who was seeking a position at the Port of Baltimore for his brother-in-law, realized that a recommendation by a Maryland lawmaker would be beneficial to his cause. In a letter to Washington, Maclay urged the president to consult with several members of the Maryland delegation about the propriety of the appointment.[48]

Members of the House of Representatives were also consulted during the pre-nomination process.[49] In his dissertation on the first fourteen years of the Senate, Roy Swanstrom writes that "Washington even made [Virginia representative James] Madison a one-man council of advice in his dealings with the Senate itself."[50] For instance, Madison helped shape Washington's cabinet and was consulted by the president on various appointment matters.[51] This did not mean, however, that Madison dominated the pre-nomination process. In North Carolina, Representative Hugh Williamson offered advice on a number of offices and passed on to Washington the endorsements of other members of his state's congressional delegation.[52] Secretary of State Thomas Jefferson, whose office handled the paperwork for most domestic appointments, even drafted a memorandum to Washington detailing recommendations received from members of Congress.[53] Madison's name appeared nowhere on the list. Clearly, Madison had a strong influence on the administration, but Washington respected the advice of other lawmakers as well.

Consulting members of Congress was not the only precedent Washington set. Although political parties had not yet fully formed during his administration, Washington established the criterion of selecting only people who had supported the Revolution and the Constitution. In addition, he viewed support for the "political tenets" of the government as a key characteristic of those he appointed. "I shall not, whilst I have the honor of administrating the government," Washington wrote, "bring men into any office of consequence knowingly whose political tenets are adverse to the measures the general government is pursuing; for this, in my opinion, would be a sort of political suicide."[54] The theory underlying this statement would become the basis for the political party component in the pre-nomination process used by future administrations. Subsequent presidents, in particular Thomas Jefferson and Andrew Jackson, would agree that picking candidates regardless of their party affiliation would be "political suicide." This reasoning not only influenced the pre-nomination process but also led to the removal of officeholders by opposing-party presidents. Jefferson would be the first to remove people from office based on their political leanings. Decades later, Jackson would introduce a significantly expanded version of Jefferson's removal system. Both presidents would base their removal policies on Washington's belief in appointing only those whose political tenets supported the administration in power.

John Adams (1797–1801)

When Vice President John Adams succeeded Washington to the presidency, there had already been a definite increase in congressional pressure for appointments.[55] The problem for Adams was that his administration was largely a continuation of Washington's. Besides retaining a similar cabinet, Adams could replace only the few officials who left office and could fill only the small number of new positions created by Congress. The idea of removing officeholders at the start of each administration had not yet taken hold, and at the time, only Federalist Party members would have been affected.[56] Adams and other politicians had not yet realized that the

problem of finding positions for the party faithful would become insepa-
rably linked with the removal of incumbents.[57]

The lack of available positions, however, did not prevent members of
Congress from soliciting offices.[58] In fact, Adams was forced to accept congressional involvement in the pre-nomination process as a means of having his nominations confirmed. As one historian explained, "the Senate
was likely to refuse to confirm unless the nominee had previously been
cleared by the congressional delegation from the nominee's home State."[59]
For example, congressional delegations from Connecticut, New York, and
Vermont gave clearance notices for several judicial appointments.[60] Congressional pressure was so bad that Adams acknowledged his inability to
nominate without the consent of lawmakers. In response to an appointment request from a relative, he wrote: "Our kinsman must apply to the
senators and representatives of his own State for recommendations. If I
were to nominate him without previous recommendations from the senators and representatives from your State, the Senate would probably negative him."[61] Adams even admitted that his nominee for the surveyor post
in Portsmouth, Samuel Adams, had actually been "named by the senators
and representatives of New Hampshire."[62] The legislative branch had
clearly forced its way into the pre-nomination process to the extent that a
sitting president acknowledged his inability to freely nominate without the
consent of Congress.[63] Leonard White would conclude from such incidents
that "by the end of Adams's administration the convention had become
well established that Congressmen were normally consulted concerning
nominations to federal office."[64]

Even the former president found the system unbearable. Washington
declared in the fall of 1798 that many military "applications are made, *chiefly*
through members of Congress. These oftentimes to get *rid* of them; oftener
still perhaps, for local and Electioneering purposes, and to please and gratify their party."[65] A few months later, Congress solicited Washington's help
with several military applications, but after weeks of laboring, his recommendations were largely ignored. Washington wrote that "any Member of
Congress who had a friend to serve, or a prejudice to endulge, could set [the
appointments] at naught." In one case, Washington, along with four generals, had recommended a Revolutionary War veteran for promotion, but "the
Veto of a Member of Congress (I presume) was *more respected,* and sufficient
to set him aside." The ex-president warned, "if the practice is continued,
you will find that serious discontents, and evils will result from it."[66]

The formation of political parties by the late 1790s introduced an additional factor into the pre-nomination process. The 1796 presidential
election—a hotly contested battle between Adams and political rival Thomas
Jefferson—marked the beginning of an ideological and policy divide that led
to the establishment of the Federalist and Republican parties.[67] With political

parties came an increased hunger for offices and a need to find suitable places for party members. Adams's willingness to abide by this new partisan factor in the pre-nomination process is debatable, but as one scholar states, "if he did not wholly proscribe members of the Republican party he at least showed such a preference for Federalists that few who were not members of that party received any favors at his hands."[68] The party component came into play at the end of Adams's administration when he tried to secure federal offices for as many Federalist Party members as possible. Most of these appointments were the result of the Judiciary Act of 1801, passed by the lame-duck Federalist Senate, which, among other things, increased the number of federal judges.[69] Adams's grandson, Henry Adams, explained:

> No sooner did this Bill become law, Feb. 13, 1801, than the Federalists used their last moments of power to establish themselves in the posts it created. In Jefferson's words, they retreated into the Judiciary as a stronghold. They filled the new courts as well as the vacancies on the old bench with safe men, at whose head, as Chief-Justice of the Supreme Court was placed the Secretary of State, John Marshall. That Jefferson should have been angry at this maneuver was natural; but, apart from greed for patronage, the Federalists felt bound to exclude Republicans from the bench, to prevent the overthrow of those legal principles in which, as they believed, national safety dwelt.[70]

Adams was willing to use these "midnight appointments" to maintain his party's dominance long after he left the presidency.[71] The logic of making such appointments was based on Washington's own words: "I shall not, whilst I have the honor of administrating the government, bring men into any office of consequence knowingly whose political tenets are adverse to the measures the general government is pursuing; for this, in my opinion, would be a sort of political suicide."[72] A failure to appoint like-minded individuals would not only impede a president's agenda but also give the opposition a chance to effect change without having won an election. Such a theory was at the heart of the political party component of the pre-nomination process, and it was one that the Federalists and, subsequently, every other political party would adopt.[73]

Thomas Jefferson (1801–1809)

The 1800 election marked the rise of the Republicans (precursor of the Democratic Party) and the end of the Federalists at the national level.[74] With Thomas Jefferson's ascent to the presidency, many of his Republican followers wanted the benefits of federal jobs, but the former Federalist administrations had filled the government with their supporters.[75] Washington's maxim of not giving offices to those in disagreement with the general government remained in force. Jefferson would follow this principle and incorporate it completely into the pre-nomination process. In an attempt to both satisfy the interests of his Republican Party and rid the federal bureaucracy of Federalists, Jefferson instituted the country's first removal effort.[76] As Lance Banning wrote, "removal of the enemy from power and from public trust had come to seem sufficient, by itself, to safeguard liberty while friends of freedom worked toward gradual replacement of the Hamiltonian system with one better suited to republican ways."[77] These removals would open offices for Republican Party members who would not only support Jefferson's policies but also benefit from the patronage of federal service. "It is now perfectly just that the [R]epublicans should come in for the vacancies," Jefferson wrote, "until something like an equilibrium in office be restored."[78] Elaborating further, Jefferson explained why removals were merely a corrective to the years of Federalist rule: "The preceding administration left 99 out of every hundred in public offices of the federal sect. Republicanism had been the mark of Cain which had rendered those who bore it exiles from all portion in the trusts and authorities of their country. This description of citizens called imperiously and justly for a restoration of right."[79] Jefferson therefore had no problem removing Federalists from office. As Dumas Malone explained: "The Federalists were seeking to perpetuate [a] system [of permanent officeholding], but Jefferson, who thought of public service more as a duty than a career, was basically unsympathetic with what we now call bureaucracy."[80] Jefferson removed 106 officeholders—more than twice the number removed by Washington and Adams combined—and he also secured the repeal of the 1801 Judiciary Act, which wiped out the remaining Federalist officeholders that his administration had been unable to purge.[81]

Besides introducing removals into the pre-nomination process, Jefferson sought to place greater appointment authority under presidential control. Unlike Washington, he was willing to provide a clear appointment policy to his subordinates,[82] even when they seemingly had complete control over their departments' appointments. For instance, Jefferson wrote a letter to Postmaster General Gideon Granger stating that vacancies should be given to Republicans and instructing him to "consider nullities all the appointments (of a removable character) crowded in by Mr. Adams." Although the strict letter of the law gave the postmaster general the authority to make appointments, Jefferson inserted himself into the pre-nomination process for postal appointments to provide additional power and support to his administration and to the Republican party.[83] He believed in the "boundless patronage" of the Post Office Department and probably would have preferred having complete control over postal appointments, but he knew that this was not in his power.[84] Years after leaving office, he would write: "The true remedy for putting those appointments in a wholesome state would be a law vesting them in the President, but without intervention of the Senate. That intervention would make the matter worse. Every senator would expect to dispose of all post offices in his vicinage or perhaps the state."[85] Jefferson's statement was almost prophetic. Future presidents and members of Congress would claim a right to oversee postal appointments even without the plain legal authority. Not until Andrew Jackson, however, would a president be given statutory control over postal appointments.[86]

When dealing with appointments directly under his control, Jefferson frequently followed the customs established under Washington and Adams and consulted with home-state lawmakers. Congressional involvement in the pre-nomination process was beneficial for Republican members because they could use the patronage resources to serve electoral ends and thus strengthen their party's standing in various states.[87] Several examples serve to highlight the practical experience of the administration's pre-nomination process. In March 1801, Jefferson wrote to South Carolina senator Charles Pinckney, "The most valuable source of information we have is that of the members of the legislature, and it is one to which I have resorted and shall resort with great freedom."[88] In May 1801, he accepted Rhode Island senator Theodore Foster's recommendation of David Leonard Barnes to be a district court judge. Jefferson told Foster that he would "be happy" to receive his letters "and information of all interesting occurrences, as well as reflecting fit characters for public offices, about the proper filling of which I am most anxious of all things."[89] During the same month, he wrote to Speaker of the House Nathaniel Macon of North Carolina, acknowledging the recommendation of a district judge. Jefferson stated that "in all cases, when an office becomes vacant in your State . . . I shall be obliged to you to recommend the best characters."[90] All these men were not only members of Congress but Republicans as well.[91]

Although Jefferson introduced removals as a component of the pre-nomination process, the dominance of the Republican Party would prevent removals from becoming a permanent feature for another twenty years. Jefferson's successors, James Madison and James Monroe, were Republicans, which negated the need to make removals. Only when a viable two-party system existed at the national level would removing officeholders become a political necessity.

James Madison (1809–1817)

With the crushing defeat of the Federalists, President James Madison felt little need to build party unity.[92] As party scholar Robert Allen Rutland explained, Madison "realized that without a party organization the Jeffersonians could never have won power; but once that fight ended in their favor, Madison had no relish for cultivating unity."[93] Removals under Madison were far fewer than under Jefferson not only because of the president's unwillingness to make them but also because he succeeded a fellow Republican. During Madison's eight years as president, he forced just twenty-seven people from office.[94]

Madison, like Jefferson, understood that the Senate played an important role in the pre-nomination process. Writing in 1789, Madison stated, "The Executive power seems to be vested in the President alone, except so far as it is qualified by an express association of the Senate in appointments."[95] That qualification was limited, however, in that the president had the power to nominate freely without interference from the Senate. Writing years after he left the White House, Madison remarked that the Senate had no automatic right over appointments:

> The power of appointment, when not otherwise provided by the Constitution is vested in the President & the Senate. Both must concur in the act, but the act must originate with the President. He is to nominate, and their advice & consent are to make the nomination an appointment. They cannot give their advice & consent without his nomination, nor of course, differently from it. In doing so they would originate or nominate, so far as the difference extended, and it would be his, not their advice & consent which consummated the appointment.[96]

The president "is to nominate," and only in the confirmation or rejection of a nomination does the Senate give its "advice and consent." Despite Madison's belief that the executive alone managed the pre-nomination process, congressional influence remained a pressing reality.[97]

In one case, Republican senators Michael Leib, Warren Giles, and Samuel Smith advised Madison not to nominate Albert Gallatin as secretary of state because they each had their own candidates in mind.[98] After realizing that "he had to compromise," Madison nominated Senator Smith's brother, Robert Smith, so that "party harmony" could be restored.[99] In another example involving foreign appointments, the Senate wanted Madison to consult with a group of senators about the matter. At first, the president refused. Writing to the Senate, Madison argued:

> The Executive and Senate in the cases of appointments to office, and of treaties, are to be considered as independent of and co-ordinate with each other. If they agree, the appointments or treaties are made. If the Senate disagree, they fail. If the Senate wish information previous to their final decision, the practice, keeping in view the constitutional

relations of the Senate and the Executive, has been, either to request the Executive to furnish it, or to refer the subject to a committee of their body, to communicate, either formally or informally, with the head of the proper department. The appointment of a committee of the Senate to confer immediately with the Executive himself, appears to lose sight of the co-ordinate relation between the Executive and the Senate, which the constitution has established, and which ought therefore to be maintained.[100]

Despite this forceful message about the independence of the executive branch, Madison ended up meeting with the group of senators.[101]

Finally, clearance by members of Congress seems to have been a required custom. For example, Treasury Secretary Albert Gallatin asked Madison to review a number of collector appointments. In his letter, Gallatin detailed the congressmen endorsing each position, and two days later, Madison nominated all of the congressionally recommended individuals.[102] The fact was that lawmakers could force consultation, and at times dictation, despite theoretical objections from Madison.

During Madison's administration, there was a controversy over a postmastership that highlights the state of the pre-nomination process for departmental appointments not under the president's control. After the Philadelphia postmaster died in office, Madison and Postmaster General Gideon Granger fought over who should fill the vacancy. Specifically, Granger wanted to appoint one of the administration's biggest opponents, Pennsylvania senator Michael Leib.[103] Madison understood the implications of such an appointment, and although Granger formally held the power to appoint all postmasters, the president could choose to make his wishes known. Madison was outraged by the postmaster general's actions, and other Republicans, "including members of Congress and of the State legislature, joined in recommending another man, and warned Granger in private that his own removal from office would follow the appointment of Leib."[104] Granger failed to heed these warnings, but he soon learned that going against the wishes of the president and members of Congress would not go unpunished. Madison quickly removed Granger and nominated Jonathan Meigs Jr. to replace him.[105] Despite claims that the postmaster general was independent of both the president and Congress, this case showed that the failure to accept the two branches' wishes would ensure a quick removal.

James Monroe (1817–1825)

By the time of James Monroe's presidency, the Republicans had no serious opposition in presidential contests.[106] One historian would write that the "harmonious circumstances of James Monroe's election to the presidency and his unique public career conspired to make him, excepting only George Washington, the most nonpartisan chief executive in American history."[107] With sixteen years of Republican rule, Monroe saw little need to remove federal officeholders, as Jefferson had done, and he apparently would have preferred not to oust anyone. As Secretary of State John Quincy Adams noted, the president was "too reluctant to exercise this power at all."[108] Monroe ended up removing only twenty-seven officeholders in eight years.[109]

In matters of appointments, the administration took an almost cavalier attitude about political parties.[110] Future president Martin Van Buren noted that Monroe tried to take the political party component out of the pre-nomination process by creating a fusion policy, which held that "no difference should be made by the Government in the distribution of its patronage and confidence on account of the political opinions and course of applicants."[111] Monroe's new order would effectively end party distinctions when consulting members of Congress. As Rutland explained, "Monroe did all he could to kill the old Republicans by his disregard of parties in his federal appointments."[112]

One example of Monroe's ambivalence toward parties involved a New York domestic appointment. After the Albany postmaster was removed for misconduct,[113] a controversy arose over his replacement. As had been the case under Madison, the postmaster general had the statutory authority to make such appointments. However, from a practical and political standpoint, the president, if he so chose, could have a strong voice in deciding who was selected. In this case, Monroe seems to have taken a hands-off approach, which divided the Republican Party in New York.

When the vacancy in Albany occurred, not every Republican leader in the state was informed. For instance, Governor De Witt Clinton knew about it more than a week before any of Senator Martin Van Buren's Regency friends.[114] This lapse provided enough time for New York's Republican congressmen to sign a petition asking that Federalist representative Solomon Van Rensselaer be appointed postmaster.[115] On the basis of this recommendation, Postmaster General Meigs submitted Van Rensselaer's name to Monroe for review, telling the president that he would make the appointment unless otherwise informed.[116] At this time, the two New York senators, Van Buren and Rufus King, as well as Vice President Daniel D. Tompkins, who was also a New Yorker, became aware of the vacant postmastership. All three attempted to stop the appointment by asking for a two-week delay to come up with an alternative candidate.[117] Finding that the matter had escalated too far, Monroe called a cabinet meeting to address the issue.[118] After hearing arguments on both sides, the president denied Van Buren's request for a delay and stated that he saw no reason to interfere in this matter. Interestingly, Monroe thought that he had no right to involve himself because "Congress had given the Postmaster General full authority over all postal appointments."[119] This is strange in light of the fact that Meigs had submitted the appointment for presidential review and indicated that he would follow Monroe's decision, clearly demonstrating great deference to executive authority. After receiving Monroe's consent, Meigs appointed Van Rensselaer.[120]

During the cabinet meeting, a proposal was made to change the law to give the president power over postal appointments. Secretaries William Crawford, William Wirt, and John Quincy Adams were all supportive of the idea.[121] Monroe apparently wanted Congress to clarify the law to provide for executive appointment.[122] In his last State of the Union address, he stated that a "revision of some parts of the post office law may be necessary; and it is submitted whether it would not be proper to provide for the appointment of post masters, where the compensation exceeds a certain amount, by nomination to the Senate, as other officers of the General Government are appointed."[123] Although various bills would be submitted to change the postal law, not until 1836 did Congress pass legislation giving the executive such authority.

Another domestic appointment controversy provides further details of Monroe's pre-nomination policy. In the fall of 1820, two Illinois Republican senators, Ninian Edwards and Jesse Burgess Thomas, fought over control of federal appointments in their state. Senator Edwards thought that Senator Thomas was receiving too many offices, so Edwards wrote to Monroe and members of the cabinet asking them to appoint some of his supporters to federal positions.[124] Despite this pressure by Edwards, Monroe did not nominate any of the senator's recommendations. At first glance, this may seem like a direct refutation of the pre-nomination process, because Monroe did not follow the senator's suggestions. However, congressional dictation had not yet become a custom; consultation with lawmakers was the norm, and both Illinois senators were consulted. The administration merely preferred Thomas's nominees over Edwards's in nearly all cases. This factional rift in the Republican Party was unfortunate, but it did not constitute a change in the pre-nomination process.[125]

The reality of the pre-nomination process was that members of Congress sought to influence appointments and were upset when they did not get their way.[126] Writing in his diary, Secretary of State Adams explained: "One of the most remarkable features of what I am witnessing every day is a perpetual struggle in both Houses of Congress to control the Executive—to make it dependent upon and subservient to them. They are continually attempting to encroach upon the powers and authorities of the President."[127] Monroe himself confided to Jefferson that "in the appointment to office, I have been forc'd either to distribute the offices among the friends of the candidates, to guard myself against the imputation of favoritism, or to take my own course, and appoint those whom I knew & confided in, without regard to them. . . . I therefore adopted the latter, and have steadily pursued it."[128] The president's policy did not always lead to successful appointments, however. In the late fall of 1821, he made a Pennsylvania appointment that was not supported by the state's Republican senators William Findlay and Walter Lowrie, and unlike the Albany postmastership, this appointment was subject to Senate confirmation. The main problem with the nominee was that he was a Federalist. Both senators protested "earnestly with Mr. Monroe against this nomination on the express ground that it was made in the execution of that amalgamation policy to which they and their State were opposed."[129] Monroe would not back down, and the Senate went on to reject his nominee by a vote of twenty-six to fourteen.[130]

A significant change in the pre-nomination process occurred during Monroe's administration when Congress passed the Tenure of Office Act of 1820 (also known as the Four Years Act), which required most classes of federal employees to be confirmed every four years.[131] Up to that time, presidents needed to fill only those federal offices made vacant by death, removal, or resignation; after passage of the law, presidents were forced to either reappoint federal officeholders or make new appointments. The most apparent reason for passage of the act was given by Secretary of State Adams, who wrote: "The senate was conciliated [into supporting the act] by the permanent increase of their power, which was the principal ultimate effect of the Act, and every Senator was flattered by the power conferred upon himself of multiplying chances to provide for his friends and dependants."[132]

Former president Jefferson quickly realized the adverse impact this law would have on the pre-nomination process. After receiving a solicitation for office, Jefferson declared:

> This is a sample of the effects we may expect from the late mischievous law vacating every four years nearly all the executive offices of the government. It saps the constitutional and salutary functions of the President, and introduces a principle of intrigue and corruption, which will soon leaven the mass, not only of Senators, but of citizens. It is more baneful than the attempt which failed in the beginning of the government, to make all officers irremovable but with the consent of the Senate. This places, every four years, all appointments under their power, and even obliges them to act on every one nomination. It will keep in constant excitement all the hungry cormorants for office, render them, as well as those in place, sycophants to their Senators, engage these in eternal intrigue to turn out one and put in another, in

cabals to swap work; and make of them what all executive directories become, mere sinks of corruption and faction.[133]

Jefferson had always believed that the Senate possessed too much power in the pre-nomination process, and in his view, the new law transferred even more executive functions to the members of that chamber. In the end, nothing but "corruption and faction" could result from giving "every four years, all appointments" to the Senate.[134]

The act, however, did not have the initial impact that some had expected. Because of the Republican dominance, neither Monroe nor his successor, John Quincy Adams, tried to exploit this law for partisan ends.[135] More important, neither thought that a president should remove competent people from office. Monroe argued that "no person at the head of government has, in my opinion, any claim to the active, partisan exertions of those in office under him."[136] Not until Andrew Jackson became president did rotation in office become a major factor in the pre-nomination process.

John Quincy Adams (1825–1829)

John Quincy Adams assumed the presidency under dramatically different circumstances than his predecessors. A viable two-party system had emerged from a bitter presidential election that split the Republican Party between supporters of Adams (the National Republicans) and supporters of Andrew Jackson (the Democrats).[137] The result was that Adams "was the last president, before the triumph under Jackson of a conception of leadership tied to a positive idea of party, who aspired to embody all the dimensions of the patriot leader."[138] For instance, Adams refused to accept a party principle in the pre-nomination process, even when the new two-party system took form.[139] "Efforts had been made by some of the Senators," he noted, "to obtain different nominations, and to introduce a principle of change or rotation in office at the expiration of these commissions; which would make the government a perpetual and unintermitting scramble for office."[140] Adams refused to create a rotation system to aid his National Republicans and removed only twelve officeholders.[141] Although the 1820 Tenure of Office Act provided the executive with a number of offices to fill every four years, Adams professed that "he [was] determined to renominate every person against whom there was no complaint which should warrant his removal."[142]

Despite his refusal to remove officeholders, Adams was continually pressured by members of Congress to reward party members.[143] As historian Dorothy Ganfield Fowler notes: "Congressmen pestered President Adams with calls to present candidates for the local offices."[144] Adams would usually refuse their recommendations. He had always found dealing with pre-nomination matters trying. After an encounter with one office seeker during the Monroe administration, he had exclaimed: "There is something so gross and so repugnant to my feelings in this cormorant appetite for office, this barefaced and repeated effort to get an old and meritorious public servant turned out of place for a bankrupt to get into it, that it needed all my sense of the allowances to be made for sharp want and of the tenderness due to misfortune to suppress my indignation."[145] Although he found the pre-nomination process distasteful, Adams could not avoid the congressional pressure in a rapidly emerging two-party era.[146] Congressional pressure for appointments was increasing, and some members were even making outright demands for offices.[147]

The combination of presidential indifference and an increasingly partisan environment produced a largely failed administration because Adams was unwilling to use appointments to reward his supporters. The state of affairs was so bad that Secretary of State Henry Clay wrote: "The friends of the Administration have to contend not only against their enemies, but against the Administration itself, which leaves its power in the hands of its own enemies."[148] In two of the largest states of the Union, Pennsylvania and New York, Adams proved Clay's claims to be accurate.[149] The administration especially hurt its New York supporters, James Tallmadge and Thurlow Weed, by first offering the position of minister to England to an opposition leader, De Witt Clinton, who refused.[150] After this initial rebuff, Adams turned to Federalist Rufus King.[151] In another act that dismayed his New York National Republicans, Adams proceeded to nominate another political enemy to a federal judgeship. In a letter to Weed, Tallmadge wrote:

> Mr. Adams is pursuing a steady course, but will he succeed to keep old friends & buy up old enemies? He began by an attempt on Clinton—who sniffed at him—I suppose the price was too low. Next he selected King—a minister recalled by Jefferson for cause as head of the Federalist party—their candidate against [Daniel D.] Tompkins:—against whom all republicans are committed on printed hand bills to rise up against him—and who is now without influence in either party—Next comes [Alfred] Conklin[g] for District Judge, a quondam federalist, now a mere page to Clinton. . . . His old friends cannot retain the power to give him the votes of this state & make him President a second time as they have the first if he purs[u]es the course he has begun.[152]

Tallmadge went to the White House to advise Adams that he was harming his friends and that an appointment at least equal to the England post was needed to bring harmony to the state. These requests went unanswered, and the administration did nothing to rectify the situation.

One of Adams's final acts of political ineptness was his failure to remove Postmaster General John McLean, who was working against him and supporting his rival, Andrew Jackson, in the upcoming presidential election.[153] On various occasions, Secretary of State Clay tried to explain to Adams that McLean was using the department's patronage to assist Jackson.[154] But even when the evidence was overwhelming, the president would not act.[155] In his diary, Adams wrote: "Of [the political treachery] I can no longer entertain a doubt," but "I can fix upon no positive act that would justify the removal of him."[156] The extent of McLean's assistance to Adams's political enemy was realized after the 1828 election, when President Andrew Jackson offered to keep McLean on as postmaster general or allow him to fill the position of either secretary of war or secretary of the navy. Ultimately, McLean did not serve in Jackson's cabinet but instead took a seat on the Supreme Court—a nice reward for all his work.[157]

The fundamental problem was Adams's failure to use his appointment power in a partisan way. Robert V. Remini explains: "Had Adams used the patronage available to him in coalescing friends and independents into a workable coalition he might have had a more successful administration. But that was not his style. In general his appointments reveal a most inept politician."[158] Other scholars confirm this view,[159] but perhaps the most apt summation of Adams's pre-nomination policy and the impact of increased partisanship was provided by Ralph Ketcham:

> [Adams] kept ardently Jacksonian partisans in office, even at the cabinet level. He acted as though party organization did not exist, and he refused to use his high office to aid in his reelection. Meanwhile, Adams's opponents articulated programs attuned to popular sentiment, built party organization, electioneered assiduously, fused coalitions, and made clear their intent to use patronage to punish foes and reward friends, with the expected result: the Jacksonian movement acquired a force that swept the self-righteous president from office in 1829.[160]

Adams's principles prevented him from removing political opponents and making appointments based on party considerations. He could not reconcile the idea of the president as a "party politician" with his own belief that the president was merely "the custodian and spokesman of the whole nation."[161] This inability not only destroyed his administration but also helped to quickly dismantle the National Republican organization. In contrast, Adams's opponent, Andrew Jackson, would have no problem modifying the pre-nomination process to adapt to the emergence of a two-party system.

The early history of the pre-nomination process supports the notion that consultation between the president and Congress was a practical necessity.

Through its own interpretation of the Appointments Clause, the Senate chose to balance the president's power to nominate by providing individual senators with a veto over their home-state appointments. Senatorial courtesy would not only become a check on potential presidential abuse of the appointment power; it would also pressure the executive to consult Congress on appointments. Presidents would be mindful to involve members of Congress lest their nominations be rejected. Consultation during the pre-nomination stage would become the best means to ensure confirmation.

In addition to congressional consultation, a political party component was brought into the pre-nomination process. President Washington was the first to remark that appointing hostile officials would be "political suicide." Both Washington and Adams would go on to select people who supported their administrations. Although Jefferson would introduce the practice of removing officeholders of the opposing party, the "era of good feelings" would greatly impede the practice of removal because of the dominance of the Republican Party. Not until the election of 1824 would another political party emerge to challenged the old Republicans. The emergence of a two-party system highlighted the need for greater consideration of party affiliation in the pre-nomination process. John Quincy Adams showed that a president could no longer ignore the partisan aspect of making removals and appointments and hope to have a successful administration.

Chapter 3

The Spoils Era I (1829–1845)

The emergence of the Democratic Party with the victory of Andrew Jackson began the second two-party system. This era would last well into the 1850s and see the rise and fall of the Whig Party.[1] Previously, in the first two-party system, the Jeffersonian Republicans had dominated party politics, but in this era, the Democratic and Whig parties would continually press each other for elected federal office. The result was that party members were more dependent on federal appointments. This placed a strain on Democratic and Whig presidents that their predecessors had not experienced during the relative stability that came with one-party dominance. Consequently, numerous removals and appointments were made to give federal positions to the party faithful.

In this chapter, the concept of rotation in office, introduced by Jackson, is examined. Rotation quickly became a permanent feature of the pre-nomination process as both parties readily accepted removal as a necessary and practical reality of a competitive two-party system. In addition, congressional consultation continued and grew with both Democratic and Whig administrations. Although "reform" was used as a campaign tactic, in general, both parties believed that electoral victory required that like-minded people be placed in office to assist in carrying out party policies. Any reform of the existing system was decades away; for the time being, neither party was willing to do away with removals or congressional involvement in the pre-nomination process.

Andrew Jackson (1829–1837)

Unlike in 1824, Andrew Jackson and the Democratic Party soundly defeated John Quincy Adams and his National Republicans in the 1828 presidential race.[2] The rise of the Democrats would profoundly change the political landscape: no longer would the nation be ruled by one dominant party. As a contemporary observer of the Jacksonian period wrote: "The reign of this administration . . . is in very strong contrast with the mild and lenient sway of Madison, Monroe, and [John Quincy] Adams. . . . Our republic henceforth, will be governed by factions, and the struggle will be who shall get the offices and their emoluments—a struggle embittered by the most base and sordid passions of the human heart."[3] The political environment had changed, as had the conception of the presidency being above party politics. No longer could chief executives ignore party in the pre-nomination process. As Ralph Ketcham explained, the "positive ideas of executive leadership so deeply embedded in Jackson's vanquished foe of 1828 (and in all of his predecessors) seem so quaint and unrealistic as to belong to another age—as indeed they did."[4]

During the campaign, Jackson's message had been one of reforming government.[5] At his inaugural, Jackson spoke specifically about "the task of *reform*, which will require particularly the correction of those abuses that have brought the patronage of the Federal government into conflict with the freedom of elections, and the counteraction of those causes which have disturbed the rightful course of appointment and have placed or continued power in unfaithful or incompetent hands."[6] The "conflict with the freedom of elections" was a direct reference to the two previous presidential contests. He thought that Adams had used the pre-nomination process to promise offices to "unfaithful or incompetent" men in order to win the presidency.[7] Jackson promised to select men with the utmost "diligence and talents" and to seek "instruction and aid from the coordinate branches of the Government (i.e., Congress)."[8]

Although playing the reform candidate had been good politics and had helped secure the election, the measures professed in the inaugural address would never sustain the administration or satisfy the politicians in Jackson's newly formed political party.[9] Most knew better than to believe the noble nature of Jackson's reform message. "It was well known," John Spencer Bassett wrote, "that Jackson would favor partisan appointments. His strong and oft repeated charge that the offices were filled with inefficient and corrupt men was but laying a basis for removals."[10] Indeed, Jackson's reform message did lead to many removals, or the so-called system of rotation in office.[11] These removals were based predominantly on opposition to his administration. For example, Jackson removed future Whig senator John J. Crittenden as district attorney in Kentucky and replaced him with former representative and Democratic supporter John Speed Smith, simply because Crittenden had supported Adams for reelection.[12] In another case, future Connecticut senator and anti-Jacksonian Nathan Smith was removed from office.[13] Jackson's removals permitted him to fill more offices than any other administration up to that time. One newspaper remarked that removals "have been made with such rapidity, and have been announced to the public in so novel a manner that we find it impossible to collect or repeat them, and we have been compelled to abandon our attempt to do it."[14] The number of removals, though not as sweeping as popularly thought, exceeded those that had occurred under Jefferson, as well as the combined total of all previous administrations.[15]

While these removals were being carried out, Jackson's rhetoric made it seem as if he was leading a principled reform movement. "The people expect reform," Jackson declared, and "they shall not be disappointed; but it must be *Judiciously* done, and upon *principle*."[16] However, Jackson's words seem to be based more on partisan politics than on principle when one looks at his February 23, 1829, letter titled "Outline of Principles." This letter, written for department heads, called attention to the removal of officeholders for the purpose of making improvements "in the economy and dispatch of public business." Jackson even requested that the "moral habits" of officeholders be watched and that those found wanting in "private or public relations" be dismissed. The true purpose of Jackson's reform message, however, can be drawn from the following section: "It becomes [the department head's] duty to dismiss all officers who were appointed against the manifest will of the people or whose official station, by a subserviency to selfish electioneering purposes, was made to operate against the freedom of elections."[17] Jackson created a completely new conception of how government officials should operate. The "public business" was not one of putting the national interest above all others; rather, it was making party concerns the determining factor in every decision. Despite the occasional reference to principled reform,[18] the end result was to push out officeholders who disagreed with party ideals.[19]

By 1832, the practice of rotation in office had been established, and justifications for removals were articulated on the floor of the Senate by loyal Jacksonian senators. For example, speaking in Jackson's defense, Senator William L. Marcy of New York stated: "It may be, sir, that politicians of the United States are not so fastidious as some gentlemen are, as to disclosing the principles on which they act. They boldly preach what they practice. When they are contending for victory, they avow their intention of enjoying the fruits of it. If they are defeated, they expect to retire from office. If they are successful, they claim, as a matter of right, the advantages of success. They see nothing wrong in the rule, that to *the victor belong the spoils* of the enemy." Continuing, he explained: "General Jackson did not come in under the same circumstances that Mr. Adams did, or Mr. Monroe, or Mr. Madison. His accession was like that of Mr. Jefferson. He came in, sir, upon a political revolution."[20] This "political revolution" meant that presidents removed hostile officeholders and gave those positions to their supporters.

In relation to appointments, one popularly held belief was that Jackson was able to prevent Congress from influencing the pre-nomination process and largely appoint candidates of his choosing. Distinguished historian

Leonard D. White stated that Jackson "declined to yield to the Senate. . . . If defeated, he bided his time and again offered the same man for the same office or a different one. Negatively, the Senate was unable to protect the public service against Jackson's removals, or to compel Jackson to accept its own choice by successive rejections of the President's nominees, or to require Jackson to give his reasons for removals for its approval."[21] Although Jackson fought and won a small number of battles against the Senate, this should not be taken as a sign that he failed to consult with members of Congress or that he disregarded their opinions in most cases.[22]

In various cases, the administration consulted lawmakers about appointments from their home states. These cases reveal that congressional input was important to Jackson, and in at least one instance, he went so far as to override his own judgment and nominate the candidate backed by members of Congress. Jackson often relied on or had local congressional support when making appointments. For example, he appointed Samuel Swartwout, a Tammany Hall Democrat and a personal friend, to the prize post of New York collector.[23] Jackson, however, did not make this appointment unilaterally. Swartwout was supported by various New York congressmen and at least tacitly by the two senators, Charles E. Dudley and Nathan Sanford, who did not work against him.[24] In Pennsylvania, former representative and future senator James Buchanan sought an appointment for George B. Porter and discussed the matter with President Jackson; when time passed and no action had been taken, he complained to Secretary of State Van Buren that "still Mr. Porter is not appointed."[25] Within a year, Porter received an appointment as governor of the territory of Michigan.[26] In another case, Jackson appointed a district attorney in Ohio, remarking that the candidate had "respectable recommendations . . . with the members of Congress at its head."[27] A final example reveals that Jackson was willing to go against his own judgment and make an appointment based on congressional advice. In this case, he was about to nominate a person to a district judge position in Pennsylvania when another candidate, Thomas Irvin, was recommended by fifteen members of Congress. Jackson questioned Irvin's abilities but in the end stated, "he may not be the best, [but] they say he is so." Jackson went on to appoint Irvin.[28]

Jackson did not always select Congress's preferred candidate, but he followed pre-nomination requirements and consulted members of Congress. One Alabama case was a bit unusual because the candidate was the brother of Governor Gabriel Moore, who requested the state's senators, John McKinley and William Rufus King, to ask Jackson to appoint his brother to office.[29] After meeting with the senators, Jackson refused the request, explaining that he already had a candidate in mind. In denying the request, he was courteous, stating, "I at all times regretted in my nominations, to have to differ with the senators of a state."[30] The real reason behind Jackson's denial may have involved Governor Moore's political loyalties. The president was worried that Moore might challenge McKinley in the next Senate race and turn a solid Jackson seat into an anti-Jackson one.[31] In light of this, Jackson may have refused the appointment so as not to benefit an anti-Jackson governor.

In another case in South Carolina, Jackson again refused to nominate the preferred congressional candidate even though he had the "recommendation of seven out of eleven" of the state's congressional delegation.[32] The reason for this refusal had more to do with the political situation in the state than with Jackson's desire to take an independent course against members of Congress. In the late 1820s and early 1830s, many members of the South Carolina delegation were nullifiers, or supporters of Senator John C. Calhoun's theory that the states had the right to nullify any federal law that they deemed unconstitutional.[33] Jackson opposed this view and refused to give appointments to men who were nullifiers.[34] As in the other examples, consultation did occur, but because none of the members of Congress agreed with Jackson's political views, their candidate was not nominated.

Jackson was, at times, willing to take on Congress. A case in point was the removal of Secretary of the Treasury William J. Duane. His removal was the result of Jackson's battle with the Bank of the United States, a congressionally chartered fiscal agent that held all federal funds. Repeatedly Jackson had called for reform of the bank, but not until after his 1832 reelection victory did he press for the withdrawal of federal government funds from the institution (in the hope of killing the bank). When Duane refused to carry out Jackson's wishes, the president removed the treasury secretary and replaced him with Roger B. Taney, who immediately announced that, beginning October 1, the federal government would no longer deposit public monies in the bank. This action put the Jackson administration in direct opposition with Congress.

The proper depository for the federal government's funds would be the focus of a three-month-long debate in Senate, but an equally important concern, and one that was central to the executive's pre-nomination powers, was the propriety of Jackson's removal of Duane. As Jackson biographer Robert V. Remini explained, Duane's removal had

> opened up a problem that all previous Presidents had deftly avoided, namely, the right of a President to dismiss a member of the executive branch whose appointment had been confirmed by the Senate. Since Congress created all cabinet positions and since appointment to them required confirmation, did that not suggest that dismissal also involved legislative concurrence? Some thought so. It seemed especially true of the Treasury secretary because of his handling of public funds, which Congress exclusively controlled. But no one had ever tested the

question. No previous President had ever dismissed a cabinet officer. They simply got an offender to resign. In that way they avoided the constitutional question of the extent of the President's removal power.[35]

By early 1834, the Senate had drafted a resolution censuring Jackson. The measure called into question the reasons for withdrawing the public funds and stated that the president had "assumed upon himself authority and power not conferred by the Constitution and laws." On March 28, 1834, the Senate passed the censure resolution by a vote of twenty-six to twenty.[36] The House, where Jackson's Democrats had the majority, did not vote for censure.

Although this was not a full congressional condemnation of his actions, Jackson was unwilling to allow the censure resolution to go unanswered. On April 15 he sent a letter of protest to the Senate, stating that it had overstepped its authority by censuring him. There were only three primary means, he explained, by which the executive could be held "accountable for his official conduct": impeachment, a private lawsuit, or public opinion. "Tested by these principles," Jackson wrote, "the resolution of the Senate is wholly unauthorized by the Constitution, and in derogation of its entire spirit. It assumes that a single branch of the legislative department may for the purposes of a public censure, and without any view to legislation or impeachment, take up, consider, and decide upon the official acts of the Executive."[37]

Jackson went to the heart of the matter when he reasoned that the censure, "in its original form," was an attack on his "dismissing [of] the late Secretary of the Treasury." The Constitution, he professed, vested the executive power in the president, and "the power of appointing, overseeing, and controlling those who execute the laws—a power in its nature executive—should remain in his hands."[38] Jackson proceeded to spell out his understanding of the pre-nomination process, providing one of the most detailed explanations of the Appointments Clause given by a president since the drafting of the Constitution:

> The executive power vested in the Senate is neither that of "nominating" nor "appointing." It is merely a check upon the Executive power of appointment. If individuals are proposed for appointment by the President by them deemed incompetent or unworthy, they may withhold their consent and the appointment can not be made. They check the action of the Executive, but can not in relation to those very subjects act themselves nor direct him. Selections are still made by the President, and the negative given to the Senate, without diminishing his responsibility, furnishes an additional guaranty to the country that the subordinate executive as well as the judicial offices shall be filled with worthy and competent men.

The whole executive power being vested in the President, who is responsible for its exercise, it is a necessary consequence that he should have a right to employ agents of his own choice to aid him in the performance of his duties, and to discharge them when he is no longer willing to be responsible for their acts.[39]

Jackson's explanation of the nominating power placed all aspects in the hands of the executive. However, this statement was more for show and was not a true description of the practical application of the pre-nomination process. As detailed earlier, even Jackson's administration consulted members of Congress. Although the chief executive had the sole authority to nominate, lawmakers were never shut out of the review process.

Jackson's letter did not immediately end the controversy. The Senate refused to enter the document into its journal and denounced the president's statements. Additional correspondence between the branches took place, and a fiscal crisis occurred resulting from actions taken by the president of the Bank of the United States, who was trying to pressure Jackson to reverse his decision.[40] In less than a year, however, the Senate reversed itself and passed a measure to expunge the censure resolution by a vote of thirty-three to thirteen.[41] Jackson thus succeeded not only in removing Duane but also in forcing the Senate to reverse its attempt to punish him.

Despite this example of a daring and bold president willing to take on Congress, Jackson was not always so confident or so eager to confront the Senate. For example, he nominated Andrew J. Crawford to the federal land office in Montevallo, Alabama (on the recommendation of Jacksonian representative John Coffee of Georgia), but quickly withdrew the nomination and appointed Crawford to another position after Jacksonian senator William Rufus King of Alabama pressed for a change. Jackson regretted being unable to make the original appointment but told Crawford, "I did not believe it would be prudent to bring your name before the Senate again, and am happy you are content where you are." He explained that if anti-Jackson senators Gabriel Moore of Alabama or George Poindexter of Mississippi had "discovered that you were related to me, that would be sufficient cause, for them to reject you." (The relationship was a distant one: Jackson's aunt, on his mother's side, was married to a James Crawford, who was either Andrew's father or his uncle.) Finally, Jackson noted that although the Montevallo appointment would have been preferable to Crawford, "a rejection by the Senate might prove a greater inconvenience, and for the reasons assigned it was not done."[42]

During Jackson's administration, the Post Office Department was finally brought under the control of the executive. For most of the nation's history, postal appointments had been largely unsupervised by presidents, which had left many administrations vulnerable to hostile partisan selections (see chapter 2). Jackson understood this problem firsthand, as he had actually benefited from President John Quincy Adams's policy of allowing Postmaster General McLean to make appointments without presidential review.[43] Jackson ensured that the same would not happen to him by giving the postmaster general cabinet-level status.[44] In addition, he sought a close working relationship with his postmaster general to carry out his "reform" policy of dismissing "all officers who were appointed against the manifest will of the people." Therefore, as Jackson scholar Remini explained, "it was also necessary that the person in charge of the department work closely and intimately with the President and have a sense of what the reform was all about."[45] The great patronage of the Post Office Department was finally under Jackson's control.[46]

Congress, however, did not sit idly by, and on July 2, 1836, the Post Office Reorganization Act was passed.[47] The measure was intended primarily to root out corruption,[48] but it also served to further institutionalize congressional involvement in appointments by giving the chief executive the power to nominate postmasters "by and with the advice and consent of the Senate."[49] To further aggregate power, Congress also mandated that the department turn over its revenue to the Treasury and that the postmaster general submit an annual budget estimate for his department to be paid by congressional appropriation.[50] These measures helped give formal control over the most sought after postmasterships to the executive and legislative branches. As Dorothy Ganfield Fowler wrote, "the Postmaster General was now no longer as independent of Congress in the distribution of patronage as he had formerly been."[51] This statement was technically true, but evidence suggests that the postmaster general had rarely been completely independent from either branch.

As mentioned in the preceding chapter, by the time of the Monroe administration, the postmaster general was submitting postal appointments for presidential review. And even before passage of the 1836 postal reform bill, members of Congress were involved in the selection of postmasters. In one case, Jackson's postmaster general William Barry asked Democratic representative Francis Thomas of Maryland "to name a person to fill" a postal vacancy. Thomas secured the appointment of his preferred candidate, but he also forced the removal of that same person after finding out that there was substantial opposition to him.[52] In commenting on the matter, Whig representative Henry A. Wise said, "here a member of Congress informs us, in effect, that he appointed and he removed." Perhaps illustrating the novelty of the practice, Wise declared, "It is bad enough to be subject to the capricious wills of a President and a Postmaster General, but it is intolerable to have the independence of official station prostrated by this practical transfer of executive functions and authority to a deputy of the legislative department."[53] By the mid-1830s, the Post Office Department appears to have routinely consulted congressional representatives on postal appointments.[54]

Andrew Jackson came into the presidency touting reform and promising to clean up government. That message may or may not have been sincere, but what Jackson actually did do was finally unleash a system that had been impeded during the Republican Party era. Breaking the Republican hold on government required both a large number of removals and a large number of appointments of loyal Democrats. The increased number of appointments heightened Congress's desire to be involved in the pre-nomination process. Despite his reputation for independence, Jackson consulted with members of Congress from his own political party and often took their advice. The Jacksonians introduced not only a new era of Democratic Party rule but also a pre-nomination process based on the spoils of government.

Martin Van Buren (1837–1841)

There would be no slowdown of the Jacksonian system during Martin Van Buren's tenure in office. In his biography of Van Buren, Edward M. Shepard notes that the new president was caught in a system that had been set in motion long before he arrived: "But it must in justice be remembered, not only that Van Buren did not begin or actively conduct the distribution of spoils; not only that his acquiescence was in a practice which in his own State he had found well established; but that the practice in which he thus joined was one which it is probable he could not have fully resisted without his own political destruction, and perhaps the temporary prostration of the political causes to which he was devoted."[55] Even though caught in difficult-to-control circumstances, Van Buren followed the practice of Jackson, which he had helped produce, in making removals and appointments based on party considerations.

Former president Jackson professed to a friend that his successor would carry out his pre-nomination policy based "on principles of rotation in office" and removals.[56] Writing during his first year in office, Van Buren detailed his policy: "I should feel it my duty to [remove officers] whenever I had good reason to believe either a change in the office was necessary to carry out the general policy in the administration of gov't. in favor of which the people decided and which it was then desired to be executed."[57] Van Buren understood that he was following a Democratic administration that had already purged the federal government of many hostile officeholders.[58] This fact did not prevent him from removing individuals who were not willing to follow the administration's policies or did not have sufficient party ties to be kept on.[59] For example, Van Buren removed Federalist

Solomon Van Rensselaer, a Monroe appointee (see chapter 2), as postmaster in Albany—something that Jackson had been unwilling to do for party reasons alone.[60] Writing about Van Rensselaer's removal, former postmaster general and sitting Supreme Court justice John McLean declared:

> I have not language to express the detestation in which I hold a policy which regards neither merit qualifications nor public services, in the advancement of party views. This system which has been introduced from New York, into the federal government will, I fear, fasten itself upon the country, until the moral force of our institutions shall be utterly destroyed. And when this shall be the case, our government will not be worth preserving. Perhaps any form of government is preferable to that of a republic which is thoroughly corrupt. And this must be the inevitable result of a policy which substitutes party for principles, and which uses the patronage of the government to effectuate its objects.[61]

McLean's reference to the "system . . . introduced from New York" was an allusion to the Albany Regency established by Van Buren in the 1820s to dominate state politics through its control of local, state, and federal appointments.[62] McLean thought that Van Buren had gone too far in removing a man for no other reason than his party affiliation. But in an era when party loyalty had overtaken republican principles, McLean's understanding of politics was rapidly becoming outdated.[63]

Party loyalty was also the primary criterion when Van Buren made appointments. For instance, because lawmakers served only short terms in Congress during the nineteenth century,[64] Van Buren had a large pool of retired Democratic members of Congress to choose from. In Maine, he selected former Jacksonian representative Gorham Parks to be U.S. marshal. In Virginia, Van Buren picked another Democratic ex-congressman, John Young Mason, as U.S. district judge. Likewise, in New Jersey, he nominated former legislator Mahlon Dickerson to the federal bench. When Dickerson resigned shortly after his appointment, Van Buren selected his brother, Philemon Dickerson, another former Democratic representative, to fill the position.[65]

Consultation with congressmen was sometimes difficult for Van Buren. In Massachusetts, for example, the political climate was troublesome, to say the least. By 1838, only two of the state's fifteen-member congressional delegation were Democrats. The situation only got worse after the next congressional election, when one of the two Democratic members, Nathaniel Briggs Borden, ran unsuccessfully on the Whig ticket. This left Representative William Parmenter as the only true Democrat from Massachusetts, but in 1838, he had served for only a year and was not recognized as the leader of his state's Democratic Party.[66] That distinction was divided between two men: Marcus Morton and David Henshaw. Morton was a former Bay State representative, a future governor, and the "heir to the Jeffersonian tradition" in the state.[67] The other dominant figure, Henshaw, was a merchant by trade; he was the current collector of the Port of Boston and would later go on to become a successful railroad financier.[68] Each man controlled different factions of the Massachusetts Democratic Party, with Morton dominant in the rural areas and Henshaw in the urban sections.[69]

Morton's interests within the Democratic Party were similar to Van Buren's, so he was the primary voice in appointments. Van Buren even offered Morton the Boston collectorship, which would have meant replacing Henshaw, but Morton declined the position. However, he was able to have Van Buren appoint George Bancroft as collector in his place.[70] Because the president did not want to destroy the state's Democratic Party with this selection, he advised Bancroft "to be discreet in his dealings with his predecessor. Henshaw was not to be driven out of the party, and the new collector was not to make wholesale removals."[71]

The situation in Pennsylvania was not much better. There, the Democratic Party had split into two factions: the Family and the Amalgamators.[72] Van Buren selected former senator George M. Dallas to be the Russian minister,[73] hoping to put as much distance as possible between the two major Pennsylvania rivals: Dallas and James Buchanan. As John Niven explained: "Van Buren gambled that Dallas would be content with a mission abroad and [current Senator James] Buchanan would be so pleased to have his rival out of the country he would be pacified."[74] The gamble did not pay off. Before Van Buren had even nominated Dallas, Buchanan declared that his state needed a cabinet-level position. Sensing that no such position was forthcoming, Buchanan wrote to the president and expressed himself in "stronger" terms that "if a Cabinet Officer should not be selected from Pennsylvania, it will give great and general dissatisfaction." Buchanan, in an attempt to mask this senatorial dictate, ended the letter by noting, "I take no part in making the selection."[75]

Despite this expression of modesty, Buchanan pressed Van Buren to make selections that were beneficial to his faction. For instance, in August 1837, when a marshal position in the eastern district opened up, he complained that all "the patronage of the Custom House, the Mint, &c. &c. seems to be accorded to the City and County of Philadelphia," which was the stronghold of the Family. Buchanan proceeded to list some of the Family members who had received offices and then diplomatically stated that it was not his "intention to find any fault with this distribution of offices; but . . . merely . . . place the state of the facts before you." He then petitioned Van Buren to select "some Gentlemen in the interior" of the state (Amalgamator territory) and mentioned Samuel D. Patterson as a good choice. Similar to his first letter, Buchanan stated that he did not want to recommend but merely "to express" his general opinion about the appointment.[76] Van Buren appointed Patterson.[77]

In an attempt to rectify the absence of a Pennsylvanian in the cabinet, Van Buren selected former congressman and Amalgamator Henry A. Muhlenberg as minister to Austria.[78] That only made matters worse by angering Family member and former governor George Wolf.[79] Wolf was so outraged by the appointment (and probably jealous because he had not received a similar office) that he resigned his own position in the Treasury Department.[80] Van Buren quickly went to work to try to placate all sides of the Pennsylvania democracy by giving Wolf the Philadelphia collector position and moving the current collector, James N. Barker, into Wolf's old job.[81] Van Buren also tried to settle the matter of Pennsylvania's representation in the cabinet once and for all. The president first offered the office of attorney general to Buchanan, but the senator turned it down.[82] He then nominated Family member Henry D. Gilpin.[83] Although this selection put a Pennsylvanian in the cabinet, it was anything but helpful to Van Buren. As Senator John C. Calhoun said: "Gilpin is Attorney-General. No one seems to know by whose interest. His appointment gave much dissatisfaction to Buchanan."[84]

Another state that caused problems for Van Buren was his home of New York, where the Democratic Party was also showing signs of splintering. At the time, the two New York senators, Nathaniel P. Tallmadge and Silas Wright, were both Democrats, but only one was friendly to the administration. Senator Wright was a leader in the Albany Regency and a loyal follower of Van Buren.[85] Senator Tallmadge, in contrast, "did not harmonize on all points" with Wright and, by the late 1830s, had broken ties with Van Buren and formed a conservative faction in New York.[86] In fact, Tallmadge often sided with the Whig Party and eventually became a member in 1839.[87] Other Democrats in the New York congressional delegation, including Representative John C. Clark, would also switch to the Whig Party.[88] The loss of these conservatives placed Van Buren in a difficult situation: he had to try to stop the rest of this faction from leaving the Democratic Party while still rewarding his Albany faithful. The situation was especially acute in New York City, where the conservative Tammany Hall members and the radical Locofocos battled over the selection of a new port collector.[89] The previous collector, Samuel Swartwout, who had been appointed by Jackson over Van Buren's protest, ran off to Europe after it was discovered that he had stolen millions of dollars from public funds.[90] Although the Locofocos were loosely associated with his administration, Van Buren did not want to alienate the Tammany Hall Democrats. In an effort to placate both factions, he appointed Jesse Hoyt, "who had friends among the orthodox of Tammany and the radical Loco-Focos." The appointment was successful and paid "immediate political benefits" for Van Buren.[91]

Hoyt's appointment was made without the known support of Albany Regency members Senator Wright and Governor William L. Marcy.[92] In any other state, a senator from the president's party might have been offended by the lack of consideration for his wishes. New York, however, was an altogether different situation. President Van Buren was the recognized leader of the Albany Regency; Wright and Marcy, as lieutenants, were supposed to follow orders, and for the most part, they did. As Wright once said, "It is part of my political creed always to act with my political friends, and to let the majority dictate [the] course of action."[93] In the case of Hoyt, Van Buren chose to make party principle a higher priority than consultation with the senator. Of course, as New York senator, Wright was involved in appointment decisions in his state.[94]

William Henry Harrison (1841)

After twelve years of Democratic Party rule, a new political party was ushered into office in 1841.[95] A diverse collection of National Republicans, ex-Democrats, and states' righters, the Whigs had no unifying theme and presented no party platform or issues to stand on.[96] The 1840 election, with its "Tippecanoe and Tyler Too" campaign slogan, proved that the Whigs were good at politics but somewhat less adept at coalescing around definitive party principles. The party's standard-bearer, William Henry Harrison, was offered to the American public as a great army general from the War of 1812 and the hero of Tippecanoe, and he succeeded in defeating incumbent Martin Van Buren.[97]

As a collection of politicians, the Whigs had never controlled the presidency or had experienced only the principled rule of John Quincy Adams. As such, many Whigs were eager to gain the benefits of winning the White House, and the party's first president was willing to go along with the party faithful.[98] Harrison, to a certain extent, proceeded to remove officeholders to make room for Whig appointees; however, he was mindful of the corrupting influence of political parties in the federal bureaucracy.[99] One of Harrison's first acts as president was to instruct Secretary of State Daniel Webster to create a committee to investigate federal employment matters. Webster directed the committee to provide an accurate description and count of federal workers in Washington and to find out whether there was "any just ground of complaint against those persons." He cautioned that the committee must "inquire into no man's political opinions or preferences" but should look for employees who had been using their positions for political purposes, such as hiring or firing men based on their party standing.[100]

Despite this apparent reform effort, Whig Party members wanted to reap the benefits of federal offices and were reluctant to do away with the rotation system.[101] As one contemporary observer noted, "the horde of hungry politicians that had congregated at Washington, with . . . packages of recommendations in their pockets, clamored for the wholesale action of the politician guillotine, that they might fill the vacancies thereby created."[102] Harrison proceeded to remove more than 300 officeholders; in addition, other "officers resigned to escape removal,"[103] so the number would have been even higher if not for these "voluntary" retirements.

An accurate account of Harrison's pre-nomination process is difficult to determine, since he was in office for only a month. It appears, however, that Harrison's cabinet played a significant role in recommending and perhaps making appointments. In fact, cabinet members considered it their "right to review the President's nominations before they were sent to the Senate."[104] As Norma Lois Peterson notes, "In the Harrison administration, the Whig cabinet . . . had believed it should guide and direct all of the president's actions . . . [because it was] the Whig desire to curb or, preferably, eliminate executive usurpation." To accomplish this end, decisions were reached in cabinet meetings by majority rule, with Harrison, of course, being "first among equals" but still "having [only] one vote."[105]

Although the cabinet was on equal footing with Harrison, not all nomination decisions went through that body. Whig senator Nathaniel Tallmadge pressed Harrison to consider his input when it came to appointments in New York.[106] For example, Harrison's candidate for a marshal position was not agreeable to the senator, so Tallmadge wrote a letter of protest asserting his right to recommend appointments:

> The more I reflect on the subject, the more I am surprised at the nomination suggested to you of Mr. ——— as Marshal for the Northern district of New York. I do not know the man and I never heard of him—and *I insist upon it, that it is my right, representing the State of New York, to be heard in relation to the appointments in the state*—no man knows more about the state than myself—and I repeat that the appointment of ——— is the best appointment that can be made. . . . I am willing to take the responsibility of it.[107]

Although Tallmadge demanded "to be heard in relation to the appointments" in New York, it appears that what he really wanted was to dictate them. Harrison eventually accepted the senator's advice,[108] but only after "Tallmadge had written several letters and had secured the support of" leading members of the New York Whig Party.[109]

Other members of Congress pressed Harrison just as hard for appointments. Whig representatives Jeremiah Brown, Francis James, and Joseph Lawrence of Pennsylvania directly petitioned the president to nominate their candidate to a federal post in Philadelphia. Brown went so far as to tell Harrison that the Whig Party would be "entirely satisfied with . . . the appointment."[110] Members of the Kentucky delegation to Congress signed a letter requesting that their candidate be considered for appointment.[111] The same occurred in Connecticut, where five of the state's seven Whig members of Congress endorsed a candidate for a marshal position.[112] In Ohio, Representative Samson Mason solicited an office for his preferred candidate.[113] Other lawmakers made similar requests. Tennessee representative Thomas Jefferson Campbell sought an appointment for a marshal post.[114] Likewise, Mississippi senator John Henderson sent endorsements to Harrison and stated that he "would be gratified with" the appointment.[115]

An unusual situation occurred when Harrison bestowed on a nonmember of Congress the right to oversee, or at least review, New York appointments. The person in question was Solomon Van Rensselaer, who had served with Harrison at various times since 1794 and had fought with him in the War of 1812.[116] They were close personal friends, and during the 1840 campaign, Van Rensselaer appears to have pressured reluctant New York Whigs into supporting Harrison rather than Winfield Scott. In addition, Van Rensselaer, a popular war hero himself, had campaigned for Harrison in various parts of the country.[117] After Harrison's victory, it was rumored that Van Rensselaer would take a cabinet position, possibly secretary of war, or the powerful collector position in New York.[118] Instead, Van Rensselaer went back to his old position as Albany postmaster.[119] Although there is some evidence that Van Rensselaer would have influenced New York appointments,[120] Harrison did not live long enough for anything conclusive to occur.

One of the most prominent appointments Harrison made was that of New York collector. That appointment showed that he could seek counsel from a large group of men but make the final decision himself. After consulting New York governor William Seward and Thurlow Weed, both Whig leaders, as well as Secretary Webster, Harrison selected former Whig representative Edward Curtis as collector.[121] Whig senator Henry Clay of Kentucky protested the appointment of Curtis because he had sided against Clay in his presidency bid; the senator pushed for the selection of his friend Robert C. Wetmore.[122] It was evident that Clay believed that he could dictate appointments to Harrison.[123] Although Harrison was popularly believed to be a weak executive who would not stand up to his advisers, in this case, he showed a strong will. After being pressed by Senator Clay and receiving a rather harsh letter, Harrison shot back, "You use the privilege of a friend to lecture me & I will take the same liberty with you—You are too impetuous.

Much as I would rely upon your judgment there are others whom I must consult & in many cases to determine adversely to your suggestions." He ordered Clay to correspond with him only in writing because he preferred that "to a conversation in the presence of others."[124] As the Clay episode highlights, Harrison would fight back when pushed too far. This case, however, was not a direct refutation of the pre-nomination process norms. Harrison did consult New York party leaders; Clay was out of line trying to dictate appointments in a state that he did not represent.

In another case, Harrison showed signs of further independence from Whig leaders. Two of his cabinet members pressed for their own favored candidates for the position of governor of the territory of Iowa. Attorney General John J. Crittenden wanted the position for his friend Orlando Brown, and Secretary of State Webster sought the post for his close associate James Wilson, but Harrison had already set the position aside for former Whig representative and personal friend John Chambers.[125] Apparently unaware of this, Webster went so far as to tell Harrison at a cabinet meeting that the decision had been made to nominate Wilson to the position. Upon hearing this statement, Harrison said, "Ah! that is the decision, then is it!" The cabinet affirmed that it was. Harrison then wrote something on a sheet of paper and handed it to his secretary of state to read. Webster, looking a bit "embarrassed," read the message: "William Henry Harrison, President of the United States." Harrison then rose to his feet and declared: "And William Henry Harrison, President of the United States, tells you, gentlemen, that, by —, John Chambers shall be Governor of Iowa."[126]

Although Harrison showed independence from his cabinet officers and a willingness to respect Congress's wishes in the pre-nomination process, assessing his presidency is a difficult task because of its briefness. Shortly after Harrison's inauguration, he contracted pneumonia and died a month later.[127]

John Tyler (1841–1845)

Harrison's successor, Vice President John Tyler, was a former Democrat who had broken with Jackson over the national bank controversy. Still, Tyler retained his states' rights leanings, and as a result, he was unwilling to go along with many of his predecessor's Whig policies.[128] This placed him at odds with the majority of Whigs, and they soon broke with his administration.[129] Understanding that he did not have many allies in the Whig Party, Tyler discussed appointment matters only with members of Congress who were his personal friends.[130] This policy went against the usual pre-nomination process, whereby lawmakers from the president's party were consulted, but the circumstances were a bit out of the ordinary. As a president who had no party, Tyler was forced to build personal loyalty rather than traditional party support.

Tyler first distanced himself from the procedures devised by Harrison and his cabinet for handling policy and appointment decisions. Shortly after assuming the presidency, Tyler was informed by Secretary of State Webster that all decisions had been made by majority vote in Harrison's cabinet.[131] This was not acceptable to Tyler, and he rejected a continuation of the practice. "I beg your pardon, gentlemen," he declared, "I shall be pleased to avail myself of your counsel and advice. But I can never consent to being dictated to as to what I shall or shall not do. I, as President, shall be responsible for my administration."[132] On several occasions, Tyler proved that he meant what he said. For instance, Postmaster General Francis Granger once told a gentleman attempting to advise him on a postmaster position, "I believe I am Postmaster-General!" After the gentleman went to the White House to discuss the issue with Tyler, he came back with a note for Granger that read: "Sir,—You will abstain from making any changes in your department in the State of — without written orders from me. J. Tyler."[133] In another case, Treasury Secretary Thomas Ewing dismissed several clerks from his department, but Tyler ordered their reinstatement. Perhaps assuming that Tyler would back down if confronted on the issue, Ewing challenged the president's action during a cabinet meeting. Despite the show of force, Tyler did not relent.[134] One historian writes that the break with his department heads made it "clear that President Tyler no longer confided in his cabinet as closely as he did in certain members of Congress who had won places in his private council."[135] Obviously, the cabinet was not going to dictate to the president.[136]

Early in his presidency, Tyler made an effort not to institute removals in the fashion of his predecessors. At his first inaugural address on April 9, 1841, he stated that the "right to remove from office, while subjected to no just restraint, is inevitably destined to produce a spirit of crouching servility with the official corps, which . . . would lead to direct and active interference in the elections, both State and Federal." Tyler warned that he would press Congress to act "upon this subject." Finally, he detailed his own removal policy: "I will remove no incumbent from office who has faithfully and honestly acquitted himself of the duties of his office, except in such cases where such officer has been guilty of an active partisanship or by secret means—the less manly, and therefore the more objectionable—has given his official influence to the purposes of party, thereby bringing the patronage of the Government in conflict with the freedom of elections." Tyler finished by noting that "numerous removals may become necessary under this rule" and that he would not "neglect to apply the same unbending rule to those of my own appointment."[137]

Although Tyler tried to hold the high ground with his removal policy, he was soon forced to use the power to gain support. As a Whig president who was at heart a Democrat, he needed to win a personal following instead of traditional party backing if he was to govern effectively. For example, Tyler formally appointed Harrison's choice of former Whig representative Edward Curtis as collector of New York (one of the most sought after federal offices).[138] But the Whigs in Congress did not trust a former Democrat, nor were they willing to be led by one. Conversely, the Democrats would not accept Tyler back as head of the party he had recently abandoned. "In general," as one historian argued, "the Democrats sought to make the most of the conflict between Tyler and the Whigs, hoping to immobilize both without helping either."[139] To counter this problem, Tyler tried to form a third party based solely on his personality.[140] The result was the appointment of both Democrats and Whigs to office in an attempt to create a core group of loyal supporters. One adviser, however, explained why Tyler could not build a political party through appointments: "You possess patronage, to be sure; and you can use it, without violating any principle; but if it were ten times as extensive as it is it would not enable you to create a party of sufficient consequence to justify you in accepting a nomination even if you could obtain one. The whole Executive Patronage is but a drop in the ocean."[141]

Despite the warning, Tyler went ahead with his plan. First he used removals as a way to create vacancies for his personal friends and followers. In a letter to Treasury Secretary John C. Spencer, Tyler explained his thinking: "We have numberless enemies in office and they should forthwith be made to quit. . . . In short the changes ought to be rapid and extensive and numerous—but we should have some assurances of support by the appointees. Glance occasionally at the Marshals and D[istrict] Attorneys and let me hear from you. . . . In short my D[ea]r Sir, action is what we want, prompt and decisive action, but what I say is that we ought to know whom we appoint."[142] Tyler assumed that by removing his enemies in government and making personal appointments, he could build a viable alternative to the Whig and Democratic parties.[143] This was done primarily "to insure his own reelection."[144] At the start of the purge, Tyler "personally marked a dozen men for instant proscription, suggesting their replacements."[145] In one case, he ordered former senator and current Philadelphia collector Jonathan Roberts to remove certain hostile officeholders and replace them with Tyler men. After refusing to do so and protesting the order, Roberts himself was removed from office.[146]

Removals would not be enough, however, to assist the administration in building a third party. Although Tyler had little support in Congress, he tried to create a following as best as he could. In New York, for example, Tyler appointed John L. Graham as deputy postmaster on the basis of a recommendation by conservative Whig senator Nathaniel Tallmadge; the senator himself was appointed governor of the territory of Wisconsin.[147] Many other appointments were given to reinforce the new Tyler party. As one Tyler biographer wrote: "appointments to office were made with an eye to securing support for the President. Tyler's appointments to important offices indicated rather clearly, moreover, the extent to which he was wooing either party."[148]

Attempting to extend his network of political allies and also pass important legislation, Tyler gave some otherwise hostile Whig senators a voice in the pre-nomination process. For instance, he permitted Whig senators William C. Preston of South Carolina, William D. Merrick of Maryland, William S. Archer of Virginia, and Alexander Barrow of Louisiana to control appointments in return for their support in blocking a bill that would create a new national bank.[149] Tyler's strategy did not work, and he was forced to veto the bill.[150] The problem with using the pre-nomination process in such a fashion was that traditional practice rewarded members of Congress from the president's party not for each vote made but for being a part of the majority coalition. Arthur Schlesinger Jr. wrote that the administration "lingered affably in the middle, a President with a policy but without a party."[151]

No matter what he did, Tyler could not escape the "angry alliance of Clay Whigs and Van Buren Democrats" that proceeded to block more than a hundred of his nominations.[152] Even when he appointed members of Congress to positions of importance, the Whig-Democrat coalition would often vote for rejection. For instance, Representatives William W. Irwin, George H. Proffit, Henry A. Wise, and Caleb Cushing were all selected for office, but only one of these appointments (Irwin's) was confirmed by the Senate.[153] The lack of support from both parties was costly.[154] One historian noted, "It is not surprising that a president without a party encountered difficulty with the Senate, and that scarcely a post was filled without one or two rejections or withdrawals."[155] In addition, those individuals who accepted a "Tyler" office were quickly excluded from their former political parties. As one observer recalled, "Democrats & Whigs are standing [against] many of the late appointments and I am this day very credibly informed that [New York] Senator [Silas] Wright has written a Political friend in this country that noone who accepted office under Tyler would be any longer recognised as true Democrats!!"[156] In the end, Tyler's attempt to win the 1844 presidential election by creating an alternative political party failed. Whig and Democratic lawmakers had little reason to support the administration, and if they did accept patronage, political banishment would have been their fate. The failure to build a viable third party, coupled with the rejection of so many nominations, highlights the fact that a chief executive cannot succeed without party support in the pre-nomination process.

The presidencies of Andrew Jackson and John Tyler are pivotal to understanding the development of the pre-nomination process during this period. The introduction of the rotation principle by Jackson provided the opportunity for members of Congress to greatly increase their pursuit of federal offices. This, of course, led to more congressional consultations, which even a strong-willed chief executive like Jackson could not prevent. During Tyler's presidency, the importance of political party support became apparent. Tyler's attempt to exclude the Whig Party in appointment matters produced a backlash in the Senate, and numerous rejections were the result. Tyler's troubles not only damaged his administration but also proved that political party support is required to ensure confirmation. More important, party labels are vital during the pre-nomination process, because party affiliation clearly distinguishes which legislators are friendly and unfriendly to an administration.

The next chapter continues to document the increase of congressional influence in the pre-nomination process. In addition, the start of the third two-party system is marked by the decline of the Whig Party and the emergence of the new Republican Party,[157] which would dominate the national government from the 1860s to the 1930s.

Chapter 4

The Spoils Era II (1845–1869)

During the years leading up to the Civil War, the influence of members of Congress in the pre-nomination process greatly increased. As one account explained, this period marked "the apogee of the spoils system in the United States; the old traditions of respectability had passed away, and the later spirit of reform had not arisen; the victors divided the spoils and were unashamed."[1] Nearly every president had a difficult time dealing with the congressional pressure. From the administrations of James K. Polk through Andrew Johnson, the demand for removals and partisan appointments grew, and the extent of congressional involvement nearly took the appointment power out of the president's hands. Part of the blame for this shift should be placed on the men who occupied the White House during this time. As a group, they were generally not a distinguished lot. Zachary Taylor stands out as the least effective; although his presidency was brief, he managed to upset many of his supporters in Congress by excluding them from the appointments process. Another, Franklin Pierce, was indecisive in his nominations, which ended up angering Congress and costing his administration the support of the Democratic Party.

This period also marks the beginning of the third two-party system, with the demise of the Whig Party and the emergence of the Republican Party. During the Civil War, Republican president Abraham Lincoln was successful in managing the pre-nomination process by allowing lawmakers to dominate appointments. His successor, Andrew Johnson, was not willing to give in to such demands, and the Senate rejected many of his appointments. Congress also took away Johnson's power to remove federal officials in an attempt to protect Republican officeholders. By the end of the 1860s, Congress had reached the height of its power in the pre-nomination process.

James K. Polk (1845–1849)

After four years out of office, the Democratic Party regained control of the White House under the direction of James K. Polk.[2] Unlike President Tyler, Polk enjoyed the benefit of an allied political party. Democratic politicians, however, placed great pressure on him to remove Whig and Tyler officeholders and appoint party supporters.[3] For example, Illinois senators Sidney Breese and James Semple declared that the marshal in their state was "not acceptable to the democracy . . . and we desire, on their behalf, that a change should be made as soon as practicable."[4] Some Polk supporters even signed petitions expressing the sentiment that *"it would be the policy of this administration to remove from office, indiscriminately, all persons appointed by President Tyler*, without regard to their uniform republican principles and long services in the democratic ranks."[5] Although often called "Young Hickory," Polk did not adopt Jackson's rotation policy.[6] He did consent to the removal of "idle and worthless" Whig officeholders, but he would not systematically remove them all.[7] In his diary, Polk wrote: "Though many removals & new appointments to fill vacancies have been made by me, my administration has not been proscriptive, and the Whigs who were faithful & good officers, whom I have retained in their places, seem to appreciate my liberality towards them and many of them have called to express their gratitude."[8] Polk's removal policy left many Democrats outraged.[9] One Ohio party member told Democratic senator William Allen that the party faithful were without offices, and "hundreds of federalists who, like vampires have preyed upon the life's blood of almost every Democratic Administration, are permitted to revel in the spoils of our victories. What a Burning shame to a Democratic President."[10]

Although Polk would not remove Whigs for political reasons, he was not unconcerned about party ties in the pre-nomination process.[11] In a diary entry referring to a Supreme Court appointment, Polk wrote, "I resolved to appoint no man who was not an original Democrat and strict constructionist, and who would be less likely to relapse into the broad Federal doctrines of Judge Marshall and Judge Story."[12] He even refused to appoint one man "because he had once edited a Federalist paper in New Orleans."[13] In another case, Polk declined to give an office to a distant relative because the individual had no connections to the Democratic Party and was in fact a Whig.[14] Toward the end of his presidency, Polk expressed the party principle under which his administration operated: "the principal chief administrative officers of the Federal government should agree in opinion with the Chief Magistrate and be ready to cooperate with him in carrying out the policies of his administration."[15] This was the maxim first articulated by George Washington, and the continuation of that principle was seen as vital to Polk and all future presidents.

Despite having an allied political party, Polk still ran into difficulties when trying to manage the pre-nomination process. Most of his problems centered on the fractured state of that party. The Democratic Party was full of feuding political leaders—ranging from South Carolina senator John C. Calhoun to former president Martin Van Buren—who wanted nothing more than to control the pre-nomination process for their own personal gain. Polk was unwilling to allow one faction to dominate. In a letter to New York governor (and former senator) Silas Wright Jr., Polk acknowledged the state of the party and promised to try to keep it united: "I regret to perceive that section jealousies prevail in some parts of the country which do me great injustice & tend to weaken the party itself. In my appointments to office I resolved from the beginning to recognize & to know no divisions of the democratic party as the only means of keeping it *united* & preserving its *strength*. I was chosen, by the *United* party & without such *Union*, we must have been defeated."[16]

Although Polk tried to make unifying appointments, the divisions within his party were too great. In Pennsylvania, the appointment of Henry Horn to the collector position in Philadelphia led to a Senate rejection because Democratic senator Simon Cameron thought that he had been denied his senatorial courtesy.[17] Even Secretary of State James Buchanan became incensed over various Pennsylvania appointments.[18] In New York, the two Democratic factions—the Barnburners and the Hunkers—were at odds, and each thought that Polk preferred the other.[19] The Hunkers secured two early victories by persuading Polk to nominate William L. Marcy as secretary of war and Representative Cornelius Van Wyck Lawrence to the prized position of New York collector.[20] Martin Van Buren's son, Smith Van Buren, told Polk that Marcy's appointment would "utterly paralyze the party in our state and prostrate the Administration and its friends."[21] Polk attempted to bestow some federal appointments on the Barnburner faction, including the post of district attorney and other minor positions, but the damage had been done.[22] The Van Buren supporters never forgave Polk and even charged that his support for their rivals led to the "Democratic defeat in the New York fall elections of 1846."[23] Polk's policy resulted in a number of Senate rejections and incessant lobbying efforts from all factions of the Democratic Party.[24]

Polk's effort to devise a pre-nomination policy that rewarded all factions equally resulted in near failure. Already well into the era of congressional domination, Polk did not fully understand that Congress wanted not merely a say in the pre-nomination process; it wanted the final word. In a letter to Polk, Governor Wright explained the change:

There is, as you and I have had the strongest occasion to know, a pervading thirst for office among our population. It prevails alike with each political party, and is constantly increasing. It has, within your times and mine, extended to very large and quite numerous classes, who never thought of living by office, in the early days of the Republic. This, to much the greatest extent, is a mere passion for office, and a wish to live out of public patronage, very much regardless of principles or measures. The men who make up their minds to join this class, very soon make office seeking a business, and enter into it very much with the same spirit with which the broker commences to gamble in stocks. They become the "bulls and bears" of the political parties, and care not who loses, if they win. Of course they are the men who make the most noise; who assume to lead, and to hold influence; who praise the most freely, or condemn the most positively; and who change men, and parties, and measures, according to the prospects of the political stock market. These men are injurious to all parties, to all administrations, and to all magistrates charged with the dispensation of public patronage.[25]

Wright was correct in his assessment. Dealing with office seekers had always been part of an executive's duties, but the political climate was changing. No longer were politicians content with merely providing information and recommendations. They actually solicited offices to achieve power and influence. Members of Congress were no different, and those of the president's party actively sought and demanded the benefits of office as well.[26]

Polk understood that he could not deny congressional involvement in the pre-nomination process. In Missouri, for example, the administration gave Democratic senator Thomas Hart Benton power over appointments.[27] Polk even had to tell his brother that he could not appoint his son to a federal post in Missouri because nearly all of the state's congressional delegation had recommended another candidate.[28] Democratic senators Lewis Cass of Michigan and Daniel S. Dickinson of New York were also successful in securing the appointments of their preferred candidates.[29] In the case of a potential removal in South Carolina, Polk followed the recommendation of Democratic senator Daniel E. Huger "and the other gentleman of Congress from S.C." that the officeholder not be removed.[30] The fact was, as Polk explained, "many members of Congress assume that they have the right to make appointments, particularly in their own states," and "they often . . . fly into a passion when their wishes are not gratified."[31]

Perhaps trying to retain a measure of independence, Polk, like most presidents, ultimately excluded from the pre-nomination process those congressmen who did not follow his policies.[32] This practice seriously harmed his administration and was perhaps not the best tactic when Congress was pressing harder than ever for control over appointments. As Norman Graebner noted, Polk "did not see that the recommendations of party leaders [members of Congress] must be a necessary qualification in making appointments, for without patronage a politician is soon rendered powerless."[33] The fact was that Polk generally followed a traditional pre-nomination policy. The change was not so much with the president but with Congress and its demand for more control. Increasingly, politicians were using offices to aid in their election campaigns. Allan Nevins cites Polk's failure to give in to congressional demands as one of the main causes of the Democratic Party's collapse in the 1848 elections.[34]

Zachary Taylor (1849–1850)

The Whig Party won the presidency on the back of Mexican War hero Zachary Taylor.[35] A political novice, Taylor campaigned as a man for all the people and set out to be the "No Party" candidate, pulling together a diverse group of supporters and defeating Democratic candidate Lewis Cass of Michigan.[36] Once in office, Taylor attempted to create a new party by building common ground between Democrats and Whigs.[37] Although a good idea in theory, Taylor's nonpartisan plan created a rift between the administration and Whigs on a variety of fronts.[38]

Removals were particularly trying for the administration. Many Whig leaders found Taylor's removals and appointments deficient, even though he ousted 540 officeholders.[39] Part of the criticism was engendered by a battle within the administration over whether to retain Democratic office-holders. As Dorothy Ganfield Fowler explained: "The Postmaster General was evidently one of the most reluctant to make removals. When he took office he spoke against proscription and declared that he was going to retain the good officers, Whig or Democrat."[40] In a number of cases, Taylor chose to follow his campaign pledge and reach out to Democrats. Early in his presidency, he failed to "reverse several of Polk's last-minute Democratic diplomatic appointments."[41] In Virginia, Taylor refused to remove Polk officeholders and even appointed some Democrats, thinking that they would support his administration. This plan was anything but successful.[42] The administration eventually began removing officeholders, but the ill feelings among the Whigs would not be forgotten.[43]

Like former Whig president William Henry Harrison, Taylor tried to create a pre-nomination process that was not dominated by the president.[44] He bestowed pre-nomination authority on his cabinet and allowed them to recommend most appointments. In one rumored incident, a rebuffed office seeker asked Taylor why he had not been selected, and the president simply replied that he had "stood by him to the last, but was outvoted."[45] Although Taylor delegated much of his pre-nomination authority, the cabinet did not have total control over appointments. In several cases, he overruled the cabinet and nominated personal friends to federal positions.[46]

Criticism grew, however, that Taylor was not in charge of the pre-nomination process. As one Whig leader noted, the impression was that Taylor "shrinks from responsibility; and that the patronage . . . is prostituted to promote the ambitious aspirations of some of those who wield it with his assent."[47] More importantly, many Whigs felt that the administration had cut them off from any meaningful deliberation in the pre-nomination process. In fact, Kentucky's Whig senator Henry Clay noted: "There is very little co-operation or concord between the two ends of the avenue. There is not, I believe, a prominent Whig in either House that has any confidential intercourse with the Executive."[48] Because of this lack of interaction, many angry Whig senators "threatened to put the cabinet upstarts in their proper place."[49]

On the whole, there was no uniform pre-nomination strategy, but there were signs that the administration did give lawmakers preferential treatment. In New York, Senator William Seward was given the lead in pre-nomination decisions over Vice President Millard Fillmore.[50] The administration also tried to please Whig senators Daniel Webster, Henry Clay, and Truman Smith and former senator John Crittenden by giving their relatives federal offices.[51] But despite this deference to Congress,[52] Taylor's pre-nomination policy split the Whig Party. "Both the process by which [the administration] allotted spoils," Michael F. Holt explained, "and the selections it made produced consternation and outrage."[53] Unfortunately, Taylor was unable to rectify these problems. After a July Fourth celebration, he fell ill and died five days later.[54]

Millard Fillmore (1850–1853)

Taylor's death was a shock to the Whig Party. Like most vice presidents, his successor, Millard Fillmore, had been an afterthought, and he was almost completely unknown to many Whigs. Coming into the chief executive's office with a divided party was a daunting task, and Fillmore's first priority was to bring the fractured Whigs together. Initially, he tried a middle-of-the-road policy of securing rejections of pending appointments, making consensus nominations, and finally removing Democratic officeholders. This policy was intended to bring Whigs together while not appearing to completely reverse Taylor's pre-nomination policy.[55] Fillmore relied on Democratic senators to assist his administration in rejecting some of the more egregious Taylor appointments. For example, Postmaster General Nathan Hall suggested that Fillmore seek the aid of Democratic senator Daniel Dickinson of New York in rejecting a number of postmasters for that state. Hall advised that these appointments "must not be confirmed if it is possible to prevent it."[56] Of course, Fillmore could have simply withdrawn nominees pending before the Senate; however, in the hope of preventing further party divisions, he preferred to let the Democrats do the dirty work by rejecting his (Taylor's) nominations. After securing the rejections, Fillmore appointed nominees who had previously been blocked by Taylor's cabinet. Finally, he removed the few remaining Democratic officeholders appointed by Taylor.[57]

Fillmore's compromise policy was put to the test in New York, where Taylor had given Senator Seward dominance in the pre-nomination process. As the chief executive, Fillmore could have removed the Seward officeholders and nominated political friends. Instead, he refused to purge existing officeholders and appointed more agreeable Whig candidates only when offices became available.[58] In other appointments, Fillmore tried to bring the factions of the Whig Party closer together. For example, he filled the foreign post in Prussia by appointing former Whig representative Daniel D. Barnard to replace Taylor's choice of Democratic senator Edward Hannegan. In addition, Fillmore reversed Taylor's failed Virginia policy of appointing Democrats, replacing those Democrats with friends of southern Whig congressmen.[59] These southern appointments had the added benefit of gaining congressional support for the administration's policy goals. On several key votes, Representative Edward Carrington Cabell backed the administration's omnibus bill that created permanent boundaries for the state of Texas and established a territorial government for New Mexico.[60] In addition, Georgia senator John Berrien voted for the Compromise Act of 1850 in the hope of receiving future patronage.[61] Both bills were passed and became law.

Despite some successes, the attempt to bring the Whig Party together failed. One of Fillmore's final efforts at unification occurred at the New York convention, where his allies, the "lower law" Whigs, lost a decisive battle to the Seward faction of the party, the "higher law" Whigs.[62] The main issues were slavery and the Compromise Act of 1850. By supporting the act, Fillmore had hoped to unite the Whig Party. However, he was unable to gain enough delegates to keep antislavery elements out of the convention, and the party fell apart. After the 1852 elections, most members joined either the Democratic Party or the newly formed Republican Party.

Franklin Pierce (1853–1857)

In the early 1850s, the Democratic Party contained three main factions: Free-Soilers, southern rights advocates, and a moderate element.[63] None of these groups had enough support to garner the necessary votes to secure the Democratic nomination. As a result, Franklin Pierce became the dark-horse candidate at the 1852 Democratic National Convention when the leading contenders, James Buchanan and Lewis Cass, deadlocked.[64] Winning the nomination on the forty-ninth ballot, Pierce went on to defeat the Whig candidate, Winfield Scott, in the general election.[65]

Before Pierce's administration could get under way, Congress passed what would be considered its first pre-nomination, or civil service, reform bill. The measure, enacted on March 3, 1853, was part of an annual appropriation bill that called for the division of clerks in the Treasury, War, Navy, Interior, and Post Office departments into four classes for purposes of salary considerations. In addition, a three-member board was to be created in each department to examine the candidates for the clerical positions covered under the law.[66] Leading civil service historians agree that the so-called pass examinations were largely a failure. "Since competitive examinations were not required," Adelbert Bower Sageser stated, "the number of candidates could be easily restricted, and the character of the examination depended entirely on the discretion of the head of the department who was also the appointing officer."[67] The restrictions were usually based on whether an office seeker had the backing of a member of Congress from the president's party.[68] If an endorsement was secured, the examination was usually little more than perfunctory. Jacob D. Cox (who would become secretary of the interior under President Grant) recalled that "the sum total of the examination [consisted] of a single question, such as, 'What did you have for breakfast?' or, 'Who recommended you for appointment?' or 'Where would you go to get your pay at the end of the month?'"[69] It appears that the examinations were taken seriously only for clerks whose duties involved "fiscal" matters.[70] The law would stay on the books until passage of the Civil Service Act of 1883 (see chapter 6).

President Pierce, like many of his predecessors, ran into difficulties with the pre-nomination process. He decided not to push immediately for the removal of Whig officeholders, most of whom had good performance records. For example, in the State Department, Secretary William Marcy permitted all officeholders to stay in their posts if they were performing their jobs properly.[71] The difficulty with rewarding officeholders based on merit rather than politics was that the policy prevented Democratic politicians from filling those posts with their friends. Even when Democratic leaders pushed for the removal of Whigs, Pierce seems to have been incapable of complying. For example, despite telling a friend that he would remove "the present Secretary of the Territory of Minnesota and . . . nominate you for the office," Pierce took no such action. In another instance, he reappointed a person that he had recently removed from office.[72]

Major appointments were discussed during cabinet meetings, but Pierce allowed cabinet members to manage minor positions on their own.

Candidates backed by party leaders such as senators or representatives were, as a Pierce biographer notes, "accepted without much question."[73] For example, Illinois senator Stephen Douglas was often consulted and managed to secure various federal appointments in his state.[74] Likewise, Representative Preston King of New York solicited appointments from the president, as did Senator Henry Dodge and Representative Daniel Wells Jr. of Wisconsin.[75] In one case, Pierce asked the Democratic delegation of Iowa, Senators George Jones and Augustus Dodge and Representative Bernhart Henn, whom they "wished removed and whom appointed in Iowa." Other members of Congress were similarly consulted.[76]

Like most presidents, Pierce had trouble managing the various factions within his party. In New York and Louisiana, appointments proved to be especially difficult. In New York, Democrats were divided among Barnburners, Hardshells, and Softshells.[77] Former Hardshell senator Daniel Dickinson objected when Pierce named Softshell William Marcy as secretary of state. The president tried to split the difference among the factions by appointing Dickinson to the New York collector position, Barnburner John Dix as assistant treasurer, and Softshell Herman J. Redfield as naval officer.[78] These appointments, however, failed to satisfy any of the factions. The same problem occurred in Louisiana, where Pierce attempted to divide appointments equally between Democratic senators and factional rivals John Slidell and Pierre Soule.[79] Nevertheless, both men fought over every appointment. For example, when the New Orleans collectorship became available, Slidell tried to influence Secretary of State Marcy into siding with his preferred choice: former Democratic representative and political ally Alexander G. Penn. Slidell told Marcy that Soule's brother-in-law was Penn's chief rival for the position and that, if appointed, he would "insure the defeat of our party at the next election."[80] Neither man won the appointment. Instead, Pierce selected former Democratic senator Solomon W. Downs.[81]

Most of Pierce's appointments ended up angering all parts of the Democratic Party, which cost the administration the support of any side. Senator Slidell lashed out at Pierce, declaring: "I have no hope that any change can restore to the President the lost confidence of the party. . . . The personal unpopularity or rather the total want of consideration and influence of the administration has been the chief cause of our reverses. The mass of the party is as sound as ever, but no confidence is reposed in its nominal chief, & a party without a head is doomed to as certain destruction, as an army without a general."[82] The lack of executive leadership can be seen in Pierce's inability to make decisions. At various moments, he would reverse course when confronted by a disgruntled lawmaker. For example, Pierce had decided to remove a corrupt Chicago postmaster but backed down when Senator Douglas complained about the removal.[83] In the territory of Oregon, Pierce and delegate Joseph Lane had agreed on two appointments for judicial offices. However, Illinois senators Douglas and James Shields and the Pennsylvania congressional delegation were able to persuade the president to withdraw the nominees and appoint other candidates. Then, after discovering Pierce's reversal, Lane was able to convince him to switch again and reinstate one of the appointments.[84]

Pierce was largely a weak and ineffectual chief executive. Although even a stronger person would have been unable to deny members of Congress a role in making nominations, a person with better judgment could have ensured that his polices did not anger all parts of his party. Such unnecessary clashes prevented any possibility of a second term.[85] Pierce's use of the pre-nomination process to give every faction equal consideration and his overall independence in other policy areas produced many enemies. However, the rising sectional battles between North and South did not serve the administration well either.

James Buchanan (1857–1861)

James Buchanan was a longtime presidential hopeful and had nearly won the nomination in 1852. Four years later, he would win the Democratic nomination on the seventieth ballot as the compromise candidate.[86] Being the party standard-bearer meant trying to pull the southern and northern factions together to not only win the election but also save the Union. Buchanan easily defeated Republican candidate John C. Frémont, whose name was not even on the ballot in most southern states.[87] As president, however, Buchanan failed to stem the growing sectional divide over slavery.

In terms of the pre-nomination process, Buchanan did not make prominent use of the removal power compared with his contemporaries.[88] Coming into the presidency on the heels of another party member meant that much of the federal civil service was already Democratic. This did not mean, however, that the administration was going to forgo a Jacksonian-style rotation policy. In fact, Buchanan "announced that no one should, unless under exceptional circumstances, receive a reappointment after his commission expired." The "exceptional circumstances" referred to the South, where the political climate was not amenable to rotating officeholders.[89] In the rest of the country, Buchanan would not allow Pierce Democrats to stay safely in office. To a friend he wrote, "They say, and that, too, with considerable force, that if the officers under a preceding Democratic administration shall be continued by a succeeding administration of the same political character, this must necessarily destroy the party."[90] Therefore, he ordered anyone removed who was not in agreement with his policies.[91] The simple fact was that Buchanan was a bigger supporter of a rotation philosophy than even

Jackson himself.[92] There was no mention, however, of what the administration did with inefficient or corrupt officeholders.

In terms of appointments, members of Congress were given a voice in the pre-nomination process. For instance, five of the six South Carolina representatives pressed Buchanan for an appointment, noting that it "would be a source of great pleasure to us and very acceptable to our state."[93] In Louisiana, Democratic senator John Slidell had almost complete control of appointments in his state.[94] Local appointments were usually made by the Democratic representative, who could practically dictate candidates for positions such as postmaster.[95] In fact, for the first time, the "right" of Democratic representatives to control appointments was mentioned by an administration official. Although conceding that the "right" had "no existence in fact," Postmaster General Horatio King stated that out of "courtesy, the member, when agreeing politically with the administration, is very generally consulted in respect to appointments to his district."[96]

Like his predecessors, Buchanan had trouble dealing with various factional rivalries. In New York, the appointment of a personal friend created near chaos among Hardshells, Softshells, and Tammany Hall political leaders. Buchanan did not fare much better in his home state of Pennsylvania. Surprisingly, he ignored his political base and appointed members of rival factions.[97] In addition, the rising sectional divide of slavery produced discord within the Democratic Party. For example, in California, the party was split between a pro-slavery group, called the Chivalry, and a Free-Soil wing. Although both sides had agreed to give the Free-Soilers control of appointments in exchange for their support of Chivalry leader William K. Gwin's reelection to the Senate, Buchanan refused to go along with it. Instead, he gave Gwin control over appointments and left Free-Soil senator David C. Broderick without the patronage he thought he rightly deserved.[98] Buchanan provoked Broderick "unmercifully" by nominating, without the solicitation of Gwin, Benjamin F. Washington, a Chivalry member, as collector of the Port of San Francisco.[99] Then, when Buchanan did select a Free-Soiler to a post—naming John Bigler as minister to Chile—it did more harm to Broderick by removing "his most effective political ally from California altogether."[100] Buchanan had clearly made a decision to aid the pro-slavery element of the Democratic Party with federal appointments, but this course did more harm than good to his administration. One historian explained the impact of Buchanan's pre-nomination policy in California: "The break between the two men [was] of more than passing moment and academic interest, for Buchanan's treatment of Broderick and his section of the Democratic party had far-reaching effects. Buchanan's reputation as a 'National Democrat,' a representative of the broad middle ground of opinion within the Democracy, was destroyed in large measure in the course of his clash with Broderick."[101]

Although Buchanan's reputation may have been damaged by his handling of California patronage, he was merely following the practice of the day. Consultation in the pre-nomination process was awarded to the "regular" faction of the Democratic Party. And as a southern sympathizer, Buchanan could not be expected to hand over control of federal appointments to Free-Soil Democrats who were opposed to many of his policies.[102]

A much more unusual break with a Democratic politician occurred in Illinois when the administration proceeded to make some rather hostile moves against Senator Stephen Douglas.[103] For example, Buchanan removed a Douglas supporter from the powerful Chicago collector position, and a friendly Chicago postmaster was replaced by a former Douglas man turned political enemy, Isaac Cook.[104] Although Douglas tried to hold up the latter appointment by charging that Cook had defaulted during his previous tenure as postmaster, the papers submitted to the Senate by the administration were "evidently satisfactory," because the appointment was confirmed.[105] There are two possible explanations for Buchanan's actions. First, Buchanan may have resented the fact that Douglas had challenged him for the Democratic nomination in 1856.[106] The second reason may have been related to Douglas's belief in popular sovereignty and his refusal to support the Lecompton constitution, which was damaging to Buchanan's wing of the party.[107] Despite the hostile measures and the differences between the two men, Douglas was still considered Illinois' "most powerful spokesman" when it came to appointments and appeared to receive his due share of patronage.[108]

Abraham Lincoln (1861-1865)

The Republican Party won its first presidential election with a collection of former Whigs, ex–Free-Soilers, Union Democrats, reform politicians, and other political castoffs.[109] And like previous victors, the Republicans wanted to exploit the power over appointments and thus solidify their electoral success.[110] The new president had other concerns, however. The rising sectional crisis resulting from the bombardment of Fort Sumter would eventually cause the southern states to secede from the Union.[111] As a result, "Lincoln, engrossed by the cares of the war, systematically referred to [lawmakers] all appointments to local offices; he did little more than countersign the selections made by the Representatives or the Senators."[112]

More than any other time in the nation's history, unity of the ruling political party was paramount. As Carl Russell Fish explained: "The Republican party was new; it was composed of diverse, hostile elements; it was full of petty jealousies, and its discipline was not good; if it was to be kept together, much depended on a proper disposition of the favors the president could bestow."[113] Lincoln, perhaps aware of the need for party unity, gave Republicans the spoils of victory. For example, soon after assuming office, he sent a letter to Treasury Secretary Salmon P. Chase seeking to have one official removed and replaced with a person recommended by Thurlow Weed and Horace Greeley, two prominent New York Republicans.[114] Lincoln made this a uniform policy, and as a result, his administration made "the most sweeping removal of federal officeholders up to that time."[115] When all was said and done, Lincoln had removed 1,195 officeholders to be replaced by loyal Republicans.[116] All presidents made use of the removal power, but as Secretary of the Navy Gideon Welles pointed out, "the President and some of his Cabinet . . . were disposed to go beyond others in these respects."[117]

In terms of the pre-nomination process, the administration "regularized and universally recognized" recommendations from members of Congress. For example, announcements were made "in the newspapers that the appointment of postmasters with salaries of less than $1,000 per year would be made upon the recommendation of the Republican Congressman of that district and therefore it would be better to address applications to him rather than to the Department."[118] Even presidential appointments were usually based on the advice of representatives. The only exception to a representative's power over postal appointments was the decision to allow Republican senators to recommend candidates in their hometowns.[119] This senatorial deference may have been a result of Senate practice. As Welles explained: "there is an implied understanding—a courtesy among Senators—that they will yield to the personal appeals of a Senator in appointments to offices in his own town."[120] The result was that the administration had no desire to "flout the traditional practice of 'senatorial courtesy,' nor did [Lincoln] try to avoid the time-honored custom of heeding the wishes of representatives."[121]

Congressional influence was so powerful that Lincoln himself admitted that he would not go against the wishes of lawmakers. In a letter to Jesse K. Dubois, an Illinois politician and friend, Lincoln expressly stated that he would follow members' recommendations: "I was nearly as sorry as you can be at not being able to give Mr. Luce the appointment you desired for him. Of course I *could* have done it; but it would have been against the united, earnest, and, I add, angry protest of the republican delegation of Minnesota, in which state the office is located. So far as I understand, it is unprecedented, [to] send an officer into a *state* against the wishes of the members of congress of the State, and of the same party."[122] In another instance, he told Rhode Island governor William Sprague that he could not nominate his candidate because the state congressional delegation had not approved him.[123] Lincoln even noted that his administration had "distributed to its party friends as nearly all the civil patronage as any administration ever did."[124]

Reflecting back on this time, Republican senator George F. Hoar of Massachusetts remarked, "the Senate claimed almost entire control of the Executive function of appointment to office. Every Senator, with hardly an exception, seemed to fancy that the national officers in his State were to be a band of political henchmen devoted to his personal fortunes. What was called 'the courtesy of the Senate' was depended upon to enable a Senator to dictate to the executive all appointments and removals in his territory."[125]

Even with a policy of congressional consultation, Lincoln still experienced various problems in the pre-nomination process. For example, Senator Edward D. Baker of Oregon thought that he should control all western appointments because he was the lone Republican in Congress from the Pacific coast. Lincoln eventually had to find a solution when California Republicans took offense at Senator Baker's involvement in appointments for their state.[126] In New York, Lincoln had to manage a fight between former senator and current secretary of state William Seward and New York senators Preston King and Ira Harris. Lincoln was put in the particularly awkward position of meeting with all three men at the State Department to establish a division of the appointments.[127] During a Kansas dispute between Senator James Henry Lane and Governor Thomas Carney, Lincoln became so fed up with the political infighting that he stated, "in my opinion there is not a more foolish or demoralizing way of conducting a political rivalry, than these fierce and bitter struggles for patronage."[128] Such conflicts were soon over for Lincoln, who was shot and killed on April 14, 1865, by southern sympathizer John Wilkes Booth.[129]

Andrew Johnson (1865–1869)

Similar to the death of President Harrison in 1841, Lincoln's assassination dealt a heavy blow to the Republican Party. The new president, Andrew Johnson, had been a Jacksonian Democrat and had sided with the Union when the Civil War began.[130] Although the Republican Party hesitantly backed Johnson after Lincoln's death, open warfare broke out soon thereafter. As a former Democrat, Johnson was not willing to adhere to Republican wishes in Congress. By the summer of 1866, Johnson was planning an alternative convention made up of conservative Republicans and war Democrats.[131]

The primary divide between Johnson and Congress was over Reconstruction.[132] Each branch had its own understanding of how the southern states should be brought back into the Union and the proper means of accomplishing that end. Hans L. Trefousse explained: "the president was determined to frustrate congressional Reconstruction in order to maintain the Union as he believed the Founding Fathers had designed it and to protect Southern whites from what he considered the horrors of complete racial equality."[133] With the Reconstruction battle in full swing and a breach developing between the president and the Republican Congress, "Johnson proceeded to remove officeholders that had been appointed at the request of congressional opponents, and to appoint his own followers."[134] These supporters, in turn, would use their federal office to aid Johnson. For example, Philadelphia collector John W. Stokes told Johnson that he had "removed about twenty offices who had been and were your open and bitter enemies and put in their places as many good true and faithful men and warm supporters and defenders of yourself and measures."[135] Johnson eventually removed 903 officeholders.[136]

The problems Johnson experienced in the pre-nomination process were doubly difficult because his supporters (mostly war Democrats and a few conservative to moderate Republicans) sought federal offices while Republican officeholders fought to keep them. One Wisconsin Democrat, writing to Johnson supporter and moderate Republican senator James R. Doolittle, expressed dismay at the situation: "I feel sick at heart, when I look over the state and see the patronage of the government in the hands of . . . your enemies and Mr. Johnson's."[137] Johnson proceeded with a number of removals to appease his supporters, but the upper house would not accept the hostile attempt to purge Republicans from office.

The Senate's policy of rejecting Johnson's nominations appears to have been widely known. One supporter told Johnson "that the Senate, has determined to reject, without regard to qualification or otherwise, any & every person, who formerly belonged to the Republican party, but who dared to vindicate their manhood by a support of [your] Administration."[138] Johnson was often forced to nominate several candidates for the same vacant position. For example, the Senate rejected three nominations for a Michigan collector post before a Johnson nominee was finally confirmed.[139] Likewise, three of Johnson's candidates for a Pennsylvania naval position were rejected.[140] Missouri topped both these states: the Senate rejected six nominations for collector of internal revenue before making a confirmation.[141]

Many of the Senate's rejections were led by Radical Republicans.[142] For instance, Massachusetts senator Charles Sumner and Michigan senator Zachariah Chandler, both Radical Republicans, were directly responsible for the rejection of appointments from their states.[143] These rejections were in line with the concept of senatorial courtesy, whereby a home-state senator could call on fellow senators to reject a nominee from his state. Other appointments that were not directly opposed by home-state senators nevertheless involved varying degrees of senatorial courtesy. For example,

Hunter Brooke failed to be confirmed as deputy postmaster in Ohio when both his home-state supporters, Senator John Sherman and Representative Rutherford B. Hayes, were away from the Capitol when the vote occurred. Although the other Ohio senator, Benjamin F. Wade, was present, he refused to assist in Brooke's confirmation out of courtesy to Representative Benjamin Eggleston, who opposed him.[144]

The rejection of Brooke highlights several ancillary aspects of the pre-nomination process. The first is the deference shown to senators when considering nominations from their home states. In Brooke's case, Republican senator Alexander Ramsey confirmed that the rule of "leaving all such approvals [of local appointments] to the decision of the State Senators" was followed.[145] Ramsey's statement, however, failed to explain how a rejection could have occurred if the two Ohio senators were not in agreement. It appears that a senator's presence on the floor of the Senate was key to this custom. Since only Wade was in attendance, the Senate could rely only on his thoughts and concerns to make a determination of fitness.[146] More importantly, this outcome showed that the Senate would not extend senatorial courtesy to an absent member (in this case, Sherman). The other interesting feature of the Brooke nomination was the obvious involvement of Ohio representatives Hayes and Eggleston. This illustrated a willingness by the Senate (or at least Senate colleagues from the same state) to extend senatorial courtesy to House members. Although it is not clear whether Wade actively worked against Brooke's nomination, he was unwilling to support confirmation and therefore respected Eggleston's opposition.

Another Senate rejection supported the concept of extending courtesy to House members. President Johnson appointed James Birney to be assessor of internal revenue in the district of Republican representative John F. Driggs of Michigan, and the Senate rejected Birney's nomination.[147] The two Michigan senators, Zachariah Chandler and Jacob M. Howard, did not oppose the nomination, but as Birney explained, the rejection was "a concession which the Senate make[s] to representatives as to local offices," and Driggs used this courtesy to prevent Birney's confirmation.[148] Both the Brooke and the Birney cases show that the Senate's internal procedures served to strengthen members of Congress in their individual negotiating positions with Johnson. In all cases, however, this courtesy was extended only to lawmakers from the president's party.

In relation to the pre-nomination process, however, political party distinction was not always clear-cut. For the most part, Johnson consulted only conservative to moderate Republicans in Congress. For instance, conservative Republican senator Samuel C. Pomeroy was able to influence appointments in Kansas, securing the nomination and confirmation of George C. Snow as Indian agent.[149] Because of opposition from Radical Republicans, however, Johnson was forced to find allies from his old political party, which resulted in a number of Democratic lawmakers gaining influence in the pre-nomination process. For example, in New York, three Democratic representatives were involved in making local appointments.[150] The same occurred in Maryland, Pennsylvania, and New Jersey, where Johnson made appointments to strengthen his own standing with Congress and to build up an army of personal supporters.[151] As one Republican supporter told Johnson, these appointments led to the belief "that the Democrats are controlling to a very large extent the distribution of your patronage." And this supporter objected "to the distribution of the patronage" to Democrats, whether they are "senators or members of the House, and our [friends] here protest with great earnestness against the combinations."[152]

Despite the large number of Democrats consulted, Johnson did not completely exclude all regular, or even Radical, Republicans. For instance, regular Republican senator Simon Cameron and Radical representative Thaddeus Stevens were able to secure the appointments of Radicals.[153] Johnson may not have known that he was appointing Radical Republicans, however. As one of his Michigan supporters explained: "The Radicals here have resorted to every art to deceive you in order to obtain control of the Federal offices; and in this they have had only too much aid at Washington (i.e., members of Congress)."[154]

Even though the Republican Senate rejected many of Johnson's nominations and was able to "deceive" him into appointing Radicals, the Republicans were still concerned about losing ground to Johnson. For example, Radical House leader Thaddeus Stevens was worried that Johnson's removals would entice Republicans to ally themselves with the administration in order to secure appointments. Thus, he warned his fellow party members "to keep an eye on any professed Republican who consents to fill an *enforced vacancy*. . . . He is a moral leper whom you should not touch. He should be socially ostracized as unfit for decent society. Let him flit about in the twilight and hide his averted countenance from the light of day."[155] A more moderate voice expressed the hope that Congress would not adjourn "without passing some bills to protect themselves, and their brave constituents, men who by hundreds are being 'kicked out of office.'"[156]

On March 2, 1867, Congress did just that when it passed the Tenure of Office Act over the veto of President Johnson.[157] That act stipulated senatorial approval to remove an officeholder whose appointment had required Senate confirmation. It also provided that cabinet members should hold their offices for the full term of the president who appointed them, subject to removal by the Senate. The act thus seemingly protected Secretary of War Edwin M. Stanton, who was an ally of the Radical Republicans, and worked to prevent any presidential interference in Congress's Reconstruction policy.[158] In the words of Carl Russell Fish: "The Tenure-of-Office

Bill of 1867 marked the first definite success that the Senate had obtained in its contest with the president for the control of the patronage; it was a partisan measure, directed against a particular president."[159]

After passage of the Tenure of Office Act, ongoing differences between the president and the secretary of war over Reconstruction intensified.[160] In August 1867, Johnson demanded Stanton's resignation.[161] When the secretary refused, Johnson suspended him and appointed Ulysses S. Grant secretary ad interim.[162] In accordance with the Tenure of Office Act, Johnson sent a letter to the Senate on December 12 stating his reasons for the suspension.[163] For nearly a month, Johnson's letter was considered by the Senate; finally, on January 10, the Senate declared that it did not concur in the dismissal of Stanton.[164] Grant thus turned the office over to Assistant Adjunct General E. D. Townsend.[165] Johnson, not wanting to hand the position back to Stanton, removed him on February 21 and appointed Lorenzo Thomas as secretary ad interim.[166]

On February 24, the House voted 128 to 47 to impeach Johnson, basing its action primarily on Stanton's suspension.[167] In total, seven of the eleven articles of impeachment accused Johnson of various violations of the Tenure of Office Act. During the trial, Johnson's lawyers argued that since Stanton had been appointed by Lincoln, Johnson was not in violation of the act because "Lincoln's 'term' had ended long before the removal."[168] On May 16, enough Republican senators agreed with this argument to prevent Johnson's conviction on the major counts.[169] Hans L. Trefousse noted: "The charges against him were too flimsy; fear that conviction would destroy the tripartite form of government—the division of powers between the executive, legislative, and judicial branches—influenced several senators."[170] Once Johnson was acquitted, Stanton resigned, and John M. Schofield was nominated. Although the Senate confirmed Schofield, in its motion it declared that Stanton "has not been legally removed."[171]

For his remaining year in office, Johnson continued to experience problems with the Senate. As Trefousse explained: "While the president still had power to make appointments, the Senate could, and frequently did, reject them."[172] For example, after resigning as attorney general to defend Johnson at his impeachment trial, Henry Stanbery was renominated to that same post. The Senate, however, voted twenty-nine to eleven not to confirm Stanbery.[173] Johnson's acquittal was much more a personal victory for him than a victory for the presidency. It did not strengthen presidential power in the pre-nomination process. The fact remained that the Tenure of Office Act was the law, and it was a constant reminder to future chief executives that Congress could again try to assert legislative control over the pre-nomination process. Writing eight years after the Johnson impeachment, future president James A. Garfield summed up the immediate consequences for the executive branch:

This evil has been greatly aggravated by the passage of the Tenure of Office Act, of 1867, whose object was to restrain President Johnson from making removals for political cause. But it has virtually resulted in the usurpation by the Senate of a large share of the appointing power. The President can remove no officer without the consent of the Senate; and such consent is not often given, unless the appointment of the successor nominated to fill the proposed vacancy is agreeable to the Senator in whose State the appointee resides. Thus it has happened that a policy [rotation in office], inaugurated by an early President [Thomas Jefferson], has resulted in seriously crippling the just powers of the executive, and is placed in the hands of Senators and Representatives a power most corrupting and dangerous.[174]

This period witnessed the decline of the Democratic Party largely because of the debate over slavery and a series of weak and ineffectual presidents. The men who occupied the White House were forced to manage the resulting factional warfare among rival Democratic Party members when handling appointments. The increased desire for federal office produced a growing need for congressmen to become more involved in the pre-nomination process. By Buchanan's administration, consultation had almost given way to dictation. The new Republican Party under Lincoln required offices to solidify what could have been a one-time electoral victory. In addition, Lincoln had more pressing concerns than battling Congress over patronage issues. By the time Johnson took over the presidency, his push for some measure of independence showed the extent of congressional dominance in the pre-nomination process. In addition to rejecting many of Johnson's appointments, the Senate enacted legislation to prevent him from removing officials. The pre-nomination system at the end of the 1860s was completely unbalanced, with Congress taking over the executive's role in appointment matters. There was no longer a system of checks and balances or even separate branches sharing power. Congress had modified its interpretation of the Appointments Clause to assume almost total control over appointments.

Chapter 5

Birth of Civil Service Reform (1869–1881)

After the presidency of Andrew Johnson, the Republican Party would once again control the White House under Civil War hero Ulysses S. Grant. Grant's victory marked the beginning of Republican dominance of the executive branch. Back in power, Republican lawmakers sought and obtained substantial control over the pre-nomination process. Despite the executive's willingness to allow congressional participation, Congress would not accept the president as an equal partner in matters of appointments, having refused to repeal the Tenure of Office Act, a measure passed during Johnson's presidency to protect Republican officeholders.

Many politicians, however, believed that reform efforts should be made to take political party and congressional control out of the federal bureaucracy and, by extension, the pre-nomination process. Several reform measures were introduced in Congress during Grant's administration, intended either to ensure worthy federal officeholders or to put an end to congressional involvement in the pre-nomination process. Neither effort had much success. By the presidencies of Rutherford B. Hayes and James Garfield, the lines had hardened: Congress would not allow the executive branch to share equally in the pre-nomination process. Both Hayes and Garfield battled Congress's hold over appointments. Each would take on powerful New York senator Roscoe Conkling, and each would claim credit for weakening the congressional dominance that had grown under the presidencies of Buchanan, Lincoln, Johnson, and Grant.

Ulysses S. Grant (1869–1877)

Ulysses S. Grant was the Republicans' inevitable choice in the 1868 presidential contest, easily defeating Democratic candidate Horatio Seymour.[1] With a Republican in the White House, and after four years of feuding with a hostile chief executive, one might have expected the Republican Congress to repeal the Tenure of Office Act. Grant favored abolishing the statute and pressured the legislative branch to do so. In his diary, Gideon Welles wrote that "Grant . . . holds up [nominations] to compel the Senators to surrender their usurped power." In addition, the president "tells applicants that he wishes the law repealed and holds himself under no obligation to remove incumbents whilst it remains."[2] The House was willing to repeal the act,[3] but despite having a Republican in the White House, the Senate was not inclined to give up its power over the executive.[4] Therefore, the practice of removing officeholders under the existing law varied: "Usually, nominations in the place of officers suspended were confirmed without comment. Sometimes there was investigation, and occasionally evidence was printed for the use of the Senate. Often this was in answer to a protest on the part of the officer suspended. The result was nearly always an ultimate approval of the action of the president."[5] Perhaps sensing that Congress would not repeal the act, Grant began to remove a large number of officeholders. Welles observed that he "appears to be making an unusual change or general sweep of all official incumbents, irrespective of party."[6]

With regard to the pre-nomination process Grant experienced one major mishap early in his presidency. The Judiciary Act of 1869 created one circuit judgeship for each of the existing nine circuits,[7] and Grant relied on Attorney General Ebenezer Rockwood Hoar to supply the names of candidates to fill these new positions. This decision greatly angered Senate Republicans, who felt that they should have furnished the names. The unhappy senators soon got their revenge when the president nominated Hoar for a vacant Supreme Court seat. The Senate Judiciary Committee reported adversely on the nomination, and the Senate rejected Hoar by a vote of thirty-three to twenty-four.[8] This was Grant's first and only appointment oversight.

Following the traditional customs of the pre-nomination process was difficult even with one-party control over the presidency and Congress. President Grant had not yet decided on a division of New York appointments between rival Republican senators Roscoe Conkling and Reuben Fenton when the latter began to oppose the administration's policies. As a result, Conkling was given absolute power over appointments in his state.[9] Grant's appointment of Thomas Murphy to the New York collector position strengthened Conkling's position. Fenton opposed the nomination but was powerless to prevent Murphy's confirmation.[10] On the Senate floor, Conkling spoke in defense of Murphy and attacked his New York colleague.[11] Conkling soon became the recognized leader of New York, and Fenton never regained his standing with the administration. Matthew Josephson explained that the appointment "made Conkling one of the real rulers of the political Government. Murphy, an experienced Republican ward heeler of New York City, a notorious shoddy contractor during the war, and sometime business associate of William Tweed, helped Conkling to eliminate a rival leader from control of the Republican Organization. The administration of the New York Custom House was devoted thereafter entirely to supporting the needs of the President and the Stalwart boss."[12] Murphy would go on to remove more than 300 officials, which gave Conkling the opportunity to fill those positions with his supporters and fortify his place at the head of the New York Republican Party.[13]

At the time, Conkling and Senator Oliver P. Morton of Indiana were the leaders of the Republican faction called the Stalwarts.[14] Other Stalwarts who received the bulk of federal appointments in their states were Simon Cameron of Pennsylvania, Benjamin Butler of Massachusetts, Zachariah Chandler of Michigan, and John Logan of Illinois.[15] The opposing Republican faction was called the Half-Breeds (a term of contempt given by Conkling), led by Senator James Blaine of Maine.[16] "In the Stalwart camp," Josephson explained, "Morton and Conkling each strove to overreach the other in managing an ignorant and complaisant President toward his own ends, or they would quietly combine to undermine a common enemy within the party."[17]

The Stalwart Republicans were so powerful that one House member was able to secure control over federal appointments in the state of Massachusetts. What made this so unusual was the fact that this particular Stalwart was Representative Benjamin Butler, and Massachusetts had a sitting Republican senator at the time—Charles Sumner.[18] The extent of Butler's power can be seen in Grant's appointment of his political ally, William A. Simmons, to the collector position in Boston.[19] This was done despite the opposition of both Republican senators—Sumner and George Boutwell.[20] Simmons's appointment handed the Stalwart representative a political prize normally given to senators, and he would go on to control nearly all aspects of federal appointments in Massachusetts.[21] As Josephson explained:

> Above all, Grant's appointments strengthened the great regional machines in the more important States, those of [Simon] Cameron, [Roscoe] Conkling, and [Benjamin] Butler in the East, of [Oliver] Morton, Zach[ariah] Chandler, and [James] Logan in the West [Stalwart Republicans]. The accelerated process of centralization which party life now underwent gave to our politics more than ever a character of *automatism*. For almost a decade more, to the end of the General Grant Era (which may be said to have lasted actually up to Garfield's death in 1881), the chief business of statesmen seemed to consist in dispensing jobs and privileges to their followers, their thoughts always fixed upon the calendar of committee meetings, caucuses, and primaries, of office vacancies to be filled.[22]

Given the influence that Stalwart Republicans had over President Grant, efforts were made to curtail their power in the pre-nomination process. Starting in 1865, several civil service reform measures were introduced in Congress.[23] The early leader in this movement was Representative Thomas A. Jenckes. According to historian Ari Hoogenboom, Jenckes cited three reasons for civil service reform. First was the doubling of federal officeholders during the Civil War "to approximately 100,000 workers," who were "haphazardly recruited and haphazardly expelled." Second, the professionalism of the federal workforce was "submerged" because "many experienced Democrats were discharged for 'disloyalty.'" Finally, the timing was right. As Hoogenboom notes: "Jenckes had planned a civil service reform law earlier," but "since he was a Lincoln supporter, it was probably for party reasons that he had not pressed for reforms while Lincoln was in office."[24]

Jenckes would not submit any significant civil service legislation after Lincoln's death either. That honor fell to Democratic senator Lyman Trumbull of Illinois, who introduced the first civil service measure to receive significant congressional consideration on December 7, 1869.[25] The bill would have made it unlawful for any member of Congress to solicit or recommend the appointment of any person to office, except if acting on a request for information by the president or a cabinet member, or if a senator was carrying out his advice and consent duties as specified in the Constitution. Violators of the law would be guilty of a misdemeanor and subject to a fine of $1,000.[26] The bill was referred to the Judiciary Committee and reported, but the Senate failed to vote on the measure.

Despite the ultimate failure of the bill, the extended debate produced a wealth of information about the pre-nomination process. Some of the most direct and thorough accounts of how appointments were made can be gleaned from discussions of the bill. In the following paragraphs I cite some of the most relevant and candid statements detailing both the pre-nomination process and its justifications as seen by the very senators who used it. For instance, in his opening remarks, Senator Trumbull explained that appointments

> are dictated and controlled in a vast majority of cases by an influence unknown to the Constitution or laws. Every Senator and every Representative in the other House knows that appointments in most cases are dictated by them, and that the President and heads of Departments are not left free to make selections with an eye single to the public good. The Representative from a congressional district, if in political accord with the Administration, claims and exercises the right, as a general rule, to control all the local appointments in his district, and

in districts represented by Opposition members the Senators from the States claim and exercise the same right. Occasionally there may be deviations from this rule, but they are exceptional. In some of the States the entire delegation, harmonizing with the Administration, may confer together in regard to certain local appointments; but as a general rule no man can be appointed postmaster, or collector or assessor of internal revenue, or to any other Federal office local to the district, unless he has the recommendation of the person who happens to represent the district in Congress, if he be a friend of the Administration.[27]

Trumbull claimed: "The custom of allowing Congressmen to dictate appointments has become so firmly established as to have almost the force of law, and nothing but a positive statute can change it." Republican senator Richard Yates of Illinois spoke in favor of the bill but stated that he would give House members only the right to make recommendations. Yates thought that representatives "have the right to recommend; they represent the districts; they are elected by the people; they are responsible to the people, and they ought to recommend; but Senators, who are to decide upon confirmation, and who stand in the capacity of judges, should not be called upon to sign indiscriminately papers that are presented to them."[28]

An amended version of the bill was reported by the Judiciary Committee on December 13, 1869. The modified bill made it unlawful for any member of Congress to solicit or recommend appointments except for "the action of Senators upon nominations submitted by the President to the Senate."[29] Although Trumbull preferred the original bill's language, the committee was "intent on cutting the thing out by the roots."[30] When debate resumed, Republican senators Samuel Clarke Pomeroy, Alexander Ramsey, and Orris Sanford Ferry all questioned the wisdom of outlawing recommendations. Trying to deflect criticism of the bill, Trumbull mentioned that it did provide an exception for senators. Standing in opposition to the bill, Republican senator Jacob M. Howard of Michigan pointed out that "someone must advise the Executive as to the fitness of persons who are to be appointed to office. It is impossible for him to inform himself by his own personal exertions as to their fitness in all cases, or in even many cases. . . . I have made up my mind that there are no persons to whom he can so safely apply for advice respecting the fitness of candidates for office as members of the two Houses of Congress."[31] The bill was then passed over until the next session of the Forty-first Congress.

On January 4, 1871, the bill was taken up again. Republican senator Samuel Clarke Pomeroy of Kansas spoke of Senator Howard's concern about prohibiting the president from seeking the advice of lawmakers until *after* he submitted a nomination. This concern was never fully answered. In drawing attention to the bill's weakness, Senator George Williams of

Oregon resorted to humor, saying, "I should oppose the passage of this bill as an impracticable piece of legislation; but as I expect to retire at the end of this session and be on the outside, I rather think it will be an advantage to those on the outside to have charge of these appointments."[32]

Speaking in support of the bill, Senator John Sherman of Ohio stated that the worse abuse came from members of the House. They "claim the right to dictate local appointments," Sherman explained, "and if their wishes are not yielded to in every case it creates at once a cause of quarrel." In the Senate, he noted, "perhaps, that is not so much so; but even here we cannot deny that the power claimed by Senators and members to interfere in appointments does create a constant state of irritation between the legislative and executive departments of the Government." Sherman thought that a civil service reform bill would never pass unless "the unconstitutional habit that has sprung up in this country of allowing members of Congress to control appointments is broken up."[33]

The most articulate defense of congressional involvement in the prenomination process was given by Stalwart senator Oliver Morton. He stated his belief that the bill "is unconstitutional" because it "makes it a penal offense for me to exercise a right that belongs to every citizen of the United States." Morton explained that "the greatest security an Executive can have, who can know but a very small number of the American people, is the fact that he can rely upon members of Congress, his political friends, for recommendations to office." Arguing that congressional involvement in the pre-nomination process is a direct result of democratic principles, Morton noted that a House member would be held "directly responsible" for bad local appointments in his district. "Therefore," Morton summarized, "it becomes his interest at once to recommend good men for these offices; his reelection depends on it." As for senators, the same principle applied. In the case of "marshals, district attorneys, and other grades," a senator would be held responsible for making bad appointments.[34] The theory of democratic governance made the people's representatives directly responsible for the men they chose to recommend and gave the president added security in knowing that the appointees were good men. According to Morton, taking away the power to recommend would destroy the democratic element of the pre-nomination process.

Senator Trumbull countered the opposition by advancing a strict separation-of-powers principle. "The only interference that Congress or any member of Congress legitimately has with the appointment of officers," Trumbull insisted, "is in giving the advice and consent of the Senate to the nominations that are made by the President." He regarded the bill as "carrying out the very spirit of the Constitution [by] prohibit[ing] such [congressional] interference." With considerable exaggeration, Trumbull claimed that during "the first forty or fifty years of Government members of Congress did not interfere with appointments." He recalled reading a letter written by Attorney General William Wirt (serving under James Monroe and John Quincy Adams) "in which he regards it as highly indelicate and improper for a member of Congress to even suggest, unless his opinion was asked, to the President of the United States or the head of a Department who should be appointed to office."[35] Trumbull finished by describing the current state of affairs and the evils inherent in the prenomination process.

Two days after Trumbull's speech, Senator Morton spoke again in defense of the existing pre-nomination process and noted that "it seems to me to be somewhat fashionable to denounce members of Congress as corrupt." He refuted Trumbull's interpretation of the Wirt letter, stating that the true "implication" of the letter was that lawmakers had continually interfered in appointments, and the attorney general had simply "reprobated the practice."[36] Morton also countered Trumbull's history of the prenomination process:

> This practice of recommendations by members of Congress has existed from the very beginning of this Government. Attention was not called to it perhaps until very recently. The number of officers to be appointed was very small then compared with what it is now. The crowd, great now, was small then; but the practice the same. Our fathers, for whom I have great reverence, were governed by the same motives that govern men in these days. . . . They recommended appointments just as we do; but they had not nearly so many to recommend.[37]

Morton closed by asking, if appointments were not recommended by members of Congress, then by whom? "They must be recommended by somebody" he noted. As long as the government rests on democratic principles, Morton said, "appointments will continue to be made with reference to politics; and no system can be devised that will prevent it."[38] Debate continued, on and off, for two more days, but the Senate ultimately refused to act on Trumbull's bill.

Despite this failure to end congressional involvement in the prenomination process, Trumbull was largely responsible for a later civil service reform measure. President Grant himself called for reform in his second message to Congress in 1870. "There is no duty which so much embarrasses the Executive and heads of Departments as that of appointments," he declared, "nor is there any such arduous and thankless labor imposed on Senators and Representatives as that of finding places for constituents. The present system does not secure the best men, and often not even fit men, for public place."[39] Subsequently, Senator Trumbull made a second effort to pass civil service legislation, but instead of attacking the issue head-on, he used procedural tactics to get a bill passed. This time, Trumbull's measure was based on a resolution introduced by Representative William H. Armstrong.[40] Although Armstrong had failed to get his resolution adopted by the House, Trumbull succeeded in having a similar version attached to a civil appropriations bill before Congress adjourned.[41] Pressed for time, the House passed the bill with Trumbull's amendment.[42]

The new civil service reform law authorized the president to establish a commission to prescribe rules and regulations for the appointment of selected federal offices.[43] Grant nominated George William Curtis, a well-known civil service reformer, to chair the new commission.[44] Within a year, it produced recommendations that were accepted by Grant and applied to the federal civil service on January 1, 1872.[45] However, a few years after its creation, the commission was denied adequate funds from Congress to carry out its work. President Grant, in a December 7, 1874, message, advised Congress:

> The rules . . . have been adhered to as closely as has been practicable with the opposition with which they meet. . . . But it is impracticable to maintain them without direct and positive support of Congress. . . . Under these circumstances, therefore, I announce that if Congress adjourns without positive legislation on the subject of "civil service reform" I will regard such action as a disapproval of the system, and will abandon it, except so far as to require examinations for certain appointees, to determine their fitness. Competitive examinations will be abandoned.[46]

Despite Grant's plea, Congress refused to appropriate the necessary funds. As Perry Powers Fred explained, once "Congress found that their patronage was diminished by the new methods, they were opposed to" reform.[47] Realizing that Congress would provide no appropriations, Grant ordered the abandonment of the civil service regulations on March 9, 1875.[48] In the end, as George Haynes noted, "President Grant's enthusiasm for civil service reform, apparently at first earnest and sincere, after four years of disillusionizing experience was so chilled by congressional indifference and hostility that the failure of Congress, after due warning, to make appropriation for the work of the commission led to his order for the abandonment of civil service regulations."[49]

Even though Grant had pressed for civil service reform, he did not believe that backroom dealings with Congress were necessarily a bad thing. Reflecting years later, Grant recalled: "The impression is given by some advocates of civil service reform that most executive appointments are made out of the penitentiary. The fact is the president very rarely appoints, he merely registers the appointments of members of Congress. In a country as vast as ours the advice of congressmen as to persons to be appointed is useful and generally in the best interests of the country."[50] Despite Grant's willingness to reform the civil service, it was difficult to do so given the number of congressional Republicans who asked him for appointments. During Grant's first few months in office, congressional solicitation for offices was particularly intense.[51] Many of these requests came from Stalwart members. For example, on March 8, 1869, Stalwart senator Timothy O. Howe of Wisconsin asked for and received an appointment for Gerry W. Hazelton to a district attorney position. The same day, Indiana senators Oliver Morton and Daniel D. Pratt recommended John W. Foster to be a postmaster in their state; less than a month later, Grant nominated him.[52]

Appointment seekers were not limited to Stalwart Republicans, however. Liberal Republicans (and some Democrats) also sought to influence appointments in their states, despite their support for civil service reform. For instance, Ohio Republican senator John Sherman solicited offices from Grant.[53] Likewise, civil service reformer and Missouri senator Carl Schurz pressed the administration for offices.[54] Not surprisingly, even Senator Trumbull asked Grant for "an opportunity to present the names of a number of worthy & deserving Gentlemen, whose applications have been filed in the departments."[55]

Despite an early attempt at reform, congressional control of the pre-nomination process under Grant was as absolute as ever. One historian explained that Grant "was never, in any real sense, the head of the government, the leader of the nation. He was completely controlled by the predominant party in Congress."[56] But only one segment of the majority party was truly in power. The Stalwart Republicans dominated the legislative agenda and therefore the pre-nomination process, leaving most liberal and moderate Republicans in the same boat as members of the Democratic Party. The result was that a small group of powerful senators controlled the fate of most appointments. Josephson summarized the situation: "If one searched for the true center, the real fountainhead, of national government authority itself, one need look no further than the dominant cabal of Senator-bosses heading the Organizations of New York, Massachusetts, Ohio, Indiana, Pennsylvania. It was to the combined power of these men that Ulysses Grant in 1869 had given virtually his own unconditional surrender."[57] That surrender marked the height of the so-called congressionally dominated era.

Rutherford B. Hayes (1877–1881)

It came as a surprise when dark-horse candidate Rutherford B. Hayes, the little-known governor of Ohio, won the Republican nomination at the

Concord convention against such powerful contenders as James Blaine, Roscoe Conkling, and Oliver Morton.[58] Hayes went on to defeat Democrat Samuel J. Tilden in an election that would eventually be decided by a congressionally appointed electoral commission.[59]

Hayes entered the White House with the intention of doing away with the existing pre-nomination system. In his acceptance letter to the Republican Convention, Hayes wrote:

> At first, the President, either directly or through the heads of departments, made all the appointments. But gradually the appointing power, in many cases, passed into the control of members of congress. The offices in these cases have become not merely rewards for party service, but rewards for services to party leaders. This system destroys the independence of the separate departments of the government. . . . It ought to be abolished. The reform should be thorough, radical, and complete.[60]

Again, in his inaugural address, Hayes called attention to the "paramount necessity of reform in our civil service," pointing out that appointments should not be made "as rewards for partisan services, nor merely on the nomination of members of Congress, as being entitled in any respect to the control of such appointments."[61] He proceeded to speak about reform in all but one of his annual messages to Congress.[62]

Early on, Hayes had difficulty developing an effective removal policy. Initially he made several removals, but in time he came to believe that doing so had been a mistake. "I grow more conservative every day on the question of re-movals," he wrote in his diary. "I have made mistakes in removing men who, perhaps, ought to have been retained, and in appointing wrong men." Hayes observed that he had made few removals, "less than by any new Administration since John Q. Adams. But I shall be more cautious in future; make removals only in clear cases, and appoint men only on the best and fullest evidence of fitness." A few months into his term, Hayes stated that he wanted to give "security to official life" and insisted that no one would be removed "except for cause."[63]

As for making nominations, Hayes did not intend to go along with the practice of allowing members of Congress to dictate appointments. For example, he went against the norm and angered many congressional Republicans by not consulting them on his cabinet appointments. Indeed, it seemed that nearly every lawmaker had his own man or wanted a place for himself. For example, Senator Conkling sought the postmaster general position for his lieutenant, Thomas C. Platt; Senator Simon Cameron wanted his son, J. Don Cameron, to be continued as secretary of war; and Senator James Blaine wanted his friend, Representative William Pierce

Frye, to have a place in the cabinet.[64] Friends of defeated senator James Logan were seeking a position for him as well.[65] But Hayes would not choose any of these men. His initial refusal to select potential presidential candidates or members of Grant's cabinet, or to "take care" of anybody, precluded most of the Republican leaders in Congress.[66] The eventual selections of William M. Evarts, Carl Schurz, and David M. Key to head the State, Interior, and Post Office departments, respectively, greatly disappointed many Republicans.

These cabinet selections managed to anger the two major elements in the Republican Party—the Stalwarts and the Half-Breeds. Evarts and Schurz were well-known civil service reformers who had long fought both Republican factions over congressional involvement in the pre-nomination process. Key was probably the most egregious choice, because he was a Democrat who had fought for the Confederacy during the Civil War.[67] To "demonstrate his power for the [president's] benefit," Senator Simon Cameron went so far as to resign his seat and then had the Pennsylvania legislature appoint his son as successor.[68] To show its displeasure over Hayes's selections, the Senate broke with tradition and referred the president's cabinet nominations to committees. However, all were eventually confirmed.[69]

Hayes's effort to end congressional control of appointments should be seen as a means of furthering civil service reform. Writing in his diary toward the end of his administration, Hayes noted:

> Experience has shown the necessity of legislation by Congress to establish an effective and permanent reform of the civil service. And nothing is plainer than that Congress will enact no useful legislation on the subject, unless actually driven to it by the force of public opinion, as long as the offices of the Government are mainly under the control of Members of Congress. The offices are regarded as part of their perquisites—by far the most important part, in the case of Senators—of the emoluments of their offices. They will not voluntarily give up that part of the compensation of their offices which they most highly prize.[70]

Ending congressional dominance of the pre-nomination process was a key goal for Hayes. He believed that Congress needed to be forced into action, and only through persistent pressure could true civil service reform measures be achieved.

In addition to refusing to have his cabinet appointments dictated by members of Congress, Hayes took other steps to achieve his reform goals. At his first cabinet meeting, he appointed a committee, headed by Evarts and Schurz, to promulgate rules covering examinations for federal office seekers.[71] Members of the cabinet followed the president's lead. Interior Secretary Schurz began "competitive examinations in his department,"[72] and Treasury Secretary John Sherman "actually dismissed useless clerks from the government pay roll."[73] In addition, although Postmaster General Key expressed an intent to consult Congress, he refused to be dictated to by the legislative branch.[74] In a statement to one Democratic representative, Key revealed his thinking on various subjects, including his Democratic affiliation, Hayes's reform policy, and his relationship with lawmakers:

> A democrat, such as I am, is not very well qualified to apply, the rules of civil service reform as enunciated in the republican platform, and the special regulations under it have not yet been reported and adopted so that any construction I give may not be authoritative. The rule that members of Congress should not dictate appointments applies as strongly to democratic as republican members, and no more so. I understand it simply to mean that the members voice shall not peremptorily control the Department in the appointment, but whilst this is so, it does not prevent the Department or the member of Congress from consulting and advising with each other in regard to the proper appointments to be made. For myself I am sure that I shall stand greatly in need of all the advice and assistance I can obtain from members of Congress in regard to appointments and shall not only be happy to receive it, but shall often seek it, and I shall not care from what political source this advice and assistance come so that it is good, whether it be from a democrat or a republican. I want good officers.[75]

The intent of Hayes's administration was to consult with Congress to achieve the best appointments possible, but as Hoogenboom notes, there was a difference "between consultation and dictation." Dictation was not an option, "but his cabinet members regularly consulted with friendly congressmen . . . about appointments in their districts."[76]

Although he was known as an advocate of civil service reform, members of his party charged Hayes with using the appointment power to reward his own supporters.[77] For example, Hayes was accused of making appointments in Louisiana on the basis of who had helped him win the election.[78] According to one source, a total of ninety-six individuals involved in the 1876 election were given federal offices.[79] In addition, members of Congress were rewarded for their help in the election. Republican senator William P. Kellogg was given power over Louisiana appointments as repayment for his efforts,[80] and the same was done for Senator George E. Spencer in Alabama.[81] In the North, Half-Breed senator George F. Hoar won control over appointments in Massachusetts (although probably not because of any help provided in the 1876 election). The previous appointment "boss," Stalwart representative Benjamin F. Butler, was cut off, and many of his appointees were removed. For example, the collector of Boston, a Butler lieutenant, was replaced with Hoar's "hand-picked" choice.[82]

One of the biggest problems for Hayes was his policy of appointing Democrats to office in the South. Instead of giving federal offices to Republican candidates and furthering the South's carpetbag governments, Hayes selected Democrats in an effort to assist the "home-rule" movement and to attract southerners to the Republican Party.[83] As one historian wrote, the "rights of local self-government" in the Hayes administration "included appointment of southerners to federal positions."[84] This policy involved not only giving Democrats minor appointments in the South but also bestowing control over patronage to Democratic leaders in Arkansas, Texas, South Carolina, Georgia, and Alabama.[85] Post Office Department appointments were used to accomplish this plan,[86] but it failed to move Democrats into the Republican camp. For instance, southern Democrats in the House of Representatives violated a bargain they had with Hayes by refusing to vote with the Republicans.[87] Senator Conkling took a practical look at Hayes's southern policy by noting, "in spite of the fact that he can command no votes at the South [the president] seems possessed of the delusion that he is able to create a party of his own there."[88]

Part of Hayes's problem was that southern Republican senators had to contend with the political reality of holding office in a hostile environment. In Mississippi, black Republican senator Blanche K. Bruce had to compromise with his Democratic colleague, Lucius Q. C. Lamar. James B. Murphy explains: "They agreed, Lamar said, upon the desirability of removing 'Carpetbaggers & corrupt mischievous white men.' While concluding that Bruce could not be exploited for Democratic party purposes, Lamar did believe 'he will go with me into any reasonable plan of so distributing the Federal offices as will give recognition to both races.'"[89] Although the agreement had more to do with skin color, political considerations remained.[90] In one case, Senator Lamar asked his colleague to help secure the appointment of a Democrat. Understanding the sensitive nature of Bruce's position with his fellow Republicans, Lamar stated, "I do not wish you to do anything that would bring you into a damaging conflict with your party." Not surprisingly, as Murphy points out, "this political detente, if known to Hayes, must have destroyed any dream of a successful white Republican party in Mississippi."[91]

Hayes's southern plan did lead to some goodwill, and a few Democratic senators became friends of the administration.[92] This did not, however, endear Hayes to Republican leaders. Senator Conkling said of the southern Democratic senators, "Hayes cannot get out of their power."[93] Hayes was also accused of rewarding his own supporters. This was probably true, but such conduct was hardly new. Indeed, the Republican Party consisted of many elements that were hostile to one another (e.g., Stalwarts, Half-Breeds, and Mugwumps),[94] and Hayes was not in tune with the ruling faction, the Stalwarts. The result was that the president attacked members of his own party to accomplish his goal of civil service reform. Following the advice of Secretary of State Evarts, Hayes tried to end the dominance of politically unhelpful Senator Conkling and create a presidentially centered Republican Party.[95] The first step was to discredit Conkling.

At Hayes's request, a commission was established to investigate the condition of the New York customhouse (the heart of Conkling's political power) and report back to him.[96] The commission, chaired by John Jay (grandson of the nation's first chief justice) recommended that politics be eliminated from the operation of all customhouses.[97] Hayes endorsed this reform measure,[98] and by August 1877, he decided to remove Alonzo B. Cornell as naval officer and Chester A. Arthur as collector of the Port of New York. Both men were active in the New York Republican Party; Cornell was chairman of the Republican State Committee,[99] and Arthur was a known Conkling supporter. Almost immediately, the Conkling forces began to fight the administration. In September, during the Republican state convention at Rochester, Conkling managed to have Hayes's reform platform rejected and went on to denounce the administration.[100]

Hayes refused to back down. In October he nominated Theodore Roosevelt Sr. and L. Bradford Prince to replace Cornell and Arthur.[101] The appointments were clearly hostile to Conkling,[102] and the administration and the senator were locked in a struggle over the control of patronage in New York. Hayes summarized the importance of this fight in his diary:

> I am now in a contest on the question of the right of Senators to dictate or control nominations. Mr. Conkling insists that no officer shall be appointed in New York without his consent, obtained previously to the nomination. This is the first and most important step in the effort to reform the civil service. It now becomes a question whether I should not insist that all who receive important places should be on the right side of this vital question. None who are opposed to the Cincinnati platform on this important question are to be regarded as Republicans in good standing.[103]

Upon receipt of the nominations of Roosevelt and Prince, the Senate referred them to the Commerce Committee, which Conkling chaired. Not surprisingly, the nominations were reported unfavorably on December 11, 1877.[104] On the Senate floor, Conkling "campaigned in earnest, and speedily won the sympathies of his fellow Senators."[105] Two days later, the Senate rejected Hayes's nominations by a vote of thirty-one to twenty-five.[106] During the six-hour debate, Conkling gave a passionate speech refuting the administration's claims against him and the New York customhouse, using "documentary proof" in almost every case.[107] Upon hearing of the rejection, Hayes wrote: "In the language of the press, 'Senator Conkling has won a great victory over the Administration.' . . . But the end is not yet. I am right, and shall not give up the contest."[108]

In July 1878, after the Senate adjourned, President Hayes suspended Cornell and Arthur and gave temporary appointments to Edwin A. Merritt and Silas W. Burt during the congressional recess.[109] As one observer noted about the recess appointments, the president's "gentle courtesy . . . is blended [with] the firm resolve . . . to exert his constitutional authority, during the remainder of his term."[110] When the Senate came back into session in December, Hayes submitted the nominations of Merritt and Burt for confirmation.[111] Although Conkling again tried to thwart Hayes (the Commerce Committee reported the nominations unfavorably),[112] this time, many members of his party refused to go against the administration. The reason for the switch in votes may have had to do with Hayes's formal communication with the Senate—a letter stating his reasons for the removal of Cornell and Arthur and the nomination of Merritt and Burt in their place.[113] After several months of fighting, Conkling lost the battle when the Senate confirmed Merritt and Burt on February 3, 1879.[114]

Although Hayes was ultimately successful in this case, the Senate was still prepared to fight the president if it believed that he was overstepping his authority in the pre-nomination process and failed to consult legislators. For example, in early 1880, Hayes nominated John M. Morton, the son of former Illinois senator Oliver P. Morton, to the collector position for the Port of San Francisco.[115] Not taking kindly to the administration's failure to consult them or to the selection of a non-Californian, Senators Newton Booth and James T. Farley invoked the tradition of senatorial courtesy, and the Senate rejected Morton on the basis of home-state opposition.[116] Hayes wrote: "The California Senators opposed him and under the doctrine called the Senatorial courtesy they succeeded in rallying against him a majority of both parties . . . there is an evident purpose to reestablish the doctrine that the Senators from a State are entitled to control the federal offices of their State. This has been greatly shaken during my Administration. In many conspicuous cases it has been broken down, or at least disregarded." He noted that senatorial courtesy was a powerful force, because "many Senators, political friends of Senator Morton, many of them intimate personal friends of the great leader, who had promised Mrs. Morton to sustain her son's nomination, deserted at the finish and voted against him, or dodged."[117]

Even with this defeat, Hayes could take heart in knowing that he had broken the power of the most powerful Republican in the Senate—Conkling. In addition, he had initiated several civil service measures at a time when Congress was either unwilling or unable to act. On February 4, 1879,

Hayes wrote to New York collector Merritt and directed him to institute new reform measures. "In making appointments and removals of subordinates you should be perfectly independent of mere influence. Neither my recommendation, nor Secretary Sherman's, nor that of any member of Congress, or other influential persons should be specially regarded. Let appointments and removals be made on business principles, and by fixed rules." He then told Merritt, along with naval officer Silas Burt and surveyor C. K. Burt, to "agree upon a body of rules for the government of your offices, based on the rules reported by the [1871 civil service] commission."[118] Soon afterward, new rules were established instituting competitive examinations for the New York customhouse. A year later, the practice was applied to the post office in New York as well.[119] Hayes later asked other major cities to adopt the New York reform efforts, but his request had only limited success.[120]

Writing near the end of his term, Hayes summed up what he hoped and believed had been accomplished: "The end I have chiefly aimed at has been to break down congressional patronage, and especially Senatorial patronage. The contest has been a bitter one. It has exposed me to attack, opposition, misconstruction, and the actual hatred of powerful men. But I have had great success. No member of either house now attempts even to dictate appointments. My sole right to make appointments is tacitly conceded."[121] The statement was hyperbole, because as the Morton case highlighted, Hayes did not have the "sole right to make appointments." In addition, civil service reform, even with the administration's backing, would go nowhere without a willing Congress. As Hoogenboom explained: "Without congressional legislation, however, it was impossible for him to permanently reform the civil service. Reforming the bureaucracy was merely a policy of an administration that had less than two years remaining, and the leading candidates to succeed Hayes, namely Grant, Blaine, and Sherman, would mobilize the civil service for their own advantage."[122] Any further reform efforts would be left to Hayes's successor, James A. Garfield.

James A. Garfield (1881)

Like Hayes four years earlier, James A. Garfield was a dark-horse candidate at the 1880 Republican National Convention.[123] Stalwart Republicans, including Roscoe Conkling, Simon Cameron, J. Don Cameron, and James Logan, tried to nominate Ulysses S. Grant for a third term but were opposed by party moderates.[124] Garfield, a Half-Breed, was selected as the compromise choice. To bring balance to the ticket and mollify the Stalwarts, New York Republican Chester A. Arthur was selected as his running mate.[125]

Despite the rise of the "solid south," Garfield was able to defeat Democratic candidate Winfield Scott Hancock.[126]

Although Garfield's presidency was brief—after less than six months in the White House, he would be shot by an irate office seeker—it had a profound impact on the pre-nomination process. In his acceptance letter to the Republican National Convention, Garfield stated his understanding that making appointments "is, perhaps, the most difficult of all duties which the Constitution has imposed on the Executive." After acknowledging that civil service reform was needed, he admitted that it was also important for the president to receive "knowledge of the communities" during the pre-nomination process.[127] This was an indirect reference to the tradition of consulting with members of Congress. The message was Garfield's attempt to gratify both the spoilsmen in his party (Stalwarts and Half-Breeds) and the civil service reformers.[128]

In addition to trying to appease the various factions, Garfield had to deal with the always contentious issue of federal offices in New York. Senator Conkling, of course, wanted complete control over his state's appointments, but Garfield was unwilling to go along. Although hoping to avoid open warfare with Conkling, Garfield insisted on making some selections in New York. Conkling refused, and neither side would compromise. Which branch would control appointments?

The controversy between Garfield and Conkling can be traced to a letter the president-elect sent to the senator on January 31, 1881. Garfield told Conkling: "I would be glad to consult you upon several subjects relating to the next administration, and especially in reference to New York interests."[129] The two men met, and in a two-and-a-half-hour session, they discussed various New York appointments.[130] At the close of the meeting, Conkling reportedly said to Garfield, "Whatever appointments you make, I ask you not to appoint any of my enemies to positions in the State of New York."[131] Although he wanted to accommodate the New York senator, Garfield told Conkling, "I must recognize some of the men who supported me at Chicago [at the Republican National Convention]."[132]

Garfield soon nominated several candidates to various posts. Along with nominating Conkling men to the positions of postmaster general, postmaster of New York, minister to France, and other minor offices, Garfield also decided to select one of his New York supporters, William H. Robertson.[133] Conkling was completely opposed and wanted Robertson's nomination withdrawn; Robertson was not part of Conkling's Stalwart faction, and he had opposed Conkling's third-term movement for Grant during the Republican convention.[134] Garfield refused: "To have [allowed Conkling to dictate appointments] would have been regarded as not only a surrender to him but as putting to the sword all those Independent Republicans who followed me at Chicago in resisting the unit rule and in advocating the right of individual delegates to the free exercise of their judgment in the Convention."[135]

The main issue appeared to be Garfield's failure to consult Conkling on this nomination. The significance of the conflict was not lost on Garfield. On several occasions he wrote about the impact this battle would have on the pre-nomination process. On March 27, 1881, he noted in his diary: "The President is authorized to nominate, and did so. A senator considers it a personal affront that he was not previously told of the purpose. I stand joyfully on that issue—let who will, fight me." A week later he wrote in a letter: "This [appointment] brings on the contest at once and will settle the question whether the President is registering clerk of the Senate or the Executive of the Nation."[136]

Former president Grant also weighed in on this matter. In a letter to Garfield, Grant stated that he thought the administration should consult home-state senators. Grant advised, "To nominate a man to the most influential position within the gift of the President in their state, without consulting them, would be an undeserved slight." Garfield replied, "Now while I agree substantially with you that 'it is always the fair thing to recognize the representatives chosen by the people,' I am not willing to allow the power of the Executive in selecting persons for nomination to be restricted to the consideration of those only who may be suggested by the Senators from the State from which the selection is to be made."[137] A few days after writing to Grant, Garfield summed up what the Conkling battle meant: "The issue now is, whether the President in making nominations to office shall act in obedience to the dictation of the Senators from the State where the office is to be exercised. I regard this assumption as at war with the Constitution, and destructive of the true principles of administration."[138]

Unlike the battle with Hayes, this time around, Conkling's allies deserted him quickly. The senator lost support from Stalwart governor Alonzo B. Cornell and the New York senate (usually under the control of Conkling men). Governor Cornell telegrammed Conkling advising him that there was no support in New York for his opposition to the nomination,[139] and the New York senate even adopted a resolution endorsing Robertson.[140] At that time, Garfield began to lobby the Senate, explaining to Republican senators "that the vote on [Robertson's] confirmation was a test of friendship or hostility to the administration."[141] When it became apparent that Conkling would lose the battle and that Robertson would be confirmed, both he and fellow New York senator Thomas C. Platt resigned on May 16, 1881.[142] They returned to New York fully confident that they would be reappointed to the Senate. Instead, the New York legislature voted to replace them.[143] There being no opposition left, the Senate confirmed Robertson without a roll-call vote on May 18, 1881.[144]

The struggle over New York appointments proved that a president could win a battle of wills with one of the most powerful leaders of the Senate. In his autobiography, liberal Republican senator John Sherman remarked on the consequences if things had turned out differently: "If [Conkling and Platt] had been returned to the Senate, the President would have been powerless to appoint anyone in New York without consulting the Senators, practically transferring to them his constitutional power."[145] Garfield's victory was even more remarkable, wrote Theodore Clarke Smith, "when it is realized that every member of [the Republican] party in the Senate sympathized with Conkling and Platt on their right to be 'consulted,' [so] it is not too much to say that no President ever won a more striking victory."[146]

Garfield, however, did not live to see the benefits of his victory. On July 2, 1881, a disappointed office seeker, Charles J. Guiteau, shot the president. He died more than two months later, on September 19.[147] With Garfield's death, civil service advocates felt that they had lost their best chance to implement genuine reform. Waiting in the wings was Garfield's vice president, Chester Arthur, a Stalwart Republican and Conkling supporter from New York. It seemed that the victories of Hayes and Garfield would be reversed by the new administration, and Congress would most likely fail to turn the positive actions of the past into legislative reform measures.

The period from 1869 to 1881 marked the beginning of a concerted reform movement. Despite some early signs of civil service reform and presidential independence, the pre-nomination process was still largely controlled by Congress. Unlike in previous periods of the nation's history, the Republican Party had complete control of the executive branch and could hand out appointments freely to party members in Congress. The dominance of the Republicans in the executive branch and the absence of any serious civil service reform assisted in the control of appointments by lawmakers. As explained in the next chapter, the passage of the first substantial civil service legislation and the reemergence of a two-party system brought balance to the pre-nomination process. Although the "boss" days had not yet passed, there were no longer figures in Congress who could dominate presidents and the pre-nomination process, as Senator Conkling and others once had.

Chapter 6

The Pendleton Act:
Patchwork Reform (1881–1897)

The late nineteenth century is known as the period of reform for the pre-nomination process. After the assassination of James A. Garfield, the political climate triggered congressional changes in the way federal offices were appointed. The result was the Pendleton Act, which provided for competitive examinations for entrance into the federal civil service and, to a certain extent, attempted to limit interference by members of Congress in the pre-nomination process. This act, however, did not end consultation between the president and lawmakers. In fact, it covered only a small number of federal offices, leaving most others subject to the political bargaining process. As such, Presidents Chester A. Arthur, Grover Cleveland, and Benjamin Harrison still had to touch base with members of Congress when making appointments.

Chester A. Arthur (1881–1885)

The death of President Garfield shocked the country and left the political landscape in disarray. The central figure in the first customhouse battle between President Rutherford B. Hayes and New York senator Roscoe Conkling was now president of the United States. Not only that, but Arthur was a product of the very spoils system that had reportedly been responsible for Garfield's death.[1] Although a tragic event for the nation, it was a blessing for those who sought civil service reform. The public's deep disgust for the factional war between the Stalwarts and the Half-Breeds, and the horror inspired by the president's assassination, produced a groundswell of public opinion in favor of civil service reform that was so energetic as to overcome congressional antipathy (as had also occurred in 1872; see chapter 5). One historian aptly summed up the situation: "Garfield dead proved more valuable to reformers than Garfield alive."[2]

At his first State of the Union address on December 6, 1881, President Arthur expressed the need to change the existing system. He wanted the federal government to conduct itself like a "successful private business" and cited the British civil service system as a good model for the United States to emulate. Arthur understood that the "evils which are complained of can not be eradicated at once," but if there was "a failure to pass any other act upon this subject," he threatened to re-create the 1871 Civil Service Commission (subject to congressional funding).[3] This message was well received by civil service reformers.[4]

Just a year later, Congress moved on Arthur's request for action when it adopted a merit system bill that had been introduced by Democratic senator George H. Pendleton of Ohio.[5] The legislation, popularly known as the Pendleton Act, was passed in the Senate on December 7, 1882, by a vote of 38 to 5; less than a month later, the House agreed to the measure by a vote of 155 to 47.[6] The intent of the act was to reform the federal civil service by administering entrance examinations to candidates for federal office. To accomplish this goal, the Pendleton Act established a three-member bipartisan commission, selected by the president with the approval of the Senate. The commission was instructed to devise rules for examinations, keep records, investigate any violations, and submit an annual report to Congress. Examinations were to be "practical in their character" so as to "fairly test the relative capacity and fitness of the persons examined."[7] Those applicants graded highest would be selected to fill vacant positions. The law also called for the classification of offices to be examined, and the president could, if he wished, expand the classification system. Drunkards were excluded from officeholding, and the admission of more than two members of the same family was prohibited. Initially, the rules applied only to the departments in Washington and any customhouse or post office with more than fifty employees.[8]

Of particular relevance to the pre-nomination process was an amendment offered to restrict legislators' ability to influence appointments. The provision read as follows: "That no recommendation of any person who shall apply for office or place under the provisions of this act, which may be given by any Senator or member of the House of Representatives, except as to the character of the applicant, shall be received or considered by any person concerned in making any examination or appointment under this act."[9] The amendment was intended to eliminate the so-called spoils system while allowing Congress to retain a voice in the pre-nomination process. Although similar to the bill introduced by Senator Trumbull in 1869, this measure was narrowly tailored to apply only to the offices classified under the Pendleton Act. In addition, because members of Congress could freely attest to the character or qualifications of potential candidates, continued congressional involvement in the pre-nomination process was ensured.

The amendment was introduced by Democratic senator John Tyler Morgan of Alabama, who stated that he wanted to end the "evil practice" of patronage. Morgan believed that the Constitution "confided the appointing power" in the executive alone and that Congress had no right to interfere. Morgan's statement sheds some light on how the pre-nomination process functioned in a day-to-day fashion. He explained that lawmakers "usurp" the executive's power by pressing for appointments in the various departments. As a result of this solicitation, the departments had adopted the practice of keeping books to record every appointment given to members of Congress "so that they shall not largely overdraw their accounts." This practice, Morgan declared, "is a shame to the country that any books should be kept in a Department to show how the patronage is divided among Congressmen and to apportion to each man of the administration party his due proportion of the spoils."[10]

Morgan believed that the Pendleton Act in its present form was defective. "If we would compel the heads of Departments to purify and regulate the civil service in accordance with the welfare of the country they have at least the right to ask us that we will abstain from interfering with their right to make the employments for which the country holds them responsible." Finally, Morgan warned that reform would be a "vain" effort unless lawmakers were "prepared to yield this power of personal control over the civil service." The Senate approved the amendment by a vote of twenty-six to sixteen.[11]

The restrictions placed on members of Congress and the appointing authority were meant to bring about better officeholders in the civil service. Approximately 14,000 custom, postal, and departmental clerical positions were initially covered under the Pendleton Act,[12] and examinations were administered to anyone seeking these positions. However, the president, department head, or bureau chief had some discretion in making appointments based on examination scores. The relevant provision required that selections be made "among those graded highest as the result of such competitive examinations." Under the law, the Civil Service Commission would aid the president in creating "suitable rules for carrying this act into effect."[13] Thus, a so-called rule of three was established, which permitted the appointing official to select from among the three highest-scoring candidates. This rule was based on an opinion by Attorney General Amos T. Akerman that had been written to answer questions pertaining to the 1871 Civil Service Act.[14]

The attorney general's opinion provided the newly established commission with an authoritative interpretation of how civil service examinations would function in light of various constitutional questions raised by the Pendleton Act. As a whole, Akerman saw "no constitutional objection to an examining board," as long as that board rendered "no imperative judgments, but only [aided] the appointing power with information." In his view, there could be no "legal obligation to follow the judgment of such a board" because that would be "inconsistent with the constitutional independence of the appointing power." Akerman, however, admitted that Congress had the "right to prescribe qualifications" for offices, but the "right . . . is limited by the necessity of leaving scope for the judgment and will of the person or body in whom the Constitution vests the power of appointment."[15]

Turning to the question of the appointing power's discretion, Akerman said, the notion "that the President shall appoint to a certain office the person adjudged by the examiners to be the fittest, is not different in constitutional principle from an enactment that he shall appoint John Doe to that office. In neither case are his judgment and will called into exercise." Under such a system, the civil service board "would virtually be the appointing power." Although Akerman believed that "a competitive examination may be resorted to in order to inform the conscience of the appointing power," it could not be the final authority on the "judgment and will" of the appointing power.[16]

Qualifications could be made that did not limit the discretion of the appointing power, however. For instance, either the president or Congress could "require that the designation shall be made out of a class of persons ascertained by proper tests to have those qualifications" for appointment. Qualifications such as citizenship, age, and professional restrictions would "still leave room to the appointing power for the exercise of its own judgment and will" in making selections.[17]

Out of Akerman's opinion and the commission's own interpretation of the "those graded highest" provision rose the rule of three.[18] The rule, as Paul P. Van Riper explained, was "based upon constitutional necessity, rather than upon administrative desirability."[19] In short, the Constitution was the controlling authority, and any law intending to reform the civil service would have to adhere to the Article II requirements of the Appointments Clause and the separation-of-powers doctrine. Under the rule of three, the appointing official retained a level of discretion implicit in exercising the constitutional power of making appointments, but qualifications could be placed on the candidates under consideration without upsetting the balance between the executive and legislative branches.[20]

Even with the primary constitutional question settled, the Pendleton Act was essentially an enabling act, and its practical efficacy was contingent on executive discretion. Presidential apathy could end the reform effort, but this would not be the case. President Arthur appointed Dorman B. Eaton, John M. Gregory, and Leroy D. Thoman as members of the new Civil Service Commission.[21] Eaton's selection was especially gratifying to civil service reformers because of his chairmanship of the original Civil Service Commission under President Grant and his aid in drafting the 1883 Civil Service Act for Senator Pendleton.[22] By May 1883, the commission had created a set of civil service rules that were adopted by President Arthur.[23] Initially, these rules applied to 13,924 offices, but the service was soon extended through presidential order to include another 1,649 positions. As a result, by the end of Arthur's administration, approximately 15,573 positions, or 10 percent of federal offices, were covered under the Pendleton Act.[24]

The creation of civil service examinations did not necessarily take politics out of the pre-nomination process. Appointing officers and members of Congress could easily circumvent the newly created examinations, most commonly through the use of "backdoor" appointments.[25] For instance, many positions had not yet been placed under civil service protection or had been exempted altogether. Offices that were initially exempted included clerks and secretaries for department or office heads, cashiers of collectors and postmasters, and superintendents of money-order divisions in post offices, among others.[26] An appointing officer could simply select someone to fill a position that was not covered by the Pendleton Act. If there was a desire to appoint someone to a civil service position but that individual had not passed the examination, the appointing officer merely gave the person an unclassified position and had him or her do the work of the classified post.[27] Temporary appointments were also used to give candidates time to learn on the job and thus ensure a top-three score once an examination did occur.[28] In some cases, examinations would be repeated until the preferred candidate scored in the top three.[29] Finally, Congress became involved in backdoor appointments by merely exempting certain candidates from examinations.[30] Although these exemptions were justified by "emergency" conditions, such as the Spanish-American War or World War I,[31] the Civil Service Commission had lists of eligible persons sufficient to meet unexpected demands.[32]

Bypassing the civil service rules was usually done at the request of lawmakers who wanted particular offices for their supporters. Most of the time, presidents and department heads were more than willing to go along with these requests, even if they violated the Pendleton Act. For instance, although the Morgan amendment forbade congressmen to make recommendations based on political considerations, both branches worked around the provision. Forty years after passage of the Pendleton Act, the Post Office Department issued "circulars" to representatives asking for their opinions about the "character and residence" of candidates; respondents were explicitly instructed not to base their recommendations "upon political considerations," or the circulars would not be accepted. In reality, these recommendations were implicit endorsements of said candidates, and the department's wording was merely hiding "the real [political] influences at work."[33]

At the start of Arthur's administration, many observers thought the president would hand over his appointment power to former New York senator Roscoe Conkling, but this did not occur. Conkling pressed Arthur to appoint him to the cabinet and to remove his enemy William H. Robertson as New York collector; Arthur did neither.[34] In a long meeting between the two men, Arthur told Conkling that this was not the time to start a factional war over appointments.[35] The rebuff to the former Stalwart leader did not mean that Arthur had completely forgotten his Republican allies, however.[36] In Pennsylvania, he permitted Stalwart senator J. Don Cameron to dominate appointments after a long absence of influence under Hayes and Garfield. This was done against the wishes of Cameron's colleague and Half-Breed senator John I. Mitchell.[37] In fact, Mitchell tried to explain to Arthur the harm such a course would have on the Republican Party, but the president replied "that he had been a practical politician for twenty-five years and neither understood nor appreciated 'abstract politics.'"[38] Another Stalwart senator, John A. Logan of Illinois, said that he would "have no trouble with Arthur" and professed that "anything I want done in Chicago he will do."[39]

In addition to rewarding Stalwart members, Arthur punished some rather hostile Half-Breed senators. In Massachusetts, Arthur suspended Boston collector Alanson Beard and selected Roland Worthington in his place, based on the request of former senator George Boutwell and Navy Secretary William E. Chandler.[40] This was seen as a hostile act by the two Half-Breed Republican senators, George F. Hoar and Henry L. Dawes, who protested the appointment. However, as Richard E. Welch Jr. explained, neither senator could "exercise the weapon of senatorial courtesy" in forcing a rejection because "their protests against its use by Conkling denied them the right—but they remained bitterly aggrieved."[41] The situation was so bad for Half-Breed Republicans that Ohio senator John Sherman wrote to former president Hayes: "It seems the purpose of the Adm'n not only to undo all you did, but to remove from office all your appointees. . . . Three or four Senators control most of the appointments at large while local appointments are made by Congressmen. This rule is not applicable to Ohio, for most of us (I especially) are ignored."[42]

Despite the ongoing factional war with the Half-Breeds, by and large, Arthur consulted with most Republican lawmakers. For example, the policy of the Post Office Department was to rely on the advice of "the Member of Congress—if a Republican—or a Senator, if the Member is not a Republican," in appointments.[43] In some cases, the pre-nomination process became almost dictatorial. For instance, at a meeting with Republican senators Philetus Sawyer and John C. Spooner of Wisconsin, Arthur was hesitant to make a decision about an appointment in their state and said that he would consider their advice. Sawyer exclaimed, "No, we don't want it considered; we want him appointed." The Wisconsin senators prevailed.[44]

Political necessity also governed the application of the pre-nomination process. Unlike his predecessor, Arthur was more than willing to use the appointment power to make alliances in the South.[45] Despite the fact that Senate Republicans, hoping to gain control of the upper house, had offered Readjuster senator William Mahone of Virginia a committee chairmanship, Garfield had refused to hand over control of federal appointments to Mahone.[46] Upon Garfield's death, however, the "complexion of matters in Virginia" greatly changed. Arthur went ahead and directed

> each Federal office holder in the State, that he must cooperate with the Readjusters, or his official head would pay the penalty, and a few obstinate ones were actually removed, and their places filled with Readjusters. It did not take many lessons of this sort to teach the new political faith. The scenes changed as if by magic. All semblance of organized Republican opposition to the Readjusters disappeared, and the Readjuster party of Virginia swallowed the Republican party of Virginia, body and bones, at one gulp.[47]

The Readjuster movement would not last, however. By 1884, even with Republican support, Senator Mahone decided to abandon the hope of sustaining a third political party in Virginia.[48] At a jointly held Republican-Readjuster state convention, the two political parties finally merged. The platform read: "That, from and after this day, our party shall be known as the Republican party of Virginia; that in National affairs we shall follow the banner of the National Republican party, and shall support with zeal and fidelity its nominees for President and Vice-President."[49] Thus the Readjusters went to the 1884 Republican National Convention in Chicago declaring, "We are for Arthur because Arthur is for us."[50] The Readjusters gave the Republican Party a built-in support structure. And although the victory was only temporary, the administration succeeded in reviving republicanism in a southern state through its use of the pre-nomination process.[51]

Grover Cleveland (1885–1889)

At the 1884 Republican Nation Convention, President Arthur lost the Republican nomination to Half-Breed Republican senator James G. Blaine of Maine.[52] The Democratic Party selected Grover Cleveland, the governor of New York, which was a key swing state. Although Cleveland lost support from Tammany Hall and other machine politicians, he gained the votes of the reform element in the Republican Party—the Mugwumps—because of their dislike for Blaine.[53] The campaign was fairly evenly matched until Blaine supporter Samuel D. Burchard characterized the Democrats as the party of "rum, Romanism, and rebellion," which was so offensive to many Roman Catholics and liberal Republicans that it was largely blamed for Blaine's defeat.[54]

As the first Democrat to control the White House since James Buchanan, Cleveland was particularly pressed by the need to reward the party faithful with federal offices.[55] The greatest pressure came from Democratic members of Congress, who "believed, and with good reason, that they held their jobs at the sufferance of party men back home. The party workers and financial contributors who had sent them to Washington expected to share in the distribution of the patronage."[56] Not wanting the president-elect to succumb to this pressure, Democratic reformers and Mugwumps arranged for the National Civil Service Reform League to send a letter to Cleveland declaring that, because of the change in party power, his presidency would be a true test for the reform moment.[57] In a reply letter, Cleveland stated:

> I am not unmindful of the fact to which you refer, that many of our citizens fear that the recent party change in the National Executive may demonstrate that the abuses which have grown up in the civil service are ineradicable. I know that they are deeply rooted, and that spoils system has been supposed to be intimately related to success in the maintenance of party organization; and I am not sure that all those who profess to be the friends of this reform will stand firmly among the advocates when they find it obstructing their way to patronage and place.
>
> But fully appreciating the trust committed to my charge, no such consideration shall cause a relaxation on my part of an earnest effort to enforce the law.[58]

Cleveland also vowed to follow not only the letter of the law but also its spirit in handling the majority of federal employees not covered by the Pendleton Act. As president, he would not remove officeholders unless they were inefficient, unscrupulous, or partisan.[59]

At his first inaugural address, Cleveland again professed a strong belief in the civil service reform effort. "The people demand reform in the administration of the Government and the application of business principles to public affairs," he stated.

> As a means to this end, civil-service reform should be in good faith enforced. Our citizens have the right to protection from the incompetency of public employees who hold their places solely as the reward of partisan service, and from the corrupting influence of those who promise and the vicious methods of those who expect such rewards;

and those who worthily seek public employment have the right to insist that merit and competency shall be recognized instead of party subserviency or the surrender of honest political belief.[60]

During his first term, Cleveland would expand the civil service network by 11,757 offices, bringing the total number of positions classified under the Pendleton Act to 27,330.[61]

Although Cleveland supported the civil service reform movement, he was forced to give way to practical politics in the pre-nomination process. "The Democratic party had been starved for a quarter of a century and was not to be denied," Van Riper explained. The "spoils system was still very much alive in the minds of the politicians, not to mention a considerable portion of the general public."[62] Cleveland attempted to blend civil service reform with the need to reward loyal Democrats by removing Republican officeholders only after they had served full four-year terms. However, he believed that those who were openly hostile to the Democratic Party "should go without regard to the time they have served, and that we should gladly receive all resignations offered to use and fill the vacancies thus created by our friends."[63] Cleveland restated this policy in an un-mailed letter noting that officeholders "should be of the same political creed and party as the Administration"; although good officers would not be removed, "no protection" would be given to those who used their "influence and power . . . to carry out partisan designs."[64]

Part of Cleveland's removal policy, as Horace Samuel Merrill explained, was born out of necessity: "The administration's removal and appointive machinery, following a period of slowness imposed by inexperience, inde-cision and caution, finally began to operate smoothly and rapidly. More important, patronage-hungry Democrats relentlessly put pressure on Cleve-land to function definitely as a member of the Democratic party. Fellow Democrats told him, in effect, that on matters involving politics he was bound to perform as a Democrat."[65] And perform he did. Ninety percent of the federal officeholders not protected by the Pendleton Act were replaced within a year and a half.[66] In Cleveland's mind, he was following the civil service reforms mandated by the Pendleton Act, but many civil service reformers were angered by his removal of nonclassified officials.[67] They believed that these removals went against "his promise that the principles of the Pendleton Act would guide him respecting the entire service."[68]

Despite the criticism, these removals not only gave Cleveland the opportunity to reward fellow Democrats with federal offices but also allowed him to challenge the propriety of the Senate's involvement in removals. Cleveland's task, however, would not be easy. The Republican Senate hoped to use the Tenure of Office Act restrictions to prove that Cleveland was failing to follow his own reform pledges and to "placate many of the ousted Republican officeholders."[69] In fact, early in Cleveland's administration, Republican senators openly declared that many of the suspended officeholders had been the victims of a partisan purge.[70] Once Congress came back into session, an investigation began. Senate committees responsible for appointments sent letters to the department heads requesting all documents relating to the suspensions; these requests were based implicitly on the repealed "evidence and reasons" provision of the original 1867 act.[71] By invoking the revoked provision, Republican senators stated that they did not want to prevent the confirmation of Cleveland's nominations but merely to compel the president to admit that he was replacing Republican officeholders with Democrats. If a confession occurred, "they would confirm his appointees without further ado."[72]

The only problem with this plan was that Cleveland believed that the Tenure of Office Act was unconstitutional and could not withstand a judicial test. Therefore, he directed the department heads to refuse to deliver any papers relating to the suspensions, but they did hand over documents pertaining to the nominations pending before the Senate. The Senate committees refused to move the majority of the nominations forward without the documents relating to the suspensions, and as a result, only 15 of the 643 pending nominations were confirmed, and 2 were rejected outright.[73]

During this time, one suspension became the focal point of this constitutional impasse. On December 26, 1885, the Senate Judiciary Committee sought all information from Attorney General Augustus Garland regarding the suspension of George M. Duskin as the district attorney in Alabama and the appointment of John D. Burnett in his place.[74] The attorney general submitted, on January 11, 1886, all documents relating to Burnett's nomination but refused to turn over "papers touching the suspension of Duskin from office," as he had "as yet received no direction from the President in relation to their transmission."[75] The Senate passed a resolution on January 25, 1886, directing the attorney general to deliver "all documents and papers" relating to Duskin's removal.[76] When the attorney general again refused the Senate's demand (at the direction of Cleveland), the Judiciary Committee sent a report to the Senate framing the issue as an executive encroachment on legislative rights: "The important question, then is whether it is within the constitutional competence of either House of Congress to have access to the official papers and documents in the various public offices of the United States, created by laws enacted themselves." The committee recommended that the Senate condemn the attorney general for refusing "under whatever influence, to send to the Senate copies of papers" relating to Duskin's removal and also to refuse "its advice and consent to proposed removals of officers" until all requested documents were delivered.[77]

These measures were intended to be a declaration of war by the Senate. As Allan Nevins wrote, "the Republicans would block the whole appointive machinery unless Cleveland surrendered."[78] Cleveland found the committee report unacceptable, and on March 1, 1886, he sent a message to the Senate stating:

> These suspensions are my executive acts based upon considerations addressed to me alone, and for which I am wholly responsible, I have had no invitation from the Senate to state the position which I have felt constrained to assume in relation to the same, or to interpret for myself my acts and motives in the premises.
>
>   In this condition of affairs I have forborne addressing the Senate upon the subject, lest I might be accused of thrusting myself unbidden upon the attention of that body.

Continuing, he noted that the "demands and requests" for information were issued so that the Senate could "sit in judgment upon the exercise of my exclusive jurisdiction and executive function, for which I am solely responsible." Cleveland then drew a distinction between documents that were official in nature and those that were purely unofficial: "the papers and documents withheld and addressed to me or intended for my use and action [are] purely unofficial and private, not infrequently confidential, and having reference to the performance of a duty exclusively mine. I considered them in no proper sense as upon the files of the Department, but as deposited there for my convenience, remaining still completely under my control." In conclusion, he remarked, "I am not responsible to the Senate and I am unwilling to submit my actions and official conduct to them for judgment."[79]

After two weeks of debate, the Senate passed a resolution condemning the attorney general by a vote of thirty-two to twenty-five. On a narrower vote of thirty to twenty-nine, the Senate agreed not to confirm Burnett without receiving the documents relating to Duskin's removal.[80] At the moment of victory for the Senate Republicans, however, the reason for battling Cleveland vanished. During the Senate debate, Democrat James Lawrence Pugh pointed out that Duskin's term had expired before the controversy even began. The only question remaining was whether Duskin's successor, Burnett, should be confirmed. In the end, with no conflict arising from the case, Burnett was confirmed.[81]

The entire matter was ultimately a defeat for the Senate. "The Senate lost prestige in this contest with the President," Joseph P. Harris explained. "Public opinion responded to the vigorous message of the President defending the executive power and regarded the controversy as merely a maneuver by Republican senators to keep Republican officeholders in office until their terms expired."[82] By the end of the year, "the efforts to interfere with the President's powers of removal and appointment" had nearly ended.[83] Not only that, but Republican senator George F. Hoar introduced a bill on July 21, 1886, to repeal the Tenure of Office Act.[84] The House and Senate passed the bill, and Cleveland signed the act out of existence on March 3, 1887.[85]

The repeal of the Tenure of Office Act returned to the executive the independence in appointment matters that had been lost during the presidency of Andrew Johnson. Alyn Brodsky noted, "With Cleveland having restored the constitutionally established bounds of executive power, Presidents were again free to deal with subordinates without senatorial hindrance."[86] The most unusual aspect of the repeal was that it took a Democratic president in a Republican-dominated era to finally bring the matter to a close.

In terms of appointments, Cleveland thought that they "had been titled in the direction of congressional domination during the presidencies of Andrew Johnson, Ulysses S. Grant and that the efforts of Hayes, Garfield, and Arthur had failed to right that balance."[87] Although Cleveland at times excluded some Democratic lawmakers from the pre-nomination process,[88] he retained a Jacksonian belief that the people should be involved in governmental decisions. In a letter to one of his supporters, Cleveland stated that he might go against the advice of a member of Congress, "but to make an appointment in the face of the wishes of the people of the place as they are expressed here seems a little high-handed for a man who believes this is the People's Government."[89]

Cleveland's administration used the pre-nomination process to consult with Democratic lawmakers. For example, in various "confidential circular" letters, Postmaster General William F. Vilas sought "no more proof" on which to base a removal than the "affirmation of knowledge on the part of a Representative or Senator that the Postmaster has been an active" partisan.[90] In a particularly revealing letter, Democratic senator Francis M. Cockrell of Missouri explained the specific relationship between the administration and Democratic congressmen in managing local appointments:

In Congressional Districts having Democratic Representatives, Senator [George G.] Vest and I leave the removal and selection of Post Masters therein entirely to such Representative, the Democratic patrons of the office, and the Administration, take no part, are not consulted, and not looked to for advise and information. Were we under such circumstances to attempt to interfere, we would be at once charged with intermeddling, and attempting to boss and dictate all the appointments in the State. As I understand the rule of the Departments, it is this: In Congressional Districts having Democratic Representatives, where such Representative informs the Department, that he has investigated and inquired into the particular case, and that he is satisfied that a certain applicant is honest, competent and faithful, and will be generally acceptable to the patrons of the office, and his appointment recognized as a good one; and so recommends him in preference to others, his recommendation will be followed, and the appointment will be made, provided such applicant has a reasonable indorsement from the patrons of the office.[91]

The practice clearly gave control of local appointments to representatives of the administration's party. Interference from senators was not welcomed and seems to have been bad form. As Senator Cockrell later explained: "I do not believe that it would be right, to place myself in a position of attempting to dictate to the Department the appointments to the local offices in Congressional Districts in the State in which they look to the Democratic Representatives for advice and information."[92] This understanding assumes that in districts without a friendly representative, the administration relied on the home-state senator (provided he was of the same party).

In states dominated by the Republican Party, Cleveland was often forced to choose between Democratic factions. In Minnesota, as in most midwestern states, the Democratic Party was divided into the Grangers and the Bourbons.[93] Former representative Ignatius Donnelly controlled the Granger element, and national Democratic committeeman Patrick H. Kelly, Minnesota Democratic chairman Michael Doran, and railroad giant James J. Hill ran the Bourbon organization.[94] During the 1884 election, Donnelly was able to bring a number of rural votes into the Cleveland camp, and he expected the administration to reward him with patronage. However, because Cleveland came from the Bourbon wing of the Democratic Party, he decided to bestow state appointments on the Kelly-Doran-Hill faction instead.[95]

One unique problem that arose during Cleveland's administration involved his Mugwump supporters, who sought to influence appointments over the protests of loyal Democrats.[96] In Massachusetts, for example, a Mugwump-Democrat controversy ensued over the appointment of the Boston collector. Representative Patrick Collins thought that his recommendations should receive proper consideration, since he was the "official head" of the Democratic Party in the state.[97] Even with Collins's repeated protests, however, Cleveland would not totally abandon the Mugwumps in this appointment. In a letter to the Democratic leader, Cleveland wrote, "I want very much to please you, and yet all the time my judgment and inclination lead me in a direction which thus far you have not approved."[98] Collins replied that if his choice was not followed, he would "abstain in future from troubling the President with any advice or suggestion as to executive appointments in Massachusetts."[99] Despite this veiled threat, Cleveland went ahead and appointed the Mugwump choice, Leverett Saltonstall. Later on, Cleveland told the losing Democratic candidate, "There never have been two better candidates for a position pressed upon me; and never have I been more embarrassed in making a selection."[100]

Benjamin Harrison (1889–1893)

By the 1888 presidential election, the Republican Party was no longer divided between the Stalwarts and the Half-Breeds. Instead of a dominant factional candidate such as Ulysses S. Grant or James G. Blaine, the Republican National Convention would see nineteen men attempt to win the nomination.[101] Fierce lobbying and backroom politicking over a five-week period eventually led to the selection of Indiana's favorite son, Benjamin Harrison, as the Republican candidate. The Democrats would renominate President Grover Cleveland as their standard-bearer, but despite winning the popular vote by 80,000, he would lose in the electoral college by a margin of 233 to 168.[102]

At his inaugural address, Harrison sought to build public confidence in his ability to faithfully carry out civil service reform. "I shall expect," he stated, "those whom I may appoint to justify their selection by a conspicuous efficiency in the discharge of their duties." In addition, "party service" would not be "a disqualification," but "it will in no case be allowed to serve as a shield of official negligence, incompetency, or delinquency" either. Harrison explained that his administration would "enforce the civil-service law fully and without evasion." However, he thought that only by increasing the offices classified under the Pendleton Act would the number of removals diminish.[103] Harrison ended up increasing the classified civil service by 10,535 offices. In total, 37,865 positions were protected under the Pendleton Act by the end of his administration.[104]

Despite his professed commitment to the Pendleton Act, many civil service reformers gave Harrison a failing grade.[105] This was primarily because of the numerous removals in the unclassified service.[106] For example, in the Post Office Department, the administration removed incumbent Democratic postmasters to make room for "30,000 Republican successors."[107] One of the few decisions that redeemed Harrison in the eyes of the reformers was his choice of Theodore Roosevelt as civil service commissioner.[108] His appointment of Roosevelt upset many Republican lawmakers, however. As Elisabeth P. Myers explained, "Roosevelt stepped on Republican toes in state after state, and the person most blamed for the action was Harrison himself. Congressmen, who had to answer to the constituents in their various states, told the President he had to do something to step on Roosevelt in turn."[109]

Harrison could not escape the paradox. While reformers were criticizing him for inattention to the Pendleton Act, Republicans were attacking him for his faithfulness to it. Party members wanted removals, but the administration was not making them fast enough.[110]

In addition to drawing criticism for his civil service record, Harrison was often attacked for his handling of the pre-nomination process. The root of the problem, according to Homer E. Socolofsky and Allan B. Spetter, was his inability to "delegate the responsibility for filling federal offices" while also possessing a disdain for the task.[111] As one observer of the period wrote: "It was said of Mr. Harrison that when he gave a man an office he did it in such a churlish way that the recipient went away angry."[112] Several Republican lawmakers confirmed this view. Senator Shelby M. Cullom of Indiana recalled: "I suppose he treated me about as well in the way of patronage as he did any other senator, but whenever he did anything for me it was done so ungraciously that the concession tended to anger rather than please."[113] Nevada senator William M. Stewart said that although he was able to influence appointments, whenever such consultation occurred, he felt that Harrison treated him badly for his efforts.[114] New York Republican "boss" Thomas C. Platt provides an apt summary of Harrison's demeanor: "in his reception of those who solicited official appointments, he was as glacial as a Siberian stripped of his furs. During and after an interview, if one could secure it, one felt even in torrid weather like pulling on his winter flannels, galoshes, overcoat, mitts and earlaps."[115]

Harrison's approach angered many Republicans and led to some open breaks between party leaders and the administration.[116] Besides Platt of New York, such powerful men as Speaker of the House Thomas Reed of Maine and Senator Matthew Quay of Pennsylvania "were routinely hostile to the administration, most prominently because of Harrison's active control of the federal patronage trough."[117] Speaker Reed once commented, "I had but two enemies in Maine; one of them Harrison pardoned out of the penitentiary, and the other he appointed Collector of Portland."[118] When Senator Quay, who had been Harrison's campaign manager, encountered presidential resistance to some Pennsylvania appointments, Quay remarked, "Mr. President, you cannot afford to ignore those people who made your election possible." Harrison merely replied, "Senator, God Almighty made me President."[119] Both Platt and Quay were so angry over pre-nomination rebuffs that they worked behind the scenes to oust Harrison in the 1892 Republican primary.[120] Although their efforts were unsuccessful, the lack of support from these two powerful Republicans and others was thought to be one of the reasons for Harrison's defeat in the presidential election.[121]

Despite his lack of pleasantries, Harrison followed the practice of accepting the endorsements of Republican members of Congress.[122] Harrison, like most presidents, might have wished to nominate independently of

Congress, but he understood the custom and necessity of conferring with lawmakers in making appointments. A few years after leaving the White House, Harrison detailed the pre-nomination process and the repercussions if a chief executive went against it:

> It has come to be a custom that, in the appointment of officers whose duties relate wholly to a Congressional district, or some part of it, the advice of the Congressman—if he is of the President's party—is accepted. This is a mere matter of custom, but it has become so settled a custom that the President finds himself in not a little trouble if he departs from it. In the Congressional districts represented by Congressmen of the party opposed to the President the custom is that the Senator or Senators—if of the President's party—make the recommendations for the local appointments; as they also do for appointments in their States not of a local character. These recommendations are followed as a rule, unless something against the character or fitness of the applicant is alleged. In such case the President exercises his prerogative to make a selection of his own upon such other representations and recommendations as are made to him.
>
> When he does this the confirmation of the appointment, however good and unexceptionable in itself, is often held up in the Senate upon the objection of the Senator whose recommendation has not been followed, and the nomination is sometimes rejected—not upon the merits, but out of "Senatorial courtesy." The power and duty of selection are vested by the Constitution in the President, but appointments are made "by and with the advice and consent of the Senate." It would seem that the power vested in the Senate relates only to competency, fitness, and character of the person appointed, but this view is much varied in practice. Some Senators practically assert the right to select as well as to consent.[123]

No chief executive before or since has given a more enlightening description of how the pre-nomination process functions. Consultation between the two branches was expected, and if a president failed to cooperate with Congress, his nominations would most likely be rejected. Harrison also explained the practical rationale for seeking congressional advice: "But as the President can, in the nature of things, know but little about the applicants for local offices, and must depend upon some one better informed than he to give him the necessary information, it is natural that he should give great weight to the advice of the Senator or Representative."[124] Great pressure was therefore placed on a president to involve Congress not only out of tradition but also because of the practical need to receive good information about candidates.

Harrison's normal pre-nomination procedure was to consult with Republican lawmakers, but like in most administrations, the process differed from state to state, depending on the congressional delegation. If a state had split-party representation in the Senate, Harrison would consult with the lone Republican senator. For instance, in Ohio, Senator John Sherman was the point man on appointments.[125] The same was true in California, where Senator Leland Stanford was referred to as the state's "supreme arbiter in the distribution of patronage."[126] When a state had two Republican senators, Harrison often gave both lawmakers influence over appointments. This was the case in Colorado, with Senators Henry M. Teller and Edward O. Wolcott, and in Wisconsin, where Senators Philetus Sawyer and John C. Spooner controlled patronage.[127]

The benefit of having a senator who was friendly to the administration cannot be overstated. Besides controlling statewide appointments, Republican senators could also influence local offices in districts represented by Democrats. When a state did not have a senator of the president's party, House members often asserted control over more territory than they represented. This could produce various problems for the White House. For example, an interesting agreement arose in Missouri, where the four Republican representatives (Nathan Frank, William M. Kinsey, Frederick G. Niedringhaus, and William H. Wade) tried to divide "the State into four districts, each attempting to look after two or three congressional districts, besides his own." The plan was to have applicants for local positions apply to either the present or defeated representative for an endorsement. Upon hearing about this arrangement, Harrison said that although he wanted the representatives to "consult and to harmonize," he "did not mean to confer on them any authority to control or distribute the offices."[128]

Harrison might have been correct in stating that representatives did not have the right to control appointments outside their districts, but they did have near dictatorial power when it came to local patronage in the territories they represented. This was particularly true in the Post Office Department.[129] A book written by Marshall Cushing, the personal secretary of Postmaster General John Wanamaker, detailed the pre-nomination process for postal appointments, referred to as the "referee" system: "In Republican districts the members of Congress are the referees; in Democratic districts, in states where one or both of the senators are Republican, the cases are referred to them for recommendation. Where there are neither members nor senators to represent a district, the Department has referees appointed,—usually men who have been members of Congress or candidates for Congress." Cushing reported that the practice had been in "vogue for many years and through many different administrations." The referee system was built on the assumption that it would be "impossible" for the appointing officer "to have personal knowledge of the merits of the various candidates," so advice was secured through local leaders, who were almost always members of Congress.[130]

The administration had clearly deferred to lawmakers on postal appointments, but the situation for U.S. attorney and marshal selections was not as well settled. The problem centered on the fact that a judicial district did not conform to the borders of one congressional district. There was often territorial overlap, with representatives from different districts claiming the right to recommend candidates in the same judicial district. For example, Harrison explained that for the eastern judicial district of Missouri alone, there were six congressional districts covering the area, with three Republican representatives claiming the right to decide who was selected as U.S. attorney or marshal for that judicial district.[131] Such situations were problematic, because there could be no uniform rule devised to determine which representative should have the primary say (other than party considerations). Limiting the involvement of a Republican lawmaker would most likely produce a congressional enemy, but permitting the same person to control appointments in another member's congressional district did not make sense either. The situation would be analogous to a Republican senator from New Hampshire influencing appointments in Maine. The Maine Republicans would be offended, and they would most likely take their anger out on the administration that had permitted such an offense to occur.

Despite the problems of conformity between congressional and judicial districts, it appears that representatives were usually able to come to some mutually beneficial agreement. For instance, all three Republican representatives in Tennessee—Henry C. Evans, Alfred A. Taylor, and Leonidas C. Houk—united in support of one U.S. attorney candidate.[132] In another case, the North Carolina Republican leadership worked out a compromise so that Representative John M. Brower and "a large proportion of the Republican members of the [state] Legislature" would collaborate on state appointments.[133] The administration endorsed similar arrangements in other states that had no members of Congress from the president's party. In the South, for instance (primarily in Arkansas, Kentucky, Georgia, Texas, and West Virginia), Harrison relied on party leaders in appointment matters.[134] For territorial appointments, either the Republican delegate or the Republican political leader was consulted.[135]

Grover Cleveland (1893–1897)

The 1892 presidential election brought a reversal of fortunes for the Democratic Party, as former president Grover Cleveland defeated incumbent Benjamin Harrison. Once again, Cleveland proved that he was the only Democratic candidate who could win a presidential election during this period. In fact, Cleveland won by a vote of 277 to 145 in the electoral college, and for the third time, he obtained a majority of the popular vote as well.[136] As Brodsky explained: "Grover Cleveland's election victory positioned him to be the strongest President since the Civil War. His party had not only carried the doubtful states of New York, New Jersey, Connecticut, and Indiana but the Republican strongholds of Illinois, Wisconsin, and California as well. Most of the influential papers nationwide had supported him, as had the eastern financial establishment. Of greater significance, for the first time since 1856 the President's party would control both houses of Congress."[137]

Once he was back in the White House, Cleveland again pressed for civil service reform.[138] At his State of the Union address on December 4, 1893, he made reference to a number of measures that he hoped Congress would enact to further the Civil Service Commission's work. In addition, Cleveland stated that he was "convinced of the incalculable benefits conferred by the civil-service law, not only in its effect upon the public service, but also, what is even more important, in its effect in elevating the tone of political life generally."[139] This conviction was borne out in the expansion of offices protected by the Pendleton Act. Welch explained the significance of Cleveland's actions:

> Cleveland brought under the protection of the Pendleton Act a larger *percentage* of the federal bureaucracy than has any other American president. By the time Cleveland left Washington for a second time, more than 40 percent of a now-enlarged corps of federal employees were on the classified list. When he had first entered office, less than 12 percent had enjoyed that protection, and only a small part of the increase had occurred during the interim presidency of Benjamin Harrison.[140]

The large number of federal offices becoming classified angered many "spoilsmen, congressmen, and Republican partisans," but there was little they could do because of the decrease in the "organized opposition to the merit system in Congress."[141] By the end of his second term, Cleveland had expanded the classified civil service by 49,179, which increased the total number of protected federal offices to 87,044.[142]

Even with the growth of the protected service, a large number of federal offices still fell under the influence of lawmakers, whose traditional bargaining approach to the pre-nomination process burdened the White House. Early in his presidency, Cleveland wrote, "[I have] a hungry party behind me, and they say I am not grateful."[143] Despite an effort to limit the portion of each day spent on appointments, many members of Congress monopolized the president's time in their attempts to influence him. By

May 8, 1893, Cleveland issued an executive order asking senators and representatives not to "introduce their constituents and friends when visiting the Executive Mansion during the hours designated for their reception."[144] That limitation, however, did not stop consultation from occurring.

Congressional involvement in the pre-nomination process was as strong as ever. For example, in a letter to Attorney General Judson Harmon, Cleveland stated that he had sought the advice of Democratic representative Josiah Patterson for a "sound and able man" to fill a vacant district attorney position in Tennessee, and the president would be "inclined to follow [Patterson's recommendation] when received."[145] In another case, Democratic senator John Martin of Kansas pressed Cleveland for foreign appointments for his constituents.[146] Sometimes a lawmaker merely wanted the courtesy of a delay in an appointment, as occurred in Pennsylvania for Representative William Henry Hines.[147]

At times, President Cleveland displayed an independent streak. For instance, he declined to make one Connecticut appointment because Democratic representative James P. Pigott had recommended a "saloon-keeper." In fact, Cleveland was disgusted with the recommendations coming from Connecticut and stated, "What I want is somebody in Connecticut who knows the men applying and who knows their character and who believes it is better politics to appoint a fit man than to appoint one merely and solely on the score of partisan activity."[148]

Although professing a desire for sound home-state information, Cleveland failed to follow his own advice. In the summer of 1893, he nominated William B. Hornblower, "a highly respected New York attorney," to the Supreme Court.[149] The Senate, however, rejected Hornblower out of courtesy to Democratic senator David Hill of New York, who disliked Hornblower and was not happy about the president's failure to consult him on the appointment.[150] Despite being an "anti-Cleveland" member of the Democratic Party,[151] Senator Hill had a right to be involved in the pre-nomination process because he was the nominee's home-state senator. Republican senator George F. Hoar, though no supporter of senatorial dictate, agreed in his autobiography that Cleveland should have consulted Hill before making such an appointment.[152] No doubt, the Senate's rejection was aided by Cleveland's weakened political condition as a result of the panic of 1893.

Despite this setback, Cleveland could be very calculating, using the pre-nomination process to promote his own agenda. For instance, during the fight to repeal the Sherman Silver Purchase Act of 1890,[153] he used appointments to encourage members of Congress to support the administration. In fact, Cleveland explained that any Democratic lawmaker who opposed repeal should "not expect me to 'turn the other cheek' by rewarding their conduct with patronage."[154] Those who did assist the administration were rewarded with control over appointments. For example, Senator Daniel W. Voorhees, a onetime Sherman Act supporter, secured several positions in his state because he reversed course and voted for repeal.[155] Through the use of patronage, Cleveland was ultimately successful in having the act rescinded in what Van Riper called the "most spectacular manipulation of public office."[156]

Despite passage of the first significant civil service reform measure in U.S. history, the effort to end political bargaining in the pre-nomination process was limited. Reformers could not simply separate the civil service from the give-and-take process inherent in the practical operation of the Appointments Clause. Through our constitutional system of governance, the president and Congress are responsible to the people, and as such, they possess the power to make tough choices. Primary responsibility for nearly all actions of the federal government, no matter how corrupt they may be, rests with either the executive or the legislative branch. In terms of appointments, the Constitution implies a collective responsibility to work together and make good selections. By instituting entrance examinations, the Pendleton Act formalized the effort to provide qualified candidates for federal office, but it did not lessen the role of either branch. Although civil service reform can limit, to a certain extent, the most egregiously inappropriate appointments, it cannot separate all appointments from what is an essential democratic process of government. In such a system, it is preferable for federal appointments to be subject to political compromising between the president and members of Congress than for them to be left to an unelected official or body. Congressional consultation, even after passage of the Pendleton Act, continued to be the primary starting point in appointment matters.

Chapter 7

McKinley to Ford: The Tradition Continues (1897–1977)

This chapter continues the study of the pre-nomination process by examining the administrations from William McKinley through Gerald Ford. These presidents, like their recent predecessors, had to wrestle with the legacy of both the pre-nomination process and civil service reform. Statutory reforms narrowed the number of appointments available, but they did not lessen the need for consultation and compromise between the president and Congress. In addition, starting in the mid-twentieth century, there was a pronounced effort by various elements of the minority party to participate more fully in the pre-nomination process.

William McKinley (1897–1901), Theodore Roosevelt (1901–1909), and William Howard Taft (1909–1913)

President William McKinley maintained the tradition of vetting postal and other local appointments through congressmen, while statewide offices were generally left to senators.[1] The administration's policy was "that no state or district appointments would be made . . . except upon the recommendation of a senator or congressmen."[2] As one McKinley biographer wrote, he "was punctilious in his regard for senatorial prerogatives, and observed the courtesy of consultation, even in cases in which it was not customary."[3] Senator Marcus Hanna was a central figure in advising the president, particularly concerning appointments in Ohio.[4] His influence was perceived to be so strong that members of Congress often sought his help in securing appointments. For example, Republican representative Isaac A. Barber of Maryland wrote to Senator Hanna about an appointment. Hanna forwarded the message to the White House, and McKinley noted that the nomination "ought to be done" for Barber.[5] Another lawmaker with substantial influence was Republican senator Nelson W. Aldrich, chairman of the Finance Committee.[6] In one case, Secretary of the Treasury Lyman J. Gage informed the senator of a vacancy and asked

Aldrich "to consider the question of [a] successor and to make your recommendation accordingly."[7] In another instance, the head of the Bureau of Pensions notified Aldrich that an appointment had been made and that the former officeholder had been "removed by your request."[8]

Other members of Congress were given a voice in appointment matters as well. In Pennsylvania, McKinley accepted the recommendations of Republican senator Matt Quay,[9] and New York Republican senator Thomas Platt controlled federal positions in his state.[10] According to one scholar, this latter arrangement worked well, "and throughout McKinley's administration harmony prevailed between the administration and the Platt organization."[11] Additional Republican lawmakers in states from Maine to Washington were given recognition in their appointment requests as well.[12]

The lack of Republican members of Congress in the solid South forced the McKinley administration to manage appointments differently there. Defeated Republican congressmen were recommended for local offices. The positions of U.S. marshals, attorneys, and federal judgeships were filled by a Board of Referees that consisted of "the defeated candidate for Governor, the chairman of the State Committee, and the member of the National Committee from the state."[13] In some cases, carpetbag or black Republican ex-congressmen controlled appointments in their states. This occurred in Mississippi, where ex-senator Blanche K. Bruce gave appointment advice to the administration.[14]

Despite being known as an independent reformer, President Theodore Roosevelt also followed the customs of the day.[15] In fact, he once wrote, "I naturally feel pleased whenever I have the chance to show 'favor' to a Senator or a Congressman."[16] Although there were some rumors that the Roosevelt White House would deny Senator Platt control over appointments in New York, they turned out to be unfounded.[17] After Roosevelt had nominated one of Platt's lieutenants to office, the senator exclaimed, "the President has assured me that it is his purpose to act in harmony with me in making New York appointments."[18] The norm was to listen to the recommendations of legislators, and Roosevelt followed it. In Delaware,[19] Kansas,[20] Maryland,[21] North Carolina,[22] Ohio,[23] Pennsylvania,[24] and South Dakota,[25] Republican senators were consulted about appointments. As for local offices, Roosevelt continued the tradition of permitting Republican representatives to name candidates.[26]

Roosevelt's adherence to pre-nomination custom was not done only out of necessity to survive the political realities of his day. On at least two occasions, he set forth the constitutional reasoning for involving members of Congress in the pre-nomination process:

> I must in each State act in conjunction with the Senators. Now and then for exceptional places I can get men appointed to whom the Senators object, or at least as to whom they are indifferent. But these cases

are exceptional. . . . I accept the Senators' recommendations, provided
they recommend decent men. This is not a case of personal peculiarity on my part or of usurpation of authority on theirs. It is a compliance not merely with the letter but with the spirit of Article 2, Section
2, of the Constitution.[27]

I understand perfectly that under the first article of the Constitution,
the Senators are part of the appointing power, and that therefore the
appointment must represent an agreement between them and me,
and, as the acquaintance of the Senator with his State is always much
greater than the knowledge of the President can possibly be, it is the
normal and natural thing that I should listen to his advice as to these
appointments, and I generally do so.[28]

Here are two examples of a sitting president proclaiming that there is a practical as well as a constitutional duty to consult Congress. Finally, Roosevelt
stated in another letter that he merely set "the standard"; the lawmakers
made the appointment: "Senators and Congressmen shall ordinarily name
the men, but I shall name the standard, and the men have got to come up
to that."[29] This was quite a candid statement from one of the most "independent" Republican presidents of the twentieth century.

The rare appointments that Roosevelt made semi-independently of
Congress were judicial. In those cases, he told Republican senator Knute
Nelson, "I exercise both an initiative and a scrutiny which I would not
dream of trying to exercise with most other appointments."[30] However, the
"exercise" of power was limited. In one case, the Senate Judiciary Committee held up a judicial nomination because Roosevelt broke with tradition by not consulting Senator Nelson.[31] At the end of the session, the
nomination was returned to the White House. Neither Roosevelt nor his
successor would attempt to renominate against Nelson's wishes.[32]

Coming into the presidency on the heels of McKinley and Roosevelt,
William Howard Taft also adhered to the practice of consulting lawmakers from his own party.[33] Like Roosevelt, Taft understood the constitutional
and practical need to involve members of Congress in the pre-nomination
process:

The usual contention is that these words require that the President,
before making a nomination, consult the Senate. . . . Such a construction of the term "advice and consent" easily leads one imbued with the
sacred awfulness of the Senate's function in the government to the conclusion that a Republican President under the Constitution and the
courtesy of the Senate must consult the Republican Senators from a
state before making an appointment in that state, although no such

constitutional or statutory obligation is upon him in respect of Democratic Senators. The Constitution thus varies in its application to the power of Senators of one political party and to the Senators of another.[34]

Two successive presidents thus articulated not only a practical but also a *constitutional* reason why chief executives must consult legislators. Understanding the built-in pressure to continue the practice, Taft noted, "an attempt on the President's part to break up the custom would create a factional opposition which would interfere with the passing of the bills he recommends, and endanger the successful carrying out of the policies to which he is pledged."[35]

In discussing the "factional opposition" of cutting off patronage, Taft may have been referring to his battle with the progressive wing of his party when he denied appointments to Republican members of Congress who had fought against the Payne-Aldrich tariff in the Senate and the dictatorial rule of Speaker Joseph Cannon in the House of Representatives. After a long, drawn-out fight that damaged not only Taft but also the Republican Party, the administration restored control over patronage to the insurgent congressmen.[36] Even maverick Republicans were entitled to appointments.

Despite continuing this well-established practice, Taft also attempted to extend civil service protection. In his second State of the Union address, he announced that he had placed all assistant postmasters under the civil service. Taft recommended that Congress give first , second , and third-class postmasters similar protection as well.[37] Realizing that there would be congressional resistance to such a policy, Taft acknowledged "that this is inviting from the Senate a concession in respect to its quasi executive power that is considerable, but I believe it to be in the interest of good administration and efficiency of service. To make this change would take the postmasters out of politics; would relieve Congressmen who now are burdened with the necessity of making recommendations for these places of a responsibility that must be irksome and can create nothing but trouble."[38] The plan failed to win congressional backing.

The only major change Taft made to the pre-nomination process occurred in the South, where the White House tried to break the hold that traditional black Republican organizations had on federal appointments. For the most part, Republican presidents and candidates had promised southern black "referees" control over patronage in return for assurances that they would deliver their state's delegates to the president at the Republican National Convention.[39] Southern whites claimed that this system resulted in political corruption and produced bad appointments. Sympathetic to this charge, Taft modified the existing pre-nomination process presumably to ensure better appointments and alleviate these concerns of southern whites.[40] In reality, this policy largely meant that the administration would refuse to nominate blacks when doing so would upset the local population, and that the president would consult Democratic members of Congress.[41]

Taft's actions greatly upset the black community and destroyed or weakened the few Republican organizations there were in the South.[42] After more than a year and a half of implementing this policy, Postmaster General Frank H. Hitchcock tried to appoint candidates who might rebuild the Republican Party. After receiving a list of appointments from Hitchcock, Taft exclaimed:

> I will not be swerved one iota from my policy to the South, and I want Hitchcock to understand it now, once and for all. I shall not appoint Negroes to office in the South, and I shall not appoint Republicans unless they be good men. I shall not relinquish my hope to build up a decent white man's party there, politics or no politics. That section of the country is entitled to have high-class men in federal offices as much as any part of the country, and if I cannot find good Republicans for the offices, then I will fill them with Democrats.[43]

This new southern appointment policy would eventually produce an entire movement to exclude blacks from the Republican Party in the South, known as the "lily-white" movement.[44]

To summarize, the first three Republican administrations of the twentieth century largely continued the practice of consulting members of Congress. Two of the three presidents actively proclaimed that this was a well-established system that had been created out of a constitutional interpretation of the Appointments Clause. Civil service reform did not significantly change how appointments were made. If anything, the pre-nomination process was streamlined so that the administration and members of Congress could better coordinate appointments. As Dorothy Ganfield Fowler explained:

> In the twentieth century the custom of Congressional "advice" was thoroughly systematized by the Republicans. Not only were Senators officially recognized as the "referee" in the case of state-wide positions; but if there were two administration Senators, and especially if they were not harmonious, they made formal agreements dividing the patronage—that is one Senator would be the "advisor" for certain counties or a judicial district and the other for the rest of the state. Frequently these agreements were made after consultation with the President and filed with the various Departments which had officers in the state.[45]

Woodrow Wilson (1913–1921)

Woodrow Wilson, the first Democratic president in sixteen years, emulated his Republican predecessors by accepting recommendations from members of Congress. In several early statements, Wilson and his administration expressed their commitment to recognize congressional influence over appointments. For instance, shortly after the election, the Wilson White House declared, "the recommendations of Senators and Representatives will be followed."[46] In addition, Wilson drafted a statement on patronage that read: "The rule receiving recommendations and endorsements by Senators for Federal appointments to offices to be filled within the State, and permitting recommendations from Members of Congress for postmasters within their respective Districts will be observed."[47] After a year in office, Wilson would write, "I am bound by the old practice in Washington to respect and accept the recommendations of Congressmen and Senators."[48]

Initially, Wilson wanted to reward the progressive elements in his party and widen the consultation base by conferring with both Democrats and Republicans. In addition, he sought to weaken conservative Democrats by taking away their patronage. At one point, Wilson told Postmaster General Albert S. Burleson that what he needed were candidates with "progressive policies."[49] However, after much debate, Burleson convinced Wilson that practical politics required the acknowledgment of all Democrats:

> Mr. President if you pursue this policy, it means that your administration is going to be a failure. It means that defeat of the measures of reform that you have next to your heart. These little offices don't amount to anything. They are inconsequential. It doesn't amount to a damn who is postmaster at Paducah, Kentucky. But these little offices mean a great deal to the Senators and Representatives in Congress. If it goes out that the President has turned down Representative So and So and Senator So and So, it means that that member has got bitter trouble at home. If you pursue the right policy, you can make the Democratic Party, progressive.[50]

A year later, Wilson told Burleson, "What you told me about the old standpatters is true. . . . They at least will stand by the party and the administration. I can rely on them better than I can on some of my own people [i.e., progressives]."[51]

With regard to widening the consultation base, Wilson met with his close adviser Edward M. House on January 25, 1913, and remarked that the practice would be "to consult the Senators regarding district attorneys, marshals and collectors, and the Congressmen as to postmasters." Wilson also noted, "when a state was represented by republican senators, he would consult them to the extent of asking them whether they knew of any reason why an appointment should not be made. In the event they objected, it was his purpose to inquire further into the fitness of the applicant."[52] There is no way to know whether all senators were treated equally, regardless of party,[53] and in any case, the practice was discontinued within two years.

Warren G. Harding (1921–1923), Calvin Coolidge (1923–1929), and Herbert Hoover (1929–1933)

The Republican Party returned to power in 1921 and retained control of the presidency for more than a decade. As a former senator, President Warren G. Harding understood that consultation was vital to keeping peace with members of Congress. In most cases, he was personally involved in appointment matters and sought to include members of Congress in the pre-nomination process.[54] For instance, shortly after taking office, Harding remarked that he wanted recommendations to come "from the ground up." This was understood to mean that "an applicant for office must have the endorsement of the party leaders in the locality where he resides and the approval of their choice by others occupying higher positions in the party organization in their States." But the ultimate decision-making authority would come from "the Republican Senator or Senators from the State . . . [who would make the] final judgment as to the wisdom of the appointment."[55] Joseph Harris explained that a "more explicit renunciation of the authority of the President to nominate federal officers can hardly be imagined."[56]

Of particular importance during this time was President Harding's rescinding of Wilson's executive order that had required postmaster positions to be given to the highest scorers on the civil service examination.[57] Under the new system, the appointing official had the discretion to select one of the three highest-scoring candidates. To alleviate civil service reform backlash, a statement accompanying Harding's executive order explained that this change merely conformed the process of making postal appointments to that applicable to other civil service positions.[58] Although Wilson's order had never really removed postal appointments from the pre-nomination process,[59] Harding was largely blamed or credited—depending on whether one was a politician or reformer—with returning these positions to the political process.[60] Despite the fact that a postal candidate had to score within the top three to be considered for an appointment, the system was easily manipulated to ensure that only those recommended by Republican congressmen were selected.[61] For instance, if the preferred candidate of a lawmaker failed to score high enough, a "second examination" would often take place.[62] Nothing in the civil service rules prevented a candidate from retaking the examination again and again until he or she achieved a top-three score.

Harding's successor, Calvin Coolidge, adhered to these pre-nomination customs and practices as well.[63] He was steadfast in consulting with Republican members of Congress. A few months after taking office, he issued a memorandum to all departments, declaring: "I have notified the Republican Senators that I intended to consult them about appointments in their own states. Some of them have suggested to me that many of these appointments come up from the Departments, and that it might save embarrassment if Senators could be notified before such appointments are made. I therefore suggest that you try to carry out that policy."[64] This policy would be repeated and adhered to throughout his administration.[65] As for local appointments, such as postmasters, they continued to be made by Republican representatives.[66] The practice of consultation persisted despite the fact that Coolidge, like Taft, recommended abolishing four-year terms for postmasters and placing first-, second-, and third-class postmasters under the civil service.[67]

In some cases, the administration went above and beyond the traditional requirements. When considering a candidate for assistant secretary of commerce, Commerce Secretary Herbert Hoover solicited the advice of Illinois Republicans—Senator Charles S. Deneen and Representative Martin B. Madden—because the person in question was a resident of Chicago.[68] In another case, Hoover consulted Republican senator James Couzens of Michigan about a candidate from that state being considered for director of the Bureau of Mines.[69] An endorsement list for another Commerce Department position contained eight senators and three representatives.[70] Coolidge even told Attorney General John G. Sargent and Secretary Hoover to consult Republican senator Charles Curtis of Kansas about a District of Columbia appointment.[71]

One of President Herbert Hoover's campaign promises was to appoint well-qualified candidates to federal positions. Most observers of his presidency have concluded that he was more interested in the qualities of candidates than in the political realities that necessitated consultation with legislators.[72] For judicial appointments, this meant limiting Congress's traditional control.[73] In his memoirs, Hoover explained his intended purpose:

> Appointments of district and circuit judges, district attorneys and marshals offer a special problem in political pressures to all Presidents. As the Senate must confirm these officials, the senators over the years had assumed that they could make unofficial nominations. If the President did not accept their views, then, because of the common interest among senators, anyone not of their selection stood little chance of

securing confirmation. With this club the judicial appointments below the Supreme Court had become practically a perquisite of the senators. And conversely the custom of the President asking the senators for suggestions as to such appointments had become a basis of amity.[74]

Taking account of political realities, but still wanting to select officers on the basis of merit,[75] the administration gave Republican senators a list of candidates that the president considered acceptable before a vacancy was announced. This procedure was intended to prevent senators from receiving local political pressure to back unworthy candidates for office. "The senator," as Hoover explained, "could thereupon take credit both with the appointee and with the appointee's friends for his support."[76]

This modification worked well in states with no Republican members of Congress. For instance, Hoover was able to rebuff the Florida Republican organization by passing over its candidate and selecting another.[77] In a letter to the secretary of the Republican State Committee, he wrote: "I cannot believe that you. . . overlook the primary responsibility which rests upon the President of the United States. That responsibility is one of the most sacred which he assumes upon his oath of office. It is that he shall, to his utmost capacity, appoint men to public office who will execute the laws of the United States with Integrity and without fear, favor, or political collusion. The appointment responsibility rests in the President, not in any organization."[78] Hoover could afford to be trite with politicians who had no power to affect the fate of his appointments. This approach also worked in the District of Columbia, where there were no members of Congress to interfere with the administration's selections.[79]

Although Hoover could stand up to state party organizations, he was forced to be more accommodating when dealing with Republican members of Congress. For instance, he made a judicial appointment under pressure from Republican senators Joseph R. Grundy and David Reed of Pennsylvania, despite protests from a senior federal circuit judge and state bar members that he had "abandoned his position concerning the necessity of appointing fit men."[80] Senator Reed actually forced Hoover's hand by visiting the White House and stating that the administration would no longer receive support from the Pennsylvania congressional delegation unless his candidate was selected.[81] The same occurred in Kansas, where Republican senator Arthur Capper told the president that "under no circumstances would he endorse any other lawyer for the place." Despite Hoover's reluctance, he nominated Capper's candidate.[82] In Delaware, Republican senators Daniel Oren Hastings and John Gillis Townsend Jr. were able to secure the selection of their preferred candidate as well.[83] After much grandstanding and hype about changing the custom of selecting judges, the White House was eventually forced to bend to practical politics and permit senators to have a strong voice in judicial appointments.[84]

Franklin D. Roosevelt (1933–1945)

The second Democratic president in the twentieth century, Franklin D. Roosevelt, understood the importance of the pre-nomination process. His top political adviser, James A. Farley, was head of the Democratic National Committee and Roosevelt's choice to be postmaster general. Farley, too, grasped the value of building a political consensus behind a nominee.[85] At first, however, both Roosevelt and Farley failed to see the need to involve members of Congress in that process. Instead, the administration sought the "endorsement of local Democratic organizations, from county committee to State committee."[86] But under pressure from Democratic senators, the pre-nomination process was changed.[87] In a meeting at the White House, Roosevelt, Farley, and Edward J. Flynn, the Democratic boss of the Bronx, agreed that Democratic senators would be consulted before the administration announced a nominee.[88] The simple fact was that unless legislators' wishes were "followed the administration would run the danger of the Senators banding together and preventing appointments."[89]

Roosevelt was not above using offices to assist his administration. For instance, he would withhold appointments from Democratic lawmakers who opposed his legislative agenda.[90] In one case, the threat of denying patronage to members of Congress who did not vote for his emergency relief bill was enough to secure its passage.[91] However, this was not a sign that the administration had complete freedom over appointments. Senators from Connecticut,[92] Nevada,[93] South Carolina,[94] Texas,[95] and Virginia[96] were able to prevent Roosevelt from running roughshod over their traditional prerogatives and did not allow themselves to be excluded from patronage considerations.

Those pre-nomination mishaps were the exceptions. Roosevelt understood that members of Congress expected to participate in appointments, and he sought to address any problems that arose. In one instance, after a Democratic congressional delegation complained to Roosevelt "about the treatment they had got on patronage from departments, he promptly asked the cabinet to be as helpful as possible with congressmen on this matter."[97] Even the conservative elements within his party were not cut off from patronage. For the most part, Roosevelt was forced to use appointments to appease these congressmen.[98] The established pre-nomination process was just too powerful for any chief executive to challenge, even one as popular as Roosevelt.

One important modification in how appointments were handled occurred during this time. Congress passed the Ramspeck-O'Mahoney Act of
1938, which placed postal appointments under civil service protection.[99] Postmasters were now appointed to indefinite terms (as opposed to four years),
with the appointing officer selecting from among the three highest scorers
on the civil service examination. Incumbent postmasters were given non-
competitive examinations. The act also permitted temporary appointments
of up to six months before an examination had to take place.[100] Although intended to end political influence over these appointments, the act had only a
nominal effect. As the 1955 Hoover Commission report described:

> Appointment by the President and confirmation by the Senate is the
> foundation for the system of political clearance which still prevails.
> The [Post Office] Department does not rely upon its own judgment
> but normally yields to the recommendations of its political advisers,
> Members of Congress or political party committees.
>   Political clearance has an adverse effect upon competition for
> appointment:
>   1. Persons belonging to the minority party generally do not com-
>   pete, whether competitive employees or outside citizens.
>   2. Persons belonging to the majority party are given to under-
>   stand that the man preferred by the local party organization
>   will be appointed if he passes the examination.
>   3. If he fails to pass the examination, efforts are made (often suc-
>   cessfully) to call another examination:
>   a. By finding reasons why one or more of the successful
>   competitors may be disqualified;
>   b. By inducing one or more to withdraw, indicating that
>   they will not be cleared;
>   c. By returning the eligible list if less than three names are
>   available. (The Civil Service Rules permit the agency to
>   request a new examination when less than three eligibles
>   are available for selection.)
>   4. Meanwhile, the acting postmaster (who is usually the party
>   nominee) is building up knowledge and experience which
>   make for ultimate success in passing the examination.
>   For these and perhaps other reasons, competition for appointment
> to the largest post offices is meager and unsatisfactory.[101]

This practice would continue until Richard Nixon's administration in the
late 1960s (discussed later).
   The expansion of federal government employment to an all-time high
as a result of Roosevelt's New Deal program also had a great impact on the

pre-nomination process.[102] This was a political blessing for the new Democratic administration, which was able to reward various party members "only because the new emergency agencies were hiring employees outside the classified civil service (about a hundred thousand such jobs by July 1934)."[103] This system produced a mini–spoils era during the New Deal and allowed Democratic Party members to fill the many agencies and relief bureaus that had been created without civil service requirements. For instance, Postmaster General Farley established an office to oversee appointments in the Public Works Administration (PWA), and every potential candidate had to receive political clearance before being selected.[104] In a letter to one applicant, a PWA administrator wrote, "It will be necessary to have a letter of endorsement from some Democratic Senator or Congressman, not necessarily from your State."[105] According to civil service scholar Donald R. Harvey, this period "was not a particularly bright one for the Civil Service Commission or the merit system it administered." Harvey noted that the Roosevelt administration consisted of practical politicians and "political realists who were no less partisan in their approach than all professional politicians have been." The simple fact was that Republicans had controlled the White House for twelve years, and "Democrats were eager for patronage."[106]

Harry S Truman (1945–1953)

Roosevelt's death thrust Vice President Harry Truman into the presidency. Truman respected the tradition of the pre-nomination process, in part because of his service in the Senate and in part because of his interest in maintaining party harmony.[107] One Truman biographer noted that he "often acted more like a prime minister than a president" because he "was aware of how senators resented the prominence of the executive branch and how angered they had been over FDR's arm-twisting tactics." Dismissing this approach, Truman dealt "with the congressional leadership on a personal basis, assum[ing] that negotiation and consultation would avoid an impasse between Congress and the White House."[108]

Although Truman generally followed the practice of consultation, he would sometimes nominate without seeking the support of Democratic senators; in each case, the nomination would be rejected by the Senate.[109] Professor Sheldon Goldman explained that President Truman, despite being "appreciative of senatorial prerogatives," believed that he was defending "the prerogatives of his office."[110] History shows that the executive branch has never had an absolute prerogative to make unilateral appointments without congressional participation. Truman, like Roosevelt at times, attempted to defend a presidential prerogative that he never had.

During his administration, Truman managed to cause a minor uproar over one civil service proposal. On April 10, 1952, he sent to Congress three reorganization plans that, as he described them, "would take postmasters out of partisan politics by abolishing the requirement that they be appointed by the President and confirmed by the Senate." In addition, "all political offices in the Bureau of Customs would be eliminated and the work would be carried on by qualified civil service appointees." Finally, "the positions of United States marshals" would be placed "under Civil Service" protection.[111] Congress refused to go along. Democratic senator Walter F. George of Georgia proclaimed that these plans would "'concentrate more power' in the executive departments and urged that 'Congress should be more responsible, rather than less, for appointments.'" Truman's plans were eventually rejected "by substantial margins" in the Senate.[112]

Dwight D. Eisenhower (1953–1961)

Dwight D. Eisenhower, the first Republican president in twenty years, was unfamiliar with Washington practices and did not follow the established custom of consulting Republican members of Congress before announcing nominations.[113] Initially, he vested primary power over investigating and recommending federal appointments in the Republican National Committee.[114] However, this practice soon caused problems when Eisenhower failed to consult key Republican senators about cabinet-level appointments.[115] For instance, Republican Majority Leader Robert Taft professed to friends that Eisenhower had appointed Cleveland steel company executive George Humphrey to head the Treasury Department without even consulting him about naming an Ohioan.[116] The White House was soon forced to issue a directive that outlined a "clearance" policy, explaining that "Republican Senators and State Republican leaders" would be consulted about "all top appointments."[117] Although Eisenhower met with Republican congressional leaders and assured them that "adequate consultation" would take place,[118] there was still "uncertainty over whether Senators or the National Committee men and state Chairmen should get first consideration in filling federal jobs."[119] A second meeting took place at which Eisenhower announced that his administration would "adhere to past practice in clearing patronage appointments with the members of his party in Congress."[120] The administration would consult not only with Republican senators but also, at times, with House members and national committeemen:

> Republican Senators will be consulted on all Federal appointments of persons within their home states. In the case of postmasters or other appointments within a Congressional District, Republican Represen-

tatives also will be consulted. In states without Republican Senators or Congressmen, Republican national committeemen will be advised, as well as Governors if they are Republican. Special rules will apply in the normally Democratic states that voted for General Eisenhower, such as Virginia, Texas, Florida and Tennessee.[121]

According to one historian, the "arrangement did not work too well."[122] In fact, "senators still grumbled that Eisenhower ignored them in matters of patronage" and retained Democratic postmasters who were undermining the administration's policies.[123] Some of these difficulties had to do with the president's personal dislike of the politics involved in appointments,[124] as well as the party's general anger over the lack of new federal job openings.[125] As a result, Eisenhower was forced to spend a significant amount of time consulting unhappy Republicans.[126]

John F. Kennedy (1961–1963) and Lyndon B. Johnson (1963–1969)

Despite being a former senator, John F. Kennedy did not give legislators the deference one might have expected. Part of the reason, as G. Calvin Mackenzie explained, was the "momentum toward centralized presidential control of the appointment process and away from reliance on party patronage." According to Mackenzie, "Kennedy, like Eisenhower, had won the presidential nomination by setting up his own organization and capturing the party. His was not a life of deeply committed partisanship nor did he grant the Democratic party organization much credit for his narrow victory in the 1960 election."[127] The failure to consult members of Congress also had to do with the lack of any clear guidance from the administration.[128] This problem reflected Kennedy's preference "to operate in a more informal, collegial setting."[129] At least in terms of judicial appointments, it was "difficult to assess with any precision the impact of each or any of the participants" in Kennedy's pre-nomination process.[130] The administration acknowledged that it would consult Democratic leaders of a particular state, but they would not be the only participants in the process. State and local bar associations would also be included when reviewing potential nominees.[131] Despite the initial effort to limit the participation of Democratic members of Congress, Attorney General Robert Kennedy could state in 1964 that the process has "grown up as a senatorial appointment with the advice and consent of the President."[132]

Clear evidence supporting this view comes from several states where the administration had to deal with hostile Democratic senators. In Virginia, Kennedy was forced to consult with Senator Harry F. Byrd, chairman of the

Finance Committee, despite Byrd's opposition to most of the administration's policies.[133] Similarly, in Mississippi, conservative senator James O. Eastland was able to exert a powerful influence over appointments because he chaired the Senate Judiciary Committee.[134] In other cases, Democratic senators were able to get appointments for otherwise objectionable candidates. Senator Thomas J. Dodd of Connecticut was successful in having his law partner named to a federal judgeship.[135] Even after his preferred candidate received negative reports from the Justice Department, the FBI, and the American Bar Association, Democratic senator Robert Kerr of Oklahoma prevailed.[136]

Other appointments were effectively controlled by members of Congress. In his autobiography, Kennedy's postmaster general J. Edward Day described legislators' power over postmasters: "Even today every vacancy that occurs among the 35,000 postmasters and 33,000 rural letter carriers is filled by political appointment, that is, on the recommendation of the local member of the House of Representatives, if he is of the party that controls the White House, or if he is not, on the recommendation of local officials of the party in the White House." Upon assuming the position of postmaster general, Day thought that he would be leading a reform movement to change how Post Office Department appointments were made—in effect, severing the relationship between members of Congress and postmasters. Day stated that since "I had no standing in the national party organization and had never dealt with patronage except in a minor way in my state position, many people—I was among them—concluded that my appointment as PMG represented a complete departure from the old pattern [of making postal appointments]."[137] That was a misguided assumption. Previous reform efforts had failed to abolish the traditional pre-nomination process, and this one was no different.

After Kennedy's assassination, Lyndon B. Johnson took more direct control of the pre-nomination process and "indicated to his team that he wanted greater deference to senatorial prerogative in judicial selection."[138] Harold W. Chase explained Johnson's decision to rely on senators: "It is not difficult to reconstruct reasons for President Johnson's deference to senators. Johnson, both as a senator and as Senate majority leader, insisted on his senatorial prerogatives because he believed in them. Further, perhaps more than any other president in our history, he was closely attuned to the political process in which senatorial prerogative plays a crucial part."[139] On several occasions, President Johnson overruled his staff on appointment decisions and told them that the home-state senators "make the choice," not the White House.[140] As one observer noted, "Everybody in the world makes recommendations to Johnson, then" the senators get to choose.[141]

There was one major White House mishap concerning an appointment that caused a permanent break between Johnson and his longtime friend and Senate colleague Richard Russell of Georgia. To gain Senate support for Johnson's Supreme Court nominees Abe Fortas and Homer Thornberry, Attorney General Ramsey Clark held up the nomination of Alexander Lawrence, Russell's choice for a Georgia district court position, in order to pressure the senator to vote with the administration. The effort backfired. Greatly angered by this move, Russell wrote to Johnson:

> To be perfectly frank . . . even after so many years in the Senate, I was so naïve I had not even suspected that this man's nomination was being withheld from the Senate due to the changes expected on the Supreme Court of the United States until after you sent in the nominations of Fortas and Thornberry. . . . This places me in the position, where, if I support your nominees for the Supreme Court, it will appear that I have done so out of my fears that you would not nominate Mr. Lawrence.[142]

Russell declared himself "released from any statements that I may have made to you with respect to your nominations."[143] Johnson was not happy and observed that this appointment may very well have "destroyed one of the great friendships I've had with one of the great men that has ever served this country." Although Johnson quickly nominated Lawrence and called Russell to explain the situation, the Georgian no longer supported the White House, and "the long-standing Johnson-Russell friendship . . . largely came to an end."[144] The resulting fallout between the two men ended with a Senate filibuster with regard to Fortas and the eventual withdrawal of both Supreme Court nominations.

During the 1960s, there appears to have been greater minority party involvement in the pre-nomination process. That is, the traditional method of consulting only lawmakers of a president's party underwent a slight modification as Republican politicians sought to play a role in appointments in their home states. This change occurred primarily in the area of judicial appointments, most likely as a direct result of the 1961 Judgeship Act.[145] That statute, which created more than seventy judicial posts, had been lobbied for since the late 1950s but did not actually pass until after Kennedy's election. To convince Democratic members of Congress to support the bill, the Eisenhower administration had promised to nominate equal numbers of Republicans and Democrats to the federal bench and "to consult Democrats" about the selections.[146] Although Kennedy's administration decided that it would be politically useful to make some Republican appointments, no uniform process was established.[147] Probably the most well-known Republican to receive patronage from Kennedy was Senate Minority Leader Everett Dirksen.[148] By 1967, Republican senator Jacob Javits of New York was able to pressure President Johnson to nominate a

Republican to a district court position.[149] Although previous administrations had sometimes taken into consideration the wishes of home-state
senators of the opposing party, this was the first known example of a "bipartisan arrangement" being publicly documented and acknowledged by
an administration.[150]

Richard M. Nixon (1969–1974)

Richard M. Nixon's practical experience in the federal government (a
former member of both houses of Congress and a onetime vice president)
might suggest that he would follow traditional pre-nomination customs.
That, however, was not the case. Like previous administrations, the Nixon
White House made several missteps. Although selecting an all-Republican
cabinet and generally picking party members for top posts, Nixon "seemed
to shun the local organizations." For instance, Republican representative
John Anderson of Illinois was unable to secure several positions for his
supporters.[151] In Maryland, Senator Charles Mathias was forced to block an
appointment of a U.S. attorney because the administration had failed to
consult him. Mathias explained that "many of his Republican Congressional colleagues are becoming impatient about the lack of meaningful
communication between them and the Administration."[152]

Several times, Nixon also angered Senator Dirksen. For example, in
the first few weeks of the administration, the White House misplaced Dirksen's appointment recommendations.[153] Even worse was the near retention
of Johnson's Veterans Affairs administrator William J. Driver at the urging
of Democrat Olin E. Teague, chairman of the House Veterans Affairs Committee. After strong protests from Dirksen, Driver was forced to resign.[154]
The Driver episode convinced Dirksen and other Republicans that Nixon
was seeking to co-opt Democrats because they controlled both houses of
Congress.[155] In other cases, Dirksen was able to block the administration's
candidates.[156] To mollify Dirksen, Nixon met with him weekly to discuss
appointment issues.[157]

There were also some appointment problems at the department level.
For instance, Secretary of State William P. Rogers angered Republican senator Barry Goldwater when he attempted to appoint Arthur J. Olsen as
director of press relations, a position that was not subject to Senate confirmation. Goldwater notified the administration that the appointment was
"personally obnoxious" to him because of a 1964 article written by Olsen
linking the senator, who was then the Republican candidate for president,
to a right-wing German extremist. The State Department, with the White
House's approval, complied with Goldwater's wishes and canceled the ap-

pointment.[158] The *New York Times* asked whether "the State Department [is] run by Secretary of State William P. Rogers or by Senator Barry Goldwater?"[159] In a more direct statement, the *Washington Post* declared: "There is something distinctly erratic, not to say pusillanimous, about an administration which turns furiously defensive when Congress seeks to invoke its rights to a voice in the conduct of war, and then turns to jelly when a single senator moves, in a singularly mean-minded way, to block an appointment in the executive branch which doesn't happen to please him personally, even though it is not one over which the Senate has the slightest right of control."[160] Neither newspaper understood or fully appreciated the historical relationship between the two branches in making appointments. Accommodation and compromise on personnel matters often lead to better interbranch relations and public policy in the long term.

Following these early missteps, the Nixon administration generally adhered to traditional customs of pre-nomination review.[161] However, political reality forced unusual arrangements in some situations. For example, Nixon refused to give liberal Republican senators Jacob K. Javits and Charles E. Goodell of New York a role in the pre-nomination process because both had opposed his nomination and actively campaigned against him.[162] In another case, Democratic senators Alan Cranston and John Tunney of California pressured the administration into allowing them to fill every third judicial vacancy with their candidates, or they would have blocked all California nominations.[163]

More than any other president, Nixon sought to minimize congressional patronage by placing the postal service completely under civil service protection.[164] At the start of his administration, Nixon had Postmaster General Winton Blount announce an end to the practice of consulting senators and representatives of the president's party about local postal positions.[165] Nixon also requested that Congress formally take the postal service out of the pre-nomination process by transforming the Post Office Department into a government corporation.[166] In making this announcement, he declared: "The tradition of political patronage in the Post Office Department extends back to the earliest days of the Republic. In a sparsely populated country, where postal officials faced few of the management problems so familiar to modern postmasters, the patronage system may have been a defensible method of selecting jobholders. As the operation of the postal service has become more complex, however, the patronage system has become an increasingly costly luxury. It is a luxury that the nation can no longer afford."[167] To win congressional support, Blount "was forced to call leading congressmen to reassure them that reform would begin with the scrapping of the current list of eligible (mostly Democrats) and the replacement of some of the 2,200 acting postmasters appointed by Kennedy and

Johnson."[168] Despite this effort, Republican members of Congress were still upset by Nixon's proposal.[169] However, the Postal Reorganization and Salary Adjustment Act of 1970 eventually passed.[170]

The act entrusted the new Postal Service to make all appointments of "officers and employees" within its power and attempted to limit the types of recommendations that members of Congress could make regarding hiring, promotions, and other personnel matters. The operative provision reads that members of the Senate and House of Representatives are "prohibited from making or transmitting to the Postal Service, or to any other officer or employee of the Government of the United States, any recommendation or statement, oral or written, with respect to any person who requests or is under consideration for any such appointment, promotion, assignment, transfer, or designation." Exemptions are laid out in a subsequent section, albeit in a rather confusing and disjointed manner. These exceptions allow the Postal Service "or any authorized officer or employee" to "solicit, accept, and consider" recommendations. In addition, it declares that "any other individual or organization" can provide information on personnel decisions. For instance, recommendation statements can include descriptions of a person's performance, ability, aptitude, character, residence, loyalty, and suitability.[171]

These different sections produce a puzzling effect, since one directly excludes members of Congress from making recommendations and the other creates an opening for such actions. Distinguishing members of Congress from "any other individual" appears to be the primary difficulty in making sense of this law. Members of Congress do not give up their status as private citizens when taking the oath of office. They have the same freedom enjoyed by other citizens to solicit information and lobby the federal government. Therefore, the exception provision appears to cancel out the prohibition of congressional recommendations.

Even if one dismisses this inherent flaw in the act, there are constitutional difficulties in totally excluding members of Congress from the pre-nomination process. One can reasonably assume that the Article I legislative functions of the House and Senate give lawmakers the right to recommend in their official capacity. The natural implication of creating laws is to see that they are faithfully carried out. In this case, Congress's legislative role does not end with the creation of the Postal Service. Each member has a constitutional duty to see that the Postal Service and its employees serve the public. Whether that entails inquiring about personnel matters (e.g., hiring, firing, promotion) or other functions of a governmental entity, these actions are valid and proper duties of each and every legislator.

Despite this criticism of the act, these changes removed a large number of political appointments from the pre-nomination process,[172] leaving the judiciary as the primary source of congressional patronage.

Gerald R. Ford (1974–1977)

When Gerald R. Ford became president after Nixon's resignation, Republican Party leaders warned him "not to repeat mistakes the Nixon White House made in handling federal patronage." According to some observers, Republican presidents did not understand the concept of enjoying the spoils of victory. As one Republican congressman stated, "When the Democrats get it [power], they appoint Democrats, do it proudly, and nobody objects. When our people get top jobs, they seem to think the thing to do is to appoint Democrats to give a bipartisan image."[173] The overriding problem in the Nixon administration, as one Ford biographer noted, was "the disdain with which Nixon treated Congress throughout his administration—not as an adversary but as an enemy to be vanquished completely."[174] Nearly every appointment at both the cabinet and lower levels had been the focus of congressional and media attention.[175] Another issue for Ford was that his administration "did not have the clean sweep of an election victory from which to develop a coherent appointment policy."[176] As a result, the lack of open and available positions greatly impaired his relationship with Congress.

For the most part, Ford respected congressional input. For instance, the administration followed the recommendations of New York Republican senators Jacob Javits and James Buckley, New Jersey Republican senator Clifford Chase, and Alaska Republican senator Ted Stevens.[177] However, as Goldman explained, "the Ford administration had one major problem with a Republican Senator and learned the hard way to respect senatorial courtesy."[178] In that case, Ford went against the wishes of Senator William L. Scott of Virginia in a judicial appointment.[179] Without Scott's support, the nomination stood little chance, and it was tabled in the Senate Judiciary Committee.[180] When a state had no senators of the president's party, the highest-ranking Republican often controlled appointments. "For example," Goldman noted, "in West Virginia, Republican governor Arch Moore made the recommendations; in Wisconsin, the Republican national committeeman; and in California, Governor Ronald Reagan."[181]

During his time in office, Ford had to deal with minority party involvement as well. For instance, Florida Democratic senators Richard Stone and Lawton Chiles declared that only nominees they had recommended would receive their endorsement. At first, Ford tried to bypass them and make a nomination independently of the senators, but his candidate was not acted on. After that failure, Ford picked the preferred candidate of Stone and Chiles.[182]

By the end of the Ford administration, consultation between the two branches was still an important feature of the pre-nomination process.

Despite various reforms, "politics" had not been taken out of the appointment process. If anything, these changes show the adaptability and usefulness of the system itself. For instance, even when positions were given civil service protection, Congress found ways to remain involved and fulfill its constitutional role.

Chapter 8

Carter to Bush II: A Lasting Legacy (1977–2007)

The acceptance of the pre-nomination process by both the executive and legislative branches underscores the enduring role that practical politics plays in making appointments. Despite pressure to move toward a civil service model, the two branches have continued to follow the traditional practice of working together in the selection process. Although there are now a reduced number of politically appointed positions, the adaptability of the pre-nomination process highlights its usefulness and resiliency. Throughout the twentieth century, every administration acknowledged through words or actions that congressional involvement in appointments is the proper model to follow. This chapter brings the study up to current president George W. Bush.

Jimmy Carter (1977–1981)

While campaigning for the presidency, Jimmy Carter openly expressed his desire to dramatically transform the pre-nomination process by selecting federal judges based on merit, not politics.[1] Once he reached the White House, Carter said that he wanted to use merit selection commissions to review circuit court candidates to ensure that well-qualified and more diverse nominees would be chosen for office without any political considerations.[2] However, this plan could work only with the consent of senators. At a December 1976 meeting with his soon-to-be attorney general Griffin Bell and Senate Judiciary chairman James O. Eastland, Carter was able to get the senator's consent to this arrangement.[3] Despite this apparent victory for the White House, there was an underlying weakness in Carter's bargaining position. As Justice Department spokesman Marvin Wall explained, "Actually it was not so much an agreement as Sen. Eastland telling 'em [Carter and Bell] what the Senate would sit still for."[4] The Senate retained the power to prevent any and all judicial nominations from being confirmed if Carter chose to venture too far from pre-nomination norms. The administration understood this and sought legislative counsel and consent.

After receiving approval from Eastland, Carter issued two executive orders establishing nominating commissions for circuit court appointments and for other federal judicial officers.[5] A third executive order encouraged senators to create their own commissions for the district courts,[6] but this plan ran into Democratic opposition and was not universally applied.[7] Carter's Associate Attorney General Michael J. Egan recalled that "some senators did it; some did not."[8] A Dallas newspaper reported that Democratic senator Lloyd M. Bentsen referred to himself as "the merit commission for Texas."[9] Another Democratic senator, Paul Sarbanes of Maryland, chose not to establish a merit commission and declared, "I don't see it [a panel] as meeting my constitutional responsibility of providing advice to the president."[10]

Despite the reference to "merit," these nominating bodies did not exclude senators from the pre-nomination process, nor did they reduce partisanship in any measurable way. An aide to one senior Democratic senator explained, "the commissions are only as good or as bad as the senators who have set them up. A selection commission is only a little more pomp and flair on the underlying senatorial participation."[11] The Constitution and history could not be dismissed, no matter how hard Carter and others tried. Senators who wanted to be involved in the process were still given great deference.

The first test of the new system, according to some career Justice Department officials, came with the selection of U.S. attorneys. In those cases, the question was whether Carter would "fight against political pressures" and choose not to remove capable men and women.[12] The answer came in both words and practice. Nearly a year after taking office, Attorney General Bell stated that U.S. attorneys would be left "in the patronage system."[13]

Several examples prove this statement correct. In Michigan, Carter removed a Republican U.S. attorney and proceeded to nominate James K. Robinson at the request of Democratic senator Donald W. Riegle Jr.[14] Asked to explain this removal in light of Carter's campaign pledges to end partisan selections, Bell remarked, "The main reason is that we had an election last November, and the Democrats won. You can use your imagination after that."[15] In New Jersey, Democratic senator Harrison A. Williams Jr. wanted Republican U.S. attorney Jonathan Goldstein replaced. When Goldstein chose to remain in office, Senator Williams remarked, "Goldstein got his position out of the raw force of political appointment. . . . Sure, a lot of people who are in jobs want to keep them, but I don't see any compelling need to change the way things were done before."[16] Eventually the administration forced Goldstein to submit a letter of resignation.[17] Carter then nominated Robert J. Del Tufo, who was endorsed by Senator Williams and Representative Peter W.

Rodino Jr., chairman of the House Judiciary Committee.[18] Finally, in Pennsylvania, Carter removed Republican U.S. attorney David W. Marston at the request of Democratic representative Joshua Eilberg.[19] Bell summed up the political realities of the removal: "I have nothing against Marston. He's a fine young man. But this is the political system in this country."[20]

Some observers were shocked that the Senate had so much power over these appointments. For instance, when Senator Sarbanes forced the selection of a certain U.S. attorney over Carter's wishes, the *Washington Post* editorialized: "From that account, who, would you guess, has the legal right to nominate federal officers like United States Attorneys? Obviously, it is not the President, for he appears in these reports as a mere lobbyist and conduit through which the choice of a senator must pass."[21] Some in the Carter administration agreed with this assessment, but they understood the political realities. As Egan explained, "these appointments ideally should be made purely on the basis of ability and achievement, without even asking whether the man's a Democrat or Republican. But the time for that has not yet come, and it won't until there's a change in the perceptions of the Senate."[22]

Merit selection for judges was even more important to President Carter. However, he understood that senators would play a key role in that process as well. "Because of the ability of any Senator to prevent the appointment of a district judge in his or, now, her State," Carter said, "the district judgeships have to be a partnership agreement between the Senators and the President. Either the Senator or I can, in effect, veto the appointment of a judge."[23] At times, individual senatorial power appears to have overwhelmed Carter's merit intent. For example, Senator Sarbanes of Maryland made all his recommendations without a merit commission.[24] Democratic senator Robert Morgan of North Carolina was able to ensure a judicial appointment for his 1974 campaign manager, Charles Winberry, despite questions about his qualifications.[25] North Carolina's other Democratic senator, Sam J. Ervin Jr., secured the selection of his son to the Fourth Circuit.[26] In another case, a person accused of "racist behavior" was confirmed because he was a friend of Senator John C. Stennis, a Mississippi Democrat.[27] Finally, after winning the 1980 Democratic nomination over Senator Edward Kennedy, Carter negotiated a deal whereby the next First Circuit judgeship would go to Kennedy's choice, in exchange for the senator's support (this ended up being Kennedy's chief counsel to the Senate Judiciary Committee, Stephen G. Breyer).[28] On the Senate floor, Morgan attacked this political bargain and derided those who spoke of "merit selection" when they knew "full well the shenanigans that went on."[29]

Carter's inability to remove political bargaining from judicial appointments was also hindered by a 1978 law that created an additional 117 district court and 35 circuit court positions.[30] The establishment of so many new posts produced a great deal of excitement among Democratic senators. For instance, Senators Thomas Eagleton, Thomas McIntyre, and John Durkin each submitted their choices before Carter even received the legislation. Senator Bentsen was a bit more restrained; he waited a few days after Carter signed the bill to send his recommendations to the Justice Department.[31]

The end result was that the administration could not push senators out of the pre-nomination process. Congressional recommendations were accepted, and, as Egan noted, the administration "didn't have much choice because a senator pretty well had the last word on that because if you didn't appoint the guy the senator wanted, he wouldn't get confirmed and that was pure and simple, that was it."[32] In comparing the selection outcomes of the traditional process with those under the merit commissions, Sheldon Goldman concluded that "party affiliation played the same role it has played traditionally: the merit-type nominating process was essentially merit selection of Democrats."[33] This assessment was confirmed by Egan: the selections "were largely political in nature," he said. "These appointees were people who had worked for the President in his campaign and who were prominent in the Democrat[ic] party in their particular states."[34] Another observer remarked, "It's really not a merit system, but a new form of cronyism."[35]

Ronald Reagan (1981–1989)

Ronald Reagan entered office with the intent to steer the federal judiciary in a more conservative direction. As a first move, he abolished the circuit court nominating commissions and established the procedure of having senators submit the names of several candidates to fill vacant appellate and district court positions.[36] Attorney General William French Smith and Deputy Attorney General Edward C. Schmults reached an agreement on the selection process with Senate Majority Leader Howard H. Baker Jr. and Senator Strom Thurmond, chairman of the Committee on the Judiciary. The agreement, as Goldman noted, "was designed to give the administration more flexibility in naming district judges while retaining senatorial influence."[37] Instead of permitting pluralistic commissions to choose federal judges, Reagan placed the selection power back into the hands of home-state senators. A memorandum by Smith described the arrangement:

> By virtue of the Senator's familiarity with the members of the Bar in their respective States, the Attorney General, in making recommendations to the President for judicial appointments, will invite Republican members to identify prospective candidates for federal district judgeships. Senators are strongly encouraged to submit the names of several candidates, preferably from three to five names, to the Attor-

ney General for a particular vacancy. This information should be shared at the earliest practicable time with the Attorney General's designated representatives so that any questions or reservations as to merit or appropriateness of the proposed candidates can be identified sufficiently early to allow meaningful consultation.

With respect to States with no Senators from the majority party, the Attorney General will solicit suggestions and recommendations from the Republican members of the Congressional delegation, who will act in such instances as a group, in lieu of Senate members from their respective States. It is presumed that Congressional members in such cases would consult with the Democratic Senators from their respective States.[38]

This message was a useful compromise, but it was also a powerful call to the Senate to fall in line with the administration's method of selecting judges. In addition to refocusing its relationship with senators, however, the White House sought to revamp the selection process altogether. Reagan would consult home-state senators, but there would be no dictation of appointments. Republican senators would submit the names of their candidates to the attorney general for consideration, and in states with no senators from the majority party, the administration would solicit suggestions and recommendations from Republican House members or governors.[39] This system would last throughout the administration.[40]

Immediately after Reagan's presidential victory, speculation began about the appointments to be made. For instance, Republican job seekers in New England were focused on the "35 top-level positions . . . including those of U.S. attorney" in their region.[41] In particular, there was concern about which members of Congress would control these appointments. Many Democratic officeholders felt the pressure to resign, including Oregon's longtime U.S. attorney, who gave up his post after serving for twenty years. Although he had escaped various political purges since the Kennedy administration, he realized "that the new Republican Administration was playing a different kind of ball" and would not accept a Democrat in office.[42] Certainly, Reagan wanted to see good Republicans in office, but the decision to remove a U.S. attorney was also dependent on the wishes of the home-state senator.[43] Without the clear approval of Republican senators, the Justice Department was unlikely to act. Once that decision was made, however, senatorial recommendations occurred rapidly. In Connecticut, Maryland, New York, Pennsylvania, and Virginia, Republican senators secured the removal and replacement of their states' U.S. attorneys.[44]

As for district and circuit court candidates, the selection system changed little during most of Reagan's presidency.[45] In the case of district court judges, when a vacancy occurred, the Republican home-state senator would submit three to five candidates to the Justice Department.[46] For example, in 1986, Senator John Warner proposed three candidates for a Richmond judgeship.[47] Despite the submission of multiple names, it appears that senatorial prerogatives were respected. In one case, Reagan rebuffed Secretary of Labor Raymond J. Donovan in a battle over a district court vacancy in New Jersey. Although Donovan "felt he had an ownership of New Jersey," Reagan selected the candidate of New Jersey Republican senator Nicholas Brady.[48] In Alabama, judicial appointments went through Republican senator Jeremiah Denton, with the acceptance of the state's conservative Democratic senator Howell Heflin.[49] Republican senators Pete Wilson and Paula Hawkins in California and Florida, respectively, were in control of appointments in their states.[50] In fact, Senator Hawkins chose to bypass Florida's advisory panel and submit names directly to the president.[51] In Kentucky, Republican senator Mitch McConnell decided to create a judicial selection commission with his Democratic colleague Wendell Ford. This did not mean, however, that the senator handed over his traditional power to either the commission or the White House. McConnell would oppose anyone who was not on his list of recommendations.[52]

Reflecting on the Reagan years, Republican senator James Jeffords recalled, "although there was clear criteria set out, the President, in no instance that I have been made aware of, interfered with the prerogative of a Senator."[53] This assessment was not accurate. Increasingly, Republican senators began to question the administration's refusal to nominate their candidates on the grounds that they were "insufficiently conservative."[54] In at least two cases, Republican lawmakers forced Reagan to appoint their recommendations through legislative tactics. Senator Gorton of Washington used his vote on the controversial nomination of Daniel A. Manion to the Seventh Circuit Court to pressure the White House to nominate William Dwyer, a "liberal Democrat," for a district court judgeship.[55] Using a different method, Minnesota's Republican senator David F. Durenberger threatened to "put a procedural block on all White House appointees" unless Reagan followed his recommendation.[56] The administration finally gave in to Durenberger's demand when the senator declared that he would block the confirmation vote of Manion.[57]

There was greater flexibility in appellate-level nominations, since a circuit covers several states.[58] As Jonathan Rose, assistant attorney general and head of the Office of Legal Policy, explained, "Our pride in our circuit court appointments in large part [was] due to the fact that we [were] . . . able to get by the senatorial courtesy system."[59] That statement may contain a measure of truth, but the administration often had to bend to political realities. For instance, Reagan deferred to Republican senator Alfonse M. D'Amato of New York in order to avoid harming a political ally who was "more politically conservative than the state he represents."[60] Senator Thurmond secured the appointment of his former aide to the Fourth Circuit,[61] his leverage no doubt reflecting his position as chairman of the Senate Judiciary Committee.

In one of the more unusual appointment episodes during the Reagan administration, Senator D'Amato endorsed the candidacy of Stuart Summit for a Second Circuit judgeship. After Reagan nominated Summit and the Senate Judiciary Committee voted favorably on him, D'Amato placed a hold on the nomination, giving no reason for doing so. This event reflects the power of a senator not only to nominate but also to change his mind and kill that nomination. As the nominee explained, "That a single Senator, never mind one who introduced me to the committee, could simply stop the entire process only a few days before my confirmation without having to explain himself to anyone and without the courtesy of explaining himself to me is simply beyond my understanding."[62]

In assessing the involvement of lawmakers in the pre-nomination process, Assistant Attorney General Rose remarked: "I don't think you can eliminate politics from the selection of judges. . . . The question is whether it plays an improperly large role as opposed to the qualifications and merits of the candidates. . . . Senators sometimes feel obligated to reward political associates as opposed to the most distinguished lawyer in their state."[63] This appraisal may be rather harsh, but it indicates the frustration associated with being unable to significantly weaken a senator's power and involvement in appointments.

The passage of the 1984 Bankruptcy Amendments and Federal Judgeship Act reduced the number of positions subject to the pre-nomination process during the Reagan presidency.[64] Before the new law, members of Congress had the power to recommend bankruptcy court candidates in a manner similar to other judicial nominations.[65] However, because a 1982 Supreme Court decision had held that parts of the existing bankruptcy law were unconstitutional,[66] Congress had to draft new legislation for these courts. These modifications included transferring the appointment of bankruptcy court judges from the president and Senate to the applicable circuit court of appeals.[67] The law had no impact on district or circuit court appointments.

George H. W. Bush (1989–1993)

The transfer of the presidency from Reagan to Bush marked the first electoral transition of power between administrations of the same party in sixty years.[68] Because of the continuation of one-party rule, many of Reagan's pre-nomination policies remained intact. For instance, power over U.S. attorney positions was left to home-state senators; thus, in California,

Pete Wilson recommended these appointments as his state's lone Republican senator.[69] In Missouri, Republican senator John Danforth succeeded in removing the U.S. attorney he had helped put in office under Reagan. In discussing the rather odd request, Danforth stated that the system is based on politics, and there "are no political appointments I know of that are lifetime appointments."[70] Other changes appeared to be based on personal rather than political interests. For instance, Senator McConnell recommended his girlfriend for a U.S. attorney post in Kentucky.[71]

In terms of district court positions, Republican senators continued their custom of selecting judges. This was the case in Oregon, where Senators Robert Packwood and Mark Hatfield were successful in having their recommendations appointed,[72] and in Missouri, where Senators Danforth and Christopher Bond controlled appointments.[73] In states with divided party representation in the Senate, the Republican senator usually made the appointment decision; this was true in Florida, where Senator Connie Mack was in charge.[74] However, in some states, appointment agreements were worked out between Republican and Democratic senators. In New York, for example, Senator D'Amato and his Democratic counterpart, Daniel Patrick Moynihan, maintained an arrangement whereby the senator whose party was not in control of the White House could recommend every fourth judicial vacancy.[75] During the Reagan and Bush administrations, this meant that Republican D'Amato selected three judicial candidates to Moynihan's one.[76]

Although senators had less control over circuit court nominations, they still had a significant voice in the process. For instance, Senators Packwood and Hatfield provided Bush with their choice for a Ninth Circuit seat.[77] If there were no Republican senators, the administration would seek advice from "state party leaders and Republican House members."[78] In Illinois, House Minority Leader Robert Michel chose judicial candidates as the top Republican in his state.[79] With Democrats Edward Kennedy and John Kerry representing Massachusetts in the Senate, Republican governor William Weld made judicial recommendations to the White House. However, because governors have little power over a president, their choices can be easily disregarded; this occurred in Weld's case.[80] Finally, merit commissions persisted in some states, even though Reagan had done much to dissuade their use.[81]

Despite generally adhering to pre-nomination customs, the Bush White House did not always have a good relationship with Congress. In fact, early in his administration, Bush ran into trouble with Republican senators over his policy of requiring three names to be submitted to the Justice Department.[82] Although this was a continuation of Reagan's policy, it appears to have been enforced more rigidly during Bush's presidency. During the first year of the administration, various Republican senators were angered by the president's failure to consult them and his disregard for their suggestions. The controversy eventually boiled over into the Senate when Republican James M. Jeffords of Vermont used a hold (a request by a senator to delay or prevent Senate action) to block two judicial nominations from Alabama because President Bush "was refusing to nominate the [district court] candidate Jeffords favored."[83] In fact, Jeffords had submitted the name of only one candidate, Fred I. Parker, for the district court vacancy, and the Justice Department was demanding that he provide at least three. Jeffords would eventually add two more names, but he "informed the Justice Department that only Parker would be an acceptable choice."[84]

After interviewing Parker for ten hours, Justice Department official Murray Dickman determined that he was unacceptable.[85] In the Senate, both Republicans and Democrats objected to the administration's action. The Senate Republican Conference pressed Bush to support "Jeffords' choice."[86] Democrat Joseph Biden, who chaired the Judiciary Committee, warned "that unless the administration has consulted with, discussed with, and had the input of the Senators from the States from which these judges originate, they will have a great deal of difficulty moving through the committee."[87] Ultimately, the controversy came down to who was more competent to ascertain the qualifications of judicial candidates in the states. Senator Jeffords regarded himself as "much more eligible to determine as to who the best judge will be for the Vermont district court." In addition, he refuted the White House's arguments and identified the principles at stake:

> I can find no way that the people within the administration could have conceivably come up with the determination they did [to refuse my candidate] for any legitimate purpose. However, this is a personal issue to me. It also affects every Senator in this body for if I am to consent to what I believe is abuse of the process, every Senator is at risk in the future, for once that precedent is broken, once we lie down and roll over, there is no doubt in my mind that this administration, which has created the biggest challenge to this, will not be the last to take away from Senators the prerogative to assume they have the right and the full right to appoint district court judges.[88]

Initially, the administration would not give in. Attorney General Dick Thornburgh argued: "It should shock no one that the president is asserting his constitutional duty to nominate judges 'with the advice and consent of the Senate.' Consistent with that provision, presidents have routinely consulted with senators of their party from the home state of district judgeships in the selection of nominees, but the final choice has always been the president's." Thornburgh then refuted the statements of Jeffords and other senators that they had a proper role in making appointments.

"Apart from its lack of historical or constitutional support," Thornburgh explained, "the view that presidents should defer to senators on district judges is also politically untenable. The people hold the president, not the senators, responsible for the appointments."[89]

Republican principles also spoke to the Senate's responsibility to see that good candidates filled the judiciary. Jeffords and other senators understood this duty and were unwilling to accept the Bush administration's stance. Consultation and compromise—not isolation and dictation—had always been the default position of the pre-nomination process. Not only history but also institutional leverage was on Jeffords's side. In the end, the Vermonter was successful. "After 18 months of a contentious debate over the prerogative of Senators to have their recommendation respected by the administration," Jeffords proclaimed, "Fred Parker was confirmed as a Federal district judge in Vermont. The long and arduous process forced me to exercise the often criticized filibuster. In this case, it clearly resulted in the public good being served, notwithstanding a rather hostile White House and a few very angry Senators."[90]

At the Supreme Court level, the retirement of Associate Justice William J. Brennan forced the administration to consider a replacement. To avoid a repetition of the 1987 Robert Bork confirmation debacle,[91] the nominee could not have any controversial writings to alarm Senate Democrats (unlike Bork, who had a long paper trail). The ultimate pick was little-known First Circuit judge David H. Souter of New Hampshire.[92] Souter's primary supporter was the Republican senator from his home state, Warren Rudman, who had continually backed his candidacy for various posts since the late 1970s.[93] Rudman had first mentioned Souter for a Supreme Court vacancy in 1987 and had been involved in his eventual First Circuit selection.[94] When another Supreme Court seat became available, Rudman "urged Bush to choose [Souter] this time."[95] Souter's selection not only pleased Rudman but also helped ensure that a swing Republican vote in the Judiciary Committee would go the president's way.[96]

William J. Clinton (1993–2001)

Like his two recent predecessors, President Bill Clinton understood that much of his legacy would rest on his judicial nominations. "There are few things that I will do," said Clinton, "that will have more lasting effect than the appointment of Federal judges."[97] He was also mindful that "federal district court judges are appointed by the President but recommended to the President by Senators, if they are Senators of the President's own party, in the States."[98] Thus, he sought to involve Democratic lawmakers in consultations as much as possible.[99] For instance, Assistant Attorney General Eleanor Acheson continually tried to reach "out to senators for candidates" to fill positions in the judiciary.[100] Most likely, this endeavor was a necessity rather than an optional task for the White House.

Being part of the political party that had been out of power for more than a decade put great pressure on the White House and Democratic legislators. For instance, a Minnesota newspaper noted that, after being "wedged behind the dam during 12 years of Republican rule in Washington, [Democrats] are nipping at [Senator Paul] Wellstone's heels."[101] The first great wave of appointments to be considered consisted of ninety-three U.S. attorney positions to be selected by the administration with the consent of home-state senators. By May 1993, Democratic senators had sent the Justice Department replacement names for "roughly three-quarters" of those posts.[102] In Minnesota, Senator Wellstone picked his state's U.S. attorney replacement,[103] as did Senator Harris Wofford in Pennsylvania.[104] Other Democratic senators in California, Delaware, Maryland, Massachusetts, New Jersey, New York, and South Carolina were also responsible for these appointments.[105]

District court selections continued to be made by home-state senators as well. When a state had divided party representation in the Senate, the Democratic senator made the recommendations. Senator Wellstone thus became the chief dispenser of district judgeships in Minnesota.[106] Senator Patty Murray of Washington managed a similar arrangement, as did Democratic senators Wendell Ford, Jeff Bingaman, and Daniel Patrick Moynihan in their respective states.[107] States with two senators of the president's party either made recommendations jointly or worked out some other accommodation. This occurred in Connecticut, Illinois, Louisiana, Nebraska, New Jersey, West Virginia, and Wisconsin.[108]

Like previous presidents, Clinton enjoyed more leeway in making appellate court selections than he did in making district court appointments. As Senator Biden explained, "Every President is more interested in the appeals courts because that's where policy is made."[109] Clinton's latitude did not mean total control, however; consultation with Democratic lawmakers was still required. Senator Patrick Leahy was able to secure the appointment of a Vermonter to a Second Circuit vacancy, and Senator Wofford of Pennsylvania got his pick onto the Third Circuit; senators in Florida and West Virginia were successful with their appointments as well.[110]

If there were no Democratic senators in a state, recommendations originated with "the Democratic members of the House of Representatives or other high-ranking Democratic Party politicians."[111] In Texas, Democratic governor Ann Richards recommended appointments.[112] After the retirement of Senator Ford from Kentucky, Governor Paul Patton made the selections.[113] Elsewhere, no clear appointment authority emerged, which produced problems for the administration. For instance, Clinton was forced to deal with two different sets of recommendations for a circuit court vacancy from Maine.[114] Judicial selection commissions continued to function in states such as Florida, New York, and Oregon, even though they were not required.[115] Clinton's one minor modification to the pre-nomination process was that the Justice Department no longer requested home-state "senators to recommend three potential nominees for a district court vacancy"; instead, one name would do.[116]

Minority party involvement in appointments was also apparent during the Clinton administration. Senator Orrin Hatch of Utah, because of his position as ranking member on the Judiciary Committee (he later became chairman when the Republicans won control of Congress), was deeply involved in selections for the Supreme Court and other federal judgeships. In 1993, Clinton met with Hatch to discuss a Supreme Court vacancy,[117] and the senator described the meeting in his autobiography: "Clinton indicated he was leaning toward nominating Bruce Babbitt, his Secretary of Interior . . . [and] asked for my reaction." Hatch "told him that [Babbitt's] confirmation would not be easy" and indicated that Stephen Breyer or Ruth Bader Ginsberg "would be confirmed easily."[118] Clinton decided against Babbitt and nominated Ginsberg for the first opening and Breyer for the next.[119]

Senator Hatch also worked closely with the administration on lower court appointments. Sheldon Goldman and Elliot Slotnick described Hatch as exhibiting "substantial professionalism and, as attested to by administration sources as well as by both Republican and Democratic Senate staff, he pursued a commitment to work with the administration to see nominations through to confirmation."[120] Hatch was not above using his position as chairman to secure places for his friends, however. In fact, he forced Clinton to appoint his preferred candidate to a district court seat in Utah.[121]

Other Republicans created additional problems for the White House in the pre-nomination process. For instance, in Idaho, Senators Larry Craig and Dirk Kempthorne opposed district court nominee John Tait, who had been recommended by Democratic representative Larry LaRocco.[122] After the 1994 Republican takeover of Congress, Craig and Kempthorne used a blue slip to block Tait's nomination in the Senate Judiciary Committee (blue slips are discussed later in this chapter). LaRocco said, "I've talked to the White House counsel and it is clear that the president will not move ahead with a number of qualified judicial nominations, including John's, because of opposition in the Senate."[123] The Senate never acted on the nomination and returned it at the end of the session.

In Pennsylvania, Republican involvement in the pre-nomination process was limited during the first few years of the Clinton administration. Senator Wofford effectively excluded his Republican colleague, Arlen Specter, just as Wofford had been cut out of appointment decisions during the Bush years. A local newspaper reported, "In a judiciously worded letter to Specter earlier this month, Wofford signaled that the Republican could expect a similarly limited role in federal judicial recommendations throughout the Clinton administration."[124] However, after Wofford lost his 1994 reelection bid, Republican senators Specter and Rick Santorum asked the Justice Department to include them in pre-nomination decisions. Santorum claimed that the administration had violated an agreement permitting the Republican senators to recommend one of every three judgeships in their state.[125] Accordingly, Specter and Santorum began to block Pennsylvania's judicial nominations not only because of the broken agreement but also because, in their opinion, "the President made too many unacceptable" selections.[126]

By the end of Clinton's presidency, the impasse had turned into a battle of words between Republicans and Democrats. One member of the Pennsylvania judicial selection commission established by Specter and Santorum argued that Clinton should take a practical look at the situation: "The Senate's role is to advise and consent. If nominees who will not be approved by a majority of the Senate are put forth, then it is up to the White House and the Senate to reach common ground. Sen. Santorum is correct when he says the White House has failed to keep its end of the common ground reached between it and our senators."[127] Others saw the situation differently. Democrat Leahy declared that the "Senate is not fulfilling its constitutional responsibility. It is interfering with the president's authority to appoint federal judges and it is hampering the third co-equal branch of our government."[128] Clinton never rectified the impasse. Pennsylvania appointments would be left to his successor to fill.

These were not isolated incidents. Appointment controversies occurred in other states as well. In North Carolina, Republican senator Jesse Helms held up the confirmation of a Fourth Circuit nomination in the name of "judicial economy."[129] He claimed that the appellate court had enough judges for its caseload, despite the fact that his Democratic colleague, John Edwards, disagreed.[130] There was also a problem in the Sixth Circuit, where Republican senator Spencer Abraham blocked appellate court judgeships in Michigan by failing to turn in the nominees' blue slips. He cited the lack of consultation by the administration as his reason, and one of his staffers said that the senator was troubled by the way the White House "conducted the nomination and consultative process."[131] The Pennsylvania, North Carolina, and Michigan situations highlighted a growing expectation of minority party involvement in the pre-nomination process, which would continue in the next administration.

George W. Bush (2001–2007)

George W. Bush entered the presidency understanding that he would have to attend to many of the lingering appointment difficulties the Clinton administration had faced. At a news conference introducing his first eleven nominations to the federal judiciary, Bush stated that a "President has few greater responsibilities than that of nominating men and women to the courts of the United States." Continuing, he explained, "For many weeks now, we have sought and received advice from Senators of both parties. I now submit these nominations in good faith, trusting that good faith will also be extended by the United States Senate. Over the years, we have seen how the confirmation process can be turned to other ends. We have seen political battles played out in committee hearings, battles that have little to do with the merits of the person sitting before the committee. This is not good for the Senate, for our courts, or for the country." He sought a "return of civility and dignity to the confirmation process."[132] But no matter how sincere or hopeful Bush's comments were, the same political atmosphere persisted. Some problems resulted from the administration's decision to end the American Bar Association's role in screening potential nominees before they reached the Senate. This caused considerable outcry among various groups and created tension between the White House and some Democratic senators.[133]

Bush began his administration by seeking to replace all the existing U.S. attorneys. "The changing of the guard in the White House," one newspaper observed, "means a similar transition soon will be under way in federal courthouses."[134] Local pressure greatly increased for members of Congress to fill these positions. In Virginia, Republican senator John Warner proclaimed, "You've never seen so many guys, and women, wanting to be U.S. attorney."[135] Recommendations for these positions continued to be made by home-state senators of the president's political party.[136] Changes were made in nearly every state from Alabama to Rhode Island, and senatorial say was virtually absolute.[137] In South Carolina, Republican senator Strom Thurmond even managed to secure the nomination of his twenty-eight-year-old son.[138]

Home-state senators were similarly involved in district court appointments.[139] When representation was split between the two parties, Republican senators often made the recommendation. This was the case for Georgia'a Senator Saxby Chambliss and Illinois' Senator Peter Fitzgerald.[140] In other states such as Minnesota, Missouri, New Mexico, Oregon, and Rhode Island, Republican senators maintained a significant voice in who was nominated.[141] In some cases, this power bordered on a right to force the nomination of their favorite candidates. For instance, Kentucky senator Jim Bunning secured an appointment for his son on the federal bench, and Senator Thurmond got Bush to give a district court judgeship to his former chief counsel for the Judiciary Committee.[142] States with two Republican senators had similar control over appointments.[143]

As for the appellate courts, although candidates "tend[ed] to be generated more by the administration," this did not mean that Republican senators lacked power.[144] Senator Thurmond succeeded in placing a former aide on the Fourth Circuit, and in Iowa and New Mexico, Senators Charles Grassley and Pete Domenici were able to get their respective circuit court choices appointed.[145] Despite his frequent votes against the administration, liberal Republican senator Lincoln Chafee of Rhode Island succeeded in getting his candidate a First Circuit judgeship, and other senators could boast comparable records.[146]

When a state did not have a Republican senator, usually the highest-ranking officeholder from the president's party made the recommendations. In Massachusetts, this meant that Governor Mitt Romney controlled appointments in his state.[147] Other governors played similar roles, including Jodi Rell in Connecticut, Linda Lingle in Hawaii, and Donald Carcieri in Rhode Island.[148] Elsewhere, the situation was quite different. During the first two years of the Bush administration, Minnesota's senior Republican representative Jim Ramstad recommended federal appointments.[149] In New Jersey, the entire party organization became involved, "including Acting Gov. Donald T. DiFrancesco and the six Republican members of Congress."[150] In Florida, Governor Jeb Bush and Representatives C. W. Bill Young and Clay Shaw created a nominating panel to make judicial selections; this arrangement was modified when Republican Mel Martinez was elected to the Senate in 2004.[151] Although individual lawmakers often made recommendations, merit commissions existed in Colorado, Maine, and Pennsylvania.[152]

The only significant change in the pre-nomination process made by Bush was the reinstatement of the three-name rule followed by the Reagan and Bush I White Houses. This did not mean that President Bush enjoyed more control over appointments than his predecessor Clinton had. As Deputy White House Counsel David Leitch declared, senators "were not bashful of telling us who they preferred." And if a "senator expressed an interest in a particular candidate on the list of three . . . we would defer to the senator." According to Leitch, "senators still have the overwhelming say in who gets appointed."[153]

Bush encountered pre-nomination difficulties arising from the political tension that had dominated judicial appointments during the Clinton administration.[154] Indeed, Democratic senators blamed the increased combativeness in the Senate on "Republicans for taking the downward spiral of partisanship . . . to a new low during President Clinton's second term."[155] Some Republicans, including Pennsylvania's Arlen Specter, agreed that he and his party members had gone too far in blocking Clinton's judicial appointments.[156] Democrats now decided to adopt the same strategy.

As a result, the concept of consulting with the minority party was advanced to a greater extent than ever before. *Washington Post* columnist E. J. Dionne Jr. articulated the rationale behind it: "If the goal is to have good judges confirmed without ugly fights, the White House and Senate Democrats should sit down and agree on lists of nominees." He cited ample precedents of presidents conferring with senators, "including those from the opposition party, before making appointments in their states or regions," and he correctly pointed out the history of minority party involvement in the pre-nomination process.[157] As far back as the 1880s, presidents had made practical accommodations with legislators from other political parties. For instance, President Arthur handed control of appointments over to Readjuster senator William Mahone in Virginia (see chapter 6). In the early twentieth century, Presidents Taft and Wilson made efforts to consult members of the minority party, and by the 1960s, Presidents Kennedy and Johnson even rewarded Republican senators who supported their policies by giving them a voice in appointments (see chapter 7).

Traditionally, majority party members played the primary role in making appointments, with those from the minority party putting up little opposition to this arrangement. That process began to break down during the Reagan administration. Goldman concluded that prior to the 1980s, "appointments to the lower federal courts were fairly routine," but during the Clinton and Bush II administrations, ideological and partisan disagreements in the Senate transformed "lower-court confirmations, particularly to the appeals courts, into epic struggles between Democrats and Republicans. Obstruct and delay has replaced advise and consent."[158] During the Bush II administration, the situation escalated. Democratic senators protested White House actions that tried to prevent their involvement in the pre-nomination process.[159] For instance, Senator Edwards of North Carolina forced consultation because he was unhappy with the way his home-state nominations had been treated by Republicans during the Clinton administration.[160] The administration seemed to be mindful of these concerns. Deputy White House Counsel Timothy Flanigan urged sensitivity "to the winds that blow in the Senate, which is evenly divided." Consultation benefited the White House because "it doesn't do the president any good to send up nominees who are on suicide missions."[161]

Senate Democrats continued to press for greater involvement. Senator Charles Schumer of New York explained that "in a 50–50 Senate and a 9–9 Judiciary Committee, there's going to have to be some kind of accommodation, but I think the feeling among Democrats has been up to this point the White House has not consulted people at all."[162] Giving voice to their frustration, Democrats on the Senate Judiciary Committee wrote to President Bush asking for more consultation.[163] White House Counsel Alberto Gonzales replied that the administration believed in "pre-nomination consultation between the Administration and the home-state Senators, regardless of party." He reminded the senators:

> We have already engaged in the sort of process that your letter encourages. We have had numerous discussions with home state Democratic and Republican Senators regarding process and existing vacancies. In most cases, we have shared the names of individuals under consideration for federal judicial appointment with home state Senators at least a month prior to the earliest conceivable date for nomination. In several cases, our consultation has included face-to-face meetings with the home state Senators. A number of additional such meetings are scheduled to take place in the coming days. We have taken the Senators' reactions to potential nominees very seriously, and we will continue to do so.[164]

Whether it was willing to consult Democrats or not, the White House eventually had to face the political realities in various states. Nowhere was this more true than in California, where Democratic senators Barbara Boxer and Dianne Feinstein pressured the administration into agreeing to a plan that allowed their involvement in appointments.[165] Although the plan did not cover appeals court candidates, Boxer and Feinstein were able to influence those appointments as well; in fact, they prevented the administration from nominating conservative Republican representative Christopher Cox to a Ninth Circuit seat before the bipartisan agreement was even worked out.[166] Under the plan, a twenty-four-member judicial selection committee was created for district court appointments. The committee was divided into four panels of six members: three appointed by Gerald Parsky, the White House's chair for California judicial appointments, and three appointed jointly by Senators Boxer and Feinstein.[167] It appears that the arrangement has been a success.[168]

Three other states made similar compromises. In New York, Democratic senator Charles Schumer, Republican governor George Pataki, and the White House reached a deal to fill that state's judicial vacancies. Schumer explained in a press release that he would back "all of the White House's pending New York nominees and all of the nominees who were undergoing background checks." In exchange, the White House agreed to nominate Schumer's choice, Paul A. Crotty, for the next vacancy in the southern district and allow him to choose the next nominee for the eastern district.[169] In Wisconsin, Democratic senators Herb Kohl and Russ Feingold forced the administration to accept recommendations from a commission they had established with Republican representative James Sensenbrenner.[170]

A judicial nominating commission was also established in Washington after Democratic senators Patty Murray and Maria Cantwell reached a compromise with the White House. That commission secured the appointment of a Ninth Circuit judge and three district court judges.[171] The White House's acceptance of minority party involvement in the pre-nomination process might have something to do with the political leverage of these legislators. For instance, Senators Feingold, Feinstein, Kohl, and Schumer all sat on the Judiciary Committee, which is charged with reviewing judicial nominations. Senators Murray and Cantwell were members of the powerful Appropriations and Finance committees, respectively.

Others senators threatened to block action on nominees to ensure some level of participation. In Minnesota, for instance, Democratic senator Mark Dayton forced the Justice Department to arrange a meeting between him and the nominee for that state's U.S. attorney post before the senator would agree to a confirmation vote.[172] In New York, Senator Schumer's opposition to potential nominee Judith Hand as U.S. attorney forced the White House to select another candidate.[173] In other states, the parties were a bit more accommodating. For instance, similar to the arrangement between New York senators D'Amato and Moynihan in the 1980s and early 1990s, Nebraska senators Chuck Hagel and Ben Nelson developed a good working relationship for the selection of judicial nominees.[174]

The Bush presidency also highlighted two important Senate procedures related to the pre-nomination process. One is the blue slip, which is linked to the tradition of senatorial courtesy. Under this informal custom, the Senate will not confirm an executive nomination unless the nominee has been approved by the home-state senators of the president's party (see chapter 2). The Senate Judiciary Committee created the blue slip (so called because of its color) in the early 1900s to allow senators, regardless of their party affiliation, to voice an opinion on a president's nomination.[175] The use of blue slips is an informal practice unique to the Judiciary Committee—it is not mentioned anywhere in the committee's rules—and it is applicable to all U.S. attorney, U.S. marshal, U.S. district court, and U.S. court of appeals nominations (except for the District of Columbia and territorial courts). Blue slips can be employed to block a nomination in two ways, depending on the preferences of the Judiciary Committee chairman: a senator can stop committee action on a nomination by returning a blue slip with a negative endorsement or by refusing to return it altogether. These practices have been modified over the years.[176]

During the Bush II administration, the process changed because of shifting party control in the Senate. Initially, with the Republican Party in power, chairman Orrin Hatch required the return of negative blue slips from both home-state senators in order to stop committee action on a judicial nomination.[177] This policy was attacked by Democrat Richard J. Durbin of Illinois, who said that during his four years in the Senate, a single home-state senator "could stop a nominee," and at times, members of the Judiciary Committee, "not even from the same state as the nominee, could stop a nomination."[178] For example, Republican Jesse Helms used the blue slip to block Clinton's judicial nominees in North Carolina despite the fact that they had the approval of Democrat John Edwards.[179]

Party control of the Senate changed on June 6, 2001, when Senator James Jeffords of Vermont bolted from the Republican Party and became an independent. The Judiciary Committee's new chairman, Democrat Patrick Leahy, moved quickly to modify the blue-slip policy to allow one home-state senator to block committee action.[180] Subsequently, Democratic senators in California and North Carolina were able to stop the consideration of judicial nominations from their states by using the blue slip.[181] Remarkably, Michigan senators Carl Levin and Debbie Stabenow blocked not only their own state nominations to the Sixth Circuit but all nominations to that circuit, regardless of state.[182]

At the start of the 108th Congress, power in the Senate changed hands again, and Hatch reinstated his previous policy of requiring two negative blue slips to block committee action.[183] This principle would stay in place until the 110th Congress, when Democrats retook the Senate and Leahy again reversed the blue-slip policy.[184] The ebb and flow of power during the Bush II administration has meant a battle between the two parties in terms of delineating the relationship between the executive and legislative branches. When the Republicans controlled the Senate, they wanted a tougher blue-slip policy, because their party controlled the presidency. When the Democrats took over, they sought to strengthen senatorial rights largely so that Bush could not dictate appointments. With a Democratic majority in the Senate, the power of home-state senators, regardless of party, has greatly increased. Perhaps understating the importance of the blue-slip process, Arkansas senator Mark Pryor called it "a nice, informal system that gives the home-state senators some say."[185]

The second measure used by Senate Democrats to force consultation is the filibuster, invoked to prevent a bill or nomination from being voted on.[186] With Democrats controlling the Senate for most of the 107th Congress (June 6, 2001, to November 22, 2002), the filibuster was not required. Home-state senators possessed the ability to block any nominee at the Judiciary Committee level through the use of a blue slip. Not until the 108th Congress did the filibuster become a necessary tool, and Democratic senators used it to block several of Bush's judicial nominations. The first occurred on March 6, 2003, when Senate Republicans tried to pass a cloture motion to force a vote on D.C. Circuit nominee Miguel Estrada.[187] Democrats would filibuster five more nominations during the 108th Congress.[188]

For most of the 108th Congress, Democrats appeared to have the upper hand, because Senate Republicans failed to overcome any of the filibusters.

During a legislative adjournment, however, President Bush relied on his recess appointment power to bypass the Senate and place several of his nominees on the federal bench.[189] Although Democrats were angered by this action,[190] they reached an accommodation with Bush: the White House agreed not to make any more recess appointments until after the November 2004 elections, and in return, Democrats would allow votes on twenty-five judicial nominations.[191] The deal made no sense for the Democrats, who held all the power and had been able to block any nomination they found objectionable. Bush's only option had been to make recess appointments, which were only temporary designations that lasted until the end of the next session. Why did the Democrats not seek more?

The appointments battle remained at a standstill until after the 2004 elections, when the Republicans picked up four Senate seats and gained solid control of the Senate. They began to insist on "up-or-down" votes on judicial nominations and even threatened a "nuclear option," under which the presiding officer of the Senate would declare filibusters of judicial nominations unconstitutional and thus out of order. If Democrats challenged the ruling, Republicans would need only a simple majority to prevail. For the rest of the 108th Congress, both sides dug in. Republican Majority Leader Bill Frist declared, "One way or another, the filibuster of judicial nominees must end." Democrat Schumer warned that efforts to implement the nuclear option "would make the last Congress look like a bipartisan tea party. For the sake of country and some degree of comity, I would hope and pray that the majority leader would not take away the Senate's time-honored, 200-year-old tradition."[192]

With Senate leaders at loggerheads, a bipartisan group of fourteen senators drafted an agreement to end the impasse. Seven Republicans and seven Democrats (better known as the "Gang of Fourteen") signed the compromise on May 23, 2005.[193] Under the "Memorandum of Understanding on Judicial Nominations," the seven Democratic senators committed to vote for cloture on Janice Rogers Brown, William Pryor, and Priscilla Owen. The seven Republicans agreed not to support the nuclear option or to filibuster judicial nominees except in "extraordinary circumstances." They all urged President Bush to consult closely with senators before nominating judges: "We believe that, under Article II, Section 2, of the United States Constitution, the word 'Advice' speaks to consultation between the Senate and the President with regard to the use of the President's power to make nominations. We encourage the Executive branch of government to consult with members of the Senate, both Democratic and Republican, prior to submitting a judicial nomination to the Senate for consideration."[194]

This agreement most likely influenced President Bush's actions when he was required to select a nominee to replace Justice Sandra Day O'Connor on the Supreme Court. At a news conference, Bush stated that his administration would continue to consult home-state senators (no party distinction was made).[195] The administration spoke with a number of senators from both parties, and Bush met with Senate Republican and Democratic leaders and the chairman and ranking member of the Judiciary Committee.[196] At the meeting, the Democratic leaders offered names for him to consider.[197] The Gang of Fourteen did not try to dominate the selection process. Democrat Mark Pryor explained, "We do not want to be a new Judiciary Committee. We do not want to be a superbody within the Senate."[198]

President Bush would go on to nominate John G. Roberts to replace O'Connor, but another vacancy occurred shortly thereafter with the death of Chief Justice William Rehnquist.[199] Bush decided to nominate Roberts as chief justice and invited Senate party leaders and the chairman and ranking member of Judiciary Committee to discuss another nomination.[200] Some Democrats seemed pleased with Bush's choice of White House Counsel Harriet E. Miers. Minority Leader Harry Reid praised the selection; Senator Ben Nelson, a Gang of Fourteen member, called it a "smart pick"; and the ranking Democrat on the Judiciary Committee, Patrick Leahy, remarked that this was the first time a president had taken his advice to make a selection outside "the judicial monastery."[201]

Despite this initial praise from Democrats, Republican senators were angered and disappointed by the selection. Conservatives felt that the administration had excluded them from the consultation process and picked someone who was unqualified and lacked strong conservative views. Miers eventually requested that her name be withdrawn.[202] Conservatives then mounted a campaign to ensure the selection of a nominee with a clear conservative record. The *Washington Post* reported that the White House "appeared intent on avoiding a repeat of the Miers fiasco and on testing reactions among conservative activists before making an announcement, rather than pulling a surprise."[203] Bush would not make the same mistake twice and selected Samuel A. Alito Jr., a conservative judge from the Third Circuit. Although the nomination initially appeared to be the showdown many had predicted, Alito's confirmation was almost completely assured by the second day of the Senate Judiciary Committee hearings.[204] The nomination was reported from committee (on a party-line vote) and confirmed by a vote of fifty-eight to forty-two on the Senate floor.[205]

The pre-nomination process has adapted through the centuries to the changing political realities of the day. Civil service and merit-based limitations have not prevented congressional involvement in appointments. Although some contend that the Appointments Clause precludes any interference in a president's right to make nominations independently of Congress, that is not how the system works in practice. The assumption that congressional involvement is not constitutionally permissible not only dismisses the advice-and-consent component of the Appointments Clause but also conveniently neglects the overwhelming historical evidence presented in this study. The Constitution does not restrain the legislative branch from participating in the pre-nomination process. In fact, our republican government empowers Congress to check the executive branch when necessary. This is especially true when carrying out important shared constitutional responsibilities such as the appointment power.

Chapter 9

Analysis and Conclusions

This book has focused on negotiations between the executive and legislative branches during the pre-nomination process. Despite the express language in Article II of the Constitution that the president "shall nominate" and Alexander Hamilton's assertion that the Senate shall have "no exertion of *choice*" in appointments, the strict interpretation of that power has not been followed.[1] The practices of presidents and legislators have shown that Hamilton's theoretical position failed to understand how a newly formed constitutional democracy would carry out the appointment function.

Since the early days of the Union, the two branches have found three general ways to manage the pre-nomination process. First, and in the strictest sense, the threat of senatorial courtesy—combined with a weak executive or a strong Congress—served to transfer a president's nominating power to individual senators of his own party.[2] Second, if a president refused to respect the custom of senatorial courtesy or decided that he had no responsibility to consult members of Congress, the pre-nomination process collapsed and the likelihood of the Senate's rejection of nominations greatly increased. Usually a third option was chosen, with the two sides reaching an accommodation.

This book demonstrates that presidents most often choose compromise over conflict. The resulting norm for the pre-nomination process has been that the two branches develop mutually beneficial arrangements to allow for consultation when considering appointments. Such a course best embodies the system of checks and balances and results in a shared-power arrangement.

This concluding chapter analyzes a number of issues, some of which were identified in the introduction. These controversies include the procedures followed for the pre-nomination process, the consequence of civil service reform and the unitary executive model, and the impact of originalism and textualism in constitutional interpretation. Such points are important to practitioners of politics, political scientists, lawyers, and historians, among others.

Republicanism and Constitutional Legitimacy

The constitutional duty to consult has little meaning unless it is carried out jointly by the executive and legislative branches. More than 200 years of history have shown that both the president and Congress have interpreted the Appointments Clause to include consultation between the branches before a nomination is submitted to the Senate. Regardless of a president's formal authority to nominate, the Senate's advice-and-consent role dictates how he fulfills that task. The word *advice* provides individual lawmakers with the constitutional justification, and presumable right, to involve themselves in the pre-nomination process. As Benjamin Goodhue noted in the First Congress, "there was a propriety in allowing the Senate to advise the President in the choice of officers; this the constitution had ordained for wise purposes."[3]

There is also an implicit component of checks and balances in the matter of consultation. The rationale for creating this principle was the fear of executive abuse. "It has been asked," Congressman Alexander White said in the First Congress, "whether a person in the elevated station of the President would abuse his trust? I do not presume he will, but I presume he may: to prevent such evils, the constitution has wisely guarded the exercise of every power." On the same day, Congressman James Jackson articulated the checks-and-balances safeguard that White alluded to: "I consider [the president and Congress] as checks upon each other, to prevent the abuse of either; and it is in this way the liberties of the people are secured. I appeal for the truth of this sentiment to the writings of Publius. He has proved that the Senate is a check upon the Executive, for the express purpose of securing the freedom of the people."[4] If the president consults Congress, ill-conceived appointments can be minimized.

Along with providing a check on executive appointment power, republicanism creates a connection between citizens and government. As the elected representatives of the people, members of Congress have a constitutional duty to express the people's opinions on various matters, including appointments. This not only provides protection against unworthy candidates holding office but also gives legitimacy to the unelected officials who make up the bureaucracy. As law professor Harold H. Bruff reasons, "From a separation of powers standpoint, the very legitimacy of what appointed bureaucrats do depends on the nature and strength of the links between them and the constitutional officers who are the intermediaries between them and the people."[5] Therefore, a close link between the elected and the unelected helps reassure citizens that the government is responsive to their wishes. Perhaps nothing is more important in a republican form of government.

The Practical Duty to Consult

Even if one dismisses the constitutional justifications for consulting with Congress during the pre-nomination process, there are practical reasons that make it wise to do so. For instance, exercising sole control over nominations places a great administrative burden on both the president and the Senate. If the two sides do not work closely together, the chance of sending up a failed nominee greatly increases. Unlike a piece of legislation, a nomination cannot be amended; once it is submitted, the Senate must consider the merits of the individual nominee. In cases of rejection or final adjournment, the nomination is returned to the president. The process could go on indefinitely without some sort of interbranch agreement before an appointment is made.

If the pre-nomination process were run on a strict separation-of-powers basis, the administrative costs in terms of time, money, and other resources would be formidable. Consultation gives individual lawmakers the opportunity to dissuade a president from making an ill-starred selection and provides each branch with the opportunity to carry out its constitutional responsibilities in a reasonable and useful way. Practically, legislative advice to the president is necessary because of the great number of positions to be filled in the federal government. It is impossible for a president to know every candidate for office, so he often seeks advice from outside sources. Members of Congress play an important role in supplying such information to the president. James Madison's proposition that lawmakers, "from their nature, [tend to be better] acquainted with the character of the candidates" than the president has survived the test of time.[6] That is why senators are usually consulted about statewide appointments, and representatives are responsible for district-level offices.

Institutional and Political Influences

The pre-nomination process also turns on the bargaining or political strength of individual legislators. A president is more apt to pay close attention to the suggestions of members of Congress who play pivotal roles in the legislative process. For instance, a chairman of a powerful committee and the majority or minority leader in the House or Senate are substantially more important in the legislative arena than a first-term congressman. Such power may force a president to negotiate with a skilled lawmaker. Thus, President John Kennedy sought advice from Democratic senators Harry F. Byrd and James Eastland, who opposed his administration's policies, because they chaired the powerful Finance and Judiciary committees, respectively. In a similar manner, Democratic senator John C. Stennis of Mississippi was able to convince President Jimmy Carter to nominate a candidate charged with "racist behavior." No doubt the senator's chairmanship of the Armed Services Committee and the appropriations subcommittee on defense helped him win that selection.[7]

Minority party members may force consultation as well. During both the Kennedy and Lyndon Johnson administrations, Senator Everett Dirksen received significant patronage, despite being the Republican leader (see chapter 7). In more recent years, Republican Orrin Hatch was able to influence Supreme Court and lower court appointments during Bill Clinton's presidency because of his position as chairman of the Senate Judiciary Committee.[8] White House Counsel Eleanor Acheson admitted that the Clinton administration had to work out deals "with the Chair of the Judiciary Committee" and also with Republican home-state senators "in very powerful positions."[9]

Even if a member of Congress does not chair a committee or hold some other position of power, he or she may still be able to influence appointments through the practice of senatorial courtesy. For instance, during the administration of William Howard Taft, Senate Finance Committee chairman Nelson W. Aldrich held up the consideration of a Massachusetts appointment because the White House had failed to consult with the nominee's home-state senators Winthrop Crane and Henry Cabot Lodge.[10] In a more recent example, Judiciary Committee chairman Joseph Biden told the George H. W. Bush administration that he would stop the consideration of judicial candidates if the White House did not consult lawmakers.[11] In that case, Biden was protecting the senatorial prerogative of Vermonter James Jeffords (see chapter 8).

The power to nominate gives a president great influence over Congress as well. Presidents Millard Fillmore and Grover Cleveland used their control over appointments to secure the passage of administration-backed measures (see chapters 4 and 6). This power, however, does not always yield the desired outcome. Presidents John Tyler and Andrew Johnson tried to use patronage to create third-party movements built around personal loyalty rather than traditional party support, but in both cases, they failed spectacularly (see chapters 3 and 4). As one historian noted about the perils of the pre-nomination process:

> The distribution of patronage necessarily occasions many personal disappointments and grievances, which weaken the President with certain individuals and factions in his party. Any disposition on the part of the President or his responsible advisers to play favorites or to cherish grudges, any tendency to misjudge men and to be deceived by plausible misrepresentation, any failure to distinguish properly between the more influential and the less influential factions, has a damaging effect upon party harmony and its power of effective cooperation.[12]

Participation in the Pre-nomination Process

Although the primary participants are senators of the president's party, others play a role. Members of the House have historically had significant influence in a variety of appointments, beginning with President George Washington.[13] In the 1850s, representatives were given the exclusive right to select postal candidates for office.[14] During Benjamin Harrison's administration (1889–1893), Republican House members were considered the "referees" for their districts; senators had power only in Democratic districts or over postal positions in their hometowns.[15] This practice continued well into the twentieth century.[16] Although postal patronage was formally abolished in the late 1960s, representatives have not lost their power to control other types of appointments.[17] Often a representative of the president's party controls judicial appointments if there are no friendly home-state senators. For instance, during the late 1980s and early 1990s, House Minority Leader Robert Michel of Illinois chose judicial candidates as the top Republican in his state.[18] Under President Clinton, Representatives Diana DeGette and David Skaggs of Colorado, along with Governor Roy Romer, created a bipartisan commission to screen candidates for a vacant judgeship.[19] In 2004, President George W. Bush authorized Representatives Bill Young and Clay Shaw of Florida, along with his brother, Governor Jeb Bush, to submit names for various judicial positions.[20] Thus, House members can and do play a significant role in the pre-nomination process.

Presidents typically consult with home-state senators or representatives of their own party; however, there are occasional anomalies. At times, the process narrows to certain factions of the president's political party, as was the case in the late 1800s when the Republican Party found itself split between the Stalwarts and the Half-Breeds. At various points, one faction or the other would control appointments. In Massachusetts, during the presidency of Ulysses S. Grant, Stalwart representative Benjamin Butler controlled most of his home-state appointments, overruling the wishes of Republican senator Charles Sumner, because of this factional war (see chapter 5). During the Progressive Era, President Taft excluded many insurgent Republicans from patronage because of their opposition to the Payne-Aldrich tariff in the Senate and the dictatorial rule of Speaker Joseph Cannon in the House of Representatives.[21] In a letter to one insurgent lawmaker, George W. Norris of Nebraska, President Taft explained why he was refusing to bestow appointments:

What I declined to do was to join those who differed from the majority of the Republican Party and stayed out of the caucus, when as leader of the party I am dependent upon party actions to secure the legislation that has been promised. It did not then seem to me, as it does not now seem to me, that as titular leader of the party I should take sides with fifteen or twenty who refused to abide by the majority votes of the party, but that I should stand by whatever the party decides under the majority rule, whatever my views as to the wisdom of the rules, which are peculiarly a matter for settlement in the House itself. It has been a custom for a Republican administration to honor the recommendations of Republican Congressmen and Senators with respect to local appointments, subject, however, to the condition that the candidates recommended should be fit for the place. This custom has grown up with a view to securing a party solidarity in acting upon party questions. The only indication that I have given has been that with respect to legislation which I have recommended, there should be party action to discharge the promise of the party platform, and that those who feel no obligation in respect to it can not complain if their recommendations are not given customary weight.[22]

When the policy of denying patronage to insurgents failed, Taft quickly restored the traditional rights given to members of Congress in appointment matters.[23]

Failure to Consult: Congressional Responses

If a president decides not to consult, Congress possesses the institutional power to persuade him to change his mind at various points in the appointment process. Before a nomination is even made, Congress has legislative tools at its disposal to stop administration-backed measures and thus convince the president to consult or even to nominate a particular candidate. As President Taft noted, any "attempt on the President's part to break up the custom [of consulting] would create a factional opposition which would interfere with the passing of the bills he recommends, and endanger the successful carrying out of the policies to which he is pledged."[24] Such a scenario unfolded in 1986 when Republican senator David F. Durenberger of Minnesota threatened to block a confirmation vote on Daniel A. Manion, a controversial judicial nominee, to force President Reagan to nominate David Doty, whom the White House considered "too liberal."[25] Three years later, Republican senator James Jeffords placed a hold on several nominations to convince President Bush to select a candidate of his choosing.[26]

If a president feels strongly about a candidate, he may very well go ahead and submit the nomination to the Senate. The president must be mindful, however, that the Senate can use a number of mechanisms to slow a nomination or prevent its confirmation. Blue slips, committee questionnaires, financial disclosure statements, American Bar Association reports, hearings, committee votes, holds, floor votes, and filibusters have been used to delay or kill nominations and thus punish presidents for failing to consult. For example, blue slips were used during the chairmanship of Senator Eastland to prevent certain nominations from moving through the Senate Judiciary Committee. A negative report on a nominee from the Justice Department can prevent further committee action as well.[27] Even if the committee or the full Senate votes, rejection is always a possibility.[28] Finally, a filibuster can stop Senate action or pressure a president to withdraw a nominee. This happened when President George W. Bush withdrew the nomination of Miguel Estrada after two years of Democratic filibustering.[29]

There have been attempts to eliminate or change some of these legislative tools.[30] In recent years, the filibuster has been attacked by senators who call it an illegitimate and unconstitutional way to prevent votes on judicial nominations. During the last days of the 109th Congress, Senate Majority Leader Bill Frist presented the basic argument for this position: "During my tenure as majority leader, the most vexatious and constitutionally challenging issue confronting the Senate was judicial filibusters. This tactic threatened to disrupt fundamentally the Senate's relationship with coordinate branches of Government and to impair the Senate's ability to discharge its constitutional obligation to advise and consent. In the process, Senate traditions were damaged."[31]

Proposals were introduced to limit or even prevent the use of filibusters on judicial nominations.[32] For the most part, proponents of such restrictions argue that the Senate is a majority institution with no room for minority opposition if such action prevents a vote on judicial nominations. Frist and others believe that "the Senate lived by the principle that filibusters would not impede the exercise of constitutional confirmation powers and that a majority of Senators could vote to confirm or reject a nominee brought to the floor. The unparalleled filibusters undermined that tradition, denying nominees the courtesy of an up or down vote. They represented an effort by a Senate minority to obstruct the duty of the full Senate to advise and consent."[33] This is faulty reasoning based on bad history. The Senate has traditionally been an institution where the minority has been able to prevent action through the use of near unlimited debate. For most of its history, the Senate did not even have a mechanism to end a filibuster.[34]

Opponents of the use of filibusters say that the majority is being thwarted, but a minority voice in a democratic institution does not mean that the majority cannot rule. Instead, as George Reedy reasoned, "it merely prevents the majority from doing everything it wants to do when it wants to do it."[35] In that sense, the threat is not from the minority but, as James Madison said in *Federalist* No. 10, from the majority. A minority, Madison believed, "may clog the administration, it may convulse the society; but it will be unable to execute and mask its violence under the forms of the Constitution."[36] Some argue that impeding action in the Senate is a threat because it goes against the public interest of the nation. Ross K. Baker acknowledges this point but counters that one should not view the Senate as embodying all values implicit in a democracy. "It would appear at first glance that obstructionism and the public interest are totally incompatible. But dismissing the hyperindividualism of the Senate as no more than a symptom of the fragmentation of American democracy would be a mistake. It would likewise be inappropriate to conclude that the absence of such strong checks on the will of the majority in the House necessarily promotes the public interest."[37] Opponents of filibusters on judicial nominations miss the point. The Senate does not embody strict majority rule; rather, it represents important values set forth in the Constitution, especially minority rights. The framers designed a system of government suited to frustrate the concentration of political power. Madison concluded that the "accumulation of all powers, legislative, executive, and judiciary in the same hands . . . may be justly pronounced the very definition of tyranny."[38] The three branches were given different elements of shared power to prevent the excessive concentration of power and, most importantly, to protect the people from the tyranny of governmental abuse.

The Senate discovered that one of the most effective ways to protect and support minority rights was to adopt tools to delay or stop legislative action. In the case of judicial nominations, the most important techniques are filibusters and holds on the Senate floor and blue slips in the Senate Judiciary Committee. Without these safeguards, the upper house would cease to be an institution of deliberation and would merely embody the sole principle of majority rights. That is not what the founders intended when establishing our constitutional framework.

Filibusters, holds, and blue slips should not be seen merely as devices for enforcing minority rights. They are also used to give the legislative branch leverage in conflicts with the executive. Despite the fact that the Constitution established three separate and equal branches, it did not create self-enforcing mechanisms to protect each institution from encroachment by the others. Each branch was left to defend itself. Without these legislative instruments, the Senate would be less effective in confronting the president.

Congressional Specification of Qualifications

The Senate's ability to influence a nomination is not limited to delaying tactics. In various cases, the upper house has stipulated certain qualifications for particular offices to ensure that the president does not nominate unilaterally or irresponsibly. Although Congress cannot formally name candidates for office,[39] it can narrow the field of choices to the point where the description fits only one individual. Presidents have traditionally adhered to such restrictions.[40] For example, in a 1916 army reorganization bill, Congress provided for an office to be filled by a person "from civil life, not less than forty-five nor more than fifty years of age, who shall have been for ten years a Judge of the Supreme Court of the Philippine Islands, shall have served for two years as a Captain in the regular or volunteer army, and shall be proficient in the Spanish language and laws." Not surprisingly, the only person qualified to fill the position lived in the district of the chairman of the House Committee on Military Affairs, who was also in charge of the House conferees for the bill.[41]

The power of Congress to limit the field of candidates has been used throughout this country's history. During the Revolutionary War, the Continental Congress first began issuing restrictions on appointments.[42] Similarly, after the establishment of a new national government, Congress passed the 1789 Judiciary Act, requiring that the U.S. attorney general and U.S. attorneys be "learned in the law."[43] This was the first major congressional stipulation guiding a president's selection decision. There are other examples as well. In an 1849 law, Congress mandated that a commission's secretary be "versed in the English and Spanish languages."[44] Twenty-one years later, after reorganizing the Marine Hospital Service and creating the position of supervising surgeon (the title was later changed to surgeon general), Congress ordered that the person appointed be "a surgeon."[45] Currently, all "permanent officers and employees" of the Census Bureau must be "citizens of the United States," and the director of the U.S. Patent and Trademark Office must both be a U.S. citizen and have a "professional background and experience in patent or trademark law."[46]

Not everyone agrees on the history or constitutionality of such restrictions. In an article titled "Regulating Presidential Powers," Saikrishna Prakash objects to any appointment limitation and states that a president "has the constitutional right to select whomever he pleases." In particular, Prakash challenges the validity of using the "learned in the law" provision of the 1789 Judiciary Act as supporting evidence for congressional restrictions. He states that one could "read the lack of controversy [over this provision] as reflecting a consensus that Congress could regulate the President's power to nominate." However, Prakash rejects this reasoning by declaring that "the provision generated no heat because no one ever focused on the constitutional question. It is easy to see why, for the requirement was certainly inconsequential. It seems obvious that the President naturally would nominate only those learned in the law to offices representing the United States in the courts. The provision was not too far removed from one stipulating that any appointee must have a pulse."[47] Although the natural assumption might be that the most qualified experts and those best fit to serve in a particular position would be selected, the general history of appointments does not bear this out.[48] Instead, the record reveals many officials who were marginally qualified and known more for their loyalty to the president than for the credentials they brought to the office.[49]

Finally, Prakash argues that the 1789 Judiciary Act was "a relatively harmless anomaly that was subsequently (albeit implicitly) rejected as an unconstitutional encroachment on the appointment power."[50] Rejected by whom? Not only have presidents explicitly endorsed such measures by signing them into law; they have, as Supreme Court Justice Louis Brandeis stated, "consistently observed them" as well. In his dissenting opinion in *Myers v. United States,* Brandeis noted a number of instances in which Congress

> restricted the President's selection by the requirement of citizenship. It has limited the power of nomination by providing that the office may be held only by a resident of the United States; of a State; of a particular State; of a particular district; of a particular territory; of the District of Columbia; of a particular foreign country. It has limited the power of nomination further by prescribing specific professional attainments, or occupational experience. . . . It has imposed the requirement of age; of sex; of race; of property; and of habitual temperance in the use of intoxicating liquors. Congress has imposed like restrictions on the power of nomination by requiring political representation; or that the selection be made on a nonpartisan basis. It has required in some cases, that the representation be industrial; in others, that it be geographic. It has at times required that the President's nominees be taken from, or include representatives from, particular branches of departments of the Government. By still other statutes, Congress has confined the President's selection to a small number of persons to be named by others.[51]

Constitutional scholar Edward S. Corwin called such measures "by far the most important limitation on presidential autonomy in this field of power" and observed that Congress has the right to "stipulate the qualifications" on offices that it creates.[52]

Despite the executive branch's historical acceptance of these congressional restrictions, in recent years, presidents have used their signing statements to resist efforts by Congress to place qualifications on their appointment power. In signing a bill, chief executives have "set boundaries on legislation by interpreting provisions that were clearly intended to be mandatory as advisory only."[53] To take a recent and dramatic example, the 2007 Department of Homeland Security Appropriation Act authorized the president to nominate, with the advice and consent of the Senate, an administrator of the Federal Emergency Management Agency (FEMA).[54] President Bush, however, declared the bill inconsistent with the Appointments Clause because it limited the pool of available candidates.[55] The act required the president to nominate a person who has "a demonstrated ability in and knowledge of emergency management and homeland security" with "not less than 5 years of executive leadership and management experience in the public or private sector."[56] Although those qualifications seem designed to ensure that the pool of potential candidates will have the experience most appropriate for the job, Bush argued that the act "rules out a large portion of those persons best qualified by experience and knowledge to fill the office."[57]

The belief that a chief executive must have unlimited authority to nominate anyone he chooses has no basis in history. Statutory qualifications were first formally addressed in the early 1870s, when Congress passed the first civil service legislation (see chapter 5). President Grant's attorney general, Amos T. Akerman, set forth his views on Congress's constitutional authority to place limits on appointments by the executive branch. Akerman said that Congress can "prescribe qualifications" for offices; however, that "right . . . is limited by the necessity of leaving scope for the judgment and will of the person or body [in] whom the Constitution vests the power of appointment." He believed that qualifications were perfectly responsible and constitutionally justifiable. For instance, an appointment could be restricted by citizenship, age, and professional restrictions and "still leave room to the appointing power for the exercise of its own judgment and will."[58] His legal opinion became the basis for the civil service criteria, or what is popularly termed the "rule of three" (see chapter 6).

Seventy-two years after Akerman wrote his opinion, and sixty years after the rule of three was adopted, Civil Service Commissioner Arthur S. Flemming explained that Akerman's opinion "has come down through the years, has never been challenged and has constituted the legal basis for . . . the 'rule of three.'"[59] Only in recent years has the executive branch challenged the constitutionally permissible and traditional right of Congress to place qualifications on offices it establishes. Beginning with at least the Reagan administration, every president has objected to limits placed on the nomination power.[60] They have denied that Congress, in creating an office, can specify qualifications and standards for the person who will fill the office.

The constitutionality of such restrictions has never been resolved by the judicial branch,[61] and it is unlikely that the courts will ever want to venture into this area. As a result, Congress and the president must come to some sort of accommodation. One might argue that the president can ignore a statutory qualification to protect the institutional integrity of the executive branch, but the costs would be prohibitive. For example, suppose the president nominates a FEMA administrator who does not have the "demonstrated ability in and knowledge of emergency management and homeland security" or has only two years' experience rather than the required five. The Senate could announce that it will not hold hearings on that individual and will await a nominee who satisfies the law. In this type of confrontation, the president is likely to take a public beating. This would be particularly true in the case of appointing a FEMA administrator. Critics of former FEMA administrator Michael D. Brown, who had no prior emergency management or homeland security experience, were quick to point out a relationship between his lack of credentials and FEMA's failure to respond adequately to Hurricane Katrina.[62]

Nonstatutory Limits to the President's Appointment Power

Formal legislative controls over the executive branch are numerous; however, much more prevalent are the informal methods of limiting a president's appointment power. Prakash and others have objected to these statutory restraints, but they assume that the legislative challenge to a chief executive's power will come through formal congressional action.[63] Battles over nominations rarely involve statutory language, however. Congress is much more likely to limit a president by informal measures, and most of the time, appointments occur after unofficial agreements between the two branches.

As this book has shown, informal methods—such as the threat to delay or reject a nomination—are much more prevalent and are often used to prevent an executive from making nominations without consulting members of Congress. At times, even the appointment of cabinet officials has been contested by Congress. During the 1800s, cabinet posts were often "used to placate political factions or satisfy regional demands."[64] Presidents were careful not to upset powerful congressional leaders in making such appointments. Republican Benjamin Harrison's defeat in the 1892 presidential election was partially attributed to his refusal to permit Pennsylvania senator Matt Quay and New York's Republican boss Thomas Platt to dictate his cabinet appointments four years earlier.[65] As late as the 1950s, President Dwight Eisenhower was forced to deal with congressional members of his own party who assumed that they had a right to assist in choosing a cabinet. Republican Majority Leader Robert A. Taft was particularly incensed by Eisenhower's lack of respect in not consulting him.[66]

In more recent decades, the norm has been to give presidents greater freedom in choosing their cabinets, but there are limits. Democratic senator Gary Hart declared, "that freedom should not extend to an agency which is, at least in part, an extension of Congress. The make-up of such commissions should reflect to some degree the various views represented in Congress."[67]

Minor posts are even more susceptible to informal congressional influence. At present, home-state senators have almost dictatorial power when it comes to naming judges. As Attorney General Robert Kennedy once declared, the process has "grown up as a senatorial appointment with the advice and consent of the President."[68] The current Bush administration has professed that when a senator wants a particular candidate selected, it will defer.[69]

The above-stated practice demonstrates the durability of both branches following a mutually beneficial understanding that does not break with the constitutional design of separation of powers, check and balances, or republican principles. More importantly, it shows that nonstatutory controls on a president's appointment power are common and useful means of influencing the pre-nomination process. Our constitutional system is based not only on what can be easily read from the Constitution but also on political actors working out informal accommodations to balance the power provided in the Appointments Clause. Practical experience often guides governmental action, not a narrow or one-sided view of constitutional provisions.

Reformers Seeking Nonpolitical Remedies

Looking back over 200 years, civil service reform has had a major impact on the pre-nomination process. A bill proposed by Democratic senator Lyman Trumbull in 1869 would have prohibited members of Congress from soliciting or recommending people for federal appointments unless requested to do so by the administration or as part of a senator's advice-and-consent duties (see chapter 5). This bill was part of an ongoing civil service movement that promoted nonpartisan examinations and selections. Many reformers believed that only through the development of a merit-based system within the executive branch would more expert and qualified officeholders emerge.

The campaign for a merit system invited a confrontation between good-government groups and elected members of Congress. Civil service scholar John G. Sproat explained: "Some [civil service reformers] thought it meant nothing more than strict adherence to the 'natural laws' of political economy. Others viewed it as government by the enlightened few for the ignorant many [or, more importantly] . . . government operated on 'businesslike' principles. All of them insisted it meant government free from graft, bribery, lobbying, and other forms of actual or potential corruption."[70] Although many civil service reformers thought that the spoils system produced bad appointments,[71] they failed to see that lawmakers embody republican values implicit in the Constitution. Senators and representatives carry out the functions of majority rule and minority rights in their respective legislative institutions, and they do so while representing the American people.

This point was lost on civil service reformers. They believed that congressional involvement in the pre-nomination process was a corrupting
influence on good government. Their only solution was to create a merit
system that would override democratic impulses.[72] Taking politics out of
the pre-nomination process, they thought, would end corruption.[73] Instead
of a system of negotiation and compromise, they wanted to use rational scientific methods to find the most qualified person for office.[74] This attitude
of reformers—that patronage was an evil that needed to be destroyed—
largely resulted from their place in the pre-nomination process. Being out-
siders gave them a built-in incentive to destroy the existing system and
create a new one. Why involve oneself in elected politics when one can
merely exclude the people's representatives and create a new process suited
to one's own goals? Civil service reformers did not appreciate the tension
between a republican form of government and government by self-styled,
unelected experts.

Despite their efforts, the pre-nomination process of political accommodation persists. Civil service reform had its last major victory more than
thirty-five years ago when President Richard Nixon signed the Postal Reorganization Act (see chapter 7). Currently, there appears to be no political
will or desire to place the remaining federal offices (mainly in the judicial
branch, but also cabinet and subcabinet positions in the various executive
departments) within the civil service system. Both branches see the political value of retaining power over judicial appointments (most notably
Supreme Court justices, circuit and district court judges, and U.S. attorneys). The merit commission approach instituted during the Carter administration appeared to limit the pre-nomination leverage of lawmakers, but
it has had only modest impact. There is a limit to how much one can (or
should) remove politics from government.

Rise of the Unitary Executive School

Like civil service reformers, unitary executive scholars have a deep
distrust for anyone or anything outside the executive branch. The ultimate
aim of both groups is to concentrate political and constitutional decisions
within the White House and to marginalize the role of elected members of
Congress. This attitude extends to the pre-nomination process because
these reformers deny that the legislative branch has any legitimate right to
influence the administrative or executive process. Only executive branch
officials, they say, have the ability and competence to make scientific and
rational decisions to ensure an efficient and proper administrative environment. What is the reason for this attitude? Blame for corruption and
waste in appointments has traditionally fallen on Congress. Unitary exec-

utive and merit reform advocates believe that ending patronage and the spoils system will cure all evils. This is a misguided answer to serious concerns about governmental accountability and fraud. Federal employees should receive more, not less, oversight from Congress.

Republicanism and the implied values of that principle have little meaning for either group. However, the Constitution was not designed to allow one person or one group to decide what is in the best interests of the country. Instead, the framers' intention was to frustrate any such concentration of power. Shared power among separate branches of government was not a misguided, archaic, or shortsighted design. Based on human nature, it was the structure of government that the framers thought most effective and reliable. Allowing one branch to dominate was certainly what the framers tried to prevent. Nonetheless, civil service reformers and unitary executive scholars believe that one branch must dominate to produce an efficient government. In the area of appointments, both groups have resisted a significant role for the elected members of Congress.

Unitary executive advocates differ significantly from civil service reformers. Whereas the latter focused primarily on appointments and the desire to take politics out of the process (with *politics* representing a code word for backroom dealings, compromise, and interference of the legislative branch), unitary executive scholars reach much deeper into government. Rather than using code words or hidden meanings, they make their objectives clear. Consider their position on appointments: John C. Yoo, one of the leading unitary executive scholars, argues that the Appointments Clause places "the power to nominate solely in the hands of the President."[75] Yoo and his colleagues believe that any legislative involvement in the pre-nomination process violates the Constitution and long-standing practice. Civil service reformers would largely agree, but the unitary executive school presses executive power to greater limits.

In one of the first attempts to show the historical underpinnings of the unitary executive theory in practice, Steven G. Calabresi and Christopher S. Yoo portray George Washington as a president bent on unifying all executive authority under his command. After claiming that the Constitutional Convention at Philadelphia created "the unitary presidency," Calabresi and Yoo argue that President Washington "was determined as the first President to give it structure and life both through his actions and through his public and private utterances."[76] Yet with regard to appointments, a unitary executive was not what Washington pursued either in theory or in practice. He clearly followed Congress's wishes when it created the Post Office Department and gave appointment authority to the postmaster general (see chapter 1). President Washington respected not only the law but also the intent of Congress: "I have uniformly avoided interfering with any appointments which do not require my official agency, and the Resolutions and Ordinances establishing the Post Office under the former Congress, and which have been recognized by the present Government, giving power to the Postmaster General to appoint his own Deputies, and making him accountable for their conduct, is an insuperable objection to my taking any part in this matter."[77]

Calabresi and Yoo insist that John Adams expressed strong views on the president's powers under the Appointments Clause.[78] However, they fail to explain that once Adams reached the White House, he did not endorse the unitary executive model for appointments and in fact gave Congress substantial control over such matters. In response to an appointment request from a relative, Adams wrote: "Our kinsman must apply to the senators and representatives of his own State for recommendations. If I were to nominate him without previous recommendations from the senators and representatives from your State, the Senate would probably negative him."[79]

Without directly mentioning the appointment power, Calabresi and Yoo declare that "the Jackson administration marks . . . the start of a period that culminates in the strong modern presidencies that have characterized much of the twentieth century."[80] They neglect to note that Andrew Jackson was not as strong a president as popularly depicted. On various occasions he consulted members of Congress and agreed that they had a powerful influence in the pre-nomination process (see chapter 3). Calabresi and Yoo also misinterpret a dispute between President William H. Harrison and Senator Henry Clay of Kentucky involving the appointment of a New York collector. Although Calabresi and Yoo are correct when they say that Harrison did not nominate Senator Clay's preferred candidate,[81] they fail to mention that it was the custom for the president to consult *home-state* party leaders, which Harrison did. Clay was at fault for trying to dictate appointments in a state he did not represent (see chapter 3). Finally, Calabresi and Yoo point to the battle between President Rutherford B. Hayes and New York senator Roscoe Conkling as another example of a strong executive overcoming congressional pressure.[82] In this case, Hayes clearly won a great victory over a powerful Republican senator; however, the president's authority was not absolute. As explained in chapter 5, the Senate was willing to reject nominations when Hayes failed to follow the pre-nomination process.

The importance of a president giving strong direction to the pre-nomination process should not be overlooked. However, one must also understand the pivotal role of Congress in making appointments. From an early date, lawmakers insisted on a prominent voice in the decision-making process. That is why the "framers of the Government had confidence in the Senate, or they would not have combined them with the Executive in the performance of his duties."[83] Precedents have accumulated over time and continue to this day. Unitary executive scholars largely ignore this history and its lasting impact on the basic constitutional principles involved in making appointments.

Interpretive Value of Originalism and Textualism

Unitary executive scholars often use the text of the Constitution, or the views of the framers, to support their claim that the presidency should function separately from the legislative branch. For instance, Calabresi and Prakash note, "We believe that the original meaning of the constitutional text unambiguously supports the unitary Executive, making . . . historical excursion[s] unnecessary."[84] However, history and practice often guide constitutional government. Life must be breathed into the Constitution to give it meaning beyond words, which may have subjective and uncertain meanings. A claim that originalism or textualism produces clear intent does not make it so.

In an attempt to show that the Senate should have no role in the appointment process before a nomination is made, presidential scholar David A. Crockett begins by examining "Founding-era arguments." After determining that many of the early documents were inconclusive, Crockett claims that the *Federalist Papers,* or, more specifically, Alexander Hamilton's contributions to that work, provide substantial evidence of the framers' intent. Crockett argues that Hamilton wanted "effective governance," and as "a unitary actor, the president can more easily" provide that. "In fact," Crockett reasons, "Hamilton's discussion of the Senate's inability to force the president to appoint its choice, makes clear that there is an element of deference to the president in this process."[85] One must be mindful that Hamilton's interpretation of the Appointments Clause was based on his preference for concentrating power and responsibility in the president. It was a theoretical and reasoned position, but one that did not square with republican principles or the reality of the legislative branch seeking involvement in the pre-nomination process.

Crockett insists that textualism supports the notion that there is no legislative role before a nomination is made. "The grammar of the clause makes clear that advice and consent comes at the appointment stage of the process, not at the nomination stage."[86] Others, including some chief executives, have disagreed with this assessment. President Theodore Roosevelt wrote that the Constitution provides for a more expanded view of how the Appointments Clause operates. "I accept the Senators' recommendations," he stated, "provided they recommend decent men. This is not a case of personal peculiarity on my part or of usurpation of authority on theirs. It is a compliance not merely with the letter but with the spirit of Article 2, Section 2, of the Constitution."[87] In another letter he wrote: "I understand perfectly that under the first article of the Constitution, the Senators are part of the appointing power, and that therefore the appointment must represent an agreement between them and me, and, as the acquaintance of the Senator with his State is always much greater than the knowledge of the President can possibly be, it is the normal and natural thing that I should listen to his advice as to these appointments, and I generally do so."[88] As Roosevelt reasoned, constitutional standards are made with the view that one should consider not only the letter but also the spirit of the Constitution. Republican principles provide for a useful balance and check on a president during the pre-nomination process, and Roosevelt's acknowledgment that home-state senators are better informed about local candidates speaks to the utility of the legislative branch. The executive should view Congress's involvement not as a burden but as a way to produce effective government.

Crockett dismisses this kind of legislative involvement. Again, using Hamilton as support, he states, there "is 'no exertion of *choice* on the part of the Senate . . . they cannot themselves *choose*—they can only ratify or reject the choice [the president] may have made.'" Crockett concludes that "the Senate's role in the appointments process is to make sure that the president does not base his choice solely or primarily on the fact that the nominee is from his state, or because he is related to or good friends with the nominee, or because the nominee will be the president's willing tool."[89] Although some senators may regard those standards as reasonable, the use of Hamiltonian criteria for the selection of appointments is not a constitutional standard, nor have the *Federalist Papers* come down through the ages as the framers' definitive word.

There are fundamental problems with founding-era arguments. Many constitutional provisions are so ambiguous that no standard was set during that time. The Appointments Clause is no different. By the end of the ratification process and the start of the new federal government, there was no uniform understanding of how the pre-nomination process would function. Just as Hamilton can be used to validate a constitutional assertion, one can easily cite another framer to support the opposite conclusion. For instance, Roger Sherman can reasonably be used to make an originalist counterargument. He was a signer of the Declaration of Independence (and a member of the committee that drafted it), a member of the committee that prepared the Articles of Confederation, a member of the Continental Congress, and a delegate to the Constitutional Convention; he was elected to the House of Representatives in the First Congress and elected to the Senate in the Second Congress, where he served until his death. Few, if any, men were more involved in the founding of this country. On July 20, 1789, Sherman provided a framer's insight into how the pre-nomination process should operate. In a private exchange with John Adams, he noted:

[The Senate] is the most important branch in government, for aiding and supporting the executive, securing the rights of the individual states, the government of the United States and the liberties of the people. The executive magistrate is to execute the laws. The senate, being a branch of the legislature, will naturally incline to have them duly executed, and, therefore, will advise to such appointments as will best attain that end. From the knowledge of the people in the several states, they can give the best information as to who are qualified for office; and though they will . . . in some degree lessen [the president's] responsibility, yet their advice may enable him to make such judicious appointments, as to render responsibility less necessary.[90]

Here, Sherman argued that effective government results from the legislative branch supplying a president with information to enable him to make "judicious appointments."

It is not necessary to conclude that Sherman's views are superior to Hamilton's. The point is that understanding the framers' intent is a difficult task and cannot be achieved by citing only one person. As chapter 1 of this book notes, the Constitutional Convention, state ratification conventions, and other founding-era documents did not generate a consensus and provided few guidelines as to how the pre-nomination process would be managed. At least in terms of appointments, one can reasonably conclude that no one has a monopoly on original intent. Only when the Constitution was put into practice did the operation of this power become clear.

Perhaps Crockett's most central argument, based on Hamilton's *Federalist* No. 76, is that the overriding concern of the appointment process is to ensure "effective governance." Crockett claims that the Senate's "task is not to be obstructive or protect minority rights or allow for unending debate, but to complete a process that results, again, in good administration." To do that, the Senate must hold "a simple majority vote," because that is the "constitutional standard."[91] Good administration is a valid goal, but it is only one of many in the Constitution. However, giving maximum latitude to the president and his aides, unhampered by legislative intrusion, goes against the republican nature of the Constitution, which gives the two branches shared powers.

The Senate, Crockett argues, provides an important role "by checking the president's work, guarding primarily against parochialism, nepotism, and cronyism, especially with respect to protecting the independence of the judicial branch from inappropriate presidential influence in the execution of its duties."[92] That vital function can be better performed before a president nominates. The pre-nomination process permits a president and lawmakers to determine whether a candidate possesses those fatal qualities. Catching a presidential misjudgment before the Senate stage reduces nomination missteps and provides for greater effectiveness and efficiency in governmental operations. Responsibility does not rest solely with the president. Both branches are joined in the appointment process to see that the best people serve in the federal government.

Some call for an end to the existing pre-nomination process and for mandatory up-or-down votes because they are dissatisfied with republican institutions. Civil service reformers, unitary executive scholars, and others seek—either by implication or by direct advocacy—a process that is unfettered by democratic participation. A republican system is too messy for experts to manage. Therefore, in order to appoint efficiently, one must take politics out of that process. There is no better way to do that than by claiming to pursue the honorable and noble goal of "good administration." For these scholars, an appointment should not be jeopardized by the traditional methods of negotiation and accommodation inherent in the existing pre-nomination process. Those who believe that democracy has failed to produce good appointments want to justify, or rationalize, the president acting on his own responsibility. The belief comes down to the notion that if good government is to occur, appointments must be made by an official who does not have to respond or be accountable to democratic pressures.

I believe that a more likely and effective way to ensure good administration is through a vigorous system of checks and balances. Providing a check after a nomination is submitted does not serve the president, Congress, or the people well. The two branches should come together to build a consensus that is acceptable to all. If a president wants to faithfully carry out republican principles during the pre-nomination process, he will make the necessary accommodations, as is done in other areas of governing. Endless negative votes on bad appointments do not produce good administration or effective government. Good administration occurs when the president and Congress consult so that needless delays and repetition do not waste valuable time and resources.

A "healthy constitutional process," according to Crockett, "will lead to resolution."[93] Here we agree. However, the Constitution does not isolate the president from legislative consultation during the pre-nomination process. Claiming a unitary executive model for the appointment process ignores important republican principles that direct the governmental institutions of the United States. Strict originalism and textualism result in impractical separation and needless distrust between Congress and the president. The governing process does not function in such a fragmented, compartmentalized manner. Neither the text of the Constitution nor the framers' intent provides sufficient guidance for the pre-nomination process. Only through the establishment of important precedents did implementation of the Appointments Clause become possible. Repeated practice, not rigid adherence to vague claims of originalism and textualism, was required. Custom and convention won initially, and they prevail to this day.

Final Remarks

At the start of this book, I offered two countervailing views concerning the operation of the Constitution. The first represents a highly theoretical and impractical conception of how nominations are made. It claims that the consideration of appointments "is granted exclusively to the President and is beyond Congress's power." The practice of the last two centuries thoroughly refutes this argument. The record demonstrates that legislators and presidents understand that the Constitution calls for congressional involvement in the selection of nominees. The duty and responsibility of carrying out the functions of the Appointments Clause have proved the necessity of receiving advice from members of Congress. They, being the elected representatives of the people, are better qualified than the president to choose the individuals to fill positions in their states and districts. That is why the following is a misguided argument: "Congress's ability to address the nominee or recommendation directly renders Congressional intrusion into the pre-nomination or pre-recommendation process unnecessary as well as unconstitutional."[94] The very necessity and constitutional responsibility of giving advice explains why Congress must be involved in the pre-nomination process. The claim that congressional participation is unneeded and unconstitutional ignores the most important part of our constitutional system—the republican and representative values that give life and meaning to American democracy.

Constitutional powers that are not strictly reserved to one branch are intended to function with republican principles in mind. This is accomplished through close consultation between the president and Congress. As explained by Supreme Court Justice Robert H. Jackson, the Constitution cannot be reasonably interpreted and applied by using a literal analysis:

> The actual art of governing under our Constitution does not and cannot conform to judicial definitions of the power of any of its branches based on isolated clauses or even single Articles torn from context. While the Constitution diffuses power the better to secure liberty, it also contemplates that practice will integrate the dispersed powers into a workable government. It enjoins upon its branches separateness but interdependence, autonomy but reciprocity. Presidential powers are not fixed but fluctuate, depending upon their disjunction or conjunction with those of Congress.[95]

This book reflects that understanding of how the Constitution is intended to function. The idea that interdependence and reciprocity win out over separateness and autonomy is not new. Our federal government was designed to guarantee that separate branches share power. Republican principles direct this process by ensuring that the government derives its authority from the consent of the governed and functions through representatives of the people. Lawmakers participate in the nomination process at the initial decision-making stage. That is why a president should be mindful of the democratic values that dominate the exercise of the Appointments Clause.

No matter how obvious such a proposition may be, it continually needs to be restated and defended. This book has presented evidence to challenge the claims made by civil service reformers, unitary executive scholars, and other opponents of a constitutional government based on shared powers and republican principles. This study will not end the debate, but I trust that it will explain why Congress plays a crucial and ongoing role in governmental operations and, in particular, in the making of appointments.

Notes

Abbreviations

BHP   Benjamin Harrison Papers, Library of Congress, Manuscript
             Reading Room
GPO   Government Printing Office
MVBP   Martin Van Buren Papers, Library of Congress, Manuscript
             Reading Room
NARA   National Archives and Records Administration
RG   Record Group
WMP   William McKinley Papers, Library of Congress, Manuscript
             Reading Room

Introduction

1. *Annals of Congress*, 1st Cong., 1st sess., vol. 1 (June 18, 1789), 551–552.

2. *Buckley v. Valeo*, 424 U.S. 1, 132 (1976). Under Article II, Section 2, Congress can prescribe the mode of appointment for "inferior" officers, subject to certain limitations.

3. Mitchel A. Sollenberger, "The Law: Must the Senate Take a Floor Vote on a Presidential Judicial Nominee?" *Presidential Studies Quarterly* 34 (June 2004): 420–436; Sheldon Goldman, "Is There a Crisis in Judicial Selection?" in *Readings in Presidential Politics*, ed. George C. Edwards III (Belmont, CA: Thomson Wadsworth, 2006), 337–354; David A. Crockett, "The Contemporary President: Should the Senate Take a Floor Vote on a Presidential Judicial Nominee?" *Presidential Studies Quarterly* 37 (June 2007): 313–330.

4. *Annals of Congress*, 1st Cong., 1st sess., vol. 1 (May 19, 1789), 393, 395; ibid. (June 18, 1789), 555. See also Louis Fisher, *Constitutional Conflicts between Congress and the President*, 5th ed. (Lawrence: University Press of Kansas, 2007), 32.

5. Louis Fisher, *Constitutional Dialogues: Interpretation as Political Process* (Princeton, NJ: Princeton University Press, 1988), 245. One source of the "judicial supremacy" model is the 1803 statement by Chief Justice John Marshall: "It is emphatically the province and duty of the judicial department to say what the law is." *Marbury v. Madison*, 5 U.S. (1 Cr.) 137, 177 (1803). Is it not also the province and duty of Congress and the president to say what the law is?

6. 462 U.S. 919, 959 (1983).

7. Louis Fisher, "The Legislative Veto: Invalidated, It Survives," *Law and Contemporary Problems* 56 (autumn 1993): 273–291.

8. Those who advocate originalism believe that the judicial branch should be guided by the intent of the founders when interpreting the Constitution, treaties, or laws. See Dennis J. Goldford, *The American Constitution and the Debate over Originalism* (New York: Cambridge University Press, 2005); Johnathan G. O'Neill, *Originalism in American Law and Politics: A Constitutional History* (Baltimore: Johns Hopkins University Press, 2005); Jack N. Rakove, *Original Meanings: Politics and Ideas in the Making of the Constitution* (New York: Vintage Books, 1996). Textualists, in contrast, argue that only an examination of the written text or the precise language used—not some general interpretation of the thoughts and beliefs of the framers—is the best method. See Ralph A. Rossum, *Antonin Scalia's Jurisprudence: Text and Tradition* (Lawrence: University Press of Kansas, 2006); Jonathan T. Molot, "Exchange: The Rise and Fall of Textualism," *Columbia Law Review* 106 (Jan. 2006): 1–69; Caleb Nelson, "What is Textualism?" *Virginia Law Review,* vol. 91 (Apr. 2005): 347–418; William N. Eskridge Jr., "All about Words: Early Understandings of the 'Judicial Power' in Statutory Interpretation, 1776–1806," *Columbia Law Review* 101 (June 2001): 990–1106.

9. *Youngstown Sheet & Tube Company v. Sawyer,* 343 U.S. 579, 610 (1952) (concurring opinion).

10. *Federalist* No. 10, in *The Federalist,* ed. Terence Ball (Cambridge: Cambridge University Press, 2003), 252.

11. Christopher S. Yoo, Steven G. Calabresi, and Anthony J. Colangelo, "The Unitary Executive in the Modern Era, 1945–2004," *Iowa Law Review* 90 (Jan. 2005): 601–731; Christopher S. Yoo, Steven G. Calabresi, and Laurence D. Nee, "The Unitary Executive during the Third Half-Century, 1889–1945," *University of Notre Dame* 80 (Nov. 2004): 1–109; Steven G. Calabresi and Christopher Yoo, "The Unitary Executive during the Second Half-Century," *Harvard Journal of Law and Public Policy* 26 (summer 2003): 667–800; John C. Yoo, "The New Sovereignty and the Old Constitution: The Chemical Weapons Convention and the Appointments Clause," *Constitutional Commentary* 15 (spring 1998): 87–130; Steven G. Calabresi and Christopher S. Yoo, "The Unitary Executive during the First Half-Century," *Case Western Reserve University* 47 (summer 1997): 1451–1561; Steven G. Calabresi and Saikrishna B. Prakash, "The President's Power to Execute the Laws," *Yale Law Journal* 104 (Dec. 1994): 541–665; Saikrishna Prakash, "Hail to the Chief Administrator: The Framers and the President's Administrative Powers," *Yale Law Journal* 102 (Jan. 1993): 991–1017; Steven G. Calabresi and Kevin H. Rhodes, "The Structural Constitution: Unitary Executive, Plural Judiciary," *Harvard Law Review* 105 (Apr. 1992): 1153–1216.

12. Statement by Deputy Assistant Attorney General Michelle E. Boardman on presidential signing statements, Office of Legal Counsel, U.S. Department of Justice, Committee on the Judiciary, U.S. Senate, June 27, 2006. Available at http://judiciary.senate.gov/print_testimony.cfm?id=1969&wit_id=5479 (accessed Mar. 2, 2007).

13. For studies on the formal, public record, see Richard Davis, *Electing Justice: Fixing the Supreme Court Nomination Process* (New York: Oxford University Press, 2005); Task Forces of Citizens for Independent Courts, *Uncertain Justice: Politics and America's Courts* (New York: Century Foundation Press, 2000); Charles H. Sheldon and Linda S. Maule, *Choosing Justice: The Recruitment of State and Federal Judges* (Pullman: Washington State University Press, 1997); George L. Watson and John A. Stookey, *Shaping America: The Politics of Supreme Court Appointments* (New York: HarperCollins, 1995); Stephen L. Carter, *The Confirmation Mess: Cleaning up the Federal Appointments Process* (New York: Basic Books, 1994); Paul Simon, *Advice and Consent: Clarence Thomas, Robert Bork, and the Intriguing History of the Supreme Court's Nomination Battles* (Washington, DC: National Press Books, 1992); Herman Schwartz, *Packing the Courts: The Conservative Campaign to Rewrite the Constitution* (New York:

Scribner, 1988); Laurence H. Tribe, *God Save This Honorable Court: How the Choice of Supreme Court Justices Shapes Our History* (New York: Random House, 1985).

14. Henry J. Abraham, *Justices, Presidents, and Senators*, 4th ed. (Lanham, MD: Rowman and Littlefield, 1999).

15. Harold W. Chase, *Federal Judges: The Appointing Process* (Minneapolis: University of Minnesota Press, 1972); Kermit L. Hall, *The Politics of Justice: Lower Federal Judicial Selection and the Second Party System, 1829–1861* (Lincoln: University of Nebraska Press, 1979); Rayman L. Soloman, "The Politics of Appointments and the Federal Courts' Role in Regulating America: U.S. Courts of Appeals Judgeships," *American Bar Foundation Research Journal* 2 (1984): 285–343; Alan Neff, "Breaking with Tradition: A Study of the U.S. District Judge Nominating Commission," *Judicature* 64 (Dec.–Jan. 1981): 256–278; Joan Gottschall, "Reagan's Appointments to the U.S. Courts of Appeals: The Continuation of a Judicial Revolution," *Judicature* 70 (June–July 1986): 48–54; Christopher Wolfe, "The Senate's Power to Give 'Advice and Consent' in Judicial Appointments," *Marquette Law Review* 82 (winter 1999): 355–379; Michael J. Gerhardt, "Norm Theory and the Future of the Federal Appointment Process," *Duke Law Journal* 50 (Apr. 2001): 1687–1715; Tracey E. George, "Court Fixing," *Arizona Law Review* 43 (spring 2001): 9–62; Stephen B. Burbank, "Politics, Privilege and Power: The Senate's Role in the Appointment of Federal Judges," *Judicature* 86 (July–Aug. 2002): 24–27; Roger E. Hartley and Lisa M. Holmes, "The Increasing Senate Scrutiny of Lower Federal Court Nominees," *Political Science Quarterly* 117 (summer 2002): 259–278. See also the various articles by Sheldon Goldman on every presidential administration's lower federal court nominations from Jimmy Carter to George W. Bush in *Judicature*.

16. Dorothy Ganfield Fowler, "Congressional Dictation of Local Appointments," *Journal of Politics* 7 (Feb. 1945): 25–57.

17. Sheldon Goldman, *Picking Federal Judges: Lower Court Selection from Roosevelt through Reagan* (New Haven, CT: Yale University Press, 1997).

18. George H. Haynes, *The Senate of the United States: Its History and Practice*, 2 vols. (Boston: Houghton Mifflin, 1938); Joseph P. Harris, *The Advice and Consent of the Senate* (Berkeley: University of California Press, 1953).

Chapter 1. Constitutional Principles

1. Jennings B. Sanders, *The Presidency of the Continental Congress, 1774–89: A Study in American Institutional History* (Gloucester, MA: Peter Smith, 1971), 33.

2. Louis Fisher, *The Politics of Shared Power: Congress and the Executive*, 4th ed. (College Station: Texas A&M University Press, 1998), 4.

3. Julian E. Zelizer, *The Reader's Companion to the United States Congress: The Building of Democracy* (New York: Houghton Mifflin, 2004), 7–8.

4. John Rutledge explained: "We have no legal Authority and Obedience to our Determinations will only follow the reasonableness, the apparent Utility, and Necessity of the Measures We adopt. We have no coercive or legislative Authority. Our Constituents are bound only in Honour, to observe our Determinations." John Adams's Notes of Debates, Sept. 6, 1774, in *Letters of Delegates to Congress*, ed. Paul H. Smith (Washington, DC: Library of Congress, 1976), 1:29.

5. Article IX, Articles of Confederation.

6. Marc W. Kruman, *Between Authority and Liberty: State Constitution Making in Revolutionary America* (Chapel Hill: University of North Carolina Press, 1999), 116.

7. Gordon S. Wood, *Creation of the American Republic, 1776–1787* (Chapel Hill: University of North Carolina Press, 1998), 145, 143.

8. Gordon Wood explained, "Americans in 1776 were resolved to destroy the capacity of their rulers ever again to put together such structures of domination or to determine the ranks of the social order [through appointments]." Wood, *Creation of the American Republic*, 148. See also William B. Michaelsen, *Creating the American Presidency, 1775–1789* (Lanham, MD: University Press of America, 1987), 3–5.

9. *Journals of the Continental Congress*, ed. Worthington C. Ford (Washington, DC: GPO, 1905), vol. 2 (July 26, 1775), 208. For a history of the Post Office Department during the Continental Congress, see Wesley Everett Rich, *The History of the United States Post Office to the Year 1829* (Cambridge, MA: Harvard University Press, 1924), 48–67.

10. *Journals of the Contintental Congress*, vol. 22 (Feb. 19, 1782), 80.

11. Ibid., vol. 23 (Oct. 18, 1782), 670.

12. Benjamin Franklin to Ebenezer Hazard, Aug. 3, 1775, in *Letters of Delegates*, 25:558, and *The Papers of Benjamin Franklin*, ed. William B. Willcox (New Haven, CT: Yale University Press, 1982), 22:146–147.

13. "Diary of Richard Smith in the Continental Congress, 1775–1776," *American Historical Review* 1, (1896): 291.

14. There may have been other, similar correspondence, but many Post Office Department documents from this period were destroyed by a fire on Dec. 15, 1836. One of the only records saved was Franklin's original ledger book, which details the accounts of all the post offices in the United States from 1776 to 1778. Mary Clemmer, *Ten Years in Washington: Life and Scenes in the National Capital, as a Woman Sees Them* (Hartford, CT: A. D. Worthington, 1874), 396–397; Wayne E. Fuller, *The American Mail: Enlarger of the Common Life* (Chicago: University of Chicago Press, 1972), 58–59.

15. One explanation for the reluctance to create more executive departments was that "leading figures in the revolution against Great Britain did not want to trade one type of autocratic rule for another." Harold J. Krent, *Presidential Powers* (New York: New York University Press, 2005), 89.

16. For examples of appointments under the Board of Treasury, see *Journals of the Continental Congress*, vol. 17 (June 12, 1780), 504; for examples of appointments under the Board of War, see ibid., vol. 12 (Sept. 21, 1778), 939; for examples of appointments under the Committee for Foreign Affairs, see ibid., vol. 8 (July 2, 1777), 523.

17. Harold J. Krent explains that "problems of both accountability and efficiency arose, principally due to turf battles and lack of coordination." Krent, *Presidential Powers*, 89.

18. Louis Fisher, *President and Congress: Power and Policy* (New York: Free Press, 1972), 11.

19. "Actually, Congress had for years leaned ever more definitely towards granting decisive authority to its executive officers. The Congress of 1781 went the whole distance." E. James Ferguson, *The Power of the Purse* (Chapel Hill: University of North Carolina Press, 1961), 118.

20. The Continental Congress created standing committees to oversee these executive departments and make reports twice a year. As Samuel Wharton noted, "it is expected, much Benefit will result to the United States by these stated Checks upon the separate Boards." Samuel Wharton to John Dickinson, June 20, 1782, in *Letters of Delegates*, 18:596.

21. For the secretary of foreign affairs, see *Journals of the Continental Congress*, vol. 19 (Jan. 10, 1781), 44; for the secretary of war, see ibid., vol. 22 (Jan. 17, 1782), 36; for the attorney general, see ibid., vol. 19 (Feb. 16, 1781), 156.

22. Ibid., vol. 19 (Feb. 20, 1781), 180; Robert Morris to the President of Congress, Mar. 3, 1781, in *The Papers of Robert Morris, 1781–1784*, ed. E. James Ferguson (Pittsburgh: University of Pittsburgh Press, 1973), 1:17–19.

23. Ferguson, *Power of the Purse*, 118.

24. Clarence L. Ver Steeg wrote: "there is little evidence that Morris determined the appointment of other department heads, there is no question that the Superintendent of Finance overshadowed the other executive departments." Clarence L. Ver Steeg, *Robert Morris: Revolutionary Financier* (New York: Octagon Books, 1972), 83.

25. *Journals of the Continental Congress*, vol. 19 (Mar. 29, 1781–Apr. 21, 1781), 326–327, 337–338, 429, 432–433; ibid., vol. 20 (Apr. 27, 1781), 455–456. See also Fisher, *President and Congress*, 12–13.

26. During the early 1780s, there was a controversy about how various armed services departments could incur debt. Although the Revolutionary War was going on at the time, many public officials were alarmed that so much money was being spent. E. Wayne Carp, *To Starve the Army at Pleasure: Continental Army Administration and American Political Culture, 1775–1783* (Chapel Hill: University of North Carolina Press, 1984), 132–133.

27. Robert Morris to the President of Congress, Feb. 18, 1782, in *The Diplomatic Correspondence of the American Revolution*, ed. Jared Sparks (Boston: Nathan Hale and Gray and Bowen, 1830), 12:119, 120.

28. *Journals of the Continental Congress*, vol. 22 (Feb. 27, 1782), 102–103.

29. Ibid., vol. 22 (Feb. 20, 1782), 83, 84.

30. Diary entry, Sept. 2, 1782, in *Papers of Robert Morris*, 6:293.

31. Robert Morris to Alexander Hamilton, Aug. 28, 1782, in ibid., 270.

32. Diary entry, Oct. 23, 1782, in ibid., 647.

33. Robert Morris to James Lovell, Dec. 17, 1782, in ibid., 7:212 n. 3.

34. Robert Morris to the President of Delaware (John Dickinson), Aug. 15, 1782, in ibid., 6:214; Robert Morris to Governor of Rhode Island (William Greene), Oct. 21, 1782, in ibid., 643–644; Governor of Maryland (William Paca) to Robert Morris, Apr. 4, 1783, in ibid., 7:672–673.

35. G. Alan Tarr, *Understanding State Constitutions* (Princeton, NJ: Princeton University Press, 2000), 86–87.

36. Delaware Constitution of 1776, in *The Federal and State Constitutions, Colonial Charters, and Other Organic Laws of the States, Territories, and Colonies Now or Heretofore Forming the United States of America*, ed. Francis Newton Thorpe (Washington, DC: GPO, 1909), 2:563–564; Pennsylvania Constitution of 1776, in ibid., 5:3086; South Carolina Constitution of 1776, in ibid., 6:3243, 3247; Virginia Constitution of 1776, in ibid., 7:3817–3818; Georgia Constitution of 1777, in ibid., 1:781; New Jersey Constitution of 1776, in ibid., 5:2596–2598; North Carolina Constitution of 1776, in ibid., 5:2792–2793; Maryland Constitution of 1776, in ibid., 2:1693, 1698–1699.

37. Michaelsen, *Creating the American Presidency*, 12.

38. New York Constitution of 1777, in *Federal and State Constitutions*, 5:2633–2634; Wood, *Creation of the American Republic*, 433; Tarr, *Understanding State Constitutions*, 87.

39. The Council of Appointments consisted of the governor and four senators elected by the New York Assembly. New York Constitution of 1777, in *Federal and State Constitutions*, 5:2633.

40. James Madison declared in the *Federalist Papers* that in New York's "council of appointment, members of the legislative are associated with the executive authority in the appointment of officers both executive and judiciary." *Federalist* No. 47, in *The Federalist*, ed. Terence Ball (Cambridge: Cambridge University Press, 2003), 238.

41. Michaelsen, *Creating the American Presidency*, 16.

42. *Federalist* No. 77, in *The Federalist*, 374. See also Jabez D. Hammond, *The History of Political Parties in the States of New York*, 3rd ed. (Cooperstown, NY: H. and E. Phinney, 1844), 1:32.

43. Evan Cornog, *The Birth of Empire: DeWitt Clinton and the American Experience, 1769–1828* (New York: Oxford University Press, 2000), 37.

44. The first case involved a 1794 challenge to Republican governor George Clinton by Federalist senators. In 1800, the roles were reversed, with Republican senators going against Federalist governor John Jay. Walter Stahr, *John Jay: Founding Father* (New York: Hambledon and London, 2005), 350–353; Howard Lee McBain, "DeWitt Clinton and the Origin of the Spoils System in New York" (Ph.D. diss., Columbia University, 1907), 33–38, 75–96; Hammond, *History of Political Parties in New York*, 1:83–86; John Bach McMaster, "The Political Depravity of the Fathers," *Atlantic Monthly* 75 (May 1895): 630.

45. The Council of Appointments continued to exist until a subsequent constitutional revision in 1821. Ellen M. Gibson and William H. Manz, *New York Research Guide* (Buffalo, NY: William S. Hein, 2004), 11.

46. Massachusetts Constitution of 1780, in *Federal and State Constitutions*, 3:1902. According to Ronald M. Peters, the "Council was to be an advisory body to the governor. Nine members from those elected to be senators were chosen to sit on the Council by joint ballot of the Senate and House." Ronald M. Peters, *The Massachusetts Constitution of 1780: A Social Compact* (Amherst: University of Massachusetts Press, 1978), 61.

47. New Hampshire Constitution of 1784, in *Federal and State Constitutions*, 3:2464.

48. Wood, *Creation of the American Republic*, 435.

49. Max Farrand, ed., *Records of the Federal Convention of 1787*, rev. ed. (New Haven, CT: Yale University Press, 1966), 1:21, 116, 119, 120, 128.

50. Ibid., 224 (see also 232 n. 12), 232–233, 244.

51. Ibid., 2:41, 42.

52. Ibid., 42–43.

53. Ibid., 45.

54. Ibid., 80–81.

55. Ibid., 81.

56. Ibid., 82.

57. Ibid., 83.

58. Members of the Committee of Detail included John Rutledge (chair), Edmund Randolph, Nathaniel Ghorum, Oliver Ellsworth, and James Wilson. Ibid., 106.

59. Ibid., 538, 539. On Sept. 8, 1787, the delegates appointed a committee to revise and arrange the articles for stylistic purposes (known as the Committee of Style). The committee consisted of Samuel Johnson (chair), Alexander Hamilton, Gouverneur Morris, James Madison, and Rufus King. Four days later, the committee reported its draft; a few changes were made, and on Sept. 17, the convention accepted the newly created Constitution. Ibid., 554–667.

60. New York Convention debates, in *The Debates in the Several State Conventions of the Adoption of the Federal Constitution*, ed. Jonathan Elliot (Washington, DC: J. B. Lippincott, 1836), 2:408.

61. North Carolina Convention debates, in ibid., 4:110.

62. Pennsylvania Convention debates, in ibid., 2:466, 480.

63. North Carolina Convention debates, in ibid., 4:46.

64. Ibid., 116.

65. Ibid., 131–132.

66. Ibid., 134.

67. *Federalist* No. 66, in *The Federalist*, 325 (emphasis in original).

68. *Federalist* No. 76, in ibid., 371.

69. Ibid.

70. *Federalist* No. 77, in ibid., 373–374 (emphasis in original).

71. John C. Miller, *Alexander Hamilton: Portrait in Paradox* (New York: Harper-Collins, 1959), 164–168.

72. John Adams to Roger Sherman, July 17, 1789, in *The Works of John Adams,* ed. Charles Francis Adams (Boston: Little, Brown, 1854), 6:427–436.

73. Roger Sherman to John Adams, July 20, 1789, in ibid., 440. Sherman served on the committee that drafted the Declaration of Independence and was also a delegate to the Constitutional Convention.

Chapter 2. Establishing the Pre-nomination Process
(1789–1829)

1. The source of this attitude is the 1803 statement by Chief Justice John Marshall: "It is emphatically the province and duty of the judicial department to say what the law is." *Marbury v. Madison*, 5 U.S. (1 Cranch) 137, 177 (1803).

2. Nor is it likely that the judicial branch will ever address such a case, for various reasons, including threshold concerns and prudential interests of the courts.

3. Michael J. Gerhardt, *The Federal Appointments Process: A Constitutional and Historical Analysis* (Durham, NC: Duke University Press, 2000), 31.

4. *Annals of Congress*, 1st Cong., 1st sess., vol. 1 (May 19, 1789), 393, 395.

5. Harold W. Chase, *Federal Judges: The Appointing Process* (Minneapolis: University of Minnesota Press, 1972), 6.

6. In particular, senators influenced the interpretation of basic constitutional maxims, such as separation of powers and checks and balances, implicit in the pre-nomination and appointment process.

7. President Washington submitted 111 nominations to the Senate for the positions of collector, naval officer, and surveyor. *Journal of the Executive Proceedings of the Senate,* 1st Cong., 1st sess., vol. 1 (Aug. 3, 1789), 9–11.

8. Ibid. (Aug. 3 and 4, 1789), 12–15; (Aug. 5, 1798), 16.

9. Thomas Hart Benton, *Abridgment of the Debates of Congress, from 1789 to 1856* (New York: D. Appleton, 1857–1861), 1:17; Joseph P. Harris, *The Advice and Consent of the Senate* (Berkeley: University of California Press, 1953), 27, 40–41, 216–217; William S. White, *Citadel: The Story of the U.S. Senate,* 2nd ed. (New York: Harper, 1957), 46–47; George H. Haynes, *The Senate of the United States: Its History and Practice* (1938; reprint, New York: Russell & Russell, 1960), 2:736–737; Henry J. Abraham, *Justices, Presidents, and Senators,* 4th ed.(Lanham, MD: Rowman and Littlefield, 1999), 19; Gerhardt, *The Federal Appointments Process,* 63–64.

10. Political scientist James Hart states that no contemporary scholar has substantiated the reason for the Senate's rejection. James Hart, *The American Presidency in Action, 1789: A Constitutional History* (New York: Macmillan, 1948), 124.

11. Benton, *Abridgment of Debates,* 1:17.

12. Lachlan McIntosh to George Washington, Feb. 14, 1789, in *The Papers of George Washington,* ed. W. W. Abbot, Presidential Series (Charlottesville: University Press of Virginia, 1987), 1:307.

13. Anthony Wayne to George Washington, May 10, 1789, in ibid., 2:262; McIntosh to Washington, Feb. 14, 1789, in ibid., 1:307.

14. Certificate from B. Fishbourn (Aug. 27, 1789), *Daily Advertiser,* Sept. 18, 1789, 1; Anthony Wayne to George Washington, May 10, 1789, in *Papers of George Washington,* 2:262; John Berrien to George Washington, May 10, 1789, in ibid., 252.

15. James Seagrove to Samuel Blachley Webb, Feb. 22, 1789, in *Correspondence and Journals of Samuel Blachley Webb, 1783–1806,* ed. Worthington C. Ford (Lancaster, PA: Wickersham Press, 1893), 3:123.

16. The collector position had originally been a state post. With ratification of the Constitution, however, the position was transferred to the federal government, and the various functions of the collector were divided into three new federal positions: collector, naval officer, and surveyor.

17. Habersham served in the Continental army and was a delegate to the Continental Congress, along with Senators Gunn and Few. See Francis B. Heitman, *Historical Register of Officers of the Continental Army during the War of the Revolution* (Washington, DC: Rare Book Shop Publishing Co., 1914), 265; Allen D. Candler and Clement A. Evans, eds., *Georgia* (Atlanta: State Historical Association, 1906), 1:483. Major John Berrien served in the Continental army and fought at Valley Forge. His father's New Jersey home was General Washington's military headquarters and was where Washington wrote his farewell address to the army. Berrien's son, John McPherson Berrien, would serve as U.S. senator from Georgia (1825–1829) and then as attorney general under President Andrew Jackson (1829–1831). See William Berrien Burroughs, "John MacPherson Berrien," in *Men of Mark in Georgia*, ed. William J. Northern (Atlanta: A. B. Caldwell, 1910), 2:140; George White, *Historical Collections of Georgia*, 3rd ed. (New York: Pudney and Russell, 1855), 371–374.

18. *Executive Proceedings*, 1st Cong., 1 sess., vol. 1 (Aug. 4, 1789), 15.

19. It should be noted that Senator Gunn served in the same regiment as Fishbourn during the Revolutionary War. See Charles C. Jones Jr., *The Life and Services of the Honorable Maj. Gen. Samuel Elbert* (Cambridge: Riverside Press, 1887), 45.

20. George Washington to the United States Senate, Aug. 6, 1789, in *Papers of George Washington*, 3:393; Terry Golway, *Washington's General: Nathanael Greene and the Triumph of the American Revolution* (New York: Henry Holt, 2005), 311–312; George W. Greene, *The Life of Nathanael Greene*, ed. W. Gilmore Simms (New York: George F. Cooledge and Bro., 1849), 351–353.

21. Extract of a letter from a friend in New York to his friend in this place, *Georgia Gazette*, Aug. 10, 1789 (Serial and Government Publications Division, Library of Congress).

22. Anthony Wayne to George Washington, Aug. 30, 1789, in *Papers of George Washington*, 3:569.

23. Benjamin Lear stated that he "received [this anecdote] from one who enjoyed Gen. Washington's most intimate friendship [his father] & to whom the Gen. Immediately on his return from the Senate Chamber, expressed his very great regret for having gone there." Stephen Decatur Jr., *Private Affairs of George Washington: From the Records and Accounts of Tobias Lear, Esquire, His Secretary* (New York: Da Capo Press, 1969), 59.

24. *Executive Proceedings*, 1st Cong., 1st sess., vol. 1 (Aug. 7, 1789), 16.

25. George Washington to James Madison, Aug. 9, 1789, in *The Writings of George Washington*, ed. Worthington C. Ford (New York: Knickerbocker Press, 1891), 11:416 (footnote).

26. "Sentiments Expressed to the Senate Committee on the Mode of Communication between the President and the Senate on Treaties and Nominations," in *The Writings of George Washington*, ed. John C. Fitzpatrick (Washington, DC: GPO, 1939), 30:374.

27. Washington to Madison, Aug. 9, 1789, in *Writings of George Washington*, ed. Ford, 11:375.

28. Washington stated, "It seems incidental to this relation between them, that not only the time but the place and manner of consultation should be with the President." "Sentiments Expressed to the Senate Committee at a Second Conference on the Mode of Communication between the President and the Senate on Treaties and Nominations," in *Writings of George Washington*, ed. Ford, 11:377.

29. Ibid., 378–379.

30. *Executive Proceedings,* 1st Cong., 1st sess., vol. 1 (Aug. 21, 1789), 19.

31. There has been only one exception to this practice. In 1921, directly after his inauguration ceremony, President Warren Harding went to the Senate chamber and submitted, in person, nominations for his cabinet. Haynes, *Senate,* 2:724.

32. *Executive Proceedings,* 1st Cong., 1st sess., vol. 1 (Feb. 9, 1790), 38.

33. Willis P. Whichard, *Justice James Iredell* (Durham, NC: Carolina Academic Press, 2000), 91.

34. *Life and Correspondence of James Iredell,* ed. Griffith J. McRee (New York: Peter Smith, 1949), 2:279–280.

35. *Executive Proceedings,* 1st Cong., 1st sess., vol. 1 (Feb. 10, 1790), 40.

36. *Journal of William Maclay,* ed. Edgar S. Maclay (New York: D. Appleton, 1890), 282.

37. George Washington to Mary Katherine Goddard, Jan. 6, 1790, in *Writings of George Washington,* ed. Fitzpatrick, 30:490.

38. Leonard D. White, *The Federalists: A Study in Administrative History, 1789–1801* (New York: Macmillan, 1948), 30, 31. See also Wayne E. Fuller, *The American Mail: Enlarger of the Common Life* (Chicago: University of Chicago Press, 1972), 282–283.

39. George Washington to Edmund Randolph, Nov. 30, 1789, in *Writings of George Washington,* ed. Fitzpatrick, 30:472.

40. George Washington to George Clinton, Mar. 6, 1792, in ibid., 31:497; George Washington to Alexander Hamilton, June 30, 1794, in ibid., 33:418; George Washington to James McHenry, Nov. 30, 1789, in ibid., 30:470–471; George Washington to James McHenry, Aug. 13, 1792, in *Papers of George Washington,* 10:655; George Washington to James McHenry, Aug. 28, 1793, in *Writings of George Washington,* ed. Fitzpatrick, 33:72; George Washington to Thomas Johnson, Mar. 6, 1795, in ibid., 34:133.

41. Alexander Martin to George Washington, Feb. 27, 1790, in *Papers of George Washington,* 5:183.

42. James Seagrove to Samuel Blachley Webb, Jan. 2, 1789, in *Correspondence and Journals of Samuel Blachley Webb,* 3:121–124 (emphasis added).

43. Levinus Clarkson to George Washington, Apr. 6, 1789, in *Papers of George Washington,* 2:26.

44. Andrew Porter to George Washington, Aug. 24, 1789, in ibid., 3:534.

45. Edward Tilghman to George Read, Sept. 21, 1789, in *Life and Correspondence of George Read,* ed. William Thompson Read (Philadelphia: J. B. Lippincott, 1870), 488; Christopher Gore to Rufus King, Sept. 13, 1789, in *The Life and Correspondence of Rufus King,* ed. Charles King (New York: G. P. Putnam, 1894), 1:368; John Parker to George Washington, Sept. 12, 1789, in *Papers of George Washington,* 4:22–23; Paul Allen to George Washington, June 18, 1790, in ibid., 5:531–532.

46. Samuel Johnston to James Iredell, Feb. 1, 1790, in *Life and Correspondence of James Iredell,* 2:281.

47. George Washington to Richard Henry Lee, Aug. 2, 1789, in *Papers of George Washington,* 3:370–371.

48. William Maclay to George Washington, July 20, 1789, in ibid., 247–248.

49. Gaillard Hunt, "Office-Seeking during Washington's Administration," *American Historical Review* 1 (Jan. 1896): 272–274.

50. Roy Swanstrom, *A Dissertation on the Fourteen Years of the Upper Legislative Body,* S. Doc. 99-19, 99th Cong., 1st sess. (Washington, DC: GPO, 1985), 94.

51. Stuart Eric Leibiger, *Founding Friendship: George Washington, James Madison, and the Creation of the Republic* (Charlottesville: University Press of Virginia, 2001), 114; Ralph Ketcham, *James Madison: A Biography* (Charlottesville: University Press of Virginia, 1990), 286–289; George Washington to James Madison, Aug. 1789, in *Writings of George Washington,* ed. Fitzpatrick, 30:393.

52. Hugh Williamson to George Washington, Feb. 5, 1790, in *Papers of George Washington*, 5:98–99; Hugh Williamson to George Washington, Mar. 22, 1790, in ibid., 268–269.

53. Memorandum of Thomas Jefferson, June 7, 1790, in ibid., 5:486–487.

54. George Washington to Thomas Pickering, Sept. 17, 1795, in *Writings of George Washington*, ed. Ford, 12:107. See also Hunt, "Office-Seeking during Washington's Administration," 282.

55. Adams would write: "It is well known that there are continued interviews between the members of the Senate and the members of the House, and the heads of departments. Eternal solicitations for nominations to office are made in this manner." Letter in the *Boston Patriot*, in *The Works of John Adams*, ed. Charles Francis Adams (Boston: Little, Brown, 1854), 9:272.

56. Gilbert Chinard, *Honest John Adams* (Boston: Little, Brown, 1964), 261; John E. Ferling, *John Adams: A Life* (New York: Henry Holt, 1996), 333–334. Adams removed twenty-one officeholders, compared with Washington's seventeen. Carl Russell Fish, "Removal of Officials by the Presidents of the United States," in *American Historical Association Reports* (Washington, DC: GPO, 1900), 2:84.

57. For evidence of people soliciting offices from members of Congress, see James Polk to Alexander Martin, Nov. 11, 1798; James Polk to Timothy Bloodworth, Mar. 11, 1798; David Barnes to Theodore Foster, Mar. 27, 1797; Caleb P. Bennett to Henry Satemen, Feb. 26, 1797; and Maxwell Bines to Henry Satemen, Feb. 8, 1797; all in General Records of the Department of State, RG 59, National Archives Microfilm Publication M406, roll 1, NARA. As White explained: "None of the leading Federalists, however, sought to make room for party adherents by removing officials and employees whose political reliability had become uncertain." White, *The Federalists*, 278.

58. See Samuel Livermore to John Adams, May 30, 1798, and James Gunn to John Adams, Mar. 27, 1797, in RG 59, M406, roll 1, NARA.

59. Swanstrom, *Dissertation on the Fourteen Years*, 109. See also White, *The Federalists*, 85.

60. James Hillhouse to Oliver Wolcott, Feb. 19, 1801, in *Memoirs of the Administrations of Washington and John Adams*, ed. George Gibbs (New York: B. Franklin, 1971), 2:493–494.

61. John Adams to Benjamin Adams, Apr. 22, 1799, in *Works of John Adams*, 8:636.

62. *Executive Proceedings*, 5th Cong., 2nd sess., vol. 1 (June 30, 1798), 283; John Adams to Benjamin Adams, Apr. 22, 1799, in *Works of John Adams*, 8:636.

63. Besides Congress, Adams had to contend with a power struggle within his own cabinet. "I soon found that if I had not the previous consent of the heads of departments, and the approbation of Mr. [Alexander] Hamilton, I run the utmost risk of a dead negative in the Senate." Letter in the *Boston Patriot*, in *Works of John Adams*, 9:272.

64. White, *The Federalists*, 83.

65. George Washington to James McHenry, Oct. 21, 1798, in *Writings of George Washington*, ed. Fitzpatrick, 36:504–505 (emphasis in original).

66. George Washington to Henry Knox, Mar. 25, 1799, in ibid., 37:160–161 (emphasis in original).

67. Noble E. Cunningham Jr., *The Jeffersonian Republicans: The Formation of Party Organization, 1789–1801* (Chapel Hill: University of North Carolina Press, 1957), 87–115; Richard Hofstadter, *Idea of a Party System: The Rise of Legitimate Opposition in the United States, 1780–1840* (Berkeley: University of California Press, 1969), 74–121. See also Matthew Q. Dawson, *Partisanship and the Birth of America's Second Party, 1796–1800* (Westport, CT: Greenwood Press, 2000).

68. Gaillard Hunt, "Office-Seeking during the Administration of John Adams," *American Historical Review* 2 (Jan. 1897): 242, 254. See also White, *The Federalists*, 271–278.

69. For further reading on the 1801 Judiciary Act, see Richard Ellis, *The Jeffersonian Crisis: Courts and Politics in the Young Republic* (New York: Oxford University Press, 1971); Kathryn Turner, "Federalist Policy and the Judiciary Act of 1801," *William and Mary Quarterly* 22 (Jan. 1965): 3–32.

70. Henry Adams, *History of the United States of America during the Administration of Thomas Jefferson* (New York: Library of America, 1986), 187.

71. Hunt, "Office-Seeking during the Administration of John Adams," 242. Years later, Jefferson would call Adams's late-term nominations "midnight appointments." Thomas Jefferson to William Johnson, June 12, 1823, in *The Writings of Thomas Jefferson*, ed. Andrew A. Lipscomb and Albert E. Bergh (Washington, DC: Thomas Jefferson Memorial Association, 1905), 15:447. It should be noted that a number of these appointments were not judicial, and the Senate approved many nominations in the final days of the administration that had been "made earlier and not yet confirmed." Page Smith, *John Adams, 1784–1826* (Garden City, NY: Doubleday, 1962), 2:1065.

72. George Washington to Thomas Pickering, Sept. 17, 1795, in *Writings of George Washington*, ed. Ford, 12:107.

73. Howard Lee McBain, "DeWitt Clinton and the Origin of the Spoils System in New York" (Ph.D. diss., Columbia University, 1907), 64.

74. One party scholar declared that the election indicated "that political parties had come of age." Cunningham, *Jeffersonian Republicans*, 248. For more information, see Susan Dunn, *Jefferson's Second Revolution: The Election Crisis of 1800 and the Triumph of Republicanism* (New York: Houghton Mifflin, 2004); John E. Ferling, *Adams vs. Jefferson: The Tumultuous Election of 1800* (New York: Oxford University Press, 2004).

75. Edward Channing, *The Jeffersonian System, 1801–1811* (New York: Greenwood Press, 1969), 11.

76. Carl E. Prince, "The Passing of the Aristocracy: Jefferson's Removal of the Federalists, 1801–1805," *Journal of American History* 57 (Dec. 1970): 565.

77. Lance Banning, *The Jeffersonian Persuasion: Evolution of Party Ideology* (Ithaca, NY: Cornell University Press, 1983), 288.

78. Thomas Jefferson to Benjamin Rush, Mar. 24, 1801, in *The Works of Thomas Jefferson*, ed. Paul Leicester Ford (New York: Knickerbocker Press, 1905), 9:230.

79. Thomas Jefferson to Benjamin Hawkins, Feb. 18, 1803, in ibid., 446.

80. Dumas Malone, *Jefferson the President, First Term 1801–1805* (Boston: Little, Brown, 1970), 4:70.

81. Jefferson removed 106 officeholders. Fish, "Removal of Officials," 84; Malone, *Jefferson*, 4:117–135; Smith, *John Adams*, 1089. For additional information on the repeal of the 1801 Judiciary Act, see William S. Carpenter, "Repeal of the Judiciary Act of 1801," *American Political Science Review* 9 (Aug. 1915): 519–528.

82. During Washington's administration, Jefferson had sought to place the Post Office Department under the president's direction. White, *The Federalists*, 226.

83. Thomas Jefferson to Gideon Granger, Mar. 29, 1801, in *Works of Thomas Jefferson*, 9:244–245. Jefferson would later write: "At present the President has some controul over those appointments by his authority over the Postmaster himself." Thomas Jefferson to James Madison, Mar. 10, 1814, in ibid., 11:392.

84. "I view [the Post Office Department] as a source of boundless patronage to the executive, jobbing to members of Congress and their friends, and a bottomless abyss of public money." Thomas Jefferson to James Madison, Mar. 6, 1796, in ibid., 8:226. Evidence suggests that Jefferson did not personally review postal

appointments. Thomas Jefferson to Thomas McKean, Feb. 19, 1803, in ibid., 9:451; Thomas Jefferson to James Madison, Mar. 10, 1814, in ibid., 11:392.

85. Jefferson to Madison, Mar. 10, 1814, in ibid., 11:392.

86. This control was subject to the advice and consent of the Senate and limited to a certain category of appointments. See the sections on James Madison and James Monroe in this chapter and the section on Andrew Jackson in chapter 3.

87. Ronald P. Formisano, "Deferential-Participant Politics: The Early Republic's Political Culture, 1789–1840," *American Political Science Review* 68 (June 1974): 479.

88. Thomas Jefferson to Charles Pinckney, Mar. 6, 1801, in *Works of Thomas Jefferson*, 9:200.

89. Thomas Jefferson to Theodore Foster, May 9, 1801, in ibid., 252, 253.

90. Thomas Jefferson to Nathaniel Macon, May 14, 1801, in ibid., 9:253. It appears that most of the federal appointments to North Carolina were made by Macon. William E. Dodd, *The Life of Nathaniel Macon* (Raleigh, NC: Edwards and Broughton, 1903), 169.

91. Marty D. Matthews, *Forgotten Founder: The Life and Times of Charles Pinckney* (Columbia: University of South Carolina Press, 2004), 97; William E. Foster, "Sketch of the Life and Services of Theodore Foster," *Collections of the Rhode Island Historical Society* 7 (1885): 111–134; Dodd, *Life of Nathaniel Macon,* xiii, 71.

92. Ketcham, *James Madison,* 468–469. Madison defeated Federalist Charles Pinckney in the electoral college by a vote of 122 to 47. Robert Brent Mosher, *Executive Register of the United States, 1789–1902* (Washington, DC: GPO, 1905), 76.

93. Robert Allen Rutland, *The Democrats: From Jefferson to Clinton* (Columbia: University of Missouri Press, 1995), 38.

94. Fish, "Removal of Officials," 84.

95. James Madison to Edmund Randolph, May 31, 1789, in *The Writings of James Madison,* ed. Gaillard Hunt (New York: Knickerbocker Press, 1904), 5:373.

96. James Madison to James Monroe, Sept. 24, 1822, in ibid., 9:111–112.

97. Carl Russell Fish, *The Civil Service and the Patronage* (Cambridge, MA: Harvard University Press, 1904), 56.

98. Ketcham, *James Madison,* 481–482; Henry Adams, *History of the United States during the Second Administration of Madison, 1813–1817* (New York: Scribner, 1891), 1:39.

99. Ketcham, *James Madison,* 482. One scholar noted that Smith's "abilities were so unequal to the position that Madison was obliged himself to perform the most important duties of the office." John P. Gordy, *Political History of the United States: With Special Reference to the Growth of Political Parties* (New York: Henry Holt, 1902), 2:12.

100. *Executive Proceedings,* 12th Cong., 2nd sess., vol. 2 (July 6, 1813), 382.

101. Harris, *Advice and Consent,* 50.

102. Albert Gallatin to James Madison, Jan. 25, 1813, in *The Papers of James Madison,* Presidential Series, ed. Robert A. Rutland (Charlottesville: University Press of Virginia, 2004), 5:619–620. In fact, there was almost no difference between the list Gallatin provided to Madison and the one submitted to the Senate. *Executive Proceedings,* 12th Cong., 2nd sess., vol. 2 (Jan. 27, 1813), 318.

103. Irving Brant, *James Madison: Commander in Chief, 1812–1836* (New York: Bobbs-Merrill, 1961), 243; Ketcham, *James Madison,* 569. This was not Granger's first transgression. The postmaster general had supported De Witt Clinton in the 1808 presidential election and had used his appointments to build his own political base. Caleb Atwater to James Madison, Dec. 20, 1809, in *The Papers of James Madison,* Secretary of State Series, ed. Robert J. Brugger et al. (Charlottesville: University Press of Virginia, 1992), 2:138–139; Evan Cornog, *The Birth of Empire: DeWitt Clinton and the American Experience, 1769–1828* (New York: Oxford University Press, 2000), 96, 133; John K. Mahon, *The War of 1812* (New York: Da Capo Press, 1991), 334.

104. Adams, *History of the United States during the Second Administration of Madison*, 1:400.

105. *Executive Proceedings*, 13th Cong., 2nd sess., vol. 2 (Feb. 25, 1814), 499; Mosher, *Executive Register*, 85; diary entry, Jan. 5, 1822, in *Memoirs of John Quincy Adams*, ed. Charles Francis Adams (Philadelphia: J. B. Lippincott, 1875), 5:481; Ketcham, *James Madison*, 569. For an account of the dismissal, see Brant, *James Madison*, 243.

106. Monroe defeated Federalist Rufus King by a vote of 183 to 34 in the electoral college. Mosher, *Executive Register*, 88. During the election, King remarked: "So certain is the [election] result, in the opinion of friends of the measure, that no pains are taken to excite the community on the subject. . . . In no preceding Election has there been such a calm respecting it." Noble E. Cunningham Jr., *The Presidency of James Monroe* (Lawrence: University Press of Kansas, 1996), 19. This period has been referred to as the "era of good feelings." See George Dangerfield, *The Era of Good Feelings* (New York: Harcourt, Brace, 1952).

107. Ralph Ketcham, *Presidents above Party: The First American Presidency, 1789–1829* (Chapel Hill: University of North Carolina Press, 1984), 124.

108. Diary entry, June 23, 1820, in *Memoirs of John Quincy Adams*, 5:158.

109. Fish, "Removal of Officials," 84.

110. Henry J. Abraham wrote: "Monroe was a good Democrat-Republican, but . . . it was widely doubted that he would be more than casually concerned with a nominee's party loyalty." Abraham, *Justices, Presidents, and Senators*, 68.

111. "The Autobiography of Martin Van Buren," in *Annual Report of the American Historical Association for the Year 1918*, ed. John C. Fitzpatrick (Washington, DC: GPO, 1920), 2:124. For more information on Van Buren's reaction to Monroe's fusion policy, see Hofstadter, *Idea of a Party System*, 226–231.

112. Rutland, *The Democrats*, 44, 49.

113. Albany postmaster Solomon Southwick had been removed for "defalcation." "Autobiography of Van Buren," 125; "New Appointment," *Connecticut Courant*, Jan. 22, 1822, 2.

114. DeWitt Clinton to Solomon Van Rensselaer, Dec. 25, 1821, in Catharina Van Rensselaer Bonney, *Legacy of Historical Gleanings*, 2nd ed. (Albany, NY: J. Munsell, 1875), 1:369; John Niven, *Martin Van Buren: The Romantic Age of American Politics* (Newtown, CT: American Political Biography Press, 2000), 111. During the 1810s, the New York Republicans divided into a number of factions. The Bucktails, headed by Martin Van Buren, were the liberal element of the Jeffersonian tradition, with a states' rights platform as their core value. They established the first true political organization, which was called the Albany Regency. The Regency was a top-down organization made up of a small group of leaders who coordinated a large system of clubs throughout the state to instill party discipline. For political strength, the group relied on patronage and press support. Members of the Regency included Benjamin F. Butler, Azariah C. Flagg, John A. Dix, William L. Marcy, and Silas Wright. See Robert V. Remini, "The Albany Regency," *New York History* 39 (Jan. 1958): 341–355; Peter W. Colby, *New York State Today: Politics, Government, Public Policy* (Albany, NY: SUNY Press, 1989), 55; David B. Cole, *Martin Van Buren and the American Political System* (Princeton, NJ: Princeton University Press, 1984), 82; Michael F. Holt, *Political Parties and American Political Development: From the Age of Jackson to the Age of Lincoln* (Baton Rouge: Louisiana State University Press, 1992), 37.

115. The petition was signed by twenty-two of the twenty-eight New York representatives to Congress. Jonathan Meigs Jr. to Rufus King and Martin Van Buren, Jan. 4, 1822, in Martin Van Buren Papers (MVBP), reel 5, Library of Congress, Manuscript Reading Room; Bonney, *Legacy of Historical Gleanings*, 1:372; diary entry, Jan. 4, 1822, in *Memoirs of John Quincy Adams*, 5:479.

116. Diary entry, Jan. 4, 1822, in *Memoirs of John Quincy Adams*, 5:479.

117. It appears that Federalist Rufus King sided against Van Rensselaer because Van Buren had supported King in his last election to the Senate. Jabez D. Hammond, *The History of Political Parties in the State of New York*, 3rd ed.(Cooperstown, NY: H. and E. Phinney, 1844), 2:96; Bonney, *Legacy of Historical Gleanings*, 1:395. Rufus King and Martin Van Buren to Jonathan Meigs Jr., Jan. 3, 1822, in MVBP, reel 5; Jonathan Meigs Jr. to Rufus King and Martin Van Buren, Jan. 4, 1822, in ibid.; Niven, *Van Buren*, 112; Daniel Tompkins, Rufus King, and Martin Van Buren to Jonathan Meigs Jr., Jan. 4, 1822, in MVBP, reel 5.

118. Diary entry, Jan. 5, 1822, in *Memoirs of John Quincy Adams*, 5:480.

119. James Monroe to Martin Van Buren, Jan. 7, 1822, in MVBP, reel 5; Harry Ammon, *James Monroe: The Quest for National Identity* (Charlottesville: University of Virginia Press, 1990), 497. In contrast, Secretary of State Adams thought that the power to remove the postmaster general gave Monroe sufficient authority over him. Diary entry, Jan. 5, 1822, in *Memoirs of John Quincy Adams*, 5:481.

120. Jonathan Meigs Jr. to Daniel Tompkins, Rufus King, and Martin Van Buren, Jan. 4, 1822; Jonathan Meigs Jr. to Daniel Tompkins and Martin Van Buren, Jan. 8, 1822; Michael Ulshoeffer to Martin Van Buren, Jan. 13, 1822, all in MVBP, reel 5.

121. Diary entry, Jan. 5. 1822, in *Memoirs of John Quincy Adams*, 5:482.

122. In fact, while in the Senate, Monroe "had recommended that all the Postmasters whose salaries amounted to two thousand dollars should be appointed by nomination to the Senate." Ibid.

123. James Monroe, State of the Union, Dec. 2, 1823, in *The Writings of James Monroe*, ed. Stanislaus Murray Hamilton (New York: Knickerbocker Press, 1903), 6:336.

124. Ninian Edwards to James Monroe, Dec. 22, 1820, in *The Edwards Papers*, ed. E. B. Washburne (Chicago: Fergus Printing Company, 1884), 3:166–176; Ninian Edwards to William H. Crawford, Jan. 11, 1821, in ibid., 181–185.

125. Ketcham noted, "In an irony as bitter to Monroe as it would have been to his predecessors, the very demise of open party opposition had surrounded him with a factionalism within his 'amalgamated' party perhaps more intense and pathological than Jefferson or Madison ever faced from openly hostile Federalists." Ketcham, *Presidents above Party*, 129.

126. For examples of appointment requests during the Monroe administration, see Ethan Allan Brown to John Q. Adams, Dec. 23, 1825; Weldon N. Edwards to John Q. Adams, Jan. 3, 1823; William Logan to John Q. Adams, Apr. 19, 1820; Thomas Newton Jr. to James Monroe, Feb. 1, 1819; Thomas Newton Jr. to John Q. Adams, Apr. 1, 1818; John Rhea to John Q. Adams, Jan. 8, 1818, all in RG 59, M439, roll 1, NARA; Mahlon Dickerson and Lewis Condict to John Q. Adams, Jan. 17, 1822; Mahlon Dickerson to John Q. Adams, Feb. 25, 1819; Joseph Bloomfield to John Q. Adams, Feb. 23, 1819, all in ibid., roll 13.

127. Diary entry, Jan. 8, 1820, in *Memoirs of John Quincy Adams*, 4:497.

128. James Monroe to Thomas Jefferson, Mar. 22, 1824, in *Writings of James Monroe*, 7:11.

129. "Autobiography of Van Buren," 234.

130. *Executive Proceedings*, 17th Cong., 1st sess., vol. 3 (Feb. 20, 1822), 274.

131. *U.S. Statutes at Large*, 16th Cong., 1st sess., vol. 3 (May 15, 1820), 582.

132. Diary entry, Feb. 7, 1828, in *Memoirs of John Quincy Adams*, 7:424. W. P. Cresson states that Treasury Secretary William Crawford "initiated and fought for the passage of the law" because he had presidential aspirations. W. P. Cresson, *James Monroe* (Chapel Hill: University of North Carolina Press, 1928), 350. See also Ammon, *James Monroe*, 494–495.

133. Thomas Jefferson to James Madison, Nov. 29, 1820, in *Writings of Thomas Jefferson*, 15:294–295.

134. Leonard D. White, *The Jeffersonians: A Study in Administrative History, 1801–1829* (New York: Macmillan, 1951), 389.

135. Ammon, *James Monroe*, 495; Harris, *Advice and Consent*, 52; Ketcham, *Presidents above Party*, 126–127.

136. James Monroe to John McLean, Dec. 5, 1827, in *Writings of James Monroe,* 7:128.

137. Robert V. Remini explained: "By 1824 all semblance of unity, vigor and discipline within the [Republican] party had vanished." Robert V. Remini, *The Election of Andrew Jackson* (Philadelphia: J. B. Lippincott, 1963), 19.

138. Ketcham, *Presidents above Party*, 130.

139. For most of his political career, Adams considered himself a nonpartisan politician. See "John Quincy Adams, Nonpartisan Politician," in Daniel Walker Howe, *The Political Culture of the American Whigs* (Chicago: University of Chicago Press, 1979), 43–68.

140. Diary entry, Mar. 5, 1825, in *Memoirs of John Quincy Adams*, 6:520–521.

141. Fish, "Removal of Officials," 84.

142. Lester M. Dorman, "A Century of Civil Service," *Scribner's Monthly* 15 (Jan. 1878): 397. See also Leonard D. White, *The Jacksonians: A Study in Administrative History, 1829–1861* (New York: Macmillan, 1954), 300.

143. Diary entry, Dec. 4, 1828, in *Memoirs of John Quincy Adams*, 8:78–79.

144. Dorothy Ganfield Fowler, "Congressional Dictation of Local Appointments," *Journal of Politics* 7 (Feb. 1945): 34.

145. Diary entry, Mar. 18, 1820, in *Memoirs of John Quincy Adams*, 5:24.

146. As one author wrote: "He was soon made to realize the impracticability of disregarding the old lines of party." Josiah Quincy, *Memoir of the Life of John Quincy Adams* (Boston: Phillips, Sampson, 1859), 148.

147. For examples of appointment requests, see Alfred Powell to Henry Clay, Feb. 26, 1827; Clement Dorsey to Henry Clay, Apr. 3, 1826; John Barney to Henry Clay, Mar. 3, 1826, all in RG 59, M531, roll 1, NARA; Josiah Johnston to Henry Clay, Jan. 29, 1827, in ibid., M439, roll 1.

148. Samuel Flagg Bemis, *John Quincy Adams and the Union* (Norwalk, CT: Easton Press, 1984), 136.

149. Ibid., 137–138.

150. Cornog, *Birth of Empire*, 154.

151. Dangerfield, *Era of Good Feelings*, 347.

152. Ibid.

153. President Adams actually retained McLean as postmaster general from Monroe's cabinet, despite the fact that he had supported Jackson in the 1824 election. Robert V. Remini, *John Quincy Adams* (New York: Times Books, 2002), 76; John T. Morse Jr., *John Quincy Adams* (Boston: Houghton Mifflin, 1882), 206–207. McLean admitted that he had made appointments on the advice of Jacksonian representatives. For example, the Philadelphia postmaster, Richard Bache, was appointed at the request of Representative Samuel D. Ingham of Pennsylvania. James Schouler, *History of the United States of America: Under the Constitution, 1817–1831*, rev. ed. (New York: Dodd, Mead, 1917), 3:436; U.S. Post Office Department, *List of Post-Offices in the United States* (Washington, DC: Way and Gideon, 1828), 92. See also Richard R. John, *Spreading the News: The American Postal System from Franklin to Morse*, 2nd ed. (Cambridge, MA: Harvard University Press, 1998), 81–83.

154. Robert V. Remini, *Henry Clay: Statesman for the Union* (New York: Norton, 1993), 316.

155. It appears that this evidence was coming from Clay's political contacts. W. Tharp to Henry Clay, May 20, 1828, in *The Papers of Henry Clay*, ed. Robert Seager II et al. (Lexington: University Press of Kentucky, 1982), 7:312.

156. Diary entry, July 7, 1828, in *Memoirs of John Quincy Adams*, 8:51.

157. Nathan Sargent, *Public Men and Events* (Philadelphia: J. B. Lippincott, 1875), 1:166; Robert V. Remini, *Andrew Jackson* (Baltimore: Johns Hopkins University Press, 1998), 2:164–165; Edward Pessen, *Jacksonian America: Society, Personality, and Politics* (Urbana: University of Illinois Press, 1985), 315.

158. Remini, *John Quincy Adams*, 76.

159. Bennett Champ Clark, *John Quincy Adams: "Old Man Eloquent"* (Boston: Little, Brown, 1932), 251; John Spencer Bassett, *The Life of Andrew Jackson* (New York: Macmillan, 1931), 442; Quincy, *Memoir of the Life of John Quincy Adams*, 149.

160. Ketcham, *Presidents above Party*, 140.

161. Hofstadter, *Idea of a Party System*, 231. See also James E. Lewis Jr., *John Quincy Adams: Policymaker for the Union* (Wilmington, DE: Scholarly Resources, 2001), 102.

Chapter 3. The Spoils Era I (1829–1845)

1. For further reading about the second party system, see Richard P. McCormick, *The Second American Party System: Party Formation in the Jacksonian Era* (Chapel Hill: University of North Carolina Press, 1966).

2. Jackson defeated Adams by a vote of 178 to 83 in the electoral college. Robert Brent Mosher, *Executive Register of the United States, 1789–1902* (Washington, DC: GPO, 1905), 106.

3. James Parton, *Life of Andrew Jackson* (New York: Mason Brothers, 1860), 3:213–214.

4. Ralph Ketcham, *Presidents above Party: The First American Presidency, 1789–1829* (Chapel Hill: University of North Carolina Press, 1984), 154.

5. See the chapter titled "Jackson and Reform" in Robert V. Remini, *Andrew Jackson* (Baltimore: Johns Hopkins University Press, 1998), 3:116–142.

6. Andrew Jackson, inaugural address, Mar. 4, 1829, in *A Compilation of the Messages and Papers of the Presidents*, ed. James D. Richardson (New York: Bureau of National Literature, 1911), 2:1001 (emphasis in original).

7. John Spencer Bassett wrote: "So much was said about the abuse of the patronage during the campaign of 1828 that Jackson himself came to believe it and heard of election results with a grim determination to make changes." John Spencer Bassett, *The Life of Andrew Jackson* (New York: Macmillan, 1931), 445. Jackson's supporters helped perpetrate this belief. In New York, Samuel Swartwout told a friend: "No damn rascal who made use of an office or its profits for the purpose of keeping Mr. Adams in and General Jackson out of power is entitled to the least leniency save that of hanging." Claude G. Bowers, *The Party Battles of the Jackson Period* (New York: Houghton Mifflin, 1922), 69.

8. Jackson inaugural address, 2:1001.

9. As one historian noted, "one of the primary changes in American life during the years after the War of 1812 was the appearance of a new class of political leaders who had a greater commitment to a political party than a dominant ideal. Lacking the antipathy towards parties which characterized many of the Founding Fathers, the organizers of the Second Party System believed that the role political parties performed in integrating the nation and in fostering democracy more than compensated for evils such as the spoils system." Herbert Ershkowitz, "Samuel L. Southard: A Case Study of Whig Leadership in the Age of Jackson," *New Jersey History* 88 (spring 1970): 24.

10. Bassett, *Life of Andrew Jackson*, 443. The call for removals was coming not only from political leaders but from the people as well. As White explained: "the

old stability in officeholding was threatened by the voice of the people themselves. The demand for appointments grew apace, and local politicians did not hesitate to tell their successful partisans in places of authority what they expected. Rotation was imposed because it was demanded from below, not merely because it was advocated from above." Leonard D. White, *The Jacksonians: A Study in Administrative History, 1829–1861* (New York: Macmillan, 1954), 301.

11. Jackson wrote in his private journal that "every man who has been in office a few years, believes he has a life estate in [office], a vested right, and if it has been held twenty years or upwards, not only a vested right, but that it ought to descend to his children, and if no children then the next of kin. This is not the principles of our government. It is *rotation in office* that will perpetuate our liberty." Bassett, *Life of Andrew Jackson*, 447 (emphasis added). For an alternative view of Jackson's reform policy, see Erik McKinley Eriksson, "The Federal Civil Service under President Jackson," *Mississippi Valley Historical Society* 13 (Mar. 1927): 517–540.

12. *Journal of the Executive Proceedings of the Senate*, 21st Cong., 1st sess., vol. 4 (Jan. 5, 1830), 42; "Letter of Invitation from Logan," 1829, in *The Life of John J. Crittenden, with Selections from His Correspondence and Speeches*, ed. Chapman Coleman (Philadelphia: J. B. Lippincott, 1873), 1:77.

13. *Executive Proceedings*, 21st Cong., 1st sess., vol. 4 (Jan. 5, 1830), 42.

14. "Reform," *Connecticut Mirror*, June 6, 1829, 3.

15. Only 213 removals were made from Washington to Adams, compared with Jackson's 252 removals (this count does not include nonpresidential appointments). Carl Russell Fish, "Removal of Officials by the Presidents of the United States," in *American Historical Association Reports* (Washington, DC: GPO, 1900), 2:84.

16. Andrew Jackson to Martin Van Buren, Mar. 31, 1829, in *Correspondence of Andrew Jackson*, ed. John Spencer Bassett (Washington, DC: Carnegie Institution of Washington, 1929), 4:19 (emphasis in original).

17. Marquis James, *The Life of Andrew Jackson* (New York: Bobbs-Merrill, 1938), 499–500.

18. Andrew Jackson to Susan Decatur, Apr. 2, 1829, in *Correspondence of Andrew Jackson*, 4:22.

19. Ketcham, *Presidents above Party*, 150–154.

20. *Register of Debates in Congress*, 22nd Cong., 1st sess., vol. 8 (Jan. 25, 1832), 1326 (emphasis added).

21. White, *The Jacksonians*, 110–111.

22. Joseph P. Harris, *The Advice and Consent of the Senate* (Berkeley: University of California Press, 1953), 53–64. Nor was Congress high-minded when it came to appointments. The rotation-in-office principle instituted by Jackson was made possible by the 1820 Tenure of Office Act. See the section on Monroe in chapter 2.

23. *Executive Proceedings*, 21st Cong., 1st sess., vol. 4 (Jan. 14, 1830), 46. Tammany Hall was the Democratic machine element in New York City. Founded in 1786 as the Columbian Order of New York City, the organization ran the local government and controlled patronage through its ability to aid new immigrants and thus win their support in local elections. See Gustavus Myers, *The History of Tammany Hall* (New York: Boni and Liveright, 1917), 63, 76, 106; M. R. Werner, *Tammany Hall* (Garden City, NY: Garden City Publishing Company, 1932); E. J. Edwards, "Tammany," *McClure's Magazine* 4 (Apr. 1895): 445–454. For a detailed account of the power and prestige of the collector position in New York, see William Hartman, "The New York Custom House: Seat of Spoils Politics," *New York History* 34 (Apr. 1953): 149–163.

24. Bassett, *Life of Andrew Jackson*, 452. The vote was twenty-five to twenty-one, with both New York senators supporting confirmation. *Executive Proceedings*, 21st Cong., 1st sess., vol. 4 (Mar. 29, 1830), 84.

25. James Buchanan to Martin Van Buren, Mar. 28, 1831, in *The Works of James Buchanan*, ed. John Bassett Moore (Philadelphia: J. B. Lippincott, 1908), 2:171.

26. *Executive Proceedings*, 22nd Cong., 1st sess., vol. 4 (Dec. 7, 1831), 178.

27. The candidate was future Supreme Court justice Noah H. Swayne (he received the appointment). Andrew Jackson to Moses Dawson, July 17, 1830, in *Correspondence of Andrew Jackson*, 4:161.

28. Andrew Jackson to Martin Van Buren, Apr. 12 [?], 1831, in ibid., 263; *Executive Proceedings*, 22nd Cong., 1st sess., vol. 4 (Dec. 7, 1831), 177.

29. John M. Martin, "The Senatorial Career of Gabriel Moore," *Alabama Historical Quarterly* 26 (summer 1964): 249.

30. Andrew Jackson to John Coffee, Dec. 28, 1830, in *Correspondence of Andrew Jackson*, 4:215.

31. At the time, Moore was spreading rumors questioning "McKinley's loyalty to Jackson." Harriet E. Amos Doss, "The Rise and Fall of an Alabama Founding Father, Gabriel Moore," *Alabama Review* 53 (July 2000): 167. See also Andrew Jackson to John Coffee, Dec. 28, 1830, in *Correspondence of Andrew Jackson*, 4:216. Jackson's fears proved to be true. Moore challenged and won McKinley's seat in 1830. By 1832, Senator Moore was supporting John Calhoun's anti-Jackson stand and voted to reject Martin Van Buren as minister to Great Britain. Doss, "Rise and Fall," 167; Martin, "Senatorial Career of Gabriel Moore," 249.

32. Robert Y. Hayne to Andrew Jackson, Feb. 4, 1831, in *Correspondence of Andrew Jackson*, 4:238.

33. The nullification movement was based on the passage of the Tariff Act of 1828, which, most southerners believed, favored the North at the expense of the South. For more information, see Chauncey Samuel Boucher, *The Nullification Controversy in South Carolina* (Chicago: University of Chicago Press, 1916).

34. Andrew Jackson to Robert Y. Hayne, Feb. 8, 1831, in *Correspondence of Andrew Jackson*, 4:241.

35. Remini, *Andrew Jackson*, 3:101.

36. *Journal of the Senate*, 23rd Cong., 1st sess. (Mar. 28, 1834), 197.

37. Andrew Jackson to the Senate, Apr. 15, 1834, in *Messages and Papers of the Presidents*, 2:1291.

38. Ibid., 1298.

39. Ibid., 1298–1299.

40. For a good account of the whole banking controversy, see Remini, *Andrew Jackson*, 3:142–178.

41. *Journal of the Senate*, 23rd Cong., 2nd sess. (Mar. 3, 1835), 224–225.

42. Ibid., 22nd Cong., 1st sess. (Feb. 28, 1833), 322; *Executive Proceedings*, 22nd Cong., 1st sess., vol. 4 (Mar. 2, 1833), 332–333; Andrew Jackson to Andrew J. Crawford, May 1, 1833, in *Correspondence of Andrew Jackson*, 5:72.

43. Gerald Cullinan, *The Post Office Department* (New York: Praeger, 1968), 41; Wesley Everett Rich, *The History of the United States Post Offices to the Year 1829* (Cambridge, MA: Harvard University Press, 1924), 132–134.

44. Richard R. John, *Spreading the News: The American Postal System from Franklin to Morse*, 2nd ed. (Cambridge, MA: Harvard University Press, 1998), 67. As one historian noted, "the Postmaster-General was too important a functionary to be treated [any] longer as one of secondary rank." James Schouler, *History of the United States of America: Under the Constitution, 1817–1831*, rev. ed. (New York: Dodd, Mead, 1917), 3:457.

45. Remini, *Andrew Jackson*, 2:165. See also *Norwich Courier*, Mar. 18, 1829, 2; Rich, *History of U.S. Post Offices*, 134–136.

46. By 1836, Senator John C. Calhoun would state that Jackson not only has "the offices and the honors" but also "has the Post Office, with all its patronage and

power of corruption." John C. Calhoun, "Remarks in Reply to Silas Wright on Admitting the Public to the Senate," Feb. 16, 1836, in *The Papers of John C. Calhoun,* ed. Clyde N. Wilson (Columbia: University of South Carolina Press, 1980), 13:78.

47. *U.S. Statutes at Large,* 24th Cong., 1st sess., vol. 5 (July 2, 1836), 80–90.

48. For information about this aspect of the act, see David B. Cole, *The Presidency of Andrew Jackson* (Lawrence: University Press of Kansas, 1993), 237–240; Amos Kendall, *Autobiography,* ed. William Stickney (Boston: Lee and Shepard, 1872), 333–347.

49. This provision was limited to postmasters who made in excess of $1,000. *U.S. Statutes at Large,* 24th Cong., 1st sess., vol. 5 (July 2, 1836), 87–88.

50. Ibid., 80.

51. Dorothy Ganfield Fowler, *The Cabinet Politician: The Postmaster General, 1829–1909* (New York: Columbia University Press, 1943), 31.

52. Francis Thomas to David Ridenour, Apr. 25, 1836, in *Register of Debates* (House), 24th Cong., 1st sess., vol. 12 (June 1, 1836), 4121, 4122.

53. Wise in ibid., 4124.

54. Dictation of postmasterships, however, was not yet the norm. Fowler, *Cabinet Politician,* 31–32.

55. Edward M. Shepard, *Martin Van Buren* (New York: Houghton Mifflin, 1899), 214–215.

56. Andrew Jackson to William B. Lewis, Sept. 9, 1839, in *Correspondence of Andrew Jackson,* 6:27.

57. John Niven, *Martin Van Buren: The Romantic Age of American Politics* (Newtown, CT: American Political Biography Press, 2000), 404–405.

58. One biographer noted that Van Buren did not want to make any immediate removals. In fact, the president's policy was to make "it a matter of 'vital importance,' to make no big changes." Major L. Wilson, *The Presidency of Martin Van Buren* (Lawrence: University Press of Kansas, 1984), 38, 39.

59. Van Buren removed eighty officeholders. Fish, "Removal of Officials," 84. One Van Buren scholar noted that this figure was "not indicative because he inherited the friendly administration of Jackson." Max M. Mintz, "The Political Ideas of Martin Van Buren," *New York History* 30 (Oct. 1949): 429.

60. Postmaster General Amos Kendall had to formally remove Van Rensselaer because he was not a presidential appointee. It appears that Jackson was reluctant to remove Van Rensselaer out of a sense of duty and honor for a fellow war veteran; Van Rensselaer had fought in the War of 1812. See J. B. Van Schaick to Solomon Van Rensselaer, Jan. 23, 1833, in Catharina Van Rensselaer Bonney, *Legacy of Historical Gleanings,* 2nd ed. (Albany, NY: J. Munsell, 1875), 54, and also 109–110, 146; "Recollections of an Old Stager," *Harper's Monthly* 45 (Sept. 1872): 601.

61. John McLean to Solomon Van Rensselaer, Mar. 29, 1839, in Bonney, *Legacy of Historical Gleanings,* 111–112.

62. Robert V. Remini, *Martin Van Buren and the Making of the Democratic Party* (New York: Columbia University Press, 1959), 7–11.

63. Richard Hofstadter, *Idea of a Party System: The Rise of Legitimate Opposition in the United States, 1780–1840* (Berkeley: University of California Press, 1969), 212–271.

64. Nelson W. Polsby, "The Institutionalization of the U.S. House of Representatives," *American Political Science Review* 62 (1968): 146–147.

65. *Executive Proceedings,* 25th Cong., 2nd sess., vol. 5 (Mar. 30, 1838), 96; ibid., 26th Cong., 2nd sess., vol. 5 (Feb. 26, 1841), 345; ibid. (July 13, 1840), 302; ibid. (Feb. 23, 1841), 342.

66. Parmenter served in Congress from 1837 to 1845.

67. Niven, *Martin Van Buren,* 430.

68. John L. Blake, *A Biographical Dictionary* (Philadelphia: H. Cowperthwait, 1859), 585.

69. For a wonderful discussion of the history of the rural-urban divide in the Massachusetts Democratic Party, see Arthur B. Darling, "Jacksonian Democracy in Massachusetts, 1824–1848," *American Historical Review* 29 (Jan. 1924): 271–287.

70. *Executive Proceedings*, 25th Cong., 2nd sess., vol. 5 (Jan. 6, 1838), 61.

71. Niven, *Martin Van Buren*, 431.

72. The Democratic split in Pennsylvania resulted from bitter fights in the 1820s among party leaders William C. Crawford, John C. Calhoun, and Andrew Jackson, each of whom hoped to secure the presidency. George M. Dallas, Trevanian Dallas, Richard Bache, William Wilkins, and Thomas Sergeant formed a group that was called the Family because so many of its members were related by blood or marriage. An alternative organization led by James Buchanan, Henry Baldwin, and Molton C. Rogers also emerged; it was called the Amalgamators because it combined Democratic members with the few remaining Federalists. See Philip S. Klein and Ari Hoogenboom, *A History of Pennsylvania* (Blacklick, OH: McGraw-Hill, 1973), 135–146; Hugh R. Slotten, *Patronage, Practice and the Culture of American Science: Alexander Dallas Bache and the U.S. Coast Survey* (New York: Cambridge University Press, 1994), 6–7; John M. Belohlavek, *George Mifflin Dallas: Jacksonian Patrician* (University Park: Pennsylvania State University Press, 1977), 6; Niven, *Martin Van Buren*, 390.

73. *Executive Proceedings*, 25th Cong., special sess., vol. 5 (Mar. 7, 1837), 13; Belohlavek, *George Mifflin Dallas*, 63.

74. Niven, *Martin Van Buren*, 407.

75. James Buchanan to Martin Van Buren, Feb. 19, 1837, in MVBP, reel 16, Library of Congress, Manuscript Reading Room.

76. James Buchanan to Martin Van Buren, Aug. 29, 1838, in *Works of James Buchanan*, 3:258–259. It appears that Buchanan often played the modesty card when requesting appointments. For instance, in offering his advice about a district attorney position, Buchanan said, "I do not intend to interfere in" the appointment. James Buchanan to Martin Van Buren, Sept. 25, 1840, in ibid., 4:323.

77. *Executive Proceedings*, 25th Cong., 1st sess., vol. 5 (Sept. 12, 1837), 28.

78. Ibid., 25th Cong., 2nd sess., vol. 5 (Feb. 6, 1838), 68.

79. In 1835, Muhlenberg challenged then Governor Wolf in his reelection bid. The split of Democratic votes cost Wolf the governorship and made possible the election of anti-Mason and Whig candidate Joseph Ritner. "The Rank and File of Democracy: Pennsylvania," *United States Democratic Review* 3 (Dec. 1838): 385–394; "Biographical Memoir of the Late Henry A. Muhlenberg," *United States Democratic Review* 16 (Jan. 1845): 67–78; Henry J. Steele, "Life and Public Services of Governor George Wolf," *Pennsylvania German Society* 39 (Oct. 12, 1928): 23.

80. Niven, *Martin Van Buren*, 431.

81. *Executive Proceedings*, 25th Cong., 2nd sess., vol. 5 (Feb. 20, 1838), 75.

82. James Buchanan to Martin Van Buren, Dec. 28, 1839, in *Works of James Buchanan*, 4:124–125.

83. *Executive Proceedings*, 26th Cong., 1st sess., vol. 5 (Jan. 8, 1840), 240.

84. Niven, *Martin Van Buren*, 468.

85. John S. Jenkins, *The Life of Silas Wright* (Rochester, NY: Wanzer, Beardsley, 1852), 107–108. For more information on the divide within the New York Democratic Party, see William Trimble, "Diverging Tendencies in New York Democracy in the Period of the Locofocos," *American Historical Review* 24 (Apr. 1919): 396–421.

86. John Arthur Garraty, *Silas Wright* (New York: Columbia University Press, 1949), 134. While still a member of the Democratic Party, Tallmadge had called on his followers "to support Whig tickets in 1837 and 1838." Michael F. Holt, *The Rise*

and Fall of the American Whig Party (New York: Oxford University Press, 1999), 74. See also Arthur M. Schlesinger Jr., *The Age of Jackson* (Boston: Little, Brown, 1948), 221–222, 233; Glyndon G. Van Deusen, *The Jacksonian Era, 1828–1848* (New York: Harper and Row, 1959), 118.

87. Horace Greeley, *Recollections of a Busy Life* (New York: J. B. Ford, 1869), 123; Niven, *Martin Van Buren,* 449, 452, 456, 457, 548, 556.

88. Greeley, *Recollections of a Busy Life,* 123; Jabez D. Hammond, *The History of Political Parties in the State of New York* (Cooperstown, NY: H. and E. Phinney, 1844), 2:476, 486; Nathan Sargent, *Public Men and Events* (Philadelphia: J. B. Lippincott, 1875), 2:86.

89. The Locofocos were a reform group created in 1835 because of a growing divide with Tammany Hall Democrats over the issue of extending Jackson's national bank fight to state banks and other monopolies. Before the break, radical members had fought to get their anti-bank policy into the Democratic Party platform. At a meeting in the fall of 1835, the radical element won control, but before the meeting could be reorganized, the gas was shut off. The radicals continued to work by candlelight—called "locofoco" matches, hence the name of the group. By the beginning of 1836, they had created a new political organization called the Equal Rights Party. The new party retained the anti-bank element but also advocated the suspension of paper money and legislative support for labor unions. During the late 1830s, Locofocos were successful in electing members in New York; however, they did not want to create a lasting party. Their intention was to have the Democrats adopt their reform measures, which occurred when President Van Buren began to agree with many of the Locofoco policies. By the end of the 1830s, the Locofoco movement had merged back into the Democratic fold. See Fitzwilliam Byrdsall, *The History of the Loco-Foco or Equal Rights Party* (New York: B. Franklin, 1967).

90. Remini, *Andrew Jackson,* 3:449.

91. Niven, *Martin Van Buren,* 432.

92. Ibid.

93. Garraty, *Silas Wright,* 31.

94. Silas Wright Jr. to John Forsythe, Dec. 30, 1840, in General Records of the Department of State, RG 59, National Archives Microfilm Publication M687, roll 20, NARA. Robert V. Remini, discussing the command structure of the Albany Regency, said: "As Van Buren conceived his machine, an order once given . . . should be obeyed right down to the last officeholder in the smallest hamlet of New York." Remini, *Martin Van Buren,* 8.

95. According to McCormick: "In 1840, for the first time, two parties that were truly national in scope contested for the presidency. In every state, politics was now established on a two-party basis. . . . The Democrats were no match for their adversaries; Van Buren could carry only six states. But more significant than the Whig victory was the evidence it gave that the second American party system had come into being." Richard P. McCormick, *The Second American Party System: Party Formation in the Jacksonian Era* (Chapel Hill: University of North Carolina Press, 1966), 341.

96. For more information on the Whig Party, see Holt, *Rise and Fall of the American Whig Party;* Lynn L. Marshall, "The Strange Stillbirth of the Whig Party," *American Historical Review* 72 (Jan. 1967): 445–468. Any centralizing focus of the Whigs was based on the dominance of Congress over the president. During the 1836 and 1840 campaigns, "Harrison made it quite clear . . . that he did not intend to be a strong Executive—that so far as he was concerned the Congress should and could run the country," but the "question, then, was how long could the lingering hatred of Andrew Jackson and the democratic principles he represented . . . serve as a cement for a coalition of ambitious leaders, competitive factions, and contradictory ideas?" Robert Seager II, *And Tyler Too* (New York: McGraw-Hill, 1963), 141–142.

See also David W. Krueger, "The Clay-Tyler Feud, 1841–1842," *Filson Club History Quarterly* 42 (Apr. 1968): 162–163.

97. Harrison defeated Van Buren by a vote of 234 to 60 in the electoral college. Mosher, *Executive Register*, 122; Dorothy Burne Goebel and Julius Goebel Jr., *Generals in the White House* (New York: Doubleday, 1945), 112–114. For a detailed account of the 1840 election, see Robert Gray Gunderson, *The Log-Cabin Campaign* (Lexington: University of Kentucky Press, 1957); Bernard Friedman, "William Henry Harrison: The People against the Parties," in *Gentleman from Indiana National Party Candidates: 1836–1940*, ed. Ralph D. Gray (Indianapolis: Indiana Historical Bureau, 1977), 3–28.

98. One historian explained: "The Whigs as a party had never before tasted victory in a presidential election, and most of their following had been banished from federal patronage for a dozen years. Consequently, they were unusually avid for spoils." Albert D. Kirwan, *John J. Crittenden: The Struggle for the Union* (Lexington: University of Kentucky Press, 1962), 140. See also Dorothy Burne Goebel, *William Henry Harrison: A Political Biography* (Philadelphia: Porcupine Press, 1974), 374; James A. Green, *William Henry Harrison: His Life and Times* (Richmond: Garrett and Massie, 1941), 394–395; Robert G. Gunderson, "A Search for Old Tip Himself," *Register of the Kentucky Historical Society* 86 (autumn 1988): 348; Gunderson, *Log-Cabin Campaign*, 259; Seager, *And Tyler Too*, 142–143.

99. H. Montgomery, *The Life of Major-General William H. Harrison* (Philadelphia: Porter and Coates, 1852), 367–368.

100. Daniel Webster to M. St. Clair Clarke, Wm. S. Murphy, and Hudson M. Garland, Mar. 27, 1841, in *The Works of Daniel Webster*, 11th ed., ed. Edward Everett (Boston: Little, Brown, 1858), 6:542–543; "Appointments by the President," *National Intelligencer*, Mar. 30, 1841.

101. Henry A. Wise to Daniel Webster, Mar. 7, 1841, and Horatio Seymour to William Henry Harrision, Feb. 10, 1841, both in General Records of the Department of State, RG 59, National Archives Microfilm Publication M687, roll 19, NARA; Kirwan, *Crittenden*, 139–140; "Suggestions of the Past: John Tyler's Administration," *Galaxy* 13 (Feb. 1872): 204; Norma Lois Peterson, *The Presidencies of William Henry Harrison and John Tyler* (Lawrence: University Press of Kansas, 1989), 33–34, 39.

102. Benjamin Perley Poore, *Perley's Reminiscences of Sixty Years in the National Metropolis* (Philadelphia: Hubbard, 1886), 1:257.

103. Carl Russell Fish, *The Civil Service and the Patronage* (Cambridge, MA: Harvard University Press, 1904), 150.

104. Poore, *Perley's Reminiscences*, 1:258.

105. Peterson, *Presidencies of William Henry Harrison and John Tyler*, 40–41.

106. Gunderson, *Log Cabin Campaign*, 270.

107. Fish, *Civil Service and Patronage*, 147–148 (emphasis added).

108. The candidate in question was Clark Robinson. *Executive Proceedings*, 27th Cong., 1st sess., vol. 5 (Mar. 15, 1841), 377.

109. Fish, *Civil Service and Patronage*, 148.

110. Jeremiah Brown to William H. Harrison, Feb. 20, 1841; Francis James to William H. Harrison, Mar. 3, 1841; Joseph Lawrence to William H. Harrison, Mar. 5, 1841, all in General Records of the Department of State, RG 59, National Archives Microfilm Publication M687, roll 2, NARA.

111. Garrett Davis, John White, [name illegible], John Pope, William J. Graves, Willis Green, and Richard Hawes to William H. Harrison, [Feb.] 1841, in ibid., roll 1.

112. William Boardman, Thomas Burr Osborne, Truman Smith, Joseph Trunball, and Thomas Williams to Daniel Webster, Feb. 27, 1841, in ibid., roll 19.

113. Samson Mason to William H. Harrison, Mar. 12, 1841, in ibid., roll 1.

114. Thomas Jefferson Campbell to Daniel Webster, Mar. 8, 1841, in ibid., roll 20.

115. John Henderson to William H. Harrison, Feb. 9, 1841, in ibid., roll 1. See also John Henderson to William H. Harrison, Mar. 8, 1841; John Henderson to William H. Harrison, Jan. 10, 1841; and John Henderson to William H. Harrison, Dec. 16, 1840, all in ibid.

116. The president was reported to have said that "he would not make any appointments in New York State without consulting Genl. Van Rensselaer." Bonney, *Legacy of Historical Gleanings*, 165.

117. Solomon Van Rensselaer to William Harrison, Jan. 8, 1840, in Bonney, *Legacy of Historical Gleanings*, 117–118; Solomon Van Rensselaer to his children, July 5, 1840, in ibid., 141–142; Letter of Invitation to Solomon Van Rensselaer from Citizens of Kentucky, July 10, 1840, in ibid., 142.

118. Silas E. Burrows to Solomon Van Rensselaer, Jan. 2, 1841, in ibid., 147; "Editors Correspondence," *National Intelligencer*, Jan. 12, 1841. There was also talk about Van Rensselaer eventually succeeding Harrison as president. See Silas E. Burrows to Solomon Van Rensselaer, Jan. 21, 1841, in Bonney, *Legacy of Historical Gleanings*, 148.

119. President Van Buren had ordered Postmaster General Amos Kendall to remove Van Rensselaer as Albany postmaster in 1839. Van Rensselaer had served in that position since 1822. Bonney, *Legacy of Historical Gleanings*, 165. Although Harrison gave Van Rensselaer a recess appointment, it was his successor, John Tyler, who would ultimately make the formal nomination to the Senate. *Executive Proceedings*, 27th Cong., 1st sess., vol. 5 (June 16, 1841), 381.

120. Catharina V. Van Rensselaer to her brother, Feb. 18, 1841, in Bonney, *Legacy of Historical Gleanings*, 154; Mrs. James Cochran to Solomon Van Rensselaer, Apr. 2, 1841, in ibid., 170; James Cochran to Solomon Van Rensselaer, Apr. 5, 1841, in ibid., 170–171.

121. Freeman Cleaves, *Old Tippecanoe: William Henry Harrison and His Times* (New York: Scribner, 1939), 339. One Harrison biographer thought that Webster's friendship with Curtis secured the appointment. Goebel, *William Henry Harrison*, 375. However, according to another historian, the support of Abbott Lawrence, a wealthy "cotton-mill capitalist" who had "personally lent the impoverished Harrison $5000 shortly after the inauguration," was probably the deciding factor in the appointment. Seager, *And Tyler Too*, 145. Although Harrison gave Curtis a recess appointment, his successor, John Tyler, ultimately made the formal appointment to the Senate. *Executive Proceedings*, 27th Cong., 1st sess., vol. 5 (June 16, 1841), 384.

122. Cleaves, *Old Tippecanoe*, 339; George Rawlings Poage, *Henry Clay and the Whig Party* (Gloucester, MA: Peter Smith, 1965), 27; "Suggestions of the Past," 204.

123. "Reminiscences of Washington: VI, The Harrison Administration," *Atlantic Monthly* 46 (Sept. 1880): 376; Seager, *And Tyler Too*, 145.

124. William H. Harrison to Henry Clay, Mar. 13, 1841, in *The Papers of Henry Clay*, ed. Robert Seager II and Melba Porter Hay (Lexington: University Press of Kentucky, 1988), 9:514. See also Henry Clay to William H. Harrison, Mar. 15, 1841, in ibid., 516–517.

125. Kirwan, *Crittenden*, 141; Lawrence Augustus Gobright, *Recollections of Men and Things at Washington* (Washington, DC: W. H. and O. H. Morrison, 1869), 49; Poore, *Perley's Reminiscences*, 1:258; John Chambers, *Autobiography of John Chambers* (Iowa City: State Historical Society of Iowa, 1908), 24.

126. "Recollections of an Old Stager," *Harper's Monthly* 47 (Oct. 1873): 754. Like his other selections, Harrison nominated Chambers during a recess of Congress, and Tyler formally submitted the nomination. *Executive Proceedings*, 27th Cong., 1st sess., vol. 5 (June 17, 1841), 386.

127. Oscar Doane Lambert, *Presidential Politics in the United States, 1841–1844* (Durham, NC: Duke University Press, 1936), 3.

128. At the Harrisburg nomination convention, Whig leaders asked Tyler "nothing of his views on the political questions of the day," and during the campaign, "he retreated to saying nothing specific enough to damage the Whig cause and nothing at basic variance with the states' rights principles for which he stood." Seager, *And Tyler Too*, 135, 136. As one Tyler biographer stated, "The anomaly of his situation was about what would have been that of W. J. Bryan had in 1896 been nominated and elected by the Republican Party. For Tyler was at heart a Democrat, and yet he was the titular head of the Whig Party." Oliver Perry Chitwood, *John Tyler: Champion of the Old South* (Newtown, CT: American Political Biography Press, 2000), 208.

129. Schlesinger wrote: "While Tyler's training had allowed him to join the Whigs in attacking executive despotism, it did not incline him to support the more arrantly Federalist items in the Whig program." Schlesinger, *Age of Jackson*, 394. For a detailed account of Tyler's break from the Whig Party, see Krueger, "Clay-Tyler Feud," 162–177.

130. One historian noted: "If Tyler was motivated too strongly by partisanship in handling the civil service, he was only taking a leaf out of the book of his enemies." Chitwood, *John Tyler*, 368.

131. Robert J. Morgan, *A Whig Embattled: The Presidency under John Tyler* (Lincoln: University of Nebraska Press, 1954), 59–60; Chitwood, *John Tyler*, 270; Seager, *And Tyler Too*, 149.

132. Interview by John Tyler Jr., *Lippincott's Monthly Magazine* 41 (1888): 417–418.

133. "Recollections of an Old Stager," 755–756.

134. Chitwood, *John Tyler*, 272; William Marcy to Martin Van Buren, July 20, 1841, in MVBP, reel 25.

135. Lambert, *Presidential Politics*, 77.

136. Eventually, Tyler's cabinet would resign en masse except for Secretary of State Daniel Webster. Lambert, *Presidential Politics*, 81–82; Irving H. Bartlett, *Daniel Webster* (New York: Norton, 1978), 176–177; Robert V. Remini, *Daniel Webster: The Man and His Times* (New York: Norton, 1997), 529–530.

137. John Tyler, inaugural address, Apr. 9, 1841, in *Messages and Papers of the Presidents*, 4:1891.

138. *Executive Proceedings*, 27th Cong., 1st sess., vol. 5 (June 16, 1841), 384.

139. Garraty, *Silas Wright*, 217.

140. The third-party plan was originally the idea of Representative Thomas W. Gilmer of Virginia. Lambert, *Presidential Politics*, 47–48.

141. Seager, *And Tyler Too*, 227.

142. Ibid., 225; Peterson, *Presidencies of William Henry Harrison and John Tyler*, 145.

143. Chitwood, *John Tyler*, 370.

144. "Origin and Growth of the Spoils System," *Century* 46 (July 1893): 473.

145. Seager, *And Tyler Too*, 225. It is difficult to differentiate Harrison's and Tyler's removals. As Fish explained, Harrison "prepared lists of removals and appointments, many of which were acted upon by Tyler. It is impossible, therefore, to disentangle the skein of their interaction." The combined removals for Harrison and Tyler are listed at 458. Fish, "Removal of Officials," 76.

146. Sargent, *Public Men and Events*, 2:190; Lambert, *Presidential Politics*, 86; Chitwood, *John Tyler*, 371.

147. "Suggestions from the Past: John Tyler's Administration," *Galaxy* 13 (Mar. 1872): 355; *Executive Proceedings*, 27th Cong., 2nd sess., vol. 6 (Mar. 8, 1842), 36; ibid., 28th Cong., 1st sess., vol. 6 (June 15, 1844), 343.

148. Morgan, *Whig Embattled*, 163.

149. Garraty, *Silas Wright*, 215.

150. Peterson, *Presidencies of William Henry Harrison and John Tyler*, 71.

151. Schlesinger, *Age of Jackson*, 395.

152. Seager, *And Tyler Too*, 227.

153. Irwin was selected as chargé d'affaires to Denmark. *Executive Proceedings*, 27th Cong., 3rd sess., vol. 6 (Mar. 2, 1843), 178. Proffitt was appointed minister to Brazil during a recess of Congress; the Senate rejected his nomination by a vote of thirty-three to eight. Ibid., 28th Cong., 1st sess., vol. 6 (Jan. 11, 1844), 209. Wise was selected as minister to France; the Senate rejected his nomination by a vote of twenty-four to twelve. Ibid., 27th Cong., 3rd sess., vol. 6 (Mar. 3, 1843), 186. Tyler later nominated him as minister of Brazil. Ibid., 28th Cong., 1st sess., vol. 6 (Jan. 19, 1844), 220. Cushing was appointed secretary of the treasury; the Senate rejected his nomination by a vote of twenty-nine to two. Ibid., 27th Cong., 3rd sess., vol. 6 (Mar. 3, 1843), 190. Tyler later appointed Cushing to the post of commissioner to China. Ibid., 28th Cong., 1st sess., vol. 6 (Dec. 15, 1843), 193.

154. Wise recounts that South Carolina senator George McDuffie was the primary backer of Tyler's appointments: "We thought of Mr. Duffie, then in the Senate, and determined to act through him. The President, in 1843, at the instance of the Hon Baillie Peyton (Representative from Tennessee, 1833–1836), had sent our name to the Senate for the mission to France, and the nomination was rejected at a moment when it was the rule of party not to allow him to have any of his own friends in appointments when the Opposition could prevent [it]. . . . And when our name for France was before the Senate, and the doctrine was openly avowed that the President should not be allowed to have his own friends in place, Mr. McDuffie had met the dogma as it deserved, and denounced it with great cogency and spirit." Henry A. Wise, *Seven Decades of the Union: A Memoir of John Tyler* (Philadelphia: J. B. Lippincott, 1872), 221–222.

155. Fish, *Civil Service and Patronage*, 153. See also Thomas H. Benton, *A Thirty Years' View* (London: D. Appleton, 1860), 2:629; Lambert, *Presidential Politics*, 142.

156. Micah Sterling to Joesph A. Scoville, Apr. 29, 1843, in *The Papers of John C. Calhoun*, ed. Clyde N. Wilson (Columbia: University of South Carolina Press, 1987), 17:156.

157. For an outline of the reasons for the decline of the Whig Party and the emergence of the Republican Party, see John H. Aldrich, *Why Parties? The Origin and Transformation of Political Parties in America* (Chicago: University of Chicago Press, 1995), 126–158.

Chapter 4. The Spoils Era II (1845–1869)

1. U.S. Civil Service Commission, *A Brief History of the United States Civil Service* (Washington, DC: GPO, 1929), 12.

2. Polk defeated Whig candidate Henry Clay by a vote of 170 to 105 in the electoral college. Robert Brent Mosher, *Executive Register of the United States, 1789–1902* (Washington, DC: GPO, 1905), 137.

3. James Buchanan to James K. Polk, Nov. 1844, in *The Works of James Buchanan*, ed. John Bassett Moore (Philadelphia: J. B. Lippincott, 1909), 6:73; Ransom H. Gillet to James K. Polk, May 3, 1845, in *Correspondence of James K. Polk*, ed. Wayne Cutler et al. (Knoxville: University of Tennessee Press, 1996), 9:339–340; Royel H. Hinan to James K. Polk, May 5, 1845, in ibid., 343–344; Benjamin F. Butler to James K. Polk, May 6, 1845, in ibid., 347–350; Sackfield Maclin to James K. Polk, July 4, 1845, in ibid., 10:16; Richard M. Johnson to James K. Polk, July 11, 1845, in ibid., 46; Charles S. Jones to James K. Polk, July 12, 1845, in ibid., 53–54; Richard M. Johnson to James K. Polk, July 13, 1845, in ibid., 56; James K. Polk to William H. Haywood Jr., Aug. 9, 1845, in ibid., 139.

4. Sidney Breese and James Semple to James K. Polk, Mar. 8, 1845, in General Records of the Department of State, RG 59, National Archives Microfilm Publication M873, roll 2, NARA.

5. Jeremiah Towle to James K. Polk, Apr. 22, 1845, in *Correspondence of James K. Polk*, 9:312.

6. According to Polk biographer Martha McBride Morrel, "Polk entered the presidency with an unorthodox policy regarding appointments. A man, he thought, should be turned out of his job only for dishonesty or incompetence. The government payroll should not be a grab-bag restocked quadrennially with prizes for the winning party. No worthy Whig or Tylerite was to be ousted simply to make way for a deserving Democrat." Martha McBride Morrel, *Young Hickory: The Life and Times of President James K. Polk* (New York: E. P. Dutton, 1949), 247. See also John Seigenthaler, *James K. Polk* (New York: Henry Holt, 2003), 114.

7. Charles Sellers, *James K. Polk: Continentalist* (Norwalk, CT: Easton Press, 1966), 268.

8. Diary entry, Mar. 2, 1849, in *The Diary of James Polk during his Presidency, 1845 to 1849*, ed. Milo M. Quaife (Chicago: A. C. McClurg, 1910), 4:360.

9. Polk removed 342 officeholders. Carl Russell Fish, "Removal of Officials by the Presidents of the United States," in *American Historical Association Reports* (Washington, DC: GPO, 1900), 2:84.

10. Norman A. Graebner, "James K. Polk: A Study in Federal Patronage," *Mississippi Valley Historical Review* 38 (Mar. 1952): 624.

11. James K. Polk to Silas Wright Jr., July 8, 1845, in *Correspondence of James K. Polk*, 10:37.

12. Diary entry, Dec. 24, 1845, in *Diary of James Polk*, 1:138.

13. Eugene Irving McCormac, *James K. Polk: A Political Biography* (Berkeley: University of California Press, 1922), 336.

14. James K. Polk to David Craighead, Sept. 13, 1845, in *Correspondence of James K. Polk*, 10:226.

15. James K. Polk to Lewis Cass, Sept. 18, 1848, in James K. Polk Papers, reel 58, Library of Congress, Manuscript Reading Room.

16. James K. Polk to Silas Wright Jr., July 8, 1845, in *Correspondence of James K. Polk*, 10:37 (emphasis in original).

17. The Senate rejected Horn by a vote of twenty-eight to twenty-one. Cameron's colleague, Daniel Sturgeon, voted for confirmation. *Journal of the Executive Proceedings of the Senate*, 29th Cong., 1st sess., vol. 7 (June 24, 1846), 104.

18. Philip S. Klein, *President James Buchanan* (University Park: Pennsylvania State University Press, 1962), 171; Henry Horn to James K. Polk, Mar. 25, 1845, in *Correspondence of James K. Polk*, 9:230; James Buchanan to James K. Polk, May 3, 1845, in ibid., 339; James Buchanan to James K. Polk, Dec. 24, 1845, in ibid., 10:437–439. See also Bill Severn, *Frontier President: James K. Polk* (New York: Ives Washburn, 1965), 153.

19. In the 1840s, the reform element within the New York Democratic Party was called the Barnburners because it was rumored that they would burn a barn to get rid of the rats. Opposed to corporations, public works, and the extension of slavery, some Barnburners had joined the Free-Soil Party by the 1850s, and the rest remained in the Democratic Party until the Civil War. See Herbert D. A. Donovan, *The Barnburners* (New York: New York University Press, 1925).

The Hunkers were the conservative element of the New York Democratic Party, so called because they "hunkered" after office. They supported internal improvements and the chartering of state banks and were opposed to antislavery legislation. See Jabez D. Hammond, *The History of Political Parties in the State of New York*, 3rd ed. (Cooperstown, NY: H. and E. Phinney, 1844), 3:510–700.

20. Actually, Polk first offered Barnburner Silas Wright Jr. the treasury secretary position, but he turned it down. John Arthur Garraty, *Silas Wright* (New York: Columbia University Press, 1949), 347–348; James K. Polk to Martin Van Buren, Jan. 4, 1845, in *Correspondence of James K. Polk*, 9:20; James K. Polk to Silas Wright Jr., Jan. 4, 1845, in ibid., 21. Polk wrote that he selected Lawrence because "he was a good and true Democrat." James K. Polk to Silas Wright Jr., Aug. 4, 1845, in ibid., 10:118; *Executive Proceedings*, 29th Cong., 1st sess., vol. 7 (Dec. 29, 1845), 12; Garraty, *Silas Wright*, 350.

21. John Niven, *Martin Van Buren: The Romantic Age of American Politics* (Newtown, CT: American Political Biography Press, 2000), 563.

22. Ibid., 563–564.

23. Graebner, "James K. Polk," 627; Donald B. Cole, *Martin Van Buren and the American Political System* (Princeton, NJ: Princeton University Press, 1984), 404–405.

24. One author wrote that Polk's policy caused "the administration's complete loss of control over Congress." Sellers, *James K. Polk*, 356.

25. Silas Wright Jr. to James K. Polk, July 21, 1845, in *Correspondence of James K. Polk*, 10:87–88.

26. For examples of solicitations from various lawmakers, see William Sawyer and Isaac Parrish to James K. Polk, Jan. 1845; William Sawyer to James K. Polk, Mar. 1845; Emery Davis Potter to James K. Polk, Mar. 1, 1845, all in M873, roll 2, NARA; Sidney Breese to James K. Polk, Mar. 10, 1845, in *Correspondence of James K. Polk*, 9:506; Chester Ashley to James K. Polk, Mar. 20, 1845, in ibid., 514; James K. Polk to Aaron V. Brown, Oct. 7, 1845, in ibid., 10:282–283.

27. William Nisbet Chambers, *Old Bullion Benton* (Boston: Little, Brown, 1956), 292.

28. James K. Polk to William W. Polk, Oct. 9, 1845, in *Correspondence of James K. Polk*, 10:286.

29. The candidates were Gansevoort Melville and Anthony Ten Eyck. Lewis Cass to James K. Polk, Apr. 26, 1845, in ibid., 9:317–318; Daniel S. Dickinson to James K. Polk, Apr. 28, 1845, in ibid., 323–324; *Executive Proceedings*, 29th Cong., 1st sess., vol. 7 (Dec. 22, 1845), 9.

30. James K. Polk to Franklin H. Elmore, July 17, 1845, in *Correspondence of James K. Polk*, 10:68. Although Huger's term had ended on Mar. 3, 1845, Polk still referred to him as a member of the South Carolina delegation, perhaps not realizing that the senator's term had expired.

31. Diary entry, July 26, 1848, in *Diary of James Polk*, 4:29.

32. Sellers, *James K. Polk*, 445.

33. Graebner, "James K. Polk," 623.

34. Allan Nevins, *Ordeal of the Union* (New York: Scribner, 1947), 1:189–190.

35. Dorothy Burne Goebel and Julius Goebel Jr., *Generals in the White House* (New York: Doubleday, 1945), 118–140.

36. Michael F. Holt, *The Rise and Fall of the American Whig Party* (New York: Oxford University Press, 1999), 270–273; Elbert B. Smith, *The Presidencies of Zachary Taylor and Millard Fillmore* (Lawrence: University Press of Kansas, 1988), 64; William E. Nott, *The Republican Campaign Text Book for 1882* (Washington, DC: Republican Printing and Publishing Co., 1882), 129. Taylor defeated Cass by a vote of 163 to 127 in the electoral college. Mosher, *Executive Register*, 144. See also K. Jack Bauer, *Zachary Taylor: Soldier, Planter, Statesman of the Old Southwest* (Baton Rouge: Louisiana State University Press, 1985), 245–246.

37. Holt, *Rise and Fall of the American Whig Party*, 414.

38. As a Clay biographer wrote of Taylor, "The man's honesty and conscientiousness won all who came into intimate association with him; but his blundering directness, his ill-conceived ideas, and his unconquerable stubbornness strewed

the path of his advisers with thorns." George Rawlings Poage, *Henry Clay and the Whig Party* (Gloucester, MA: Peter Smith, 1965), 183.

39. Goebel and Goebel, *Generals in the White House*, 134; Dorothy Ganfield Fowler, *The Cabinet Politician: The Postmaster General, 1829–1909* (New York: Columbia University Press, 1943), 68–69; Fish, "Removal of Officials," 84.

40. Fowler, *Cabinet Politician*, 69.

41. Holt, *Rise and Fall of the American Whig Party*, 422.

42. Holman Hamilton, *Zachary Taylor: Soldier in the White House* (Indianapolis: Bobbs-Merrill, 1951), 2:206.

43. Fowler, *Cabinet Politician*, 69; Goebel and Goebel, *Generals in the White House*, 134.

44. Bauer, *Zachary Taylor*, 259.

45. Hamilton, *Zachary Taylor*, 2:214–215.

46. Ibid., 207, 208; Holt, *Rise and Fall of the American Whig Party*, 419.

47. Smith, *Presidencies of Zachary Taylor and Millard Fillmore*, 163.

48. Henry Clay to James Harlan, Mar. 16, 1850, in *The Private Correspondence of Henry Clay*, ed. Calvin Colton (New York: A. S. Barnes, 1856), 604.

49. Holt, *Rise and Fall of the American Whig Party*, 457.

50. Albert D. Kirwan, *John J. Crittenden: The Struggle for the Union* (Lexington: University of Kentucky Press, 1962), 249; Robert J. Rayback, *Millard Fillmore* (Norwalk, CT: Easton Press, 1959), 201–205; Smith, *Presidencies of Zachary Taylor and Millard Fillmore*, 59, 60–61, 163.

51. Hamilton, *Zachary Taylor*, 2:206.

52. For examples of congressional appointment requests, see James Shields to John M. Clayton, Mar. 10, 1849; Thomas Henry to Zachary Taylor, Feb. 15, 1849; W. H. Ewing and Robert R. Reed to Zachary Taylor, [Feb.] 1849, all in M873, roll 2, NARA.

53. Holt, *Rise and Fall of the American Whig Party*, 418.

54. Ibid., 520–521.

55. Fillmore refused to make a "wholesale replacement" of Taylor officeholders as well. Benson Lee Grayson, *The Unknown President: The Administration of President Millard Fillmore* (Washington, DC: University Press of America, 1981), 71.

56. Holt, *Rise and Fall of the American Whig Party*, 548.

57. Fillmore removed only eight-eight officeholders. Fish, "Removal of Officials," 84; Holt, *Rise and Fall of the American Whig Party*, 545.

58. Holt, *Rise and Fall of the American Whig Party*, 546.

59. *Executive Proceedings*, 31st Cong., 1st sess., vol. 8 (Aug. 10, 1850), 214; Holt, *Rise and Fall of the American Whig Party*, 546.

60. See the House debate and votes on S. 307, "An act proposing to the State of Texas the establishment of her northern and western boundaries, the relinquishment by the said State of all territory claimed by her exterior to said boundaries, and of all her claims upon the United States, and to establish a territorial government for New Mexico," in *Journal of the House of Representatives*, 31st Cong., 1st sess. (Sept. 2–6, 1850), 1358–1413; Holt, *Rise and Fall of the American Whig Party*, 546.

61. Holt, *Rise and Fall of the American Whig Party*, 546.

62. The term *higher law* derived from a speech given by Senator William Seward that attacked claims that slavery was protected by the federal government and that proponents had an equal right to extend the practice into the territories. Seward stated that there was "a higher law than the Constitution, which regulates our authority over the domain." Those who accepted Seward's view were called "higher law" Whigs; those opposed, including President Fillmore, were called "lower law" Whigs. A recounting of Seward's speech can be found in Glyndon G. Van Deusen, *William Henry Seward* (New York: Oxford University Press, 1967), 122–124.

63. By the 1850s, there were few moderate Democrats (the moderate wing was represented by 1848 Democratic standard-bearer Lewis Cass of Michigan). See Willard C. Klunder, *Lewis Cass and the Politics of Moderation* (Kent, OH: Kent State University Press, 1996). In addition, as a result of the slavery issue, the party had split into northern and southern wings. See David M. Potter, *The Impending Crisis, 1848–1861* (New York: Harper and Row, 1976), 238–240; Ronald J. Hrebenar and Matthew J. Burbank, *Political Parties, Interest Groups, and Political Campaigns* (Boulder, CO: Westview Press, 1999), 23; Eric Foner, *Free Soil, Free Labor, Free Men: The Ideology of the Republican Party before the Civil War* (New York: Oxford University Press, 1970), 150–152.

64. For a detailed account of Pierce's candidacy, see Peter A. Wallner, *Franklin Pierce: New Hampshire's Favorite Son* (Concord, NH: Plaidswede Publishing, 2004), 181–204.

65. Pierce defeated Scott by a vote of 254 to 42 in the electoral college. Mosher, *Executive Register*, 154; Robert Allen Rutland, *The Democrats: From Jefferson to Clinton* (Columbia: University of Missouri Press, 1995), 93–96; Goebel and Goebel, *Generals in the White House*, 148–151.

66. "An Act making Appropriations for Civil and Diplomatic Expenses of Government," *U.S. Statutes at Large*, 32nd Cong., 2nd sess., vol. 10 (Mar. 3, 1853), 209–211. For more information, see Leonard D. White, *The Jacksonians: A Study in Administrative History, 1829–1861* (New York: Macmillan, 1954), 365–375.

67. Adelbert Bower Sageser, *The First Two Decades of the Pendleton Act: A Study of Civil Service Reform* (Lincoln: University Studies of the University of Nebraska, 1935), 13. See also Carl Russell Fish, *The Civil Service and the Patronage* (Cambridge, MA: Harvard University Press, 1904), 183; Paul P. Van Riper, *History of the United States Civil Service* (Evanston, IL: Row, Peterson, 1958), 52.

68. Dorman B. Eaton, "Two Years of Civil Service Reform," *North American Review* 141 (July 1885): 19.

69. Jacob D. Cox, "The Civil-Service Reform," *North American Review* 112 (Jan. 1871): 94. See also Perley Orman Ray, *An Introduction to Political Parties and Practical Politics* (New York: Charles Scribner's Sons, 1913), 300–301.

70. Van Riper, *History of the Civil Service*, 52.

71. Ivor Debenham Spencer, *The Victor and the Spoils: A Life of William L. Marcy* (Providence, RI: Brown University Press, 1959), 227; Roy Franklin Nichols, *The Democratic Machine: 1850–1854* (New York: Columbia University, 1923), 192–193.

72. Roy Franklin Nichols, *Franklin Pierce: Young Hickory of the Granite Hills* (Philadelphia: University of Pennsylvania Press, 1931), 382.

73. Ibid., 251, 252.

74. Larry Gara, *The Presidency of Franklin Pierce* (Lawrence: University Press of Kansas, 1991), 50.

75. Preston King to Franklin Pierce, Mar. 7, 1853, in M967, roll 1, NARA; Henry Dodge to Franklin Pierce, Mar. 5, 1853; Henry Dodge to Franklin Pierce, Mar. 9, 1853; Henry Dodge to Franklin Pierce, Mar. 12, 1853; Henry Dodge to Franklin Pierce, May 7, 1853; Daniel Wells Jr. to William Marcy, Mar. 10, 1853; Daniel Wells Jr. to Franklin Pierce, Mar. 10, 1853; Henry Dodge and Daniel Wells Jr. to Franklin Pierce, Mar. 10, 1853, all in ibid., roll 47.

76. Nichols, *Franklin Pierce*, 252; William McKendree Gwin to Franklin Pierce, Mar. 17, 1853; Stephen Adams, Wiliam Barksdale, William Taylor Sullivan Barry, Otho Robards Singleton, and Daniel Boone Wright to Franklin Pierce, Apr. 21, 1854, both in M967, roll 48, NARA.

77. Previously, Hardshells and Softshells were both part of a New York faction called the Hunkers. Before the 1852 election, both groups favored internal improvements, the chartering of state banks, and the abolition of slavery. The Hunkers then

divided into the Hardshells (who opposed Pierce and slavery) and the Softshells (who supported Pierce and were moderately antislavery). See Hammond, *History of Political Parties in New York*, 3:510–700.

78. Gara, *Presidency of Franklin Pierce*, 50.

79. Nichols, *Franklin Pierce*, 254.

80. John Slidell to William L. Marcy, Mar. 10, 1853, in William L. Marcy Papers, container 29, Library of Congress, Manuscript Reading Room.

81. *Executive Proceedings*, 33rd Cong., special sess., vol. 9 (Apr. 6, 1853), 151.

82. John Slidell to James Buchanan, Apr. 3, 1855, in *Works of James Buchanan*, 9:332.

83. Gara, *Presidency of Franklin Pierce*, 59.

84. Nichols, *Franklin Pierce*, 381–382.

85. Senator Slidell said that Pierce was so disliked in the Senate that he might have had only one ally (Senator Henry Dodge of Wisconsin) supporting his renomination. Louis Martin Sears, *John Slidell* (Durham, NC: Duke University Press, 1925), 119.

86. Elbert B. Smith, *The Presidency of James Buchanan* (Lawrence: University Press of Kansas, 1975), 5.

87. Buchanan defeated Frémont by a vote of 174 to 114 in the electoral college. Mosher, *Executive Register*, 159; Robert Allen Rutland, *The Republicans: From Lincoln to Bush* (Columbia: University of Missouri Press, 1996), 15.

88. Buchanan removed 458 officeholders, compared with Pierce's 823 removals. Fish, "Removal of Officials," 84.

89. Fish, *Civil Service and Patronage*, 166. See also diary entries, Mar. 17 and Apr. 6, 1857, in "Diary and Memoranda of William L. Marcy, 1857," *American Historical Review*, vol. 24 (July 1919): 642–644, 648–649.

90. George T. Curtis, *Life of James Buchanan* (New York: Harper and Brothers, 1883), 2:185–186.

91. Smith, *Presidency of James Buchanan*, 21. See also Jean H. Baker, *James Buchanan* (New York: Henry Holt, 2004), 87.

92. White, *The Jacksonians*, 313.

93. William Boyce, John McQueen, James Orr, Laurence Keitt, and Josiah Evans to James Buchanan, Mar. 2, 1857, in M967, roll 1, NARA.

94. John Slidell to Lewis Cass, Jan. 12, 1857, in ibid., roll 47; Klein, *President James Buchanan*, 284; Sears, *John Slidell*, 142; John M. Sacher, *Perfect War of Politics: Parties, Politicians, and Democracy in Louisiana, 1824–1861* (Baton Rouge: Louisiana State University Press, 2003), 260. Slidell was even successful in influencing cabinet appointments. See Sears, *John Slidell*, 141; A. L. Diket, *Senator John Slidell and the Community He Represented in Washington, 1853–1861* (Washington, DC: University Press of America, 1982), 100.

95. Fowler, *Cabinet Politician*, 91.

96. Horatio King to Albert Jenkins, Feb. 27, 1861, in Dorothy Ganfield Fowler, "Congressional Dictation of Local Appointments," *Journal of Politics* 7 (Feb. 1945): 40.

97. Klein, *President James Buchanan*, 280–281.

98. In a letter to Broderick, Gwin wrote: "Providing I am elected, you shall have the exclusive control of the patronage, so far as I am concerned." William K. Gwin to David C. Broderick, Jan. 11, 1857, in Lately Thomas, *Between Two Empires: The Life Story of California's First Senator William McKendree Gwin* (Boston: Houghton Mifflin, 1969), 179. See also David A. Williams, *David C. Broderick: A Political Portrait* (San Marino, CA: Huntington Library, 1969), 33, 154–155; Arthur Quinn, *The Rivals: William Gwin, David Broderick, and the Birth of California* (New York: Crown Publishers, 1994), 232–233.

99. *Executive Proceedings,* 35th Cong., 1st sess., vol. 10 (Mar. 1, 1858), 322; Quinn, *Rivals,* 233.

100. *Executive Proceedings,* 35th Cong., 1st sess., vol. 10 (Dec. 22, 1857), 267; Quinn, *Rivals,* 233.

101. Williams, *David C. Broderick,* 159.

102. Smith, *Presidency of James Buchanan,* 37.

103. Klein, *President James Buchanan,* 284. See also Fish, *Civil Service and Patronage,* 169.

104. Robert Walter Johannsen, *Stephen A. Douglas* (Urbana: University of Illinois Press, 1997), 553; *Executive Proceedings,* 35th Cong., 1st sess., vol. 10 (Feb. 16, 1858), 308; Fowler, *Cabinet Politician,* 93.

105. *Executive Proceedings,* 35th Cong., 1st sess., vol. 10 (Feb. 16, 1858), 328, 337–339; Fowler, *Cabinet Politician,* 93.

106. For support of this view, see Philip Gerald Auchampaugh, "The Buchanan-Douglas Feud," *Journal of Illinois State History* 25 (Apr. 1932): 19.

107. The Lecompton constitution was created by the pro-slavery Kansas legislature in two forms (neither of which made slavery illegal) and then voted on by popular referendum (with Free-Soilers boycotting). After passage, the constitution was sent to Congress for ratification. The Senate accepted the act despite the opposition of Senator Douglas; the House, with the aid of Douglas Democrats, defeated the measure and passed legislation requiring a revote under a closely watched referendum. See Richard H. Sewell, *A House Divided: Sectionalism and Civil War, 1848–1865* (Baltimore: Johns Hopkins University Press, 1988), 63–67; Fowler, *Cabinet Politician,* 92.

108. Johannsen, *Stephen A. Douglas,* 554.

109. Abraham Lincoln defeated John C. Breckinridge by a vote of 180 to 72 in the electoral college. Mosher, *Executive Register,* 164. See also the chapter titled "A New Party Arises" in George H. Mayer, *The Republican Party, 1854–1964* (New York: Oxford University Press, 1964), 23–47.

110. In a memo to Lincoln, Secretary of State William H. Seward expressed concern over the new administration's lack of direction and placed the blame on the Senate's want of patronage: "We are at the end of a month's administration, and yet without a policy either domestic or foreign. . . . This, however, is not culpable, and it has even been unavoidable. The presence of the Senate, with the need to meet applications for patronage, have prevented attention to other and more grave matters." William H. Seward to Abraham Lincoln, "Some Thoughts for the President's Consideration," Apr. 1, 1861, in Frederic Bancroft, *The Life of William H. Seward* (New York and London: Harper and Brothers, 1900), 2:132.

111. The ensuing Civil War would last through most of Lincoln's presidency. For a general history of the Civil War, see Harry Hansen, *The Civil War* (New York: Duell, Sloan, and Pearce, 1962).

112. Moisei Ostrogorski, *Democracy and the Organization of Political Parties* (New York: Macmillan, 1922), 2:133.

113. Fish, *Civil Service and Patronage,* 169. See also Carl Russell Fish, "Lincoln and the Patronage," *American Historical Review* 8 (Oct. 1902): 66.

114. Abraham Lincoln to Salmon P. Chase, May 8, 1861, in *The Living Lincoln,* ed. Paul M. Angle and Earl Schenck Miers (New York: Barnes and Noble Books, 1992), 403.

115. Harry J. Carman and Reinhard H. Luthin, *Lincoln and the Patronage* (New York: Columbia University Press, 1943), 331.

116. Fish, "Removal of Officials," 84.

117. Allen C. Guelzo, *Abraham Lincoln: Redeemer President* (Grand Rapids, MI: Eerdmans, 1999), 278.

118. Fowler, *Cabinet Politician*, 107. See also Carman and Luthin, *Lincoln and the Patronage*, 333; Fish, "Lincoln and the Patronage," 59; Ostrogorski, *Democracy and the Organization of Political Parties*, 2:133.

119. Gerald Cullinan, *The Post Office Department* (New York: Praeger, 1968), 79; Fowler, *Cabinet Politician*, 107.

120. Diary entry, Feb. 10, 1863, in *Diary of Gideon Welles, Secretary of Navy under Lincoln and Johnson*, introduction by John T. Morse Jr. (Boston: Houghton Mifflin, 1911), 1:235.

121. Carman and Luthin, *Lincoln and the Patronage*, 64.

122. Abraham Lincoln to Jesse K. Dubois, Mar. 30, 1861, in *The Collected Works of Abraham Lincoln*, ed. Roy P. Basler (New Brunswick, NJ: Rutgers University Press, 1953), 4:302 (emphasis in original).

123. Abraham Lincoln to William Sprague, May 10, 1861, in ibid., 6:270.

124. Abraham Lincoln to Carl Schurz, Nov. 10, 1862, in *Uncollected Letters of Abraham Lincoln*, ed. Gilbert A. Tracy (New York: Houghton Mifflin, 1917), 215.

125. George Hoar, in *Congressional Record*, 53rd Cong., special sess., vol. 27 (Apr. 7, 1893), 102.

126. John Denton Carter, "Abraham Lincoln and the California Patronage," *American Historical Review* 48 (Apr. 1943): 495–506.

127. Gideon Welles, *Lincoln and Seward* (New York: Sheldon, 1874), 70–75.

128. Abraham Lincoln to Thomas Carney, May 14, 1864, in *Collected Works of Abraham Lincoln*, 7:340.

129. David Herbert Donald, *Lincoln* (New York: Touchstone, 1996), 596–599.

130. At the beginning of the war, Johnson said that he "had rather be a subject of the Russian tsar than a citizen of the Southern Confederacy." Hans L. Trefousse, *Andrew Johnson* (New York: Norton, 1997), 139. See also James L. Baumgardner, "Abraham Lincoln, Andrew Johnson, and the Federal Patronage: An Attempt to Save Tennessee for the Union?" *East Tennessee Historical Society's Publications* 45 (1973): 51–60.

131. Hans L. Trefousse, *Thaddeus Stevens: Nineteenth-Century Egalitarian* (Mechanicsburg, PA: Stackpole Books, 2001), 195.

132. As two historians stated: "Among the anomalies of congressional policy in 1867 was that it left the implementation of Reconstruction in the hands of an institution—the army—controlled by its greatest adversary, President Johnson." Alan Brinkley and Davis Dyer, *American Presidency* (New York: Houghton Mifflin, 2004), 196.

133. Trefousse, *Andrew Johnson*, 272.

134. Joseph P. Harris, *The Advice and Consent of the Senate* (Berkeley: University of California Press, 1953), 73.

135. John W. Stokes to Andrew Johnson, Mar. 15, 1867, in *The Papers of Andrew Johnson*, ed. Paul H. Bergeron (Knoxville: University of Tennessee Press, 1995), 12:151.

136. Fish, "Removal of Officials," 84.

137. Trefousse, *Andrew Johnson*, 338. Senator Doolittle had been a Democrat before he broke with his party in the 1850s. He would run unsuccessfully for governor on the Democratic ticket in 1871.

138. William F. Johnston to Andrew Johnson, Feb. 15, 1867, in *Papers of Andrew Johnson*, 12:33.

139. John Atkinson was rejected twice. See *Executive Proceedings*, 39th Cong., 1st sess., vol. 14 (July 13, 1866), 922, and 39th Cong., 2nd sess., vol. 16 (Jan. 22, 1867), 136–137. The Senate also rejected Edgar G. Spalding. See ibid., vol. 15 (Feb. 25, 1867), 268. John P. Sanborn eventually was confirmed. See ibid. (Mar. 2, 1867), 328.

140. Joseph R. Flanigen, Sydenham E. Ancona, and A. L. Ashmead were all rejected by voice vote. See ibid. (Jan. 22, 1867), 136–137; 40th Cong., 1st sess., vol. 15 (Mar. 12, 1867), 426; and ibid. (Mar. 15, 1867), 452.

141. John M. Glover to Andrew Johnson, Apr. 4, 1867, in *Papers of Andrew Johnson*, 12:204–205.

142. This was the name given to Republican politicians who believed in social and political rights for blacks and sought to achieve this end through federal legislation and enforcement. During the years following the Civil War, Radical Republicans in Congress favored harsh measures to achieve racial equality in the South and an overall Reconstruction policy that neither Abraham Lincoln nor Andrew Johnson would accept. One Reconstruction historian explained that "the driving force of Radical ideology was the utopian vision of a nation whose citizens enjoyed equality of civil and political right, secured by a powerful and beneficent national state." Eric Foner, *Reconstruction: America's Unfinished Revolution, 1863–1877* (New York: Harper and Row, 1988), 230. See also Harold Hyman, *The Radical Republicans and Reconstruction, 1861–1870* (Indianapolis: Bobbs-Merrill, 1967); Hans L. Trefousse, *The Radical Republicans: Lincoln's Vanguard for Racial Justice* (New York: Knopf, 1969); David Montgomery, *Beyond Equality: Labor and the Radical Republicans, 1862–1872* (New York: Knopf, 1981).

143. Hugh McCulloch to Andrew Johnson, Mar. 5, 1867, in *Papers of Andrew Johnson*, 12:116; William Thorpe to Andrew Johnson, Sept. 25, 1867, in ibid., 13:109.

144. *Executive Proceedings*, 40th Cong., special sess., vol. 15 (Apr. 12, 1867), 697; Hunter Brooke to Andrew Johnson, Apr. 13, 1867, in *Papers of Andrew Johnson*, 12:228.

145. Brooke to Johnson, Apr. 13, 1867, in *Papers of Andrew Johnson*, 12:228.

146. The rejection was probably also aided by the Radical Republicans' effort to indiscriminately oppose Johnson's nominations.

147. *Executive Proceedings*, 40th Cong., 1st sess., vol. 15 (Mar. 14, 1867), 450.

148. James Birney to Andrew Johnson, Mar. 22, 1867, in *Papers of Andrew Johnson*, 12:173.

149. Samuel C. Pomeroy to Andrew Johnson, Feb. 12, 1867, in ibid., 24; *Executive Proceedings*, 39th Cong., 2nd sess., vol. 15 (Dec. 20, 1866), 64.

150. William E. Robinson to Andrew Johnson, Feb. 18, 1867, in *Papers of Andrew Johnson*, 12:44–45; William E. Robinson to Andrew Johnson, Apr. 6, 1867, in ibid., 207; John Morrissey to Andrew Johnson, Mar. 26, 1867, in ibid., 185; Demas Barnes to Andrew Johnson, Apr. 11, 1867, in ibid., 223.

151. Thomas Swann to Andrew Johnson, Feb. 14, 1867, in ibid., 29–30; Samuel J. Randall to Andrew Johnson, Apr. 7, 1867, in ibid., 210; Charles Milne to Andrew Johnson, Feb. 18, 1867, in ibid., 43.

152. Joseph R. Flanigen to Andrew Johnson, Apr. 3, 1867, in ibid., 202, 203.

153. Andrew J. Steinman to Andrew Johnson, Apr. 22, 1867, in ibid., 239–240.

154. William Thorpe to Andrew Johnson, Sept. 25, 1867, in ibid., 13:109.

155. H. K. Beale, *The Critical Year: A Study of Andrew Jackson and Reconstruction* (New York: Harcourt, Brace, 1930), 359 (emphasis added).

156. Trefousse, *Andrew Johnson*, 276.

157. S. 453, "An Act regulating the tenure of certain civil offices," in *Journal of the House of Representatives*, 39th Cong., 2nd sess. (Mar. 2, 1867), 578–579; *Journal of the Senate*, 39th Cong., 2nd sess. (Mar. 2, 1867), 419; *U.S. Statutes at Large*, 39th Cong., 2nd sess., vol. 14 (Mar. 2, 1867), 430.

158. Brinkley and Dyer, *American Presidency*, 196; John Hope Franklin, *Reconstruction after the Civil War* (Chicago: University of Chicago Press, 1994), 71; Kermit L. Hall, *American Legal History: Cases and Materials* (New York: Oxford University Press, 1996), 228.

159. Fish, *Civil Service and Patronage*, 197.

160. For a detailed account of Johnson's feud with Stanton, see Trefousse, *Andrew Johnson*, 255–292.

161. Diary entry, Aug. 3, 1867, in *Diary of Gideon Welles*, 3:155.

162. Chester G. Hearn, *Impeachment of Andrew Johnson* (Jefferson, NC: McFarland, 2000), 133–134.

163. *Executive Proceedings,* 40th Cong., 2nd sess., vol. 16 (Dec. 12, 1867), 95–105.

164. *Journal of the Senate,* 40th Cong., 2nd sess. (Jan. 10, 1868), 961.

165. Adam Badeau, *Grant in Peace: From Appomattox to Mount McGregor* (Hartford, CT: S. S. Scranton, 1887), 111; Hearn, *Impeachment of Andrew Johnson,* 143.

166. *Journal of the Senate,* 40th Cong., 2nd sess. (Feb. 21, 1868), 963.

167. *Journal of the House of Representatives,* 40th Cong., 2nd sess. (Feb. 24, 1868), 392.

168. James E. Sefton, *Andrew Johnson and the Uses of Constitutional Power* (Boston: Little, Brown, 1980), 174–175, 177.

169. The Senate acquitted Johnson of the remaining articles on May 26. Trefousse, *Andrew Johnson,* 327–328.

170. Trefousse, *Thaddeus Stevens,* 236.

171. *Executive Proceedings,* 40th Cong., 2nd sess., vol. 16 (May 28, 1868), 236.

172. Trefousse, *Andrew Johnson,* 335.

173. *Executive Proceedings,* 40th Cong., 2nd sess., vol. 16 (June 2, 1868), 249.

174. James A. Garfield, "A Century of Congress," *Atlantic Monthly* 237 (July 1877): 61.

Chapter 5. Birth of Civil Service Reform (1869–1881)

1. Grant defeated Seymour by a vote of 214 to 80 in the electoral college. Robert Brent Mosher, *Executive Register of the United States, 1789–1902* (Washington, DC: GPO, 1905), 188. See also William S. McFeely, *Grant* (New York: Norton, 1982), 274–284.

2. Diary entry, Mar. 19, 1869, in *Diary of Gideon Welles, Secretary of Navy under Lincoln and Johnson* (New York: Houghton Mifflin, 1911), 3:557.

3. H.R. 3, 41st Cong., 1st sess. (1869).

4. Senator Charles Sumner took the lead in defeating the president's attempt to repeal the act. David Herbert Donald, *Charles Sumner and the Rights of Man* (New York: Knopf, 1970), 370.

5. Carl Russell Fish, *The Civil Service and the Patronage* (Cambridge, MA: Harvard University Press, 1904), 202. The Tenure of Office Act was modified in 1869 to give the president more discretion over suspensions but still retained Senate involvement.

6. Diary entry, Apr. 15, 1869, in *Diary of Gideon Welles,* 3:576.

7. 16 Stat. 44 (1869).

8. Moorfield Storey and Edward W. Emerson, *Ebenezer Rockwood Hoar: A Memoir* (Boston: Houghton Mifflin, 1911), 182. Henry J. Abraham points to Hoar's support for civil service reform and his opposition to Andrew Johnson's impeachment as additional reasons for his rejection. Henry J. Abraham, *Justices, Presidents, and Senators,* 4th ed. (Lanham, MD: Rowman and Littlefield, 1999), 96.

9. William B. Hesseltine, *Ulysses S. Grant: Politician* (New York: Frederick Ungar, 1957), 211–213, 254–255. For more information, see Donald Barr Chidsey, *The Gentleman from New York: A Life of Roscoe Conkling* (New Haven, CT: Yale University Press, 1935), 140–150.

10. *Journal of the Executive Proceedings of the Senate,* 41st Cong., 2nd sess., vol. 17 (July 7, 1870), 507. Allan Nevins reported that "Senator Fenton took the appointment as a heavy personal blow. He and Murphy had been enemies for years. But Conkling, thirsty for absolute power, forced Murphy's confirmation by a vote." Allan Nevins, *Hamilton Fish: The Inner History of the Grant Administration* (New York: Dodd, Mead, 1936), 593.

11. After the speech, one southern senator remarked to Conkling, "If you had spoken of me in that way I should have killed you." Alfred R. Conkling, *The Life and Letters of Roscoe Conkling* (New York: Charles L. Webster, 1889), 374. For a more detailed account of Conkling's speech, see William M. Stewart, *Reminiscences of Senator William M. Stewart of Nevada* (New York: Neale, 1908), 255–257.

12. Matthew Josephson, *The Politicos: 1865–1896* (New York: Harcourt, Brace, 1938), 95.

13. James Schouler, *History of the United States of America: Under the Constitution*, rev. ed. (New York: Dodd, Mead, 1917), 7:206.

14. Allan Peskin stated that the Stalwarts were "characterized as 'all-out believers in party regularity and the bloody shirt,' cynical machine politicians, hungry for office, and hostile to [civil service] reform." Allan Peskin, "Who Were the Stalwarts? Who Were Their Rivals? Republican Factions in the Gilded Age," *Political Science Quarterly* 99 (winter 1984–1985): 704. See also William G. Eidson, "Who Were the Stalwarts?" *Mid-America* 52 (Oct. 1970): 235–261.

15. Josephson, *The Politicos*, 89–91.

16. Robert Allen Rutland, *The Republicans: From Lincoln to Bush* (Columbia: University of Missouri Press, 1996), 88.

17. Josephson, *The Politicos*, 180.

18. George F. Hoar, *Autobiography of Seventy Years* (New York: Scribner, 1905), 1:386. David H. Donald gives a long list of reasons why Sumner might have lost control of appointments, including his successful effort to block repeal of the Tenure of Office Act. See Donald, *Charles Sumner*, 438.

19. Josephson, *The Politicos*, 172. See also E. Benjamin Andrews, *The United States in Our Own Times: A History from Reconstruction to Expansion* (New York: Scribner, 1903), 236.

20. During this appointment battle, Butler told Representative Ebenezer Rockwood Hoar: "I have a hold over Grant and he dare not withdraw Simmons' name." William D. Mallam, "The Grant-Butler Relationship," *Mississippi Valley Historical Review* 41 (Dec. 1954): 270, 275. See also George S. Boutwell, *Reminiscences of Sixty Years in Public Affairs* (New York: Greenwood Press, 1968), 2:283–284.

21. William D. Mallam, "Butlerism in Massachusetts," *New England Quarterly* 33 (June 1960): 196–199; Mallam, "The Grant-Butler Relationship," 270, 274–275.

22. Josephson, *The Politicos*, 173 (emphasis in original).

23. For a discussion of the early civil service bills, see Ari Hoogenboom, *Outlawing the Spoils: A History of the Civil Service Reform Movement, 1865–1883* (Urbana: University of Illinois Press, 1961), 13–32.

24. Ari Hoogenboom, "Thomas A. Jenckes and Civil Service Reform," *The Mississippi Valley Historical Review* 47 (Mar. 1961): 637. Another author explains that most "of those who became reformers had failed to achieve political prominence within the existing system, which was falling under machine domination, and so determined to overthrow that system and champion a new one." John M. Dobson, *Politics in the Gilded Age: A New Perspective on Reform* (New York: Praeger, 1972), 75.

25. Mark M. Krug states: "Among the small group of public figures who gave their support and leadership to the first civil reform movement, Lyman Trumbull was one of the most prominent. The movement began immediately after the Civil War and ended in failure ten years later." Mark M. Krug, *Lyman Trumbull: Conservative Radical* (New York: A. S. Barnes, 1965), 289.

26. S. 298, 41st Cong., 2nd sess. (1869); *Congressional Globe*, 41st Cong., 2nd sess. (Dec. 7, 1869), 17.

27. *Congressional Globe*, 41st Cong., 2nd sess. (Dec. 7, 1869), 17.

28. Ibid., 18.

29. Ibid. (Feb. 7, 1870), 1077. For information on the Judiciary Committee's amendment, see Senator Trumbull's comments in *Congressional Globe,* 41st Cong., 3rd sess. (Jan. 4, 1871), 292.

30. Hoogenboom, *Outlawing the Spoils,* 86.

31. *Congressional Globe,* 41st Cong., 2nd sess. (Feb. 7, 1870), 1077, 1078.

32. Ibid., 41st Cong., 3rd sess. (Jan. 4, 1871), 293.

33. Ibid.

34. Ibid., 293, 294; ibid. (Jan. 12, 1871), 461.

35. Ibid. (Jan. 10, 1871), 399–400.

36. Ibid. (Jan. 12, 1871), 458, 460.

37. Ibid., 460–461.

38. Ibid., 461.

39. Ulysses S. Grant, State of the Union, Dec. 5, 1870, in *A Compilation of the Messages and Papers of the Presidents,* ed. James D. Richardson (New York: Bureau of National Literature, 1911), 6:4063.

40. This bill had the approval of President Grant. See Hoogenboom, "Thomas A. Jenckes," 656.

41. *Congressional Globe,* 41st Cong., 3rd sess. (Mar. 3, 1871), 1997.

42. Representative Henry L. Dawes, the manager of the bill, argued: "It would be impossible for us to submit it to conference committee and obtain a report from that committee and have it acted upon by both Houses in time to have the bill enrolled. It therefore comes to this, that after all our labor and effort to pass the several appropriation bills we shall fail upon this, the last bill, unless we are willing to concur in the amendments of the Senate." Ibid., 1935, 1936.

43. Ibid., 1935. For a detailed account of the first Civil Service Commission, see Hoogenboom, *Outlawing the Spoils,* 88–134.

44. Fish, *Civil Service and Patronage,* 213. For more information on Curtis, see Edward Cary, *George William Curtis* (New York: Greenwood Press, 1969).

45. *Messages and Papers of the Presidents,* 6:4111; *Journal of the Senate,* 42nd Cong., 2nd sess. (Dec. 19, 1871), 65–66. For the specific civil service rules, see *Messages and Papers of the Presidents,* 6:4111–4113.

46. Grant, State of the Union, Dec. 7, 1874, in *Messages and Papers of the Presidents,* 6:4255. In the Civil Service Commission's annual report, the president made another plea for congressional funding. U.S. Civil Service Commission, *Report to the President, April 15, 1874* (Washington, DC: GPO, 1874), 3.

47. Perry Powers Fred, "The Reform of the Federal Service," *Political Science Quarterly* 3 (June 1888): 258.

48. *Messages and Papers of the Presidents,* 6:4281.

49. George H. Haynes, *The Senate of the United States: Its History and Practice* (Boston: Houghton Mifflin, 1938), 1:751.

50. John Russell Young, *Around the World with General Grant* (New York: American News Company, 1879), 2:263.

51. From Jan. 1869 through May 1869, letters to Grant were heavy with appointment requests. See *The Papers of Ulysses S. Grant,* ed. John Y. Simon (Carbondale: Southern Illinois University Press, 1995), 19:334, 336–337, 368, 373, 376, 391–392, 409, 411–413, 423, 426, 428, 438–439, 450, 454, 480.

52. Timothy O. Howe et al. to Ulysses S. Grant, Mar. 8, 1869, in ibid., 366; *Executive Proceedings,* 41st Cong., 1st sess., vol. 17 (Apr. 5, 1869), 86; Oliver H. P. T. Morton and Daniel D. Pratt to Ulysses S. Grant, Mar. 8, 1869, in *Papers of Ulysses S. Grant,* 19:368; *Executive Proceedings,* 41st Cong., 1st sess., vol. 17 (Apr. 2, 1869), 62.

53. John Sherman to Ulysses S. Grant, Jan. 18, 1869, in *Papers of Ulysses S. Grant,* 19:334; John Sherman to Ulysses S. Grant, Mar. 8, 1869, in ibid., 368.

54. Nevins, *Hamilton Fish,* 119–120.

55. Lyman Trumbull to Ulysses S. Grant, Mar. 22, 1869, in *Papers of Ulysses S. Grant*, 19:391.

56. H. J. Eckenrode, *Rutherford B. Hayes: Statesman of Reunion* (Norwalk, CT: Easton Press, 1988), 278.

57. Josephson, *The Politicos*, 99.

58. It was reported that the unlikely coalition of spoilsmen and reformers (Roscoe Conkling, Oliver Morton, Simon Cameron, Carl Schurz, and Benjamin Bristow) united and voted for Hayes in order to defeat front-runner James Blaine. William Dudley Foulke, *Life of Oliver P. Morton* (New York: AMS Press, 1974), 2:400–401.

59. Hayes defeated Tilden by a vote of 185 to 184 in the electoral college. Mosher, *Executive Register*, 211. See also Hans L. Trefousse, *Rutherford B. Hayes* (New York: Times Books, 2002), 74–83.

60. Rutherford B. Hayes, letter of acceptance of the Republican presidential nomination, in *Proceedings of the Republican National Convention, 1876* (Concord, NH: Republican Press Association, 1876), 115.

61. Rutherford B. Hayes, inaugural address, Mar. 5, 1877, in *Messages and Papers of the Presidents*, 6:4396.

62. Rutherford B. Hayes, State of the Union, Dec. 3, 1877, Dec. 1, 1879, and Dec. 6, 1880, in ibid., 4418, 4514, 4555.

63. Diary entries, Aug. 5 and Nov. 5, 1877, in *Diary and Letters of Rutherford Birchard Hayes*, ed. Charles R. Williams (Columbus: Ohio State Archeological and Historical, 1922), 3:441, 450.

64. Joseph P. Harris, *The Advice and Consent of the Senate* (Berkeley: University of California Press, 1953), 80.

65. James Pickett Jones, *John A. Logan: Stalwart Republican from Illinois* (Carbondale: Southern Illinois University Press, 2001), 100–106.

66. Earlier in the selection process, Hayes wrote in his diary: "I must not take either of the leading competitors for the Presidential nomination, nor any member of the present Cabinet." Diary entry, Jan. 17, 1877, in *Diary and Letters*, 3:402. A month later, Hayes wrote that he would not select a "member of the present [cabinet,] . . . presidential candidates," or an "appointment to 'take care' of anybody." Diary entry, Feb. 19, 1877, in ibid., 419.

67. Republican fears were alleviated by an arrangement Key agreed to. Outgoing postmaster general James N. Tyner would remain as first assistant and oversee most of the appointments in the North, while Key would control the southern appointments. As one newspaper account explained: "We are to have in effect a Dual Post Office Department." Albert V. House Jr., "President Hayes' Selection of David M. Key for Postmaster General," *Journal of Southern History* 4 (Feb. 1938): 90.

68. James A. Kehl, *Boss Rule in the Gilded Age: Matt Quay of Pennsylvania* (Pittsburgh: University of Pittsburgh Press, 1981), 41.

69. Josephson, *The Politicos*, 238; Harris, *Advice and Consent*, 81.

70. Diary entry, July 13, 1880, in *Diary and Letters*, 3:611.

71. Charles R. Williams, *The Life of Rutherford Birchard Hayes* (New York: Da Capo Press, 1971), 2:76; Trefousse, *Rutherford B. Hayes*, 93.

72. William Dudley Foulke, *Fighting the Spoilsmen* (1919; reprint, New York: Arno Press, 1974), 7; Chauncey M. Depew, *My Memories of Eighty Years* (New York: Scribner, 1922), 101; Henry L. Nelson, "Some Truths about the Civil Service," *Atlantic Monthly* 51 (Feb. 1883): 242.

73. Josephson, *The Politicos*, 241.

74. In a letter to Senator Augustus Merrimon of North Carolina, Key wrote: "While I shall always be glad to receive the advice of Senators and Representatives in Congress, touching matters of this kind, yet I shall not consider myself as in any way

bound to act upon it. My desire is to do the greatest good to the greatest number, and to this end I shall always be glad to have your cooperation." David M. Key to Augustus Merrimon, Mar. 17, 1877, in Williams, *Life of Rutherford Birchard Hayes*, 2:76.

75. David M. Key to Hendrick B. Wright, Apr. 1, 1877, in House, "President Hayes' Selection," 92–93.

76. Ari Hoogenboom, *The Presidency of Rutherford B. Hayes* (Lawrence: University Press of Kansas, 1988), 202.

77. In his biography of Half-Breed senator George F. Hoar, Richard E. Welch Jr. wrote: "The paradox of [Hoar's] position and that of the Hayes Administration was that righteous efforts to rid the Republican party of the taint of Stalwart politics apparently made it necessary to force the dismissal of one's enemies and promote the claims of one's friends." Richard E. Welch Jr., *George Frisbie Hoar and the Half-Breed Republicans* (Cambridge, MA: Harvard University Press, 1971), 75.

78. Fred, "Reform of the Federal Service," 253.

79. Table titled "How Hayes Has Paid the Men Who Made Him President," in *Congressional Record*, 47th Cong., 2nd sess., vol. 14 (Dec. 21, 1882), 518–519.

80. "Hayes Paying His Debts," *Washington Post*, July 22, 1878, 1; "Odd Executive Methods," *New York Times*, July 22, 1878, 1.

81. "Bulldozing Hayes," *Washington Post*, Aug. 26, 1878, 1. Senator Spencer was one of the worst "carpetbag" Republicans in the South. Sarah Van V. Woolfolk notes that in his 1872 reelection campaign, Spencer's conduct included "political betrayal of colleagues; manipulation of Federal patronage; embezzlement of public funds; purchase of votes; and intimidation of voters by the presence of Federal troops." Sarah Van V. Woolfolk, "George E. Spencer: A Carpetbagger in Alabama," *Alabama Review* 19 (Jan. 1966): 41–52.

82. Welch, *George Frisbie Hoar*, 75–76.

83. Harry Barnard, *Rutherford B. Hayes* (Indianapolis: Bobbs-Merrill, 1954), 454; Depew, *My Memories*, 101. Another theory was that, "in return for making their chieftain president, the Republicans had promised that Hayes would remove the garrisons from Louisiana and South Carolina and would appoint [Democrats] to his cabinet and to important Southern posts." Stanley P. Hirshson, *Farewell to the Bloody Shirt* (Bloomington: Indiana University Press, 1962), 42.

84. Ralph Lowell Eckert, *John Brown Gordon: Soldier, Southern, American* (Baton Rouge: Louisiana State University Press, 1989), 188.

85. Hirshson, *Farewell to the Bloody Shirt*, 36.

86. David M. Abshire, *The South Rejects a Prophet: The Life of Senator D. M. Key, 1824–1900* (New York: Praeger, 1967), 173–174.

87. Hirshson, *Farewell to the Bloody Shirt*, 40.

88. "Mr. Conkling at Home: Hayes Owned by the South," *New York World*, Apr. 17, 1878, 1.

89. James B. Murphy, *L. Q. C. Lamar* (Baton Rouge: Louisiana State University Press, 1973), 186.

90. At this time, the white carpetbag version of the Republican Party in Mississippi had disbanded. The remaining blacks went on to reconstitute the organization and came to an agreement with whites whereby black Republicans would support Democrats for office in exchange for help in retaining control of the Republican Party and federal appointments in the state. Ibid., 185–186.

91. Ibid., 187.

92. For example, Hayes wrote that his cabinet appointments would have been rejected without "the resolute support of the Southern Senators like [John] Gordon, [Lucius Q. C.] Lamar, and [Benjamin H.] Hill." Diary entry, Mar. 14, 1877, in *Diary and Letters*, 3:425.

93. "Mr. Conkling at Home," 1; "Conkling Uncorked," *Washington Post,* Apr. 18, 1878, 1.

94. The Mugwumps were one of the reform elements within the Republican Party that would fail to vote for the Republican ticket in the 1884 presidential election because of their dislike of Senator James G. Blaine. During the late 1800s, Mugwumps supported tariff reduction and civil service reform and tended to be apathetic or even hostile to civil rights, which were supported by the Stalwart and Half-Breed Republicans. Hirshson, *Farewell to the Bloody Shirt,* 12, 123, 252–253; H. Wayne Morgan, *From Hayes to McKinley* (Syracuse, NY: Syracuse University Press, 1969), 28–29; Lorin Peterson, *The Day of the Mugwump* (New York: Random House, 1961).

95. Hoogenboom, *Outlawing the Spoils,* 156–157.

96. John Sherman, *Recollections of Forty Years* (New York: Greenwood Press, 1968), 673.

97. U.S. House of Representatives, *First Report of the Commission on the New York Custom-House, and Instructions Related Thereto,* Ex. Doc. No. 8, 45th Cong., 1st sess. (May 24, 1877), 15.

98. Rutherford B. Hayes to John Sherman, May 26, 1877, in Williams, *Life of Rutherford Birchard Hayes,* 2:77.

99. Ibid., 85.

100. Ibid., 86; Hoogenboom, *Outlawing the Spoils,* 159–160.

101. *Executive Proceedings,* 45th Cong., 1st sess., vol. 21 (Oct. 24 and 29, 1877), 98–99.

102. For example, Roosevelt had led a delegation of citizens at the 1876 Republican Convention "with the special purpose of preventing the nomination of Conkling" for president. Barnard, *Rutherford B. Hayes,* 454.

103. Diary entry, Dec. 9, 1877, in *Diary and Letters,* 3:453.

104. *Executive Proceedings,* 45th Cong., 2nd sess., vol. 21 (Dec. 11, 1877), 169.

105. Josephson, *The Politicos,* 248.

106. *Executive Proceedings,* 45th Cong., 2nd sess., vol. 21 (Dec. 13, 1877), 171–172.

107. "Mr. Conkling Succeeds," *New York Tribune,* Dec. 13, 1877, 1.

108. Diary entry, Dec. 13, 1877, in *Diary and Letters,* 3:454.

109. George F. Howe, "The New York Custom-House Controversy, 1877–1879," *Mississippi Valley Historical Review* 18 (Dec. 1931): 358. While the customhouse battle was going on, Theodore Roosevelt Sr. died suddenly, thus preventing Hayes from nominating him. Josephson, *The Politicos,* 249.

110. John Jay, "Civil-Service Reform," *North American Review* 127 (Sept.–Oct. 1878): 273.

111. *Executive Proceedings,* 45th Cong., 1st sess., vol. 21 (Dec. 2 and 3, 1877), 379, 381.

112. Senator Conkling reportedly produced evidence that the Hayes administration had forced the collector, Chester Arthur, to appoint its friends to customhouse positions. Josephson, *The Politicos,* 250.

113. *Executive Proceedings,* 46th Cong., 1st sess., vol. 21 (Jan. 31, 1879), 497–498.

114. The Senate confirmed Merritt by a vote of thirty-three to twenty-four and Burt by a vote of thirty-one to nineteen. Ibid. (Feb. 3, 1879), 502–503. For an account of the proceedings in the Senate, see Eckenrode, *Rutherford B. Hayes,* 275–277.

115. *Executive Proceedings,* 46th Cong., 2nd sess., vol. 22 (Jan. 7, 1880), 156.

116. "Probable Nominations," *New York Times,* Jan. 6, 1880, 5; editorial, *New York Times,* Jan. 7, 1880, 2; editorial, *New York Times,* Jan. 8, 1880, 2; Special Dispatch, "Committee Work: The Appointment of Morton," *Chicago Daily Tribune,* Jan. 21,

1880, 1; *Executive Proceedings,* 46th Cong., 2nd sess., vol. 22 (Feb. 5, 1880), 221–222; "Fairly into It," *Washington Post,* Jan. 22, 1880, 1; "Other Matters of Importance," *Washington Post,* Feb. 5, 1880, 1; "Affairs at Washington," *New York Times,* Feb. 6, 1880, 1.

117. Diary entry, Feb. 7, 1880, in *Diary and Letters,* 3:585. Hayes was later successful in securing Morton's confirmation as surveyor of customs in California. *Executive Proceedings,* 46th Cong., 3rd sess., vol. 22 (Jan. 17, 1881), 452.

118. Rutherford B. Hayes to E. A. Merritt, Feb. 4, 1879, in *Diary and Letters,* 3:520; Rutherford B. Hayes to Silas W. Burt, Feb. 6, 1879, in ibid., 520–521. See also Rutherford B. Hayes to C. K. Graham, Feb. 6, 1879, in ibid., 521.

119. Fish, *Civil Service and Patronage,* 216. These rules would stay in place until passage of the Pendleton Act in 1883. George William Curtis and Sherman S. Rogers, "Civil Service Reform," *Atlantic Monthly* 71 (Jan. 1893): 20. See also Dorman B. Eaton, *The Spoils System and Civil Service Reform in the Custom-House and Post-Office at New York* (New York: G. P. Putnam, 1881).

120. Hoogenboom, *Presidency of Rutherford B. Hayes,* 145–146.

121. Diary entry, July 14, 1880, in *Diary and Letters,* 3:612.

122. Hoogenboom, *Presidency of Rutherford B. Hayes,* 147.

123. In fact, Hayes's treasury secretary, John Sherman, was the favorite-son candidate of Ohio. Edwin P. Hoyt, *James A. Garfield* (Chicago: Reilly and Lee, 1964), 112, 128–129.

124. Margaret Leech and Harry J. Brown, *The Garfield Orbit* (New York: Harper and Row, 1978), 202–209.

125. For an account of the 1880 Republican National Convention and the nomination of the Garfield-Arthur ticket, see Rutland, *The Republicans,* 88–90.

126. The 1880 presidential contest marked the first time the Democratic Party carried all the southern states. Leech and Brown, *Garfield Orbit,* 220. Garfield defeated Hancock by a vote of 214 to 155 in the electoral college. Mosher, *Executive Register,* 234.

127. James Garfield, letter of acceptance of the Republican presidential nomination, in *Proceedings of the Republican National Convention, 1880* (Chicago: Jno. B. Jeffery Printing House, 1880), 301.

128. Neither element was pleased with Garfield's letter. Josephson, *The Politicos,* 295.

129. James Garfield to Roscoe Conkling, Jan. 31, 1881, in *The Autobiography of Thomas Collier Platt,* ed. Louis J. Lang (1910; reprint, New York: Arno Press, 1974), 145.

130. Diary entry, Mar. 20, 1881, in *The Diary of James A. Garfield,* ed. Harry James Brown and Frederick D. Williams (East Lansing: Michigan State University Press, 1981), 4:561.

131. "What Is Said at Albany," *New York Times,* Mar. 23, 1881, 1.

132. Diary entry, Mar. 20, 1881, in *Diary of James A. Garfield,* 4:561.

133. James Garfield to Burke Aaron Hinsdale, Apr. 4, 1881, in *Garfield-Hinsdale Letters: Correspondence between James Abram Garfield and Burke Aaron Hinsdale,* ed. Mary L. Hinsdale (Ann Arbor: University of Michigan Press, 1949), 488; *Executive Proceedings,* 47th Cong., special sess., vol. 23 (Mar. 23, 1881), 39.

134. Matthew P. Breen, *Thirty Years of New York Politics* (New York: Arno Press, 1974), 648–649; E. Benjamin Andrews, "A History of the Last Quarter-Century in the United States," *Scribner's Magazine* 18 (Sept. 1895): 279; Theodore Clarke Smith, *The Life and Letters of James Abram Garfield* (New Haven, CT: Yale University Press, 1925), 963.

135. Garfield to Hinsdale, Apr. 4, 1881, in *Garfield-Hinsdale Letters,* 489.

136. Diary entry, Mar. 27, 1881, in *Diary of James A. Garfield,* 4:565; Garfield to Hinsdale, Apr. 4, 1881, in *Garfield-Hinsdale Letters,* 489.

137. Smith, *Life and Letters of James Abram Garfield*, 1132; James Garfield to Ulysses S. Grant, May 15, 1881, in Leech and Brown, *Garfield Orbit*, 315–316. For an account of the interaction between President Garfield and Grant, see McFeely, *Grant*, 485–486.

138. Diary entry, May 17, 1881, in *Diary of James A. Garfield*, 4:595.

139. Leech and Brown, *Garfield Orbit*, 230–231.

140. Diary entry, Mar. 25, 1881, in *Diary of James A. Garfield*, 4:563; Breen, *Thirty Years*, 650.

141. Diary entry, Apr. 2, 1881, in *Diary of James A. Garfield*, 4:568.

142. A copy of the letter of resignation can be found in Breen, *Thirty Years*, 657. For an account of the resignation, see *Autobiography of Thomas Collier Platt*, 152–157.

143. The New York Assembly and Senate voted in joint session for replacement candidates. Breen, *Thirty Years*, 658–660.

144. *Executive Proceedings*, 47th Cong., special sess., vol. 23 (May 18, 1881), 87.

145. Sherman, *Recollections*, 817.

146. Smith, *Life and Letters of James Abram Garfield*, 1141.

147. Andrews, "A History of the Last Quarter-Century," 286.

Chapter 6. The Pendleton Act: Patchwork Reform
(1881–1897)

1. For an account of Arthur's career as a member of Conkling's machine, see George Frederick Howe, *Chester A. Arthur: A Quarter-Century of Machine Politics* (New York: Frederick Ungar, 1957).

2. Ari Hoogenboom, *Outlawing the Spoils: A History of the Civil Service Reform Movement, 1865–1883* (Urbana: University of Illinois Press, 1961), 212.

3. Chester A. Arthur, State of the Union, Dec. 6, 1881, in *A Compilation of the Messages and Papers of the Presidents*, ed. James D. Richardson (New York: Bureau of National Literature, 1911), 6:4647–4650.

4. Hoogenboom, *Outlawing the Spoils*, 216–217; "Topics of the Time: Pubic Service and Private Business," *Century* 23 (Feb. 1882): 616–617. See also Thomas C. Reeves, *Gentleman Boss: The Life of Chester Alan Arthur* (New York: Knopf, 1975), 323.

5. Zachary Karabell argues that the Republican defeat in the 1882 congressional elections prompted Congress to act. Zachary Karabell, *Chester Alan Arthur* (New York: Henry Holt, 2004), 99–104. The New York Civil Service Reform Association drafted a bill to replace Senator Pendleton's original reform measure, which was, by all accounts, unconstitutional and impractical. Dorman B. Eaton convinced the senator to substitute his bill with the association's version. Adelbert Bower Sageser, *The First Two Decades of the Pendleton Act: A Study of Civil Service Reform* (Lincoln: University Studies of the University of Nebraska, 1935), 39.

6. *Congressional Record*, 47th Cong., 2nd sess., vol. 14 (Dec. 27, 1882), 661; ibid. (Jan. 16, 1883), 867. For a discussion of the congressional debate on the Pendleton Act, see Hoogenboom, *Outlawing the Spoils*, 236–252.

7. *Congressional Record*, 47th Cong., 2nd sess., vol. 14 (Jan. 4, 1883), 860.

8. Existing officeholders were grandfathered into the system and were not subject to the competitive examinations. In addition, positions in Washington were to be apportioned among the states and territories based on population as of the latest federal census. Hoogenboom points out that this provision was a means of making reform popular among members of Congress. Ari Hoogenboom, "The Pendleton Act and the Civil Service," *American Historical Review* 64 (Jan. 1959): 314.

9. *Congressional Record*, 47th Cong., 2nd sess., vol. 14 (Dec. 27, 1882), 656.

10. Ibid., 654, 655. Morgan's amendment was a modified version of a similar

amendment he had offered four days earlier that had been defeated by a vote of twenty-six to twenty-one. Ibid. (Dec. 23, 1882), 620.

11. Ibid., 655, 656.

12. A total of 13,924 positions were placed into the classified system (2,573 in customs, 5,699 in postal, and 5,652 in departments in Washington, DC). "Table 1. Civil Service Classifications, 1883–1901," in Stephen Skowronek, *Building a New American State: The Expansion of National Administrative Capacities, 1877–1920*, 8th ed. (Cambridge: Cambridge University Press, 1997), 70.

13. Practically, this meant that the commission itself would devise the rules necessary to determine how the examinations would affect the pre-nomination process.

14. U.S. Civil Service Commissioner Arthur S. Flemming explained that the 1871 opinion "has come down through the years; has never been challenged and has constituted the legal basis for what in normal times we refer to as the 'rule of three.'" U.S. House of Representatives, Committee on the Civil Service, *Investigation of Civilian Employment: Hearings before the Committee on the Civil Service*, part 1, 78th Cong., 1st sess. (Mar. 10, 1943), 16.

15. Amos T. Akerman, "Civil-Service Commission," Aug. 31, 1871, in U.S. Department of Justice, *Official Opinions of the Attorneys General*, ed. A. J. Bentley (Washington, DC: GPO, 1873), 13:520.

16. Ibid., 523, 524.

17. Ibid., 524–525.

18. From 1883 to 1888, a "rule of four" existed. Rule 16, May 7, 1883, in *Messages and Papers of the Presidents*, 6:4752; Departmental Rule 7, Feb. 2, 1888, in ibid., 7:5336.

19. Paul P. Van Riper, *History of the United States Civil Service* (Evanston, IL: Row, Peterson, 1958), 104.

20. The rule of three continues to be a primary feature of most civil service appointments. Section 3318(a) of Title 5 states the following: "The nominating or appointing authority shall *select* for appointment to each vacancy *from* the highest three eligibles available for appointment" (emphasis in original).

21. Sageser, *First Two Decades of the Pendleton Act*, 61.

22. Van Riper, *History of U.S. Civil Service*, 94, 117.

23. *Messages and Papers of the Presidents*, 6:4748–4753.

24. "Table 1. Civil Service Classifications, 1883–1901," 70; Van Riper, *History of U.S. Civil Service*, 105.

25. Hoogenboom, "Pendleton Act," 307.

26. Rule 19, Nov. 10, 1884, in *Messages and Papers of the Presidents*, 7:4821–4822.

27. Sageser, *First Two Decades of the Pendleton Act*, 215; Skowronek, *Building a New American State*, 80.

28. Postal Rule 4, Jan. 5, 1894, in *Messages and Papers of the Presidents*, 8:5946.

29. U.S. Senate, Committee on Civil Service, *Methods and Procedure of Civil Service Examining Division*, 67th Cong., 2nd sess. (1922), 5.

30. For example, in 1917, Congress exempted from civil service examinations "insurance experts" in the Bureau of War Risk Insurance. See U.S. Civil Service Commission, *Forty-first Annual Report* (Washington, DC: GPO, 1924), ix. Also, many of the Civil Service Commission's annual reports included an appendix that listed the positions exempt from the federal civil service. For example, see U.S. Civil Service Commission, *Thirty-seventh Annual Report* (Washington, DC: GPO, 1920), 76–88; *Thirty-ninth Annual Report* (Washington, DC: GPO, 1922), 84–95; *Fortieth Annual Report* (Washington, DC: GPO, 1923), 85–92.

31. During World War I, the Civil Service Commission reported: "The appointment of civilians from outside the civil service, without competitive tests of fitness,

as military men and women, paid from military appropriations salaries larger than are paid in the civil service, and their assignments to desks in the departments at Washington at the beginning of the war was discouraging to the great body of civil-service employees, who were continued at their prewar rates of pay while new appointees performing the same or less difficult work received higher pay." U.S. Civil Service Commission, *Thirty-sixth Annual Report* (Washington, DC: GPO, 1919), xxiii.

32. Sageser, *First Two Decades of the Pendleton Act*, 216; Hoogenboom, "Pendleton Act," 308. For insight into the problems of managing the civil service during wartime, see Civil Service Commission, *Thirty-sixth Annual Report*, v–xxxi.

33. Address by William Dudley Foulke, in *Proceedings: National Civil Service Reform League, Jan. 12, 1926* (New York: National Civil Service Reform League, 1926), 18–19. See also address by Carl Schurz, in *Proceedings: National Civil Service Reform League, Dec. 8 and 9, 1904* (New York: National Civil Service Reform League, 1904), 85–86.

34. Reeves, *Gentleman Boss*, 256, 260. One Arthur biographer wrote: "The New York Stalwarts grew particularly bitter because [Arthur] declined to change what they considered a sorry situation in his own state. His refusal to remove Collector Robertson, who prevented them from using the Custom House patronage to maintain their organization, seemed to them a breach of loyalty." Howe, *Chester A. Arthur*, 163.

35. Karabell, *Chester Alan Arthur*, 69.

36. Reeves, *Gentleman Boss*, 256. See also Dorothy Ganfield Fowler, *The Cabinet Politician: The Postmaster General, 1829–1909* (New York: Columbia University Press, 1943), 181.

37. George H. Mayer, *The Republican Party, 1854–1964* (New York: Oxford University Press, 1964), 206.

38. James A. Kehl, *Boss Rule in the Gilded Age: Matt Quay of Pennsylvania* (Pittsburgh: University of Pittsburgh Press, 1981), 52.

39. James Pickett Jones, *John A. Logan: Stalwart Republican from Illinois* (Carbondale: Southern Illinois University Press, 2001), 150.

40. Richard E. Welch Jr., *George Frisbie Hoar and the Half-Breed Republicans* (Cambridge, MA: Harvard University Press, 1971), 105; Leon Burr Richardson, *William E. Chandler: Republican* (New York: Dodd, Mead, 1940), 342.

41. Welch, *George Frisbie Hoar*, 105.

42. Howe, *Chester A. Arthur*, 195.

43. Dorothy Ganfield Fowler, "Congressional Dictation of Local Appointments," *Journal of Politics* 7 (Feb. 1945), 46. For information on the Post Office Department during the Arthur administration, see Fowler, *Cabinet Politician*, 180–187.

44. Richard Nelson Current, *Pine Logs and Politics: A Life of Philetus Sawyer, 1816–1900* (Madison: State Historical Society of Wisconsin, 1950), 202–203.

45. Reeves, *Gentleman Boss*, 309.

46. Edward Mayes, *Lucius Q. C. Lamar: His Life, Times, and Speeches* (Nashville, TN: Publishing House of the Methodist Episcopal Church, 1896), 422–430; Charles Chilton Pearson, *Readjustor Movement in Virginia* (New Haven, CT: Yale University Press, 1917), 138, 141; Nelson Morehouse Blake, *William Mahone of Virginia* (Richmond, VA: Garret and Massie, 1935), 185; Vincent P. De Santis, *Republicans Face the Southern Question* (Baltimore: Johns Hopkins Press, 1959), 150. The Readjuster Party consisted of former members of the Democratic and Republican parties. The party advocated the partial transfer of Virginia's Civil War debt to West Virginia and a lowering of the interest rate for the remaining payments. In addition, Readjusters supported equal treatment of blacks, which included the enforcement of federal

civil rights legislation and improved public schooling. See Pearson, *Readjustor Movement*; Benjamin Le Fevre, *Campaign of '84* (New York: Baird and Dillon, 1884), 263.

47. Blake, *William Mahone*, 221.

48. Howe, *Chester A. Arthur*, 216.

49. Blake, *William Mahone*, 229.

50. Pearson, *Readjustor Movement*, 168; Blake, *William Mahone*, 230.

51. Thomas C. Reeves wrote: "The administration moved quickly to forge coalitions between Republicans and independents in other parts of the South as well. In Alabama, Arkansas, Mississippi, North Carolina, South Carolina, Tennessee, and Texas, ex-Democrats won support from Washington. Several of the southern independent leaders were Greenbackers, and some sought unlimited coinage of silver." Reeves, *Gentleman Boss*, 309.

52. Arthur is the only incumbent Republican president ever to actively seek and lose the party's nomination. One historian concluded that the 1884 presidential election effectively destroyed the Stalwart and Half-Breed Republican factions. Kehl, *Boss Rule*, 57.

53. Alyn Brodsky, *Grover Cleveland: A Study in Character* (New York: St. Martin's Press, 2000), 74, 84. The word *mugwump* was established during the 1884 campaign as the popular term for Republican reformers who abandoned their party to support Cleveland. Lorin Peterson, *The Day of the Mugwump* (New York: Random House, 1961), 22; John M. Dobson, *Politics in the Gilded Age: A New Perspective on Reform* (New York: Praeger, 1972), 108–120; Gerald W. McFarland ed., *Mugwumps, Morals and Politics, 1884–1920* (Amherst: University of Massachusetts Press, 1975), 35–54.

54. Mark Wahlgren Summers, *Rum, Romanism and Rebellion: The Making of a President, 1884* (Chapel Hill: University of North Carolina Press, 2000), 281–283, 296; Norman E. Tutorow, *James Gillespie Blaine and the Presidency* (New York: Peter Lang, 1989), 79. Cleveland defeated Blaine by a vote of 219 to 182 in the electoral college. Robert Brent Mosher, *Executive Register of the United States, 1789–1902* (Washington, DC: GPO, 1905), 248.

55. "To secure [federal offices] and to enjoy their emoluments was the hope of thousands upon thousands of Democratic party 'workers,' who now swarmed like locusts in the streets of Washington and besieged the governmental bureaus and the portals of the White House." Harry Thurston Peck, *Twenty Years of the Republic, 1885–1905* (New York: Dodd, Mead, 1920), 66. See also Frank R. Kent, *The Democratic Party* (New York: Century, 1928), 291.

56. Horace Samuel Merrill, *Bourbon Leader: Grover Cleveland and the Democratic Party* (Boston: Little, Brown, 1957), 95.

57. The National Civil Service Reform League, founded in 1881, promoted civil service reform through the publication of journals and pamphlets. For a detailed account of this organization, see Frank M. Stewart, *The National Civil Service Reform League* (Austin: University of Texas Press, 1929).

58. Grover Cleveland to George W. Curtis, Dec. 25, 1884, in *Letters of Grover Cleveland, 1850–1908*, ed. Allan Nevins (New York: Houghton Mifflin, 1933), 52–53.

59. Ibid.

60. Grover Cleveland, inaugural address, Mar. 4, 1885, in *Messages and Papers of the Presidents*, 7:4887.

61. Of these offices, 5,328 were added through executive order, 1,931 by rules revision, and 4,498 through growth of the service. "Table 1. Civil Service Classifications, 1883–1901," 70.

62. Van Riper, *History of the U.S. Civil Service*, 119.

63. Grover Cleveland to Daniel Manning, June 20, 1885, in *Letters of Grover Cleveland*, 64.

64. Unmailed letter from Grover Cleveland to a western politician, Aug. 25, 1885, in ibid., 73.

65. Merrill, *Bourbon Leader*, 95.

66. Carl Russell Fish, *The Civil Service and the Patronage* (Cambridge, MA: Harvard University Press, 1904), 222. The Civil Service Commission reported that "not less than 96 per cent of the Republican [postal] employees were turned out during the four years." U.S. Civil Service Commission, *Eleventh Report* (Washington, DC: GPO, 1895), 16.

67. For example, in Indiana, civil service reformer William Dudley Foulke protested the removals that went against Cleveland's reform statements. William Dudley Foulke, *Fighting the Spoilsmen* (1919; reprint, New York: Arno Press, 1974), 38–39.

68. Hoogenboom, *Outlawing the Spoils*, 261.

69. Allan Nevins, *Grover Cleveland: A Study in Courage* (New York: Dodd, Mead, 1932), 254.

70. Grover Cleveland, "The Independence of the Executive, II," *Atlantic Monthly* 86 (July 1900), 3; Nevins, *Grover Cleveland*, 254–255.

71. As Cleveland later recalled: "These requests foreshadowed what the senatorial construction of the [Tenure of Office Act] of 1869 might be, and indicated that the Senate notwithstanding constitutional limitations, and even in the face of the repeal of the statutory provisions giving it the right to pass upon suspensions by the President [the so-called evidence and reasons provision], was still inclined to insist, directly or indirectly, upon that right." Cleveland, "The Independence of the Executive, II," 4.

72. Nevins, *Grover Cleveland*, 255.

73. Cleveland, "The Independence of the Executive, II," 3, 4.

74. Robert McElroy, *Grover Cleveland: The Man and the Statesman* (New York: Harper, 1923), 1:175.

75. Cleveland, "The Independence of the Executive, II," 5.

76. *Journal of the Executive Proceedings of the Senate*, 49th Cong., 1st sess., vol. 25 (Jan. 25, 1886), 294.

77. Cleveland, "The Independence of the Executive, II," 7.

78. Nevins, *Grover Cleveland*, 259.

79. *Messages and Papers of the Presidents*, 7:4961–4962, 4963, 4967.

80. *Congressional Record*, 49th Congress, 1st sess., vol. 17 (Mar. 26, 1886), 2810–2814.

81. Cleveland, "The Independence of the Executive, II," 11.

82. Joseph P. Harris, *The Advice and Consent of the Senate* (Berkeley: University of California Press, 1953), 90.

83. Nevins, *Grover Cleveland*, 264.

84. *Congressional Record*, 49th Congress, 2nd sess., vol. 17 (July 21, 1886), 113.

85. Brodsky, *Grover Cleveland*, 138; Henry Jones Ford, *The Cleveland Era: A Chronicle of the New Order in Politics* (New Haven, CT: Yale University Press, 1919), 119.

86. Brodsky, *Grover Cleveland*, 138.

87. Richard E. Welch Jr., *The Presidencies of Grover Cleveland* (Lawrence: University Press of Kansas, 1988), 217.

88. Nevins, *Grover Cleveland*, 237.

89. Grover Cleveland to George W. Hayward, July 21, 1885, in *Letters of Grover Cleveland*, 68.

90. Horace Samuel Merrill, "Ignatius Donnelly, James J. Hill, and Cleveland Administration Patronage," *Mississippi Valley Historical Review* 39 (Dec. 1952): 505.

91. Francis M. Cockrell to Sam M. Green, Dec. 23, 1885, in Hugh P. Williamson,

"Correspondence of Senator Francis Marion Cockrell: December 23, 1885–March 24, 1888," *Bulletin of the Missouri Historical Society* 28 (July 1969): 298.

92. Francis M. Cockrell to Sam M. Green, Mar. 18, 1886, in ibid., 299.

93. In 1885, the Republican Party controlled the entire Minnesota congressional delegation, which included two senators and five representatives. The Grangers were members of an agrarian movement that took its name from the National Grange of the Patrons of Husbandry, a social order founded in 1867. The movement grew from a social to a political organization in large part because of the panic of 1873, which caused farmers to protest corporate economic abuses. The movement was politically powerful in the Midwest, and Grangers controlled the state legislatures in Illinois, Wisconsin, Minnesota, and Iowa. In these states, Granger laws were passed establishing maximum railroad rates and state railroad commissions. In the late 1870s, the Granger movement lost ground to the Greenback Party, and by the turn of the century, the agrarian cause had been taken up by the Populist Party. See James Dabney McCabe, *History of the Granger Movement or the Farmer's War against Monopolies* (New York: A. M. Kelly, 1969); Solon J. Buck, *The Granger Movement* (Lincoln: University of Nebraska Press, 1963); Arthur Elijah Paine, *The Granger Movement in Illinois* (Urbana, IL: University Press, 1904).

The Bourbons were the conservative element in the Democratic Party and consisted primarily of those opposed to unions, welfare legislation, high taxes, and general federal interference in state matters. See Horace Samuel Merrill, *Bourbon Democracy in the Middle West, 1865–1896* (Baton Rouge: Louisiana State University Press, 1953); Allen Johnston Going, *Bourbon Democracy in Alabama, 1874–1890* (Tuscaloosa: University of Alabama Press, 1992).

94. Merrill, "Cleveland Administration Patronage," 506.

95. Ibid., 513–514. For a detailed account of this dispute, see Martin Ridge, *Ignatius Donnelly: The Portrait of a Politician* (St. Paul: Minnesota Historical Society Press, 1991), 218–225. For an account outlining Cleveland as a Bourbon, see Merrill, *Bourbon Leader*.

96. M. P. Curran, *Life of Patrick A. Collins* (Norwood, MA: Norwood Press, 1906), 100.

97. Ibid., 104. At the time, the state was represented by two Republican senators, Henry L. Dawes and George F. Hoar. For a detailed account of this controversy, see Geoffrey Blodgett, *The Gentle Reformers: Massachusetts Democrats in the Cleveland Era* (Cambridge, MA: Harvard University Press, 1966), 57–61.

98. Grover Cleveland to Patrick A. Collins, Oct. 29, 1885, in *Letters of Grover Cleveland*, 89.

99. Curran, *Life of Patrick A. Collins*, 106.

100. Grover Cleveland to Peter Butler, Nov. 22, 1895, in *Letters of Grover Cleveland*, 93.

101. Mayer, *The Republican Party*, 215–218.

102. Mosher, *Executive Register*, 262. Charles W. Calhoun explained that because of the disfranchisement of southern blacks, Democrats could claim "no moral ground" on winning the popular vote. Charles W. Calhoun, *Benjamin Harrison* (New York: Henry Holt, 2005), 58.

103. Benjamin Harrison, inaugural address, Mar. 4, 1889, in *Messages and Papers of the Presidents*, 7:5446.

104. Of these offices, 8,690 were added by executive order and 1,845 through growth of the service. "Table 1. Civil Service Classifications, 1883–1901," 70.

105. Van Riper, *History of the U.S. Civil Service*, 124; Hoogenboom, *Outlawing the Spoils*, 261.

106. Sageser, *First Two Decades of the Pendleton Act*, 171.

107. Harry J. Sievers, *Benjamin Harrison: Hoosier President* (Indianapolis: Bobbs-Merrill, 1968), 74; Foulke, *Fighting the Spoilsmen*, 51. See also Fish, *Civil Service and Patronage*, 224.

108. Foulke, *Fighting the Spoilsmen*, 289; Van Riper, *History of the U.S. Civil Service*, 124; Sageser, *First Two Decades of the Pendleton Act*, 141.

109. Elisabeth P. Myers, *Benjamin Harrison* (Chicago: Reilly and Lee Books, 1969), 129.

110. Sageser, *First Two Decades of the Pendleton Act*, 131–132.

111. Homer E. Socolofsky and Allan B. Spetter, *The Presidency of Benjamin Harrison* (Lawrence: University Press of Kansas, 1987), 34. See also Alan Brinkley and Davis Dyer, *American Presidency* (New York: Houghton Mifflin, 2004), 252–253.

112. H. H. Kohlsaat, *From McKinley to Harding: Personal Recollections of Our Presidents* (New York: Scribner, 1923), 5.

113. Shelby M. Cullom, *Fifty Years in Public Service: Personal Recollections of Shelby M. Cullom* (Chicago: A. C. McClurg, 1911), 249. Evidence suggests that the senator was treated well by the administration. W. B. Cooley to Edward Smith, Nov. 25, 1889, in National Civil Service Reform League, *Civil Service Reform in the National Service, 1889–1891* (Boston: Press of Geo. H. Ellis, 1891), 60.

114. William M. Stewart, *Reminiscences of Senator William M. Stewart of Nevada* (New York: Neale, 1908), 310.

115. Thomas Collier Platt, *The Autobiography of Thomas Collier Platt*, ed. Louis Lang (1910; reprint, New York: Arno Press, 1974), 252. See also Peck, *Twenty Years of the Republic*, 282.

116. One scholar wrote that Harrison "felt . . . a strong personal dislike for some of the most influential leaders of his party; and though, in his official intercourse with them, he tried hard to treat them with cordiality, he did it with so bad a grace that his actual sentiments became perfectly well known." Peck, *Twenty Years of the Republic*, 170–171.

117. Michael J. Korzi, *Seat of Popular Leadership: The Presidency, Political Parties, and Democratic Leadership* (Amherst: University of Massachusetts Press, 2004), 177.

118. Champ Clark, *My Quarter Century of American Politics* (New York: Harper, 1920), 1:290.

119. Kehl, *Boss Rule*, 159.

120. Harold F. Gosnell noted that "Platt's chief concern at Washington was the strength of the time-honored custom of 'senatorial courtesy' and a President who failed to consult him upon New York matters might well consider the next presidential campaign." Harold F. Gosnell, "Thomas C. Platt—Political Manager," *Political Science Quarterly* 38 (Sept. 1923): 458. See also Kehl, *Boss Rule*, 159; Peck, *Twenty Years of the Republic*, 284; Robert Miraldi, *The Pen Is Mightier: The Muckraking Life of Charles Edward Russell* (New York: Palgrave Macmillan, 2003), 60; Robert Rienow and Leona Train Rienow, *Of Snuff, Sin and the Senate* (Chicago: Follett, 1965), 193.

121. Henry L. Stoddard, *As I Knew Them* (New York: Harper and Brothers, 1927), 168.

122. Arthur Wallace Dunn, *From Harrison to McKinley* (New York: G. P. Putnam, 1922), 1:88.

123. Benjamin Harrison, *This Country of Ours* (New York: Charles Scribner's Sons, 1897), 107–109.

124. Ibid., 109.

125. John Sherman to Benjamin Harrison, Apr. 25, 1889, in Benjamin Harrison Papers (BHP), reel 19, Library of Congress, Manuscript Reading Room.

126. Socolofsky and Spetter, *Presidency of Benjamin Harrison*, 33.

127. William H. H. Miller to Benjamin Harrison, Mar. 21, 1889, in BHP, reel 19; John C. Spooner to Benjamin Harrison, Apr. 13, 1889, in ibid.; Dorothy Ganfield Fowler, *John Coit Spooner: Defender of Presidents* (New York: University Publishers, 1961), 118–122.

128. "Talk with the President," *Globe-Democrat*, Apr. 19, 1889, in BHP, reel 19.

129. Herbert Adams Gibbons, *John Wanamaker* (New York: Harper, 1926), 298–301; National Civil Service Reform League, *Civil Service Reform*, 25–63; Wayne E. Fuller, *The American Mail: Enlarger of the Common Life* (Chicago: University of Chicago Press, 1972), 314; Fowler, *Cabinet Politician*, 213–219; "'Good' John Wanamaker," *New York Times*, Oct. 3, 1892, 5; Louis Melius, *The American Postal Service: History of the Postal Service from the Earliest Times* (Washington, DC: National Capitol Press, 1917), 62.

130. Marshall Cushing, *The Story of Our Post Office* (Boston: A. M. Thayer, 1893), 281. The last known use of the term *referee* was during Franklin D. Roosevelt's administration. "McGill Patronage Referee," *New York Times*, May 1, 1933, 2.

131. "Talk with the President."

132. William H. H. Miller to Benjamin Harrison, Apr. 6, 1889, in BHP, reel 19.

133. William H. H. Miller to Benjamin Harrison, Mar. 27, 1889, in ibid.

134. William H. H. Miller to Benjamin Harrison, Mar. 26, 1889, Apr. 28, 1889, Mar. 27, 1889, Mar. 22, 1889, Apr. 8, 1889, and Apr. 11, 1889, in ibid.

135. William H. H. Miller to Benjamin Harrison, Apr. 23, 1889, and Mar. 21, 1889; Kate Field to Benjamin Harrison, Mar. 21, 1889, in ibid.

136. Mosher, *Executive Register*, 268; Robert Allen Rutland, *The Republicans: From Lincoln to Bush* (Columbia: University of Missouri Press, 1996), 107–108; McElroy, *Grover Cleveland*, 1:356–357; Merrill, *Bourbon Leader*, 167.

137. Brodsky, *Grover Cleveland*, 290. In reality, the Senate was in opposition to Cleveland. As Nevins explained: "the Democratic contingent of the Senate was controlled by men who hated Cleveland and spared no pains to block his measures." Nevins, *Grover Cleveland*, 11.

138. Nevins, *Grover Cleveland*, 519.

139. Grover Cleveland, State of the Union, Dec. 4, 1893, in *Messages and Papers of the Presidents*, 8:5889.

140. Welch, *Presidencies of Grover Cleveland*, 61.

141. Sageser, *First Two Decades of the Pendleton Act*, 200.

142. Of these offices, 15,459 were added by executive order, 27,052 by rules revision, and 6,668 by growth of the service. "Table 1. Civil Service Classifications, 1883–1901," 70.

143. McElroy, *Grover Cleveland*, 2:8.

144. *Messages and Papers of the Presidents*, 8:5831–5832.

145. Grover Cleveland to Judson Harmon, Aug. 6, 1895, in *Letters of Grover Cleveland*, 403, 404.

146. President's Private Files, "Foreign appoints. for his constituents—list etc.," Dec. 18, 1893, in Grover Cleveland Papers, reel 81, Library of Congress, Manuscript Reading Room.

147. President's Private Files, "Asks delay in appoint. of Int. Rev. Coll. 12th Pa. Dist.," Dec. 21, 1893, in ibid.

148. Grover Cleveland to E. C. Benedict, Apr. 10 and 15, 1894, in *Letters of Grover Cleveland*, 350.

149. Brodsky, *Grover Cleveland*, 326.

150. McElroy, *Grover Cleveland*, 2:132; Nevins, *Grover Cleveland*, 569.

151. Henry J. Abraham, *Justices, Presidents, and Senators*, 4th ed. (Lanham, MD: Rowman and Littlefield, 1999), 108.

152. George F. Hoar, *Autobiography of Seventy Years* (New York: Scribner, 1903), 2:172.

153. This law required the federal government to purchase 4.5 million ounces of silver a month and issue legal tender notes based on said purchase. In addition, the act permitted anyone who wanted to redeem these legal tender notes to do so in either gold or silver. If the notes were redeemed, they would deplete the government's gold reserves and effectively create a lack of confidence in the government's ability to repay its debts in gold. Nevins, *Grover Cleveland*, 466; McElroy, *Grover Cleveland*, 2:23–25. For information on the economic impact of this law, see Charles R. Geisst, *Wall Street* (New York: Oxford University Press, 2004), 110–111.

154. Grover Cleveland to John G. Carlisle, Jan. 22, 1893, in *Letters of Grover Cleveland*, 315. See also, Grover Cleveland to Henry T. Thurber, Aug. 20, 1893, in ibid., 331; Brodsky, *Grover Cleveland*, 305.

155. Nevins, *Grover Cleveland*, 466, 541–542; Brodsky, *Grover Cleveland*, 319.

156. Richard Franklin Bensel, *The Political Economy of American Industrialization, 1877–1900* (Cambridge: Cambridge University Press, 2000), 371; J. Rogers Hollingsworth, *The Whirligig of Politics: The Democracy of Cleveland and Bryan* (Chicago: University of Chicago Press, 1963), 12–18; Van Riper, *History of the U.S. Civil Service*, 129.

Chapter 7. McKinley to Ford: The Tradition Continues
(1897–1977)

1. H. Wayne Morgan, *William McKinley and His America* (Syracuse, NY: Syracuse University Press, 1964), 289; William Carl Spielman, *William McKinley: Stalwart Republican* (New York: Exposition Press, 1954), 104–105. See also Lewis L. Gould, *The Presidency of William McKinley* (Lawrence: University Press of Kansas, 1980), 51; Dorothy Ganfield Fowler, *The Cabinet Politician: The Postmaster General, 1829–1909* (New York: Columbia University Press, 1943), 253.

2. Jefferson H. Claypool to William McKinley, Apr. 1897, in William McKinley Papers (WMP), reel 2, Library of Congress, Manuscript Reading Room.

3. Margaret Leech, *In the Days of McKinley* (New York: Harper, 1959), 135.

4. Memorandum from Marcus Hanna, n.d.; Marcus Hanna to William R. Day, June 30, 1897; Robert Brent Mosher to John Addison Porter, July 17, 1897; William R. Day to John Addison Porter, Aug. 7, 1897, all in WMP, reel 2. See also Herbert Croly, *Marcus Alonzo Hanna: His Life and Work* (New York: Macmillan, 1919).

5. Executive Mansion Memo, [late Mar. or early Apr.] 1897, in WMP, reel 2.

6. John D. Long to Nelson W. Aldrich, Mar. 8, 1897, in Nelson Aldrich Papers, reel 21, Library of Congress, Manuscript Reading Room; Charles A. Wilson to Nelson W. Aldrich, Oct. 1, 1897; James Wilson to Nelson W. Aldrich, Dec. 6, 1897; Russell A. Alger to Nelson W. Aldrich, July 3, 1899; H. C. Corbin to Nelson W. Aldrich, July 10, 1899; H. C. Corbin to Nelson W. Aldrich, Aug. 28, 1899; H. C. Corbin to Nelson W. Aldrich, Oct. 12, 1899; and Charles R. Brayton to Arthur V. Shelton, June 23, 1900, all in ibid., reel 22; H. C. Corbin to Nelson W. Aldrich, Dec. 2, 1900; George B. Cortelyou to Nelson W. Aldrich, Dec. 22, 1900; James Wilson to Nelson W. Aldrich, Feb. 23, 1901; H. C. Corbin to Nelson W. Aldrich, Feb. 28, 1901; George B. Cortelyou to Nelson W. Aldrich, Apr. 17, 1901; H. C. Corbin to Nelson W. Aldrich, Apr. 17, 1901; H. C. Corbin to Nelson W. Aldrich, May 2, 1901; and H. C. Corbin to Nelson W. Aldrich, June 4, 1901, all in ibid., reel 23.

7. Lyman J. Gage to Nelson W. Aldrich, Nov. 27, 1899, in ibid., reel 22.

8. H. Jay Travis to Nelson W. Aldrich, July 22, 1897, in ibid.

9. Matthew S. Quay to William McKinley, Mar. 21, 1898, in WMP, reel 3; Matthew S. Quay to William McKinley, Apr. 28, 1898, in ibid.; "Quay to Dispense Offices: Pennsylvanians Wanting Preferment Must Go to Him," *New York Times,* Jan. 19, 1897, 2; "For Commissioner of Patents," ibid., Feb. 15, 1897, 1; "Campaign in Pennsylvania," ibid., Oct. 2, 1898, 2; "The Genesis of Quayism," ibid., Oct. 8, 1898, 6. See also Robert Rienow and Leona Train Rienow, *Of Snuff, Sin and the Senate* (Chicago: Follett, 1965), 195.

10. O. J. Hodge to William McKinley, Mar. 23, 1898, in WMP, reel 3; Thomas C. Platt to William McKinley, Apr. 23, 1898, in ibid.; "Three out of Four for Platt," *New York Times,* Apr. 12, 1897, 12; "Platt and His Captains," ibid., Apr. 18, 1897, 8; "The Old Spoils Plan," ibid., July 13, 1897, 6; "The Delusions of Platt," ibid., July 24, 1897, 6; "Hanna and Platt at Odds?" ibid., June 15, 1900, 3.

11. Roscoe C. E. Brown, *History of the State of New York: Political and Governmental,* ed. Ray B. Smith (Syracuse, NY: Syracuse Press, 1922), 4:37.

12. Richmond Pearson to William McKinley, Mar. 27, 1897; Jeter C. Pritchard to William McKinley, Mar. 27, 1897; George E. Morse to William McKinley, Aug. 25, 1897, all in WMP, reel 2; memorandum—case of the Post Office at Port Townsend, Washington, Feb. 1, 1898; Redfield Proctor to John Addison Porter, Feb. 18, 1898; Eugene Hale to John Addison Porter, Apr. 29, 1898; Charles H. Grosvenor to William McKinley, Jan. 8, 1898; and Charles H. Grosvenor to William McKinley, Feb. 17, 1898; all in ibid., reel 3; Joseph B. Foraker to William McKinley, Apr. 22, 1901, in Nelson Aldrich Papers, reel 23; George F. Hoar to William McKinley, Apr. 21, 1899, in ibid., reel 22.

13. Croly, *Marcus Alonzo Hanna,* 298.

14. Confidential Memorandum for the President, Jan. 18, 1898, in WMP, reel 3.

15. Michael J. Gerhardt, *The Federal Appointments Process: A Constitutional and Historical Analysis* (Durham, NC: Duke University Press, 2000), 97–98; Fowler, *Cabinet Politician,* 267–268; "Mr. Platt Discusses President Roosevelt," *New York Times,* Sept. 16, 1901, 7.

16. Theodore Roosevelt to Redfield Proctor, June 13, 1907, in *The Letters of Theodore Roosevelt,* ed. Elting E. Morison (Cambridge, MA: Harvard University Press, 1952), 5:689. See also Fowler, *Cabinet Politician,* 267–268.

17. Theodore Roosevelt to Thomas Collier Platt, Dec. 22, 1904, in *Letters of Theodore Roosevelt,* 4:1075; Theodore Roosevelt to William Miller Collier, Dec. 19, 1904, in ibid., 1074; Theodore Roosevelt to Thomas Collier Platt, Nov. 11, 1904, in ibid., 1029; Theodore Roosevelt to Lucius Nathan Littauer, July 22, 1903, in ibid., 3:525; Oscar Solomon Straus, *Under Four Administrations: From Cleveland to Taft* (Boston: Houghton Mifflin, 1922), 309.

18. "Mr. Van Cott Reappointed," *New York Times,* Dec. 5, 1901, 1. See also "J. S. Clarkson Surveyor," ibid., Apr. 15, 1902, 3.

19. There was an ongoing factional battle, so the administration had to contend with a division of the federal patronage in Delaware between Senators James F. Allee and Lewis H. Ball. Theodore Roosevelt to Henry Clay Payne, Sept. 5, 1903, in *Letters of Theodore Roosevelt,* 3:588; "Delaware Partitioned by Spoils Contract," *New York Times,* Sept. 5, 1903, 1; "Miss Todd's Term 'Expired' Year Ago," *Washington Times,* Sept. 8, 1903, 3.

20. Theodore Roosevelt to Philander Chase Knox, Sept. 30, 1901, in *Letters of Theodore Roosevelt,* 3:154–155.

21. Theodore Roosevelt to Louis Emory McComas, Dec. 21, 1904, in ibid., 4:1074.

22. "'Lily White' Gain Point," *New York Times,* Dec. 21, 1902, 13; "Negroes Lose Fight in North Carolina," ibid., Feb. 17, 1903, 1; "Negro Postmaster Ousted," ibid., Mar. 25, 1903, 8.

23. Theodore Roosevelt to Charles William Frederick Dick, May 31, 1905, in *Letters of Theodore Roosevelt*, 4:1198–1200; Theodore Roosevelt to Charles William Frederick Dick, Apr. 16, 1904, in ibid., 774; Theodore Roosevelt to Joseph Benson Foraker, Feb. 23, 1904, in ibid., 737–738; Theodore Roosevelt to Henry Clay Payne, Jan. 23, 1904, in ibid., 3:705; Theodore Roosevelt to Marcus Alonzo Hanna, Nov. 4, 1903, in ibid., 646; Theodore Roosevelt to Marcus Alonzo Hanna, Oct. 31, 1903, in ibid., 640; Theodore Roosevelt to William Allen White, Aug.t 27, 1901, in ibid., 135; "Foraker and Bushnell to Control Patronage," *New York Times*, Nov. 28, 1901, 1.

24. Roosevelt wrote: "I should certainly endeavor to do what the two Pennsylvania Senators wished in matters of patronage." Theodore Roosevelt to William Allen White, Aug. 27, 1901, in *Letters of Theodore Roosevelt*, 3:136. See also Theodore Roosevelt to George Kennan, Mar. 23, 1903, in ibid., 456; Theodore Roosevelt to Matthew Stanley Quay, June 7, 1902, in ibid., 270; Theodore Roosevelt to Joseph Bucklin Bishop, Nov. 27, 1901, in ibid., 201–202; "Quay Postmaster Stays," *New York Times*, Dec. 12, 1903, 4.

25. "Senators Even in Lottery for Dakota Places," *Washington Times*, Nov. 26, 1907, 8.

26. Theodore Roosevelt to Charles Sumner Gleed, Nov. 25, 1901, in *Letters of Theodore Roosevelt*, 3:201; "Sanders' Removal by the President to Aid Hughes," *Washington Times*, Apr. 19, 1907, 12.

27. Theodore Roosevelt to Winston Churchill, Feb. 13, 1907, in *Letters of Theodore Roosevelt*, 5:587.

28. Theodore Roosevelt to Augustus Peabody Gardner, Oct. 28, 1904, in ibid., 4:1002. See also "Rebuked by the President," *New York Times*, Nov. 15, 1904, 1.

29. Theodore Roosevelt to Henry Cabot Lodge, Oct. 11, 1901, in Joseph Bucklin Bishop, *Theodore Roosevelt and His Time: Shown in His Own Letters* (New York: Charles Scribner's Sons, 1920), 1:157–158.

30. Theodore Roosevelt to Knute Nelson, Apr. 14, 1908, in *Letters of Theodore Roosevelt*, 6:1007.

31. "Purdy's Nomination to Be Judge Starts Contest over Patronage," *Washington Times*, Apr. 24, 1908, 3.

32. "Senate to Delay Action on Names," *Washington Times*, Feb. 23, 1909, 5; "Charles A. Willard Gets Purdy's Place," ibid., May 8, 1909, 1.

33. Harlan Hahn, "President Taft and the Discipline of Patronage," *Journal of Politics* 28 (May 1966): 386–387. See also Charles E. Barker, *With President Taft in the White House* (Chicago: A. Kroch, 1947), 38; Joel Arthur Tarr, *A Study in Boss Politics: William Lorimer of Chicago* (Urbana: University of Illinois Press, 1971), 229–230; "Beveridge Leads Hoosier State Now," *Washington Times*, Nov. 6, 1908, 6; "Beveridge Busy on Post Offices," ibid., Nov. 16, 1909, 3; "Beveridge Offers Several Surprises," ibid., Nov. 29, 1909, 5.

34. William Howard Taft, *Our Chief Magistrate and His Powers* (New York: Columbia University Press, 1925), 63.

35. Ibid., 61–62.

36. Hahn, "President Taft and the Discipline of Patronage," 368–390.

37. Under civil service rules, it was necessary for Congress to pass legislation on any class of appointments that required Senate confirmation.

38. William H. Taft, State of the Union, Dec. 6, 1910, in *A Compilation of the Messages and Papers of the Presidents*, ed. James D. Richardson (New York: Bureau of National Literature, 1911), 10:7907.

39. "Taft to Break up Machine in South," *New York Times*, Jan. 22, 1909, 4; "Mr. Taft and the South," ibid., Apr. 13, 1909, 8; James Hay Jr., "Taft to Eliminate Power of Negroes in Southern G.O.P.," *Washington Times*, Sept. 14, 1910, 1.

40. "The 'Solid' South," *New York Times*, Dec. 29, 1909, 8.

41. "Democrats Slated for South's Plums," *Washington Times,* Mar. 24, 1909, 1; "Taft to Consult Democrats," *New York Times,* June 2, 1910, 8.

42. In a letter, Booker T. Washington wrote: "It is almost pathetic, however, to note the deep feeling of disappointment and sadness expressed by practically every man who comes here concerning the supposed attitude of President Taft. Last night in my annual address to an audience of some three thousand people in the theatre, gathered from all parts of the country, I referred to President Taft in as complimentary and strong terms as I could. You would be surprised to know that there was not a single handclap or a single move anywhere in the audience that indicated approval of my remarks." Booker T. Washington to Charles William Anderson, Aug. 20, 1909, in *The Booker T. Washington Papers,* ed. Louis R. Harlan and Raymond W. Smock (Urbana: University of Illinois Press, 1972), 10:157.

43. Archie Butt, *Taft and Roosevelt: The Intimate Letters of Archie Butt* (New York: Doubleday, Doran, 1930), 2:511.

44. Vincent P. De Santis, "The Republican Party and the Southern Negro," *Journal of Negro History* 45 (Apr. 1960): 87.

45. Dorothy Ganfield Fowler, "Congressional Dictation of Local Appointments," *Journal of Politics* 7 (Feb. 1945): 49–50.

46. William F. McCombs, *Making Woodrow Wilson President,* ed. Louis Jay Lang (New York: Fairview, 1921), 225.

47. "Proposed Statement on Patronage," Apr. 22, 1913, in *The Papers of Woodrow Wilson,* ed. Arthur S. Link (Princeton, NJ: Princeton University Press, 1978), 27:344–345.

48. Woodrow Wilson to Stephen Samuel Wise, June 4, 1914, in ibid., 30:144.

49. David F. Houston, *Eight Years with Wilson's Cabinet* (New York: Double, Page, 1926), 1:41. See also August Heckscher, *Woodrow Wilson* (New York: Charles Scribner's Sons, 1991), 286.

50. Arthur S. Link, "Woodrow Wilson and the Democratic Party," *Review of Politics* 18 (Apr. 1956): 148–149. See also Ruth Cranston, *The Story of Woodrow Wilson* (New York: Simon and Schuster, 1945), 120–121. Like most presidents, Wilson was willing to take away patronage if a member of Congress "failed to support his policies." Henry A. Turner, "Woodrow Wilson: Exponent of Executive Leadership," *Western Political Quarterly* 4 (Mar. 1951): 103. See also Adrian Anderson, "President Wilson's Politician: Albert Sidney Burleson of Texas," *Southwestern Historical Quarterly* 77 (Jan. 1974): 349.

51. Heckscher, *Woodrow Wilson,* 286.

52. Diary of Colonel House, Jan. 15, 1913, in *Papers of Woodrow Wilson,* 27:72.

53. Joseph P. Harris wrote: "It may be assumed, however, that his conferences with senators of the opposite party were quite different from conferences with members of his own party." Joseph P. Harris, *The Advice and Consent of the Senate* (Berkeley: University of California Press, 1953), 95. Wilson's secretary of the treasury, William G. McAdoo, explained that the reason for abandoning the practice was that "the Republican senators sometimes recommended the most incapable man on the list." William G. McAdoo, *Crowded Years* (Boston: Houghton Mifflin, 1931), 191.

54. Andrew Sinclair, *The Available Man: The Life behind the Masks of Warren Gamaliel Harding* (New York: Macmillan, 1965), 191, 193; Eugene P. Trani and David L. Wilson, *The Presidency of Warren G. Harding* (Lawrence: University Press of Kansas, 1977), 45.

55. "Harding to Appoint for Party Strength," *New York Times,* Mar. 9, 1921, 3. The only appointments off-limits to Republican senators were postmasters. As Senator George W. Pepper explained: "Recommending men for appointment to federal office is considered a senatorial prerogative, except for the appointment of postmasters which is regarded as the privilege of representatives." George Whar-

ton Pepper, *Philadelphia Lawyer: An Autobiography* (Philadelphia: J. B. Lippincott, 1944), 194.

56. Harris, *Advice and Consent*, 116.

57. Woodrow Wilson, executive order, Mar. 31, 1917, in author's files.

58. Warren G. Harding, executive order, May 10, 1921, in *A Compilation of the Messages and Papers of the Presidents*, supplement ed., ed. James D. Richardson (New York: Bureau of National Literature, 1925), 8964, 8965.

59. For instance, the Civil Service Commission reported that when faced with a clear violation, such as members of Congress recommending candidates for political reasons, the Wilson administration would not give in. In its annual report, the commission noted, "if the [political] appointment is permitted to stand when the facts show clearly that it was based on recommendations having their source in political considerations, virtually the only effect of the Executive order is to invite political recommendations so veiled as to hide their true character." U.S. Civil Service Commission, *Fortieth Annual Report* (Washington, DC: GPO, 1923), xxviii. As one former Wilson cabinet member wrote, that method "still left the selection to political considerations." Josephus Daniels, *The Life of Woodrow Wilson* (United States: Will H. Johnston, 1924), 207. See also U.S. Civil Service Commission, *Thirty-fourth Annual Report* (Washington, DC: GPO, 1917), ix; U.S. Civil Service Commission, *Thirty-fifth Annual Report* (Washington, DC: GPO, 1918), xv; Daniel D. Stid, *The President as Statesman: Woodrow Wilson and the Constitution* (Lawrence: University Press of Kansas, 1998), 137.

60. Sinclair, *Available Man*, 192; "Find Spoils System Is Being Revived," *New York Times*, Nov. 17, 1921, 16; "Lauds Harding Choices in Naming Postmasters," *Washington Post*, May 15, 1922, 8; "Charges of Spoils Stip up Senators," *New York Times*, Jan. 21, 1923, 6; "Wants Highest on List Named Postmasters," *Washington Post*, Mar. 26, 1923, 13.

61. Address by William Dudley Foulke, in *Proceedings: National Civil Service Reform League, Jan. 12, 1926* (New York: National Civil Service Reform League, 1926), 17. See also the discussion of the "rule of three" in the section on Chester A. Arthur in chapter 6.

62. "Roosevelt Studies Ending of Examinations for First and Second Class Postmasters," *New York Times*, Apr. 12, 1933, 2.

63. In his autobiography, Coolidge wrote: "Tradition and custom, it will be seen, are often times determining factors in the Presidential office, as they are in all other walks of life. This is not because they are arbitrary, but because long experience has demonstrated that they are the best methods of dealing with human affairs. Things are done in a certain way after many repetitions show that way causes the least friction and is most likely to bring the desired result." Calvin Coolidge, *Autobiography* (New York: Cosmopolitan Book Corporation, 1929), 214–215.

64. Memorandum from Calvin Coolidge to Heads of Departments, Dec. 10, 1923, in Calvin Coolidge Papers, box 289, Library of Congress, Manuscript Reading Room. Commerce Secretary Herbert Hoover replied that he would "be very glad to carry out your wishes in the matter." Dec. 15, 1923, in ibid., reel 6.

65. William Allen White, *A Puritan in Babylon* (Norwalk, CT: Easton Press, 1986), 283–284; Harris, *Advice and Consent*, 116; Robert Sobel, *Coolidge: An American Enigma* (Washington, DC: Regnery, 1998), 254; Robert E. Gilbert, *The Tormented President: Calvin Coolidge, Death, and Clinical Depression* (Westport, CT: Praeger, 2003), 125.

66. "Postal Appointments Protested by League," *Washington Post*, Dec. 4, 1924, 13; Calvin Coolidge, State of the Union, Dec. 6, 1923, in *Messages and Papers of the Presidents*, supplement ed., 9348.

67. Coolidge, State of the Union, Dec. 6, 1923, 9348.

68. Herbert Hoover to Calvin Coolidge, Aug. 3. 1926, in Calvin Coolidge Papers, reel 6.

69. Herbert Hoover to Calvin Coolidge, Oct. 27, 1925, in ibid., reel 7.

70. "Endorsements Given Dickerson N. Hoover for Appointment as Supervising Inspector General of the Steamboat Inspection Service," n.d., in ibid. In a letter about the appointment, Commerce Secretary Hoover said that he had consulted another senator as well. Herbert Hoover to Calvin Coolidge, Dec. 30, 1925, in ibid.

71. Memorandum, July 17, 1926, in ibid., reel 6.

72. Eugene Lyons, *Herbert Hoover* (Garden City, NY: Doubleday, 1964), 192; Edgar Eugene Robinson and Vaughn Davis Bornet, *Herbert Hoover: President of the United States* (Stanford, CA: Hoover Institution Press, 1975), 49; Donald J. Lisio, *Hoover, Blacks, and Lily-Whites* (Chapel Hill: University of North Carolina Press, 1985), 196.

73. David Burner, *Herbert Hoover: A Public Life* (New York: Knopf, 1979), 234.

74. Herbert Hoover, *The Memoirs of Herbert Hoover* (New York: Macmillan, 1952), 269.

75. Referring to Hoover's Mar. 8, 1929, statement on his appointment policy. See Walter Starr Myers and Walter H. Newton, *The Hoover Administration: A Documented Narrative* (New York: Scribner, 1936), 375.

76. Hoover, *Memoirs,* 270.

77. At the time, Florida, like most southern states, had no Republican members of Congress. "Hoover Rebukes Florida Committee," *New York Times,* Oct. 22, 1929, 18; "Appointments to Office," *Washington Post,* Oct. 25, 1929, 8.

78. Herbert Hoover to Fred E. Britten, Sept. 26, 1929, in *The State Papers and Other Public Writings of Herbert Hoover,* ed. William Starr Myers (New York: Doubleday, Doran, 1934), 1:105.

79. "Politicians and Pie," *Washington Post,* June 3, 1929, 6.

80. "Says Hoover Bows to the 'Old Guard,'" *New York Times,* Mar. 2, 1930, 6. See also "Senate Confirms Watson as Judge," ibid., Dec. 18, 1929, 2.

81. Carlisle Bargeron, "President's Plan to Keep Bench Separate from Politics Fails," *Washington Post,* June 9, 1929, 1.

82. "Judgeship to Test Senatorial Influence," *New York Times,* May 7, 1929, 4. Kansas governor Clyde M. Reed was also given credit for the selection. See "Names Nields as Judge," ibid., June 21, 1930, 4.

83. "Names Nields as Judge," 4.

84. Harold Wolfe, *Herbert Hoover: Public Servant and Leader of the Loyal Opposition* (New York: Exposition Press, 1956), 149.

85. James A. Farley, *Jim Farley's Story: The Roosevelt Years* (New York: McGraw-Hill, 1948), 35. See also James A. Farley, *Behind the Bullots: The History of a Politician* (New York: Harcourt, Brace, 1938), 234–235.

86. "Farley Promises Jobs for 150,000," *New York Times,* Dec. 23, 1932, 5. In addition, the administration announced that it would consult Democratic politicians who had supported Roosevelt during the Democratic primary. These people were referred to as F.R.B.C., or For Roosevelt Before Chicago. See Farley, *Behind the Ballots,* 233; Sean J. Savage, *Roosevelt: The Party Leader, 1932–1945* (Lexington: University Press of Kentucky, 1991), 22–23.

87. Part of the problem also centered on Roosevelt's plan to withhold appointments until after the administration's "emergency legislative program" had been passed (which, coincidentally, increased the number of federal positions available for appointment by more than 25,000). "The Gates of Patronage Are Soon to Swing Wide," *New York Times,* July 2, 1933, 1. See also "Action on Patronage Demanded of Farley," ibid., May 11, 1933, 2; "No Postmasters Nominated So Far," ibid., June 17, 1933, 3.

88. The *New York Times* reported that the "result of the conference was an agreement that Senators must and will be consulted in the first instance and a recognition of the fact that their power to refuse confirmation amounts to at least an even share in the administration's choice of its assistants." Arthur Krock, "Capitol Impatient for Patronage List," *New York Times,* Mar. 17, 1933, 2.

89. "Farley Agrees to Consult Senators on Jobs; Modifies Plan after Visit to Roosevelt," *New York Times,* Mar. 16, 1933, 1.

90. Marian C. McKenna, *Franklin Roosevelt and the Great Constitutional War: The Court-Packing Crisis of 1937* (New York: Fordham University Press, 2002), 546; Farley, *Jim Farley's Story,* 74, 121–122; "Allred Appointed a Federal Judge at 39," *New York Times,* July 12, 1938, 4.

91. Kenneth S. Davis, *FDR: The New Deal Years, 1933–1937* (New York: Random House, 1986), 58–59.

92. Senator Lonergan was able to block the confirmation of Edward G. Dolan as collector of internal revenue and Frank S. Bergin as U.S. attorney. *Congressional Record,* 73rd Cong., 2nd sess., vol. 78 (May 28 and June 1, 1934), 9718, 10224. "Prof. Ayres Seeks Senatorial Seat," *New York Times,* Aug. 34, 1934, 3; "Roosevelt Choice Blocked in Senate," ibid., June 2, 1934, 2.

93. Senator Pat McCarran prevented the confirmation of William S. Boyle as U.S. attorney. Jerome E. Edwards, *Pat McCarran: Political Boss of Nevada* (Reno: University of Nevada Press, 1982), 85–93; "Senate Rejects Nominee, Rebuffs President," *Washington Post,* June 30, 1939, 2; "Senators Reject Boyle Nomination," *New York Times,* June 30, 1939, 8. See also "McCarran Says Nevada Appointee Is 'Obnoxious,'" *Washington Post,* Apr. 19, 1939, 3; "Senators Back McCarran in 'Courtesy' Row," ibid., June 20, 1939, 1.

94. Senator Ed "Cotton" Smith successfully held up the confirmation of Rexford Tugwell as undersecretary of agriculture to force Roosevelt to nominate his candidate to a U.S. marshal position. James MacGregor Burns, *Roosevelt: The Lion and the Fox* (New York: Harcourt, Brace, 1956), 188. Later, after another appointment conflict, Senator Smith would declare: "if they do not change their method of distributing patronage the President will soon have a revolution on his hands." Frank Freidel, *Franklin D. Roosevelt: Launching the New Deal* (Boston: Little, Brown, 1973), 445.

95. Senator W. Lee O'Daniel stopped the confirmation of James Allred as U.S. district judge. "Senators Block Action on Allred," *New York Times,* Mar. 23, 1943, 21; "Committee's 9-to-9 Split Blocks Allred," *Washington Post,* Mar. 23, 1943, 1; "O'Daniel Considers Allred 'Obnoxious,'" ibid., Mar. 16, 1943, 8.

96. Senators Carter Glass and Harry Byrd blocked the confirmation of Floyd H. Roberts as U.S. district judge. Ronald L. Heinemann, *Harry Byrd of Virginia* (Charlottesville: University Press of Virginia, 1996), 193–196; Rixey Smith and Norman Beasley, *Carter Glass* (New York: Da Capo Press, 1972), 395–398. For more information, see A. Cash Koeniger, "The New Deal and the States: Roosevelt versus the Byrd Organization in Virginia," *Journal of American History* 68 (Mar. 1982): 876–896.

97. Burns, *Roosevelt,* 188.

98. Frank Freidel, *Franklin D. Roosevelt: A Rendezvous with Destiny* (Boston: Little, Brown, 1990), 153.

99. Public Law 75-719, *U.S. Statutes at Large,* 75th Cong., 2nd sess., vol. 52 (June 25, 1938), 1076.

100. For a detailed history of the act, see Harris, *Advice and Consent,* 346–351.

101. Excerpts from the 1955 Hoover Commission Report in U.S. House of Representatives, Committee on Post Office and Civil Service, *Taking Politics out of Postmaster and Other Appointments and Promotions in the Postal Service,* 90th Cong., 2nd sess. (Feb. 6, 7, 8; Mar. 26, 28, 1968), 13–14.

102. Freidel, *Franklin D. Roosevelt: Launching the New Deal,* 303.

103. Burns, *Roosevelt*, 187–188.

104. William D. Reeves, "PWA and Competition Administration in the New Deal," *Journal of American History* 60 (Sept. 1973): 367; William J. Duchaine, "Farley Picks Aide for Senate Fight," *New York Times*, Jan. 7, 1934, E6.

105. "President Is Told of 'Politics' in WPA," *New York Times*, Aug. 17, 1936, 4.

106. Donald R. Harvey, *The Civil Service Commission* (New York: Praeger, 1970), 11–12.

107. Harold F. Gosnell, *Truman's Crises: A Political Biography of Harry S. Truman* (Westport, CT: Greenwood Press, 1980), 97.

108. Robert H. Ferrell, *Harry S. Truman* (Washington, DC: CQ Press, 2003), 233.

109. The Senate rejected M. Neil Andrews after Truman went against the wishes of Georgia senators Walter F. George and Richard Russell. *Congressional Record*, 81st Cong., 2nd sess., vol. 97 (Aug. 9, 1950), 12105. On the same day, the Senate rejected another judicial candidate because Truman failed to consult Senator Guy M. Gillette of Iowa. Ibid., 12106. Finally, Senator Paul Douglas of Illinois prevented the confirmation of two district judges because of Truman's refusal to follow the pre-nomination tradition. Ibid. (Oct. 9, 1951), 12840.

110. Sheldon Goldman, *Picking Federal Judges: Lower Court Selection from Roosevelt through Reagan* (New Haven, CT: Yale University Press, 1997), 68.

111. Louis W. Koenig, ed., *The Truman Administration* (New York: New York University Press, 1956), 53.

112. Andrew J. Dunar, *The Truman Scandals and the Politics of Morality* (Columbia: University of Missouri Press, 1984), 134.

113. Robert J. Donovan, *Eisenhower: The Inside Story* (New York: Harper and Brothers, 1956), 96.

114. This was part of an agreement reached at the Republican National Convention in Chicago. Leo Egan, "Eisenhower Sets up Bureau to Handle G.O.P. Job Appeals," *New York Times*, Nov. 17, 1952, 1; Cornelius P. Cotter, "Eisenhower as Party Leader," *Political Science Quarterly* 98 (summer 1983): 266.

115. Problems arose when President-elect Eisenhower did not consult soon-to-be Senate Majority Leader Robert Taft on the appointments of George Humphrey as treasury secretary, Charles E. Wilson as defense secretary, Martin Durkin as labor secretary, and Sinclair Weeks as commerce secretary. James T. Patterson, *Mr. Republican: A Biography of Robert A. Taft* (Boston: Houghton Mifflin, 1972), 583–584; Stewart Alsop, "Ike-Taft Conflict Lulled for Present," *Washington Post*, Dec. 22, 1952, 10. See also Robert C. Albright, "Worried Legislators Get Word Ike Will Consult on Jobs, Bills," ibid., Dec. 16, 1952, 1.

116. Patterson, *Mr. Republican*, 584.

117. There was probably confusion as to whether "top appointments" meant subcabinet level or local appointments, which were traditionally the purview of members of Congress. "GOP Planning to Consult Senators on Appointments," *Washington Post*, Dec. 27, 1952, 2.

118. Russell Porter, "Taft Sees General, Predicts Harmony," *New York Times*, Dec. 31, 1952, 1. For more information about the meeting, see "'Frank Conference' Held," ibid., Jan. 5, 1953, 14.

119. "Senate Leaders Seek U.S. Jobs Showdown," *New York Times*, Jan. 9, 1953, 7. See also "Patronage Issue Rouses Taft's Ire," ibid., Jan. 11, 1953, 5; John L. Steele, "Taft Seeks to End 'Confusion' on GOP Patronage Handling," *Washington Post*, Jan. 11, 1953, M8.

120. Edward F. Ryan, "Eisenhower Puts Cabinet through 1st 'Team Drill,'" *Washington Post*, Jan. 13, 1953, 1.

121. "Consultation System Set," *New York Times*, Jan. 5, 1953, 13.

122. William S. White, *The Taft Story* (New York: Harper, 1954), 213.

123. Patterson, *Mr. Republican*, 589; Donovan, *Eisenhower*, 272.

124. Dwight D. Eisenhower, *Mandate for Change, 1953–1956* (New York: Doubleday, 1963), 119–120; Martin Tolchin and Susan Tolchin, *To the Victor . . . Political Patronage from the Clubhouse to the White House* (New York: Random House, 1971), 258; Donovan, *Eisenhower*, 94–101, 272; James P. Pfiffner, "Presidential Appointments: Recruiting Executive Branch Leaders," in *Innocent until Nominated*, ed. G. Calvin Mackenzie (Washington, DC: Brookings Institution Press, 2001), 52. One Eisenhower biographer thought that he "had no understanding of the uses of patronage and power." Marquis Childs, *Eisenhower: Captive Hero* (New York: Harcourt, Brace, 1958), 227.

125. Marquis Childs, "Dulles Attacked on Patronage Decisions," *Washington Post,* Jan. 19, 1954, 14; Robert E. Thompson, "GOP Victory Held Periled by Job Policy," ibid., Mar. 28, 1954, M2; "Patronage Dispute Still Hot One Here," ibid., Feb. 3, 1955, 2. See also, Harvey, *Civil Service Commission*, 23–24.

126. Dwight D. Eisenhower, *The Eisenhower Diaries*, ed. Robert H. Ferrell (New York: Norton, 1981), 292–294; Sidney M. Milkis, *The President and the Parties: The Transformation of the American Party System since the New Deal* (New York: Oxford University Press, 1993), 161–163; Byron C. Hulsey, *Everett Dirksen and His Presidents* (Lawrence: University Press of Kansas, 2000), 62–63; Goldman, *Picking Federal Judges*, 131–134; Patterson, *Mr. Republican*, 582–592; "Jersey Republican Named to U.S. Bench," *New York Times,* June 16, 1960, 26; "2 Maryland Senators Tiff on Patronage," *Washington Post,* May 19, 1953, 1; "Nixon-Knowland Feud Smolders," ibid., May 24, 1953, B5.

127. G. Calvin Mackenzie, "Partisan Presidential Leadership: The President's Appointees," in *The Parties Respond: Changes in American Parties and Campaigns*, ed. Louis Sandy Maisel (Boulder, CO: Westview Press, 2002), 279–280. See also Arthur M. Schlesinger Jr., *Robert Kennedy and His Times* (New York: Houghton Mifflin, 2002), 373–374; Matthew B. Coffey, "A Death at the White House: The Short Life of the New Patronage," *Public Administration Review* 34 (Sept.–Oct. 1974): 441.

128. Clayton Knowles, "Administration Faces Early Patronage Problem as State Groups Seek Bigger Role," *New York Times,* Jan. 21, 1961, 13; David Kraslow, "Senators Charge Kennedy Patronage Undercut," *Washington Post,* Aug. 9, 1961, A5.

129. John P. Burke, *The Institutional Presidency: Organizing and Managing the White House from FDR to Clinton*, 2nd ed. (Baltimore: Johns Hopkins University Press, 2000), 75.

130. Harold W. Chase, *Federal Judges: The Appointing Process* (Minneapolis: University of Minnesota Press, 1972), 61.

131. Elsie Carper, "Byrd Has Some Aces to Play," *Washington Post,* Nov. 27, 1960, E2.

132. Schlesinger, *Robert Kennedy*, 374.

133. Jack Bell, "Almond Job May Stir Byrd-Kennedy Clash," *Washington Post,* July 31, 1961, B2.

134. David Halberstam, "Kennedy Selects Eastland Friend," *New York Times,* June 21, 1961, 19; W. J. Rorabaugh, *Kennedy and the Promise of the Sixties* (New York: Cambridge University Press, 2002), 88; Victor S. Navasky, *Kennedy Justice* (New York: Atheneum, 1971), 250–252; Arthur M. Schlesinger Jr., *A Thousand Days* (New York: Fawcett Premier, 1965), 640–641.

135. "Connecticut Set on 2 Judgeships," *New York Times,* July 16, 1961, 39.

136. Navasky, *Kennedy Justice*, 252–253; Nina Totenberg, "Will Judges Be Chosen Rationally?" *Judicature* 60 (Aug.–Sept. 1976): 96; Schlesinger, *Robert Kennedy*, 374–375.

137. J. Edward Day, *My Appointed Round: 929 Days as Postmaster General* (New York: Holt, Rinehart, and Winston, 1965), 8–9.

138. Chase, *Federal Judges,* 184. See also Goldman, *Picking Federal Judges,* 173; Doris Kearns Goodwin, *Lyndon Johnson and the American Dream* (New York: St. Martin's Press, 1991), 244–245.

139. Chase, *Federal Judges,* 184.

140. Goldman, *Picking Federal Judges,* 173; Richard L. Schott and Dagmar S. Hamilton, *People, Positions, and Power: The Political Appointments of Lyndon Johnson* (Chicago: University of Chicago Press, 1983), 23. See also W. Marvin Watson, *Chief of Staff: Lyndon Johnson and His Presidency* (New York: St. Martin's Press, 2004), 5.

141. Tolchin and Tolchin, *To the Victor,* 161.

142. Robert Dallek, *Flawed Giant: Lyndon Johnson and His Times, 1961–1973* (New York: Oxford University Press, 1998), 560–561.

143. Ibid., 561.

144. Ibid. See also Gilbert C. Fite, *Richard B. Russell, Jr., Senator from Georgia* (Chapel Hill: University of North Carolina Press, 1991), 476–481.

145. Public Law 87-36, *U.S. Statutes at Large,* 87th Cong., 1st sess., vol. 75 (May 19, 1961), 80.

146. Anthony Lewis, "Rogers Pledges Democrats Parity on New Judges," *New York Times,* Aug. 28, 1959, 1; "Judgeship Plan Gains in Senate," ibid., Sept. 12, 1959, 1; Anthony Lewis, "Rogers Presses for More Judges; Promises to Consult Democrats," ibid., May 31, 1960, 24. In addition, there was a push by the American Bar Association (ABA) to appoint on a bipartisan basis. The ABA asked Kennedy to appoint Republicans to at least a third of the new positions. Anthony Lewis, "Kennedy Pledges Able U.S. Judges," ibid., May 20, 1961, 8; Austin C. Wehrwein, "U.S. Record Near in Bench Openings," ibid., Feb. 18, 1961, 20; "Mr. Kennedy and the Judges," ibid., May 22, 1961, 30.

147. Chase, *Federal Judges,* 71–78.

148. Edward L. Schapsmeier and Frederick H. Schapsmeier, *Dirksen of Illinois: Senatorial Statesman* (Urbana: University of Illinois Press, 1985), 143; Sean J. Savage, *JFK, LBJ, and the Democratic Party* (Albany, NY: SUNY Press, 2004), 108; Hulsey, *Everett Dirksen,* 151, 161; Associated Press, "Chicago Lawyer Chosen for F.P.C." *New York Times,* Jan. 24, 1962, 16. For an excellent account of the Kennedy-Dirksen relationship, see Byron C. Hulsey, "'He Is My President': Everett Dirksen, John Kennedy, and the Politics of Consensus," *Journal of Illinois History* 2 (autumn 1999): 183–204.

149. Richard I. Madden, "Javits Delaying a Judgeship Here," *New York Times,* Dec. 14, 1967, 8; "Johnson Names Travia and Judd for U.S. Bench," ibid., Apr. 26, 1968, 26.

150. Johnson continued to give Senator Dirksen appointments as well. Neil MacNeil, *Dirksen: Portrait of a Public Man* (New York: World, 1970), 282–283; Jean E. Torcom, "Leadership: The Role and Style of Senator Everett Dirksen," in *To Be a Congressman: The Promise and the Power,* ed. Sven Groennings and Jonathan P. Hawley (Washington, DC: Acropolis Books, 1973), 210; Schapsmeier and Schapsmeier, *Dirksen of Illinois,* 193–196; Hulsey, *Everett Dirksen,* 185–186; Watson, *Chief of Staff,* 5. For an account of the Johnson-Dirksen relationship, see Vaughn Davis Bornet, *The Presidency of Lyndon B. Johnson* (Lawrence: University Press of Kansas, 1983), 130–131.

151. Tolchin and Tolchin, *To the Victor,* 264.

152. Leonard Downie Jr., "Mathias Balks at Appointee," *Washington Post,* Apr. 8, 1969, C1.

153. Warren Weaver Jr., "G.O.P. Plagued by Snarl in Putting Faithful in Jobs," *New York Times,* Feb. 24, 1969, 22.

154. MacNeil, *Dirksen,* 354; "Administrator of V.A. Resigns; Opposition by Dirksen Is Hinted," *New York Times,* Apr. 9, 1969, 13; Jack Bell, "Dirksen to Oppose

Nominee," *Washington Post*, Apr. 23, 1969, A8; Rowland Evans and Robert Novak, "Dirksen Losing a Plum: Lifelong Democrat Likely to Keep VA Helm," ibid., Mar. 16, 1969, C9.

155. Rowland Evans and Robert Novak, "GOP Singing the Blues over Lack of Patronage," *Washington Post*, Feb. 12, 1969, A21.

156. Schapsmeier and Schapsmeier, *Dirksen of Illinois*, 221–222; Tolchin and Tolchin, *To the Victor*, 267–268.

157. "Job Talks Ease GOP Protests on Hill," *Washington Post*, July 17, 1969, A22. There would be only a few of these meetings. In Aug. 1969, Dirksen was hospitalized with a malignant tumor on his lung and died less than a month later. Hulsey, *Everett Dirksen*, 272.

158. "White House Reported Aware of Retreat by Rogers on Aide," *New York Times*, Sept. 1, 1970, 2; Chalmers M. Roberts, "Rogers Changed Mind on Olsen," *Washington Post*, Sept. 1, 1970, A2; Tad Szulc, "Aide's Promotion Canceled by U.S.," *New York Times*, Aug. 31, 1970, 11; Chalmers M. Roberts, "Goldwater Blocks State Dept. Choice," *Washington Post*, Aug. 31, 1970, A1. See also Louis Fisher, *Constitutional Conflicts between Congress and the President*, 5th ed. (Lawrence: University Press of Kansas, 2007), 32.

159. Editorial, "The Olsen Affair," *New York Times*, Sept. 1, 1970, 34.

160. Editorial, "The Olsen Affair: A Dangerous Retreat," *Washington Post*, Sept. 7, 1970, A18.

161. Goldman, *Picking Federal Judges*, 209; G. Calvin Mackenzie, *The Politics of Presidential Appointments* (New York: Free Press, 1981), 225; James M. Naughton, "Broderick Named a Federal Judge," *New York Times*, Aug. 25, 1976, 26; Totenberg, "Will Judges Be Chosen Rationally?" 95.

162. Steven V. Roberts, "State G.O.P. Gets Patronage Role," *New York Times*, Dec. 15, 1968, 4; "State's Senators Tread Cautiously," ibid., Dec. 27, 1968, 19; Richard L. Madden, "State G.O.P. Takes Patronage Reins," ibid., Sept. 30, 1969, 28. For a discussion of Nixon's dislike of liberal Republican senators, see Rowland Evans Jr. and Robert D. Novak, *Nixon in the White House: The Frustration of Power* (New York: Random House, 1971), 107–108.

163. Totenberg, "Will Judges Be Chosen Rationally?" 95. Another account explained that the senators named one out of every four judges; see John R. Schmidhauser, *Judges and Justices: The Federal Appellate Judiciary* (Boston: Little, Brown, 1979), 36.

164. For information on how this system operated during this period, see Harvey, *Civil Service Commission*, 64–66.

165. "Nixon Acts to End Postal Patronage," *Washington Post*, Feb. 6, 1969, A1; "Nixon Orders Postal Jobs Removed from Patronage," *New York Times*, Feb. 6, 1969, 1.

166. Richard Nixon, "Reform of the Postal Service," in *Weekly Compilation of Presidential Documents*, vol. 5 (Feb. 25, 1969), 319–320; Carroll Kilpatrick, "Nixon Message Asks Legislation on Postal Reform," *Washington Post*, Feb. 26, 1969, A2. See also Richard Nixon, "Reform of the Nation's Postal System," in *Weekly Compilation of Presidential Documents*, vol. 5 (May 27, 1969), 752–756.

167. Nixon, "Reform of the Postal Service," 319.

168. Tolchin and Tolchin, *To the Victor*, 260.

169. Editorial, "Post Office Politics," *New York Times*, Feb. 8, 1969, 30; Jack Anderson, "Blount Faces Grilling on Postal Plans," *Washington Post*, Feb. 13, 1969, E17; Drew Pearson and Jack Anderson, "Postmaster Threatens to Quit," ibid., May 16, 1969, D17. In addition, some administration officials thought that this reform effort was a politically bad idea. Melvin Small, *The Presidency of Richard Nixon* (Lawrence: University Press of Kansas, 1999), 196.

170. Public Law 91-375, *U.S. Statutes at Large*, 91st Cong., 2nd sess., vol. 84 (Aug. 12, 1970), 719.

171. Ibid., 728–730.

172. Shirley Anne Warshaw, "The Implementation of Cabinet Government during the Nixon Administration," in *Richard M. Nixon: Politician, President, Administrator*, eds. Leon Friedman and William F. Levantrosser (New York: Greenwood Press, 1991), 341. For more information on the act's impact on the pre-nomination process, see William Greider, "Postal Reform Cans an Old Political Plum," *Washington Post*, Aug. 13, 1970, A1.

173. Mike Causey, "President Warned on Patronage," *Washington Post*, Mar. 10, 1975, D11.

174. John Robert Greene, *The Presidency of Gerald R. Ford* (Lawrence: University Press of Kansas, 1995), 54.

175. David Burnham, "Democrats Assail Regulatory Agency Appointments," *New York Times*, June 25, 1975, 86; John Herbers, "Ford Now Is a President in the Recent Tradition," ibid., May 18, 1975, E4; editorial, "T.V.A., a National Asset," ibid., Apr. 9, 1975, 42; John Herbers, "In 6 Months, Ford's Style Is Set," ibid., Feb. 23, 1975, 1; John Herbers, "Mr. Ford Is Slow in Picking His Staff," ibid., Sept. 1, 1974, 1.

176. Roger G. Brown, "Party and Bureaucracy: From Kennedy to Reagan," *Political Science Quarterly* 97 (summer 1982): 289.

177. Gary Hoening, "Headlines: New Federal Judge," *New York Times*, Aug. 29, 1976, 131; Albin Krebs, "Notes on People," ibid., Dec. 1, 1976, 54; Goldman, *Picking Federal Judges*, 213.

178. Goldman, *Picking Federal Judges*, 210.

179. Bill McAllister, "Judge Nominated Despite Objections of Va. Senator," *Washington Post*, Apr. 2, 1976, C3.

180. *Legislative and Executive Calendar*, Committee on the Judiciary, 94th Cong., 2nd sess., 247. See also "'Senatorial Courtesy' Derails Ford Judgeship Nomination," *Congressional Quarterly*, May 8, 1976, 1124.

181. Goldman, *Picking Federal Judges*, 212.

182. Ibid., 210–211.

Chapter 8. Carter to Bush II: A Lasting Legacy (1977–2007)

1. Editorial, "The New Federal Judges," *Washington Post*, Nov. 15, 1978, A18; Susanna McBee, "Common Cause Head Calls Justice Dept. 'Heavily Politicized,'" ibid., May 11, 1977, A13. This was not unlike Hoover during his 1928 campaign; see chapter 7.

2. Richard E. Cohen, "Choosing Federal Judges: The Senate Keeps Control," *National Journal* 11 (Mar. 1979): 355; editorial, "Jimmy Carter on Justice," *Washington Post*, Aug. 16, 1976, A22.

3. Miller Center of Public Affairs, interview with Griffin Bell, Carter Presidency Project, Mar. 23, 1988, 20, http://webstorage1.mcpa.virginia.edu/library/mc/poh/transcripts/ohp_1988_0323_bell.pdf (accessed Aug. 6, 2007); Griffin B. Bell, *Taking Care of the Law* (New York: William Morrow, 1982), 208–209.

4. George Lardner Jr., "Bell, Carter and Merit Selection," *Washington Post*, Feb. 2, 1978, A1.

5. Executive Order No. 11972, "United States Circuit Court Judgeships," in *Weekly Compilation of Presidential Documents*, vol. 13 (Feb. 17, 1977), 214–215; Executive Order No. 11992, "Committee of Federal Judicial Officers," in ibid. (May 24, 1977), 810–811.

6. Executive Order No. 12097, "Merit Selection of United States District

Judges," in ibid., vol. 14 (Nov. 8, 1978), 1975–1976. For more information, see Alan Neff, "Breaking with Tradition: A Study of the U.S. District Judge Nominating Commissions," *Judicature* 64 (Dec.–Jan. 1981): 257–278.

7. Elliot E. Slotnick, "Reforms in Judicial Selection: Will They Affect the Senate's Role? (Part I)," *Judicature* 64 (Aug. 1980): 66.

8. Miller Center of Public Affairs, "Judicial Selection," in *The Lloyd N. Cutler Conference on White House Counsel, November 10–11, 2006* (Charlottesville, VA: Miller Center of Public Affairs, 2007), 6.

9. Martin Tolchin, "Testing the Merit of Carter's Merit Selection," *New York Times*, Dec. 31, 1978, E4.

10. Saundra Saperstein, "Sarbanes to Pick Judge Nominees," *Washington Post*, Nov. 20, 1978, C1.

11. Elliot E. Slotnick, "Reforms in Judicial Selection: Will They Affect the Senate's Role? (Part II)," *Judicature* 64 (Sept. 1980): 124. See also Robert J. Lipshutz, "Exit Interview," Sept. 29, 1979, Jimmy Carter Library and Museum Web site, http://jimmycarterlibrary.org/library/exitInt/exitLipshutz.pdf (accessed Aug. 6, 2007); Miller Center, "Judicial Selection," 5.

12. John M. Gashko, "Judicial Merit System: Only a Promise," *Washington Post*, Mar. 15, 1977, A4.

13. Lardner, "Bell, Carter and Merit Selection," A1.

14. "Carter Discharges a U.S. Attorney," *New York Times*, May 26, 1977, 16.

15. John M. Gashko, "A Question of Politics and the Law," *Washington Post*, June 26, 1977, A8.

16. M. A. Farber, "Attempts to Replace U.S. Attorney in New Jersey Stir Patronage Fight," *New York Times*, July 5, 1977, 33.

17. M. A. Farber, "Goldstein Resigns as a U.S. Prosecutor," *New York Times*, Sept. 13, 1977, 22. See also David A. Maraniss and Chris Schauble, "Finney Resigns as Prosecutor," *Washington Post*, Oct. 20, 1977, C1.

18. Farber, "Goldstein Resigns." 22; Gashko, "A Question of Politics and the Law," A8.

19. Roger Wilkins, "Parallel of Marston's Dismissal with Morgenthau Case in 1969," *New York Times*, Jan. 23, 1978, D6; William Safire, "The Philadelphia," ibid., Feb. 19, 1978, SM3; Charles R. Babcock, "Philadelphia Judge Is Forgotten Man in Marston Dispute," *Washington Post*, Feb. 5, 1978, A14. At the time, Republican senators Richard Schweiker and John Heinz represented Pennsylvania.

20. Charles R. Bobcok, "Carter: No Pressure in Firing Prosecutor," *Washington Post*, Jan. 13, 1978, A1.

21. Editorial, "Something Wrong in the Senate," *Washington Post*, Jan. 4, 1978, A18.

22. Gashko, "A Question of Politics and the Law," A8.

23. Jimmy Carter, "Interview with the President," *Weekly Compilation of Presidential Documents*, vol. 14 (Dec. 7, 1978), 2174.

24. Donald P. Baker, "Md. Lawyer Norman P. Ramsey Recommended as Federal Judge," *Washington Post*, July 1, 1980, C3; Saundra Saperstein, "Sarbanes Picks 2 as U.S. Judges," ibid., Jan. 17, 1979, C1; Saundra Saperstein, "Sarbanes to Pick Judge Nominees," ibid., Nov. 20, 1978, C1.

25. The Senate Judiciary Committee voted not to report Winberry to the Senate. Charles R. Babcock, "Senate May Slow Judges' Runner Stamp," *Washington Post*, Mar. 9, 1980, A2.

26. Sheldon Goldman, *Picking Federal Judges: Lower Court Selection from Roosevelt through Reagan* (New Haven, CT: Yale University Press, 1997), 260–261.

27. Richard L. Lyons, "Stennis Choice Rushed to Judgeship," *Washington Post*, Jan. 11, 1980, A1.

28. Goldman, *Picking Federal Judges*, 261.

29. Robert Morgan, in *Congressional Record*, 96th Cong., 2nd sess., vol. 126 (Dec. 2, 1980), 31451.

30. Public Law 95-486, *U.S. Statutes at Large*, 95th Cong., 2nd sess., vol. 92 (Oct. 20, 1978), 1629. See also Warren Weaver Jr., "Side Issues Delay Bill to Create New U.S. Judgeships," *New York Times*, Mar. 19, 1978, 21.

31. Charles R. Babcock, "Picking Federal Judges: Merit System vs. Pork Bench," *Washington Post*, Nov. 7, 1978, A4.

32. Miller Center, "Judicial Selection," 6.

33. Sheldon Goldman, "Carter's Judicial Appointments: A Lasting Legacy," *Judicature* 64 (Mar. 1981): 351–352.

34. Miller Center, "Judicial Selection," 6.

35. Robert G. Kaiser, "The 2,000 Carter Jobs: Who Got Them?" *Washington Post*, June 6, 1977, A1.

36. Executive Order No. 12305, "Termination of Certain Federal Advisory Committees," in *Weekly Compilation of Presidential Documents*, vol. 17 (May 5, 1981), 495–496; Charles R. Babcock, "Panels to Help Pick Judges Are Abolished," *Washington Post*, May 7, 1981, A32; Herman Schwartz, *Packing the Courts: The Conservative Campaign to Rewrite the Constitution* (New York: Scribner, 1988), 58–62.

37. Goldman, *Picking Federal Judges*, 287–288.

38. William French Smith, "The Attorney General's Memorandum on Judicial Selection Procedures," *Judicature* 64 (Apr. 1981): 428.

39. Maryanne Borrelli, Karen Hult, and Nancy Kassop, "The White House Counsel's Office," *Presidential Studies Quarterly* 31 (Dec. 2001): 566; Bob Campbell, "Reagan to Name Hayes for U.S. Attorney Post," *Detroit Free Press*, June 15, 1985, 2B.

40. Edwin Meese III, *With Reagan: The Inside Story* (Washington, DC: Regnery Gateway, 1992), 317.

41. George B. Merry, "New Englanders Grab for Patronage Plums Ripened by Reagan's Win," *Christian Science Monitor*, Nov. 14, 1980, 12.

42. Wallace Turner, "Oregon's U.S. Attorney since '61 Leaving Job," *New York Times*, Dec. 6, 1981, A1.

43. "Decision by Reagan Is Awaited on U.S. Attorneys Who Are Democrats," *New York Times*, Nov. 28, 1980, B11.

44. "The City; Raggi Suggested for U.S. Judgeship," *New York Times*, June 24, 1986, B2; Dick Cooper, "Montco Judge May Get Post as U.S. Attorney," *Philadelphia Inquirer*, June 5, 1982, B1; Larry Eichel, "U.S. Post Is Declined by Scirica," ibid., Jan. 22, 1982, B3; Philip Smith, "A Warner U.S. Attorney Candidate Faces Possible Disciplinary Action," *Washington Post*, July 12, 1981, B3; Donald P. Baker, "Three Proposed for Prosecutor," ibid., May 9, 1981, C1; Diane Henry, "Weicker 'Purring' for Now," *New York Times*, Dec. 21, 1980, CN1.

45. Although Reagan abolished circuit court merit commissions, district-level commissions continued to exist and created problems for the administration. See A Friend of the Constitution, "Congress, the President, and Judicial Selection: Lessons from the Reagan Years," in *Judicial Selection: Merit, Ideology, and Politics*, ed. Henry J. Abraham, Griffin B. Bell, Eugene W. Hickok, Jr., John W. Kern III, and Stephen J. Markman (Washington, DC: National Legal Center for the Public Interest, 1990), 52.

46. Miller Center of Public Affairs, interview with A. B. Culvahouse, Ronald Reagan Oral History Project, Apr. 1, 2004, 58, http://webstorage1.mcpa.virginia.edu/library/mc/poh/transcripts/ohp_2004_0401_culvahouse.pdf (accessed Aug. 6, 2007).

47. D'Vera Cohn, "Warner Expects Black Prosecutor to Get U.S. Judgeship in Va.," *Washington Post*, Feb. 6, 1986, D1.

48. David Hoffman and Lou Cannon, "Donovan Is Rebuffed on Judgeship Choice," *Washington Post,* Sept. 24, 1982, A1; David Hoffman and Lou Cannon, "Donovan Fails Again on Appointment of Judge," ibid., Mar. 11, 1983, A4.

49. Tony Freyer and Timothy Dixon, *Democracy and Judicial Independence: A History of the Federal Courts of Alabama, 1820–1994* (Brooklyn, AL: Carlson Publishing, 1995), 162, 165.

50. Associated Press, "Sen. Wilson Tells His Choice for U.S. District Court Seat," *San Francisco Chronicle,* May 3, 1986, B1; Brian Duffy, "Noted Lawyer Recommended as U.S. Judge," *Miami Herald,* Aug. 24, 1985, 1B. See also Associated Press, "Mail Pours in to Oppose Ousting Prosecutor," ibid., Feb. 13, 1987, 2C.

51. Editorial, "Slow Down, Senator," *Miami Herald,* Sept. 1, 1984, 24A; Peter Slevin, "Bar Heads Decry U.S. Judge Selection Process," ibid., Aug. 29, 1984, 1D.

52. Michael York, "McConnell, Ford Creating Judicial Selection Panel," *Lexington Herald-Leader,* June 27, 1985, B1.

53. James Jeffords, in *Congressional Record,* 101st Cong., 1st sess., vol. 135 (Nov. 21, 1989), 31326.

54. Howard Kurtz, "GOP Senators Foiled on Judicial Nominees," *Washington Post,* Feb. 20, 1987, A17.

55. Maralee Schwartz, "President Pays Manion-Vote IOU Sen. Gorton Held," *Washington Post,* Sept. 29, 1986, A8.

56. Glen Elsasser, "Senate Pal Untangles Judgeship Nomination," *Chicago Tribune,* Feb. 23, 1987, 1.

57. Kurtz, "GOP Senators Foiled," A17; Philip Shenons, "Reagan May Phone Senators on Court Choice," *New York Times,* June 26, 1986, A17; Aaron Epstein, "Manion Gains Senate OK in Test of Reagan's Power," *Miami Herald,* July 24, 1986, 15A.

58. Ronald Brownstein, "With or without Supreme Court Changes, Reagan Will Reshape the Federal Bench," *National Journal* 49 (Dec. 8, 1984): 2338.

59. W. Gary Fowler, "Judicial Selection under Reagan and Carter," *Judicature* 67 (Dec.–Jan. 1984): 274.

60. Sheldon Goldman, "Reagan's Second Term Judicial Appointments: The Battle at Midway," *Judicature* 70 (Apr.–May 1987): 326; Arnold H. Lubasch, "Judge Timbers Leaving U.S. Appeals Court Post," *New York Times,* July 17, 1981, B3; "Pratt Appointment Approved," ibid., June 19, 1982, A1; Arnold H. Lubasch, "D'Amato Suggests Several as Judges," ibid., Feb. 24, 1985, A36; Arnold H. Lubasch, "Upstate Judge Is Named to U.S. Court of Appeals," ibid., June 26, 1985, B3.

61. Linda Greenhouse, "Reagan Names 6 to Federal Appeals Courts," *New York Times,* Aug. 2, 1984, A17.

62. David Margolick, "At the Bar," *New York Times,* Dec. 9, 1988, B13.

63. Howard Kurtz, "Reagan Transforms the Federal Judiciary," *Washington Post,* Mar. 31, 1985, A4.

64. Public Law 98-531, *U.S. Statutes at Large,* 98th Cong., 2nd sess., vol. 98 (Oct. 19, 1984), 333.

65. Virginia Wiegand, "Two Akron Lawyers up for Judge's Post," *Akron Beacon Journal,* Jan. 13, 1985, G1; Bankruptcy Reform Act of 1978, Public Law 95-598, *U.S. Statutes at Large,* 95th Cong., 2nd sess., vol. 92 (Nov. 6, 1978), 2549.

66. *Northern Pipeline Construction Co. v. Marathon Pipe Line Co.,* 458 U.S. 50 (1982).

67. U.S.C. 152. For more information on bankruptcy reform legislation and its impact on appointments, see Eric A. Posner, "The Political Economy of the Bankruptcy Reform Act of 1978," *Michigan Law Review* 96 (Oct. 1997): 47–126.

68. James P. Pfiffner, "Establishing the Bush Presidency," *Public Administration Review* 50 (Jan.–Feb. 1990): 68.

69. Jim Doyle, "Some Recommendations from Senator Wilson," *San Francisco Chronicle*, Jan. 10, 1991, A5; "Wilson Recommends Prosecutor for Sacramento's U.S. Attorney," ibid., Jan. 5, 1991, A8.

70. Michael Tackett, "Senator Opens Trapdoor, and U.S. Attorney in St. Louis Seeks a New Stage," *Chicago Tribune*, Feb. 4, 1990, 4. See also Mark Schlinkmann, "Dittmeier out, Says Danforth," *St. Louis Post-Dispatch*, Dec. 28, 1989, 1A.

71. Kit Wagar, "Woman McConnell Dates Gets U.S. Attorney Nomination," *Lexington Herald-Leader*, June 19, 1991, A1; Thomas Tolliver, "McConnell Defends Choice for Prosecutor," ibid., Feb. 21, 1991, A1.

72. Foster Church, "2 Senators Back Jones for Burns' Seat," *Oregonian*, May 3, 1989, D8.

73. "St. Louis Black Woman Backed for U.S. Bench," *St. Louis Post-Dispatch*, Apr. 2, 1992, 7A; Tim Bryant, "List Grows of Women on Bench; Hamilton's Name Added to Roster," ibid., Nov. 18, 1990, 9D.

74. Heather Dewar, "Conservative Sought for Judgeship; No Edge for Minorities to Replace Hastings, Mack's Office Says," *Miami Herald*, Oct. 21, 1989, 1A.

75. Al D'Amato, *Power, Pasta and Politics: The World According to Senator Al D'Amato* (New York: Hyperion, 1995), 306.

76. "Farley Backs Skretny for District Court Seat," *Buffalo News*, June 14, 1989, B14.

77. Roberta Ulrich, "Attorney General May Get Judgeship," *Oregonian*, Jan. 10, 1991, C1.

78. Sheldon Goldman, "Bush's Judicial Legacy: The Final Imprint," *Judicature* 76 (Apr.–May 1993): 285.

79. William Grady, Bill Crawford, and John O'Brien, "6 Judicial Hopes Pinned on Election," *Chicago Tribune*, Sept. 8, 1992, 3; Patrick E. Gauen, "11 Seeking Judgeship for Illinois," *St. Louis Post-Dispatch*, Jan. 7, 1991, 1A.

80. Kevin Cullen, "D.C. Judge May Fill Appellate Vacancy," *Boston Globe*, Jan. 11, 1992, 25.

81. Tim Bryant, "Contenders for Federal Judges Narrowed to 3," *St. Louis Post-Dispatch*, Apr. 3, 1990, 3A; Robert L. Koening, "Panel to Pick Nominees for U.S. Judgeship," ibid., Feb. 12, 1990, 3A.

82. Sheldon Goldman, "The Bush Imprint on the Judiciary," *Judicature* 74 (Apr.–May 1991): 297.

83. Joan Biskupic, "Senators Demonstrate They Prefer to Judge Nominees for Themselves," *Congressional Quarterly* 48 (Jan. 6, 1990), 40.

84. Ruth Marcus, "GOP Senators Feud with Administration over Naming Judges," *Washington Post*, Nov. 22, 1989, A6.

85. Ibid.

86. Ruth Marcus, "GOP Senators, Bush Administration at Odds over Judicial Appointments," *Washington Post*, Nov. 23, 1989, A25.

87. Joseph Biden, in *Congressional Record*, 101st Cong., 1st sess., vol. 135 (Nov. 21, 1989), 31327.

88. James Jeffords, in ibid.

89. Dick Thornburgh, "The President's Prerogative," *Washington Post*, Dec. 31, 1989, C6.

90. James Jeffords, in *Congressional Record*, 103rd Cong., 2nd sess., vol. 140 (Oct. 8, 1994), 29562.

91. Henry J. Abraham, *Justices, Presidents, and Senators*, 4th ed. (Lanham, MD: Rowman and Littlefield, 1999), 297–299.

92. One Bush biographer called him the perfect "stealth candidate." Herbert S. Parmet, *George Bush: The Life of a Lone Star Yankee* (New York: Scribner, 1997), 436.

93. Warren B. Rudman, *Combat: Twelve Years in the U.S. Senate* (New York: Ran-

dom House, 1996), 152–194; Mary McGrory, "Nice Guy with Powerful Friends," *Washington Post,* July 26, 1990, A2; Linda Greenhouse, "Man in the News; an 'Intellectual Mind': David Hackett Souter," *New York Times,* July 24, 1990, A1.

94. Rudman, *Combat,* 161, 162.

95. R. W. Apple Jr., "Bush's Court Choice; Sununu Tells How and Why He Pushed Souter for Court," *New York Times,* July 25, 1990, A12.

96. R. W. Apple Jr., "Bush's Move: Caution Wins," *New York Times,* July 24, 1990, A1.

97. William J. Clinton, "Nominations for United States Court of Appeals Judges," in *Weekly Compilation of Presidential Documents,* vol. 29 (Aug. 7, 1993), 1591.

98. William J. Clinton, "Remarks in a Town Meeting in Sacramento," in ibid. (Oct. 3, 1993), 1977.

99. Tinsley E. Yarbrough, "Clinton and the Courts," in *The Clinton Presidency: The First Term, 1992–1996,* ed. Paul S. Herrnson and Dilys M. Hill (New York: St. Martin's Press, 1999), 46; Sheldon Goldman, "Judicial Selection under Clinton: A Midterm Examination," *Judicature* 78 (May–June 1995): 278.

100. Miller Center, "Judicial Selection," 10.

101. Donna Halvorsen, "Wellstone Gains Say in Process of Picking Judges," *Star Tribune* (Minneapolis, MN), Nov. 15, 1992, 1B.

102. Carolyn Skorneck, "Overhaul of U.S. Attorneys Drags Hands-on Approach by Distracted Reno to Fill 93 Positions," *Pittsburgh Post-Gazette,* May 27, 1993, C7.

103. Conrad de Fiebre, "Wellstone Backs B. Todd Jones as Replacement for Lillehaug," *Star Tribune* (Minneapolis, MN), June 23, 1998, 3B.

104. Susan Caba and Steve Goldstein, "Stiles Nominated for U.S. Attorney," *Philadelphia Inquirer,* May 27, 1993, B1; Gary Cohn, "Resignation Announced by Baylson," ibid., Jan. 14, 1993, B3.

105. Associated Press, "U.S. Senate Approves Woman to Be Federal Judge in Camden," *Philadelphia Inquirer,* Nov. 12, 1999, B3; Douglas Turner, "First Woman Due to Get Nod as U.S. Attorney," *Buffalo News,* June 24, 1998, B1; Patrick H. Nemoyer, "Moynihan Has Stellar Record on Appointments," ibid., Dec. 19, 1996, B3; Schuyler Kropf, "Local Lawyer in Line to Be U.S. Attorney," *Post and Courier* (Charleston, SC), Dec. 12, 1995, A15; Skorneck, "Overhaul of U.S. Attorneys," C7.

106. Robert Whereatt, "Gardebring Withdraws Judgeship Candidacy, Citing Grams' Opposition," *Star Tribune* (Minneapolis, MN), July 1, 1995, 1A; Greg Gordon, "Tunheim Endorsed for Federal Judgeship," ibid., Mar. 17, 1995, 1A.

107. "Senator Picks Pasco Lawyer for Judgeship in Washington," *Sunday Oregonian,* Jan. 12, 1997, D5; Scott Sandlin, "Black Nominated for Federal Judicial Post," *Albuquerque Journal,* Feb. 4, 1995, B1; Ronald Sullivan, "Moynihan Recommends 3 to Be Federal Judges," *New York Times,* Nov. 11, 1993, B6; Mary Ann Roser, "Kentucky Women Lobby for Seat on Federal Bench," *Lexington Herald-Leader,* June 19, 1993, C1.

108. Associated Press, "U.S. Senate Approves Woman to Be Federal Judge in Camden," *Philadelphia Inquirer,* Nov. 12, 1999, B3; "Santa Clara County," *San Francisco Chronicle,* Mar. 18, 1998, A22; "Judge Tyson Urged for Federal Judgeship," *Advocate* (Baton Rouge, LA), Dec. 23, 1997, 1A; "Feinstein Recommends Judge for Federal Post," *San Francisco Chronicle,* June 21, 1997, A15; Mike Dorning, "Senators Offer Picks for Federal Judges," *Chicago Tribune,* May 20, 1997, 3; Craig Gilbert, "3 Nominated for Federal Bench," *Milwaukee Journal Sentinel,* Mar. 22, 1997, 1; Associated Press, "Senators Recommend 2 for Federal Judgeships," *New York Times,* Mar. 18, 1997, B4; Kenneth R. Lamke, "Federal Judge Changing Status, Creating Vacancy," *Milwaukee Journal Sentinel,* Dec. 27, 1996, 1; C. David Kotok, "Democratic Party Leader Backed for Judicial Seat," *Omaha World Herald,* Oct. 24, 1995, 1B;

"Boxer Endorses 2 for L.A. Judgeships," *San Francisco Chronicle*, Sept. 27, 1995, A22; "Clinton Nominates Judge to Federal Bench," *Pittsburgh Post-Gazette*, Aug. 16, 1995, C3; "Federal Judge Wannabe List Pared to 4," *Capital Times* (Madison, WI), July 22, 1995, 7A; David Elsner and William Grady, "Clinton Taps Nominee for U.S. Judge," *Chicago Tribune*, May 6, 1994, 8; "Clinton Nominates Judge to District Court Bench," *San Francisco Chronicle*, Apr. 29, 1994, B6.

109. Neil A. Lewis, "Unmaking the G.O.P. Court Legacy," *New York Times*, Aug. 23, 1993, A10.

110. Patrick Leahy, in *Congressional Record*, 103rd Cong., 2nd sess., vol. 140 (Oct. 7, 1994), 28950; Susan Caba and Steve Goldstein, "Stiles Nominated for U.S. Attorney," *Philadelphia Inquirer*, May 27, 1993, B1; Lawrence Messina, "W. Va.'s Senators Push King for Federal Appeals Bench," *Charleston (WV) Gazette*, Feb. 5, 1998, 2A; Joan Biskupic, "Nominee Tests Clinton's Judicial Balance Amid Crime Debate," *Washington Post*, Feb. 3, 1994, A10.

111. Sheldon Goldman and Elliot Slotnick, "Clinton's First Term Judiciary: Many Bridges to Cross," *Judicature* 80 (May–June 1997): 254–255; Sheldon Goldman, Elliot Slotnick, Gerald Gryski, and Gary Zuk, "Clinton's Judges: Summing up the Legacy," *Judicature* 84 (Mar.–Apr.): 229–230.

112. Jerry Urban, "Bentsen to Play Role in 12 Judgeships," *Houston Chronicle*, Nov. 26, 1992, A43.

113. Associated Press, "Reed Nominated as First Black U.S. Attorney," *Kentucky Post*, Oct. 8, 1999, 3K.

114. Steve Campbell, "Candidates for Judgeship Wait It Out; the White House Is Torn between the Two Men, and by Opposing Recommendations," *Portland (ME) Press Herald*, Mar. 24, 1997, 1A.

115. Bob Graham, in *Congressional Record*, 106th Cong., 2nd sess., vol. 146 (Sept. 13, 2000), 17929–17930; Daniel Patrick Moynihan, in ibid., 1st sess., vol. 145 (Oct. 22, 1999), 26615; Ron Wyden, in ibid., 105th Cong., 2nd sess., vol. 144 (Apr. 27, 1998), 6823.

116. Miller Center of Public Affairs, *Improving the Process of Appointing Federal Judges: A Report of the Miller Commission on the Selection of Federal Judges* (Charlottesville, VA: Miller Center of Public Affairs, 1996), 5; Miller Center, "Judicial Selection," 11.

117. Richard L. Berke, "2 Republicans Oppose Naming Babbitt to Court," *New York Times*, June 9, 1993, A17.

118. Orrin Hatch, *Square Peg: Confessions of a Citizen Senator* (New York: Basic Books, 2002), 180. Abraham noted that Senate Judiciary Committee chairman Joseph Biden also warned against the appointment of Babbitt. Abraham, *Justices, Presidents, and Senators*, 322.

119. In his memoirs, President Clinton did not mention Senator Hatch's involvement in Ginsberg's selection. Bill Clinton, *My Life* (New York: Knopf, 2004), 524–525, 592. For another detailed account of the pre-nomination process for this selection, see John F. Harris, *The Survivor: Bill Clinton in the White House* (New York: Random House, 2005), 58–61.

120. Goldman and Slotnick, "Clinton's First Term Judiciary," 256.

121. Dan Carney, "Clinton, Hatch Spar over Judgeships," *CQ Weekly Report*, Aug. 14, 1999, 2003; Lee Davidson, "Stewart Clears Final Hurdle in Becoming Federal Judge," *Deseret News* (Salt Lake City, UT), Nov. 13, 1999, B3.

122. Jim Fisher, "If a Democrat Chose Him, He Must Be a Bum," *Lewiston (ID) Morning Tribune*, Sept. 16, 1994, 8A.

123. Michael R. Wickline, "Lewiston Attorney; GOP Wins Halt Tait's Judicial Nomination," *Lewiston (ID) Morning Tribune*, Dec. 14, 1994, 6A.

124. Mike Bucsko, "Specter Keeps Hand in Judicial Nominees," *Pittsburgh Post-Gazette*, Jan. 22, 1993, C6.

125. Rachel Smolkin and Torsten Ove, "District Bench May Lose Another," *Pittsburgh Post-Gazette*, Sept. 8, 2001, A1.

126. Joseph A. Slobodzian, "Judges from PA and NJ Are Trapped in a Logjam," *Philadelphia Inquirer*, Oct. 26, 1998, A1.

127. Clyde H. Slease III, "The White House, Not Santorum, Has Failed Regarding Judges," *Pittsburgh Post-Gazette*, Oct. 5, 2000, A18.

128. Carol Rosenberg, "W. Palm Lawyer Backed for Federal Bench," *Miami Herald*, Mar. 19, 1997, 5B.

129. Editorial, "Helms' Reasons Don't Fly on Federal Judgeship," *News and Record* (Greensboro, NC), Sept. 23, 2000, A12.

130. John Edwards, "Judicial Emergency Declared in North Carolina, Senator Edwards Urges Senate Action on Court Nominee," press release, June 8, 1999 (in author's files).

131. Richard A. Ryan, "President Feuds with Abraham," *Detroit News*, Oct. 17, 1999, 1A. See also editorial, "Court Nominees Too Much Senate Delay," *Detroit Free Press*, May 27, 2000, 10A.

132. George W. Bush, "Remarks Announcing Nomination for the Federal Judiciary," *Weekly Compilation of Presidential Documents*, vol. 37 (May 9, 2001), 723.

133. George Lardner Jr., " 'Careful' Judicial Vetting Process; White House Shuns Politics, Counsel Says as Nominations Near," *Washington Post*, Apr. 19, 2001, A17.

134. Kurt Erickson, "Bush Likely to Replace U.S. Attorneys," *Pantagraph* (Bloomington, IL), Jan. 17, 2001, A5.

135. Peter Hardin, "Senators Expect to Help Fill Plum Job Openings," *Richmond Times Dispatch*, Jan. 27, 2001, B3.

136. Sheldon Goldman, Elliot Slotnick, Gerald Gryski, Gary Zuk, and Sara Schiavoni, "W. Bush's Judiciary: The First Term Record," *Judicature* 88 (May–June 2005): 246.

137. Scott MacKay, "GOP's Gorham Nominated for U.S. Attorney," *Providence Journal-Bulletin*, Feb. 4, 2003, A1; "Senators Nominate Attorney, Marshal," *Akron Beacon Journal*, June 26, 2002, D3; Associated Press State and Local Wire, "Bush Chooses Des Moines Lawyer for U.S. Attorney Spot," Feb. 4, 2002; Torsten Ove, "Buchanan's Story One of Success, Determination; She's State's Youngest U.S. Attorney," *Pittsburgh Post-Gazette*, Sept. 30, 2001, C1; Guillermo Contreras and Michael Coleman, "Bush Picks Top N.M. Prosecutor," *Albuquerque Journal*, Aug. 3, 2001, A1; Ed Asher, "Texas Native Suggested to Fill U.S. Attorney Post," *Houston Chronicle*, July 13, 2001, A1; Matt O'Connor, "Fitzgerald Taps an Outsider for U.S. Attorney," *Chicago Tribune*, May 14, 2001, 1; Associated Press State and Local Wire, "Senators Recommend Terry Harris of Memphis as U.S. Attorney," May 2, 2001; Associated Press, "KY.'s First Black U.S. Attorney Resigning," *Lexington Herald-Leader*, Apr. 26, 2001, B1; Carri Geer Thevenot, "U.S. Attorney: Senator Goes North for Choice," *Las Vegas Review-Journal*, Apr. 10, 2001, 1B; Terry Horne, "Lugar Submits Nominations for U.S. Marshal, Attorney Posts," *Indianapolis Star*, Mar. 5, 2001, B1; Laurence Hammack, "Warner, Allen Tap 3 Candidates for U.S. Attorney," *Roanoke Times*, Feb. 22, 2001, B1; Mark Minton and Linda Satter, "Cummins, Gean Pitched to Fill U.S. Attorney Posts," *Arkansas Democrat-Gazette*, Feb. 9, 2001, A1; editorial, "Georgia GOP Chairman Fight," *Augusta (GA) Chronicle*, Feb. 8, 2001, A5; Stan Bailey, "5 Lawyers Seek to Succeed Pitt as U.S. Attorney," *Birmingham (AL) News*, Jan. 26, 2001, 4B.

138. Steve Piacente, "Thurmond Ignores Attack on Son's Nomination," *Post and Courier* (Charleston, SC), Aug. 9, 2001, B3; "Thurmond Nominates Son, 28, to Be Their State's U.S. Attorney," *Chicago Tribune*, Jan. 24, 2001, 6.

139. Sheldon Goldman, Elliot Slotnick, Gerald Gryski, Gary Zuk, and Sara Schiavoni, "W. Bush Remaking the Judiciary: Like Father Like Son?" *Judicature* 86 (May–June 2003): 285.

140. Bill Rankin, "Senator Suggests Three for Bench," *Atlanta Journal-Constitution*, Oct. 25, 2003, 4A; Jannan Hanna, "Fitzgerald Makes Pick for U.S. Judge," *Chicago Tribune*, Jan. 21, 2002, 1.

141. Pam Louwagie, "St. Thomas Law Professor Tapped for Federal Bench," *Star Tribune* (Minneapolis, MN), Dec. 15, 2005, 1B; Ashbel S. Green, "Sen. Smith Suggests 3 for District Court Post," *Oregonian*, Jan. 29, 2003, B9; Gerald M. Carbone, "Federal Judge Smith Sworn In," *Providence Journal-Bulletin*, Dec. 17, 2002, B1; Jon Sawyer, "GOP, Democrats Hail Pick of Autrey," *St. Louis Post-Dispatch*, June 6, 2001, A1; "Domenici Recommends 11 for District Court Posts," *Albuquerque Journal*, Apr. 28, 2001, A4.

142. Jennifer A. Dlouhy, "Committee Expected to Quietly Endorse Bunning Nomination," *CQ Daily Monitor*, Feb. 7, 2002, 11; Steve Piacente, "Ex-Thurmond Aide Wooten Wins Judgeship OK," *Post and Courier* (Charleston, SC), Nov. 9, 2001, 5B; Associated Press State and Local Wire, "Bush Nominates U.S. Magistrate for Federal Bench in South Carolina," June 18, 2001.

143. Jim Myers, "Seymour to Give up Federal Court Post," *Tulsa World*, Jan. 6, 2005, A1; Mary Orndorff, "Hopkins Confirmed as Federal Judge," *Birmingham (AL) News*, June 16, 2003, 3B; Peter Hardin, "Senators Suggest Four for Virginia Judgeship," *Richmond Times Dispatch*, Jan. 18, 2003, B3; Jim Hughes, "Senators List Judge Nominees," *Denver Post*, Jan. 10, 2003, B1; Renee Ordway, "Bangor Lawyer Eyed for Bench," *Bangor (ME) Daily News*, Dec. 6, 2002, A1; Bart Jansen, "Maine to Enter Federal Judge Fray," *Portland (ME) Press Herald*, June 9, 2002, 2C; Laylan Copelin, "Texas Senators Endorse Junell for Federal Judge," *Austin American-Statesman*, Mar. 8, 2002, B3; Tom Jackman, "Fairfax Judge to Get Federal Seat," *Washington Post*, Jan. 24, 2002, B4; Associated Press State and Local Wire, "Four Nominated for Federal District Court Vacancies," Aug. 2, 2001; "Summit Judge Recommended for U.S. Court," *Akron (OH) Beacon Journal*, Nov. 22, 2001, D1; Libby Quaid for Associated Press State and Local Wire, "Three Names Sent to Bush for Kansas Federal Judgeship," May 4, 2001; Mary Orndorff, "Law Professor in Line for U.S. Judgeship," *Birmingham (AL) News*, May 1, 2001, 1B; Mary Orndorff, "Mobile-Area Man Recommended for U.S. Judgeship," ibid., Apr. 17, 2001, 2B; editorial, "A Worthy Judicial Candidate," *Lancaster (PA) New Era*, Apr. 2, 2001, A6.

144. Goldman et al., "W. Bush Remaking the Judiciary," 285; Goldman et al., "W. Bush's Judiciary," 246.

145. Amy Fagan, "Ex-Thurmond Aide Clears Hurdle to Judgeship," *Washington Times*, Nov. 19, 2002, A6; Associated Press State and Local Wire, "Iowa U.S. Attorney to Be Nominated for 8th Circuit Vacancy," Dec. 20, 2002; editorial, "Hartz Will Bolster Federal Appeals Bench," *Sante Fe New Mexican*, June 23, 2001, A9.

146. Scott MacKay and Mark Arsenault, "Flanders Nominated for Federal Court," *Providence Journal*, Mar. 18, 2006, A1; John Distaso, "Bush Picks Howard to Be Judge," *Union Leader* (Manchester, NH), Aug. 3, 2001, A1; Amy Fagan, "Judicial Nominees Have Easy Sailing in Opening Debate," *CQ Daily Monitor*, July 12, 2001, 12; Jonathan Ringel, "Role Reversal Leaves Senate Spinning," *Legal Times*, June 18, 2001, 8; Elizabeth A. Palmer, "Virginia Senators Urge Bush to Reappoint Gregory," *CQ Weekly Report*, Mar. 24, 2001, 675; Andy Sher, "No Chattanoogan Urged for 6th Circuit Court," *Chattanooga (TN) Times Free Press*, Mar. 21, 2001, A4.

147. Sean P. Murphy, "Governor Chooses 5 Nominees for Marshal," *Boston Globe*, Sept. 17, 2005, B1; Frank Phillips, "Romney Sends White House 13 Choices for US Judgeship," ibid., Apr. 11, 2003, B3; Frank Phillips, "Romney Compiles Names for US Judgeship," ibid., Apr. 1, 2003, B3.

148. David Lightman, "Bryant Gains Federal Judgeship," *Hartford Courant,* Mar. 29, 2007, A3; Edward Fitzpatrick, "Fate of Flanders' Judgeship Uncertain," *Providence Journal,* Nov. 20, 2006, A1; Associated Press State and Local Wire, "Hong Recommended for Federal Judgeship," June 4, 2004; Matt Apuzzo for Associated Press State and Local Wire, "Federal Judgeship Opens in Connecticut," Nov. 19, 2001.

149. Rob Hotakainen and Greg Gordon, "In a Letter to Bush, Ramstad Put His Sister at Top of Judgeship List," *Star Tribune* (Minneapolis, MN), Dec. 6, 2001, 1A; Randy Furst, "U.S. Attorney Search Prompts Dispute," ibid., Dec. 21, 2000, 1B.

150. Laura Mansnerus, "New Jersey G.O.P. and Legal Elite Differ on U.S. Attorney," *New York Times,* Aug. 26, 2001, A33.

151. David Wasson, "Judicial Nominees Vex Party," *Tampa Tribune,* July 15, 2001, 1; "Judicial Cooperation, Aug. 26, 2005, Mel Martinez's Web site, http://martinez .senate.gov/public/index.cfm?FuseAction=InNews.View&ContentRecord_id=1753& CFID=49674080&CFTOKEN=69596959 (accessed Apr. 15, 2007).

152. "Snowe, Collins Appoint Panel to Screen Federal Judge Hopefuls," *Bangor (ME) Daily News,* Nov. 22, 2002, B5; L. Stuart Ditzen, "Judicial-Selection Process a Private Affair," *Philadelphia Inquirer,* Mar. 25, 2001, B1; Bill McAllister, "Senators Act to Fill Court Slots; Six-Member Panel to Screen Candidates," *Denver Post,* Mar. 2, 2001, B4.

153. Deputy White House Counsel David Leitch, in Miller Center, "Judicial Selection," 15, 19.

154. Matthew Tully, "Senators Won't Rule out Filibuster of High Court Nominees," *CQ Daily Monitor,* Mar. 21, 2002, 7.

155. Stuart Taylor Jr., "More Judicial Mud Fighting," *Legal Times,* May 13, 2002, 59.

156. Arlen Specter, "Let's Agree on a Timely Basis," *Legal Times,* July 8, 2002, 38.

157. E. J. Dionne Jr., "A Judiciary Worth Fighting For," *Washington Post,* Mar. 1, 2002, A25.

158. Sheldon Goldman, "The Injudicious Senate," *Washington Post,* Aug. 13, 2001, A15.

159. Jonathan Ringel, "White House States Horse-Trading over Judicial Nominations," *Miami Daily Business Review,* May 1, 2001, A8; Douglas Turner, "Democrats Push for a Say on Judicial Nominations," *Buffalo News,* Apr. 29, 2001, A10.

160. Elizabeth A. Palmer, "Early Signs of Comity Emerge in Judicial Nomination Process," *CQ Weekly Report,* May 12, 2001, 1073–1074. See also the Clinton section in this chapter.

161. George Lardner Jr., "'Careful' Judicial Vetting Process," *Washington Post,* Apr. 19, 2001, A17.

162. Associated Press, "Democrats: Don't Change Judicial-Nomination Process," *Telegraph Herald* (Dubuque, IA), Apr. 28, 2001, A7.

163. Turner, "Democrats Push for a Say on Judicial Nominations," A10. The Senate Judiciary Committee Democrats included Patrick Leahy, Edward M. Kennedy, Joseph Biden, Herb Kohl, Dianne Feinstein, Russell D. Feingold, Charles E. Schumer, Richard J. Durbin, and Maria Cantwell (listed in order of committee seniority).

164. Letter from Alberto Gonzales to Senate Judiciary Committee Democrats, May 2, 2001, White House Web site, http://www.whitehouse.gov/news/releases/ 2001/05/20010507.html (accessed Aug. 6, 2007).

165. Michael Doyle, "Bush Set to Name Judges; New Bipartisan Panel Will Pick California Candidates for the Federal Bench," *Fresno (CA) Bee,* May 1, 2001, A11.

166. Michael Doyle, "State Tries Bipartisan Panel to Fill Judicial Nominations," *Modesto (CA) Bee,* May 1, 2001, B5.

167. Barbara Boxer, "Senate Confirms Two More San Diegans to U.S. District

Court," press release, Oct. 2, 2003 http://boxer.senate.gov/news/releases/record
.cfm?id=212771 (accessed Aug. 6, 2007); Carla Marinucci, "Feinstein, Boxer Given
a Say over Judges," *San Francisco Chronicle*, Apr. 27, 2001, A3.

168. Dianne Feinstein, "Senator Feinstein Statement on Senate Approval of
Federal District Court Judges," press release, Feb. 1, 2007, http://feinstein.senate
.gov/public/index.cfm?FuseAction=NewsRoom.PressReleases&ContentRecord_id
=c1160b7a-7e9c-9af9–762a-a309468ebb92&Region_id=&Issue_id= (accessed Aug. 6,
2007); Dianne Feinstein, "Senate Approves Nomination of Stephen Larson to the
Central District Court of California," press release, Mar. 16, 2006 http://feinstein
.senate.gov/public/index.cfm?FuseAction=NewsRoom.PressReleases&Content
Record_id=7929fcbf-7e9c-9af9–7684-ed1ac090d669&Region_id=&Issue_id= (accessed Aug. 6, 2007); Boxer press release, "Senate Confirms Two More San Diegans."

169. Charles Schumer, "Schumer Formally Asks President to Nominate Former
Staten Island District Attorney Murphy to Federal Bench," press release, July 8, 2004,
http://schumer.senate.gov/SchumerWebsite/pressroom/press_releases/2004/PR0
2738.Murphy070804.html (accessed Aug. 6, 2007).

170. Katherine M. Skiba, "U.S. Senate Approves Sykes for Federal Seat," *Milwaukee Journal Sentinel*, June 25, 2004, 1B; Craig Gilbert, "Kohl, Feingold Back
Panel's Eecommendations for U.S. Appeals Court," ibid., Sept. 19, 2003, 1B.

171. Maria Cantwell, "Cantwell Commends the Confirmation of Washington
State Federal District Judge Lonny Suko," press release, July 15, 2003, http://
cantwell.senate.gov/news/record.cfm?id=241840& (accessed Aug. 6, 2007); Patty
Murray, "Senator Murray's Ten-Month Effort Succeeds in Confirming Washington's
First Latino District Court Judge," press release, June 15, 2004, http://murray
.senate.gov/news.cfm?id=222648 (accessed Aug. 6, 2007).

172. Randy Furst, "Dayton Will Support Paulose for U.S. Post," *Star Tribune*
(Minneapolis, MN), Dec. 7, 2006, 4B.

173. John O'Brien, "Bush Expected to Nominate Suddaby," *Post-Standard*
(Syracuse, NY), Sept. 11, 2002, B2; Andrew Tilghman, "Pataki Loyalist Rejected for
U.S. Attorney Post," *Times Union* (Albany, NY), Apr. 20, 2002, A1.

174. Dick Seelmeyer, "Nebraska's Senators Praise Judge Nominee," *Lincoln
(NE) Journal Star*, Oct. 5, 2001, B2; Leslie Reed, "Judicial Nominee Wins Wide
Praise," *Omaha (NE) World Herald*, July 1, 2001, 1B.

175. The account of the history of the blue slip reflects my research in the
National Archives and Records Administration in Washington, DC, over a two-week
period (Jan. 23 to Feb. 3, 2003). The records investigated included the executive nomination files from the Fifty-sixth through Eighty-third Congresses (1899–1953) and
the correspondence and communications files of the Senate Committee on the Judiciary during those Congresses. Blue slips were found for every Congress starting
with the Sixty-fifth (1917–1918). See Nomination files, 1917–1953; Committee on the
Judiciary; 65th–83rd Congresses; Records of the United States Senate, RG 46, NARA;
Mitchel A. Sollenberger, "The History of the Blue Slip in the Senate Committee on
the Judiciary (1917–2003)," *Congressional Research Service*, RL32013 (Oct. 22, 2003), 7.

176. Sollenberger, "History of the Blue Slip," 7–22.

177. U.S. Senate, Committee on the Judiciary, *Confirmation Hearing on the Nominations of Larry D. Thompson to Be Deputy Attorney General and Theodore B. Olson to
Be Solicitor General of the United States*, 107th Cong., 1st sess., 2001, 139.

178. Ibid.

179. Amy Fagan and Elizabeth Palmer, "No Agreement Reached on Judicial
Nomination Process," *CQ Daily Monitor*, Apr. 25, 2001, 10.

180. Elizabeth A. Palmer, "Senate GOP Backs Down from Dispute over Handling
of Nominees," *CQ Weekly Report*, June 9, 2001, 1360.

181. For example, the *Legal Times* reported that Senators Barbara Boxer and

John Edwards held up two judicial nominations during the 107th Congress. Jonathan Groner, "A Major Shift in the Battle for the Bench," *Legal Times,* Nov. 11, 2002, 8.

182. Traditionally, senators can blue-slip only circuit court nominees that the president has selected from their home states. Therefore, any attempt to prevent the confirmation of every nomination from the same circuit would be very unusual. "Inadmissible," *Legal Times,* Aug. 20, 2001, 3; Jonathan Ringel, "Showtime at Senate Judiciary," ibid., Sept. 3, 2001, 1; Neil A. Lewis, "The Nation: Here Come the Judges; First the Senate, Now the Courts of Appeals," *New York Times,* Dec. 1, 2002, D3.

183. Tony Mauro, "Estrada, Sutton on the Senate Fight Card," *Legal Times,* Jan. 27, 2003, 3.

184. Editorial, "Revive Fair Deal on Michigan Federal Judges—Every Judicial Nominee Should Be Given a Vote," *Detroit News,* Jan. 19, 2007, 12A; "Senators Can Veto Judicial Picks," *Grand Rapid (MI) Press,* Jan. 5, 2007, B6.

185. Alex Daniels, "Interim Appointments Seen as a Way around Traditional Blue Slips," *Arkansas Democrat-Gazette,* Mar. 26, 2007, front section.

186. The only procedure in the Senate to stop a filibuster is a cloture motion (Rule 22), which requires sixty senators to vote in favor of it. To start a cloture motion, sixteen senators must sign a petition. After waiting two calendar days, a cloture vote can be held to end debate. If the motion is passed, no more than thirty additional hours of debate can be held before a vote on the measure must take place.

187. See *Congressional Record,* 108th Cong., 1st sess., daily ed. (Mar. 6, 2003), S3217.

188. Priscilla Owen for the Fifth Circuit, Charles Pickering for the Fifth Circuit, Janice Rogers Brown for the D.C. Circuit, William Pryor Jr. for the Eleventh Circuit, and William Myers for the Ninth Circuit. Besides the six filibustered nominees, there were a handful of others (including Henry Saad, William Haynes, and Brett M. Kavanaugh) who would have been blocked if a Senate vote had been forced. See Helen Dewar, "Democrats Ask to Recall Haynes," *Washington Post,* May 18, 2004, A17; Seth Stern, "Judiciary Approves Appeals Nominee as Stabenow, Levin Consider Filibuster," *CQ Today,* June 18, 2004, 12; Charles Hurt, "Another Judicial Pick in Cross Fire," *Washington Times,* Apr. 28, 2004, A3.

189. President Bush used his recess appointment power on Charles Pickering Sr. and William Pryor Jr. See Neil A. Lewis, "Bypassing Senate for Second Times, Bush Seats Judge," *New York Times,* Feb. 21, 2004, A1.

190. Sheryl Gay Stolberg, "Democrats Issue Threat to Block Court Nominees," *New York Times,* Mar. 27, 2004, A1.

191. Keith Perine, "Bush Blinks in War with Democrats over Stalled Judicial Nominees," *CQ Weekly Report,* May 22, 2004, 1204.

192. Carl Hulse, "Frist Warns on Filibusters over Bush Nominees," *New York Times,* Nov. 12, 2004, A21.

193. Paul Kane, "Deal on Judges Called 'Close,'" *Roll Call,* May 9, 2005, 1; The Republican senators were Lincoln Chafee, Susan M. Collins, Mike DeWine, Lindsey Graham, John McCain, Olympia Snowe, and John Warner. The Democratic senators were Robert C. Byrd, Daniel Inouye, Mary Landrieu, Joseph Lieberman, Ben Nelson, Mark Pryor, and Ken Salazar.

194. "Memorandum of Understanding on Judicial Nominations," U.S. Senate, May 23, 2005 (in author's files).

195. George W. Bush, "The President's News Conference," *Weekly Compilation of Presidential Documents,* vol. 41 (May 31, 2005), 911.

196. Dan Balz and Mike Allen, "Bush Begins Consultation with Key Senators," *Washington Post,* July 13, 2005, A8.

197. Carl Hulse and Richard W. Stevenson, "Senators Advise Bush on Picking a Court Nominee," *New York Times,* July 13, 2005, A1.

198. Sheryl Gay Stolberg, "Swing Senators Face New Test in Supreme Court Fight," *New York Times,* July 14, 2005, A16.

199. Todd S. Purdum, "Eulogies for Rehnquist Recall a Man of Many Interest," *New York Times,* Sept. 8, 2005, A20.

200. "Bush, Senators to Meet over Court," *Washington Post,* Sept. 17, 2005, A2; Sheryl Gay Stolberg, "Top Democrat Says He'll Vote No on Roberts," *New York Times,* Sept. 21, 2005, A1.

201. Sheryl Gay Stolberg, "Court in Transition: Reaction," *New York Times,* Oct. 4, 2005, A23.

202. David D. Kirkpatrick, "Court in Transition: The Overview," *New York Times,* Oct. 6, 2005, A1; David D. Kirkpatrick, "Bush Choice Gets Criticisms Rare for Nominees to Court," ibid., Oct. 24, 2005, A14.

203. Peter Baker, "President to Name Nominee for Court," *Washington Post,* Oct. 21, 2005, A1.

204. The *New York Times* reported that by "the afternoon of the second day of Judge Alito's testimony, senior Democratic aides were already conceding privately that their hopes of stopping him were essentially lost." David D. Kirkpatrick, "Two Nominee Strategies. One Worked," *New York Times,* Jan. 31, 2006, A18. See also David D. Kirkpatrick, "Court in Transition: The Overview; Wider Fight Seen as Alito Victory Appears Secured," ibid., Jan. 14, 2006, A1; Adam Nagourney and Neil A. Lewis, "Court in Transition: The Overview; After Alito's Testimony, Democrats Still Dislike Him but Can't Stop Him," ibid., Jan. 13, 2006, A19; Charles Babington and Jo Becker, "Alito Likely to Become a Justice," *Washington Post,* Jan. 13, 2006, A1.

205. *Congressional Record,* 109th Cong., 2nd sess., daily ed. (Jan. 31, 2006), S348. This was after a cloture vote (72–25) stopped a potential filibuster. David D. Kirkpatrick, "Alito Clears Final Hurdle for Confirmation to Court," *New York Times,* Jan. 31, 2006, A1.

Chapter 9. Analysis and Conclusions

1. *Federalist* No. 66, in *The Federalist,* ed. Terence Ball (Cambridge: Cambridge University Press, 2003), 325 (emphasis in original). In addition, Chief Justice John Marshall wrote that the power to nominate "is the sole act of the president, and is completely voluntary." *Marbury v. Madison,* 5 U.S. (1 Cr.) 137, 155 (1803). Also see chapter 1.

2. Joseph Harris described this custom as "the sanction by which members of the Senate of the party in power are able to dictate appointments to federal offices within their own states. In effect, it transfers the nominating function for these offices from the President to the individual senators of his party, leaving the President with only a veto on the choices of the senators." Joseph P. Harris, *The Advice and Consent of the Senate* (Berkeley: University of California Press, 1953), 236.

3. *Annals of Congress,* 1st Cong., 1st sess., vol. 1 (May 19, 1789), 393.

4. Ibid. (June 18, 1789), 538, 551–552.

5. Harold H. Bruff, *Balance of Forces: Separation of Powers Law in the Administrative State* (Durham, NC: Carolina Academic Press, 2006), 389.

6. *Annals of Congress,* 1st Cong., 1st sess., vol. 1 (May 19, 1789), 395.

7. Richard L. Lyons, "Stennis Choice Rushed to Judgeship," *Washington Post,* Jan. 11, 1980, A1.

8. Orrin Hatch, *Square Peg: Confessions of a Citizen Senator* (New York: Basic Books, 2002), 180; Dan Carney, "Clinton, Hatch Spar over Judgeships," *CQ Weekly Report,* Aug. 14, 1999, 2003.

9. Miller Center of Public Affairs, "Judicial Selection," in *The Lloyd N. Cutler*

Conference on White House Counsel, November 10–11, 2006 (Charlottesville, VA: Miller Center of Public Affairs, 2007), 13.

10. "Senators Affront Cabinet Members," *New York Times*, Dec. 11, 1909, 1; "Drop Fight on MacVeagh," ibid., Dec. 12, 1909, 4; "Say Scott Held up Hitchcock's Choice," ibid., Dec. 16, 1909, 5.

11. Joseph Biden, in *Congressional Record*, 101st Cong., 1st sess., vol. 135 (Nov. 21, 1989), 31327.

12. Herbert Croly, *Marcus Alonzo Hanna: His Life and Work* (New York: Macmillan, 1919), 297.

13. Ralph Ketcham, *James Madison: A Biography* (Charlottesville: University Press of Virginia, 1990), 286–289.

14. Dorothy Ganfield Fowler, *The Cabinet Politician: The Postmaster General, 1829–1909* (New York: Columbia University Press, 1943), 91; Horatio King to Albert Jenkins, Feb. 27, 1861, in Dorothy Ganfield Fowler, "Congressional Dictation of Local Appointments," *Journal of Politics* 7 (Feb. 1945): 40.

15. Marshall Cushing, *The Story of Our Post Office* (Boston: A. M. Thayer, 1893), 281; Gerald Cullinan, *The Post Office Department* (New York: Praeger, 1968), 79.

16. Harris, *Advice and Consent*, 355.

17. See House member involvement in appointments during the Bush I, Clinton, and Bush II administrations in chapter 8.

18. William Grady, Bill Crawford, and John O'Brien, "6 Judicial Hopes Pinned on Election," *Chicago Tribune*, Sept. 8, 1992, 3; Patrick E. Gauen, "11 Seeking Judgeship for Illinois," *St. Louis Post-Dispatch*, Jan. 7, 1991, 1A.

19. Diana DeGette, "Romer, DeGette and Skaggs Announce Judicial Appointments Panel," press release, May 8, 1998, http://www.house.gov/degette/news/releases/980508.html (accessed Aug. 6, 2007).

20. Florida Federal Judicial Nominating Commission, "Rules of Procedure," Dec. 2004, http://www.flnd.uscourts.gov/announcements/documents/20041112FJNC Rules.pdf#search='commission%20and%20district%20judges%20and%20federal' (accessed Aug. 6, 2007).

21. See Kenneth W. Hechler, *Insurgency: Personalities and Politics of the Taft Era* (New York: Columbia University Press, 1940). For a detailed account of this episode, see Harlan Hahn, "President Taft and the Discipline of Patronage," *Journal of Politics* 28 (May 1966): 368–390.

22. Richard Lowitt, *George W. Norris: The Making of a Progressive, 1861–1912* (Westport, CT: Greenwood Press, 1980), 162.

23. Hahn, "President Taft and the Discipline of Patronage," 387.

24. William Howard Taft, *Our Chief Magistrate and His Powers* (New York: Columbia University Press, 1925), 61–62.

25. Howard Kurtz, "GOP Senators Foiled on Judicial Nominees," *Washington Post*, Feb. 20, 1987, A17.

26. Ruth Marcus, "GOP Senators, Bush Administration at Odds over Judicial Appointments," *Washington Post*, Nov. 23, 1989, A25.

27. See Mitchel A. Sollenberger, "The Law: Must the Senate Take a Floor Vote on a Presidential Nominee?" *Presidential Studies Quarterly* 34 (June 2004): 420–436.

28. For an example of a committee rejection, see Mitch Sollenberger, Jack Rossotti, and Mark J. Rozell, "Reagan and the Courts," in *The Reagan Presidency*, ed. Paul Kengor (Lanham, MD: Rowman and Littlefield, 2005), 101–102; for an example of a Senate rejection, see Nancy Scherer, *Scoring Points: Politicians, Activists, and the Lower Federal Court Appointment Process* (Stanford, CA: Stanford University Press, 2005), 93–94.

29. Scherer, *Scoring Points*, 151.

30. For instance, there have been a number of proposals to eliminate "secret" holds. The most recent occurred in the 109th Congress when Senator Ron Wyden

introduced Senate Amendment 2944 as part of the Legislative Transparency and Accountability Act of 2006. See Senator Ron Wyden, in *Congressional Record,* 109th Cong., 2nd sess., daily ed. (Mar. 8, 2006), S1872–S1881.

31. Ibid. (Dec. 5, 2006), S11113.

32. See U.S. Senate, Subcommittee on the Constitution, *Judicial Nominations, Filibusters, and the Constitution: When a Majority Is Denied Its Right to Consent,* 108th Cong., 1st sess. (May 6, 2003).

33. *Congressional Record,* 109th Cong., 2nd sess., daily ed. (Dec. 5, 2006), S11114.

34. George H. Haynes, *The Senate of the United States: Its History and Practice* (Boston: Houghton Mifflin, 1938), 1:392–419; Roger H. Davidson and Walter J. Oleszek, *Congress and Its Members* (Washington, DC: CQ Press, 2000), 251–252.

35. George Reedy, *The U.S. Senate* (New York: Crown, 1986), 197.

36. *Federalist* No. 10, in *The Federalist,* 43.

37. Ross K. Baker, *House and Senate,* 3rd ed. (New York: Norton, 2001), 80–81.

38. *Federalist* No. 47, in *The Federalist,* 234.

39. *United States v. Ferreira,* 54 U.S. (13 Howard) 39, 50–51 (1852).

40. Harold J. Krent, *Presidential Powers* (New York: New York University Press, 2005), 32, 34.

41. Edward S. Corwin, *The President: Office and Powers, 1787–1957* (New York: New York University Press, 1957), 363–364.

42. For example, Congress passed resolutions requiring that two counselors be appointed who are "learned in the law" and that judges of an appeals court be "learned in the law." *Journals of the Continental Congress,* ed. Worthington C. Ford (Washington, DC: GPO, 1908), vol. 10 (Feb. 5, 1778), 125; ibid., vol. 15 (Dec. 4, 1779), 1349.

43. "An Act to Establish the Judicial Courts of the United States," *U.S. Statutes at Large,* 1st Cong., 1st sess., vol. 1 (Sept. 24, 1789), 92–93.

44. "An Act to Carry into Effect Certain Stipulations of the Treaty between the United States of America and the Republic of Mexico, of the Second Day of February, One Thousand Eight Hundred and Forty-eight," *U.S. Statutes at Large,* 30th Cong., 2nd sess., vol. 9 (Mar. 3, 1849), 393.

45. "An Act to Reorganize the Marine Hospital Service, and to Provide for the Relief of Sick and Disabled Seamen," *U.S. Statutes at Large,* 41st Cong., 2nd sess., vol. 1 (June 29, 1870), 170.

46. U.S.C. §22 (2004); U.S.C. §3 (2004).

47. Saikrishna Prakash, "Regulating Presidential Powers," *Cornell Law Review* 91 (Nov. 2005): 238, 246, 247. Prakash refers to David P. Currie's statement on the Judiciary Act: "In prescribing that each of the government's attorneys be 'a meet person learned in the law' Congress significantly if sensibly restricted the President's discretion in selecting them. Nobody seems to have suggested that in so doing Congress offended the appointment provisions of Article II." David P. Currie, *The Constitution in Congress: The Federalist Period 1789–1801* (Chicago: University of Chicago Press, 1997), 43.

48. James Eisenstein, *Counsel for the United States: U.S. Attorneys in the Political and Legal Systems* (Baltimore: Johns Hopkins University Press, 1978), 35–53.

49. Nancy V. Baker, *Conflicting Loyalties: Law and Politics in the Attorney General's Office, 1789–1990* (Lawrence: University Press of Kansas, 1992), 107–125, 166–179.

50. Prakash, "Regulating Presidential Powers," 247.

51. *Myers v. United States,* 272 U.S. 52, 265–274 (1923) (dissenting opinion).

52. Corwin, *The President,* 74.

53. Phillip J. Cooper, *By Order of the President: The Use and Abuse of Executive Direct Action* (Lawrence: University Press of Kansas, 2002), 208.

54. Public Law 109-295, *U.S. Statutes at Large,* 109th Cong., 2nd sess., vol. 120 (Oct. 4, 2006), 1394.

55. "Statement on Signing the Department of Homeland Security Appropriation Act, 2007," in *Weekly Compilation of Presidential Documents,* vol. 42 (Oct. 4, 2006), 1742–1743. This was not the only time that Bush objected to statutory requirements for an office. See "Statement on Signing the Postal Accountability and Enhancement Act," in ibid. (Dec. 22, 2006), 2196; "Statement on Signing the Safe, Accountable, Flexible, Efficient Transportation Equity Act: A Legacy for Users," in ibid., vol. 41 (Aug. 10, 2005), 1273; "Statement on Signing the Vision 100—Century of Aviation Reauthorization Act," in ibid., vol. 39 (Dec. 12, 2003), 1796.

56. Public Law 109-295, *U.S. Statutes at Large,* 109th Cong., 2nd sess., vol. 120 (Oct. 4, 2006), 1397.

57. *Weekly Compilation of Presidential Documents,* vol. 42 (Oct. 4, 2006), 1743.

58. Amos T. Akerman, "Civil-Service Commission," Aug. 31, 1871, in U.S. Department of Justuice, *Official Opinions of the Attorneys General,* ed. A. J. Bentley (Washington, DC: GPO, 1873), 13:520, 524–525.

59. U.S. House of Representatives, Committee on the Civil Service, *Investigation of Civilian Employment: Hearings before the Committee on the Civil Service,* part 1, 78th Cong., 1st sess. (Mar. 10, 1943), 16.

60. For President Ronald Reagan's objections, see "Statement on Signing the Bankruptcy Amendments and Federal Judgeship Act of 1984," in *Weekly Compilation of Presidential Documents,* vol. 34 (July 10, 1984), 1011; Public Law 98-353, *U.S. Statutes at Large,* 98th Cong., 2nd sess., vol. 98 (July 10, 1984), 333. For President George H. W. Bush's objections, see "Statement on Signing the Intelligence Authorization Act, Fiscal Year 1992," in *Weekly Compilation of Presidential Documents,* vol. 27 (Dec. 4, 1991), 1758; Public Law 102-183, *U.S. Statutes at Large,* 102nd Cong., 1st sess., vol. 105 (Dec. 4, 1991), 1260. For President Bill Clinton's objections, see "Statement on Signing the Omnibus Parks and Public Lands Management Act of 1996," in *Weekly Compilation of Presidential Documents,* vol. 27 (Nov. 12, 1996), 2383; Public Law 104-333, *U.S. Statutes at Large,* 104th Cong., 2nd sess., vol. 110 (Nov. 12, 1996), 4093.

61. Krent, *Presidential Powers,* 32.

62. Matt Stearns and Seth Borenstein, "FEMA Leader Has Unlikely Background," *Miami Herald,* Sept. 4, 2005, 23A; Spencer S. Hsu and Susan B. Glasser, "FEMA Director Singled out by Response Critics," *Washington Post,* Sept. 6, 2005, A1; Andrew Zajac and Andrew Martin, "Top FEMA Leaders Short on Experience," *Chicago Tribune,* Sept. 7, 2005, 4; Seth Borenstein, "Feds Ill-Prepared to Respond, Experts Say," *Miami Herald,* Sept. 1, 2005, 24A; Josh White and Peter Whoriskey, "Planning, Response Are Faulted," *Washington Post,* Sept. 2, 2005, A1; Marc Sandalow, "Anarchy, Anger, Desperation: The Response," *San Francisco Chronicle,* Sept. 2, 2005, A1; Frank James and Andrew Martin, "Ex-Officials Say Weakened FEMA Botched Response," *Chicago Tribune,* Sept. 3, 2005, 1; Susan B. Glasser and Josh White, "Storm Exposed Disarray at the Top," *Washington Post,* Sept. 4, 2005, A1.

63. Prakash, "Regulating Presidential Powers," 215–257. See also the discussion of the unitary executive school in this chapter.

64. Stephen K. Bailey, "The President and His Political Executives," *Annals of the American Academy of Political and Social Science* 307 (Sept. 1956): 27.

65. Henry L. Stoddard, *As I Knew Them* (New York: Harper and Brothers, 1927), 168.

66. James T. Patterson, *Mr. Republican: A Biography of Robert A. Taft* (Boston: Houghton Mifflin, 1972), 583–584; Stewart Alsop, "Ike-Taft Conflict Lulled for Present," *Washington Post,* Dec. 22, 1952, 10. See also Robert C. Albright, "Worried Legislators Get Word Ike Will Consult on Jobs, Bills," *Washington Post,* Dec. 16, 1952, 1.

67. Dean E. Mann and Zachary A. Smith, "The Selection of U.S. Cabinet Officers and Other Political Executives," *International Political Science Review* 2 (1981): 227. See also G. Calvin Mackenzie, "The Real Invisible Hand: Presidential Appointees in the Administration of George W. Bush," *PS: Political Science and Politics* 35 (Mar. 2002): 29–30.

68. Arthur M. Schlesinger Jr., *Robert Kennedy and His Times* (New York: Houghton Mifflin, 2002), 374.

69. White House Counsel David Leitch, in Miller Center, "Judicial Selection," 15.

70. John G. Sproat, *"The Best Men": Liberal Reformers in the Gilded Age* (New York: Oxford University Press, 1968), 245.

71. For a concise history of the civil service movement explaining its criticism of the spoils system, see David H. Rosenbloom, *Federal Service and the Constitution: The Development of the Public Employment Relationship* (Ithaca, NY: Cornell University Press, 1971), 70–93.

72. For insight into the reformers' antidemocratic outlook, see Ari Hoogenboom, *Outlawing the Spoils: A History of the Civil Service Reform Movement, 1865–1883* (Urbana: University of Illinois Press, 1961), 26; Sproat, *"The Best Men,"* 245.

73. Here, *politics* was a derogatory term applied to lawmakers' involvement in appointment matters—the implication being that only elected officials engaged in it.

74. Charles O. Graves, "How It Was Done in Great Britain," *Scribner's Monthly* 14 (June 1877): 242–247; Adelbert Bower Sageser, *The First Two Decades of the Pendleton Act: A Study of Civil Service Reform* (Lincoln: University Studies of the University of Nebraska, 1935), 15–16; Wayne E. Fuller, *The American Mail: Enlarger of the Common Life* (Chicago: University of Chicago Press, 1972), 310.

75. John C. Yoo, "The New Sovereignty and the Old Constitution: The Chemical Weapons Convention and the Appointments Clause," *Constitutional Commentary* 15 (spring 1998): 109.

76. Steven G. Calabresi and Christopher S. Yoo, "The Unitary Executive during the First Half-Century," *Case Western Reserve University* 47 (summer 1997): 1475.

77. George Washington to Mary Katherine Goddard, Jan. 6, 1790, in *The Writings of George Washington,* ed. John C. Fitzpatrick (Washington, DC: GPO, 1939), 30:490. See chapter 2.

78. Calabresi and Yoo, "The Unitary Executive during the First Half-Century," 1491.

79. John Adams to Benjamin Adams, Apr. 22, 1799, in *The Works of John Adams,* ed. Charles Francis Adams (Boston: Little, Brown, 1854), 8:636.

80. Calabresi and Yoo, "The Unitary Executive during the First Half-Century," 1526.

81. Steven G. Calabresi and Christopher S. Yoo, "The Unitary Executive during the Second Half-Century," *Harvard Journal of Law and Public Policy* 26 (summer 2003): 680.

82. Ibid., 775–777.

83. Alexander White, "Department of Foreign Affairs," *Annals of Congress,* 1st Cong., 1st sess., vol. 1 (June 18, 1789), 539.

84. Steven G. Calabresi and Saikrishna B. Prakash, "The President's Power to Execute the Laws," *Yale Law Journal* 104 (Dec. 1994): 559.

85. David A. Crockett, "The Contemporary President: Should the Senate Take a Floor Vote on a Presidential Judicial Nominee?" *Presidential Studies Quarterly* 37 (June 2007): 315, 316.

86. Ibid., 317.

87. Theodore Roosevelt to Winston Churchill, Feb. 13, 1907, in *The Letters of Theodore Roosevelt,* ed. Elting E. Morison (Cambridge, MA: Harvard University Press, 1952), 5:587.

88. Theodore Roosevelt to Augustus Peabody Gardner, Oct. 28, 1904, in ibid., 4:1002. See also "Rebuked by the President," *New York Times*, Nov. 15, 1904, 1.

89. Crockett, "The Contemporary President," 317.

90. Roger Sherman to John Adams, July 20, 1789, in *Works of John Adams*, 6:440.

91. Crockett, "The Contemporary President," 316, 328, 329.

92. Ibid., 328.

93. Ibid., 329.

94. Brief for the Petitioners, *Cheney v. United States District Court for the District of Columbia* (2004) (No. 03–475), 32.

95. *Youngstown Sheet & Tube Co. v. Sawyer,* 343 U.S. 579, 635 (1952) (concurring opinion).

Bibliography

Research Collections

Benjamin Harrison Papers, Library of Congress, Manuscript Reading Room.

Calvin Coolidge Papers, Library of Congress, Manuscript Reading Room.

Committee papers, 1901–1946, Committee on the Judiciary, Fifty-seventh to Seventy-ninth Congresses, Records of the United States Senate, Record Group 46, National Archives, Washington, DC.

Correspondence of Patrick (Pat) McCarran, 1947–1948, Committee on the Judiciary; Eightieth Congress, Records of the United States Senate, Record Group 46, National Archives, Washington, DC.

Executive dockets, 1901–1941, Committee on the Judiciary, Fifty-seventh to Seventy-seventh Congresses, Records of the United States Senate, Record Group 46, National Archives, Washington, DC.

Executive session minutes and other records relating to committee meetings, 1947–1968, Committee on the Judiciary, Eightieth to Ninetieth Congresses, Records of the United States Senate, Record Group 46, National Archives, Washington, DC.

General correspondence, 1955–1962, Committee on the Judiciary, Eighty-fourth to Eighty-seventh Congresses, Records of the United States Senate, Record Group 46, National Archives, Washington, DC.

General records of the Department of State, Record Group 59, National Archives, College Park, MD.

Grover Cleveland Papers, Library of Congress, Manuscript Reading Room.

James K. Polk Papers, Library of Congress, Manuscript Reading Room.

Martin Van Buren Papers, Library of Congress, Manuscript Reading Room.

Nelson W. Aldrich Papers, Library of Congress, Manuscript Reading Room.

Nomination files, 1917–1953, Committee on the Judiciary, Sixty-fifth to Eighty-third Congresses, Records of the United States Senate, Record Group 46, National Archives, Washington, DC.

Presidential messages and executive communications, 1947–1968, Committee on the Judiciary, Eightieth to Ninetieth Congresses, Records of the United States Senate, Record Group 46, National Archives, Washington, DC.

Records relating to nominations, 1947–1968, Committee on the Judiciary, Sixty-fifth to Eighty-second Congresses, Records of the United States Senate, Record Group 46, National Archives, Washington, DC.

Register of letters received on nominations, 1901–1941, Committee on the Judiciary, Fifty-seventh to Seventy-seventh Congresses, Records of the United States Senate, Record Group 46, National Archives, Washington, DC.

William L. Marcy Papers, Library of Congress, Manuscript Reading Room.
William McKinley Papers, Library of Congress, Manuscript Reading Room.

Articles and Books

Abraham, Henry J. *Justices, Presidents, and Senators*. 4th ed. Lanham, MD: Rowman and Littlefield, 1999.
Abraham, Henry J., Griffin B. Bell, Eugene W. Hickok Jr., John W. Kern III, and Stephen J. Markman, eds. *Judicial Selection: Merit, Ideology, and Politics*. Washington, DC: National Legal Center for the Public Interest, 1990.
Abshire, David M. *The South Rejects a Prophet: The Life of Senator D. M. Key, 1824–1900*. New York: Praeger, 1967.
Ackerman, Bruce A. "Transformative Appointments." *Harvard University Law Review* 101 (Apr. 1988): 1164–1184.
Adams, Henry. *History of the United States of America during the Administration of Thomas Jefferson*. New York: Library of America, 1986.
———. *History of the United States during the Second Administration of Madison, 1813–1817*. 3 vols. New York: Scribner, 1891.
Adams, John. *The Works of John Adams*, ed. Charles Francis Adams. 10 vols. Boston: Little, Brown, 1851–1865.
Adams, John Quincy. *Memoirs of John Quincy Adams*, ed. Charles Francis Adams. 12 vols. Philadelphia: J. B. Lippincott, 1874–1877.
Adler, David Gray, and Larry N. George, eds. *The Constitution and the Conduct of American Foreign Policy*. Lawrence: University Press of Kansas, 1996.
Aldrich, John H. *Why Parties? The Origin and Transformation of Political Parties in America*. Chicago: University of Chicago Press, 1995.
Ammon, Harry. *James Monroe: The Quest for National Identity*. Charlottesville: University of Virginia Press, 1990.
Anderson, Adrian. "President Wilson's Politician: Albert Sidney Burleson of Texas." *Southwestern Historical Quarterly* 77 (Jan. 1974): 339–354.
Andrews, E. Benjamin. "A History of the Last Quarter-Century in the United States." *Scribner's Magazine* 18 (Sept. 1895): 267–289.
———. *The United States in Our Own Times: A History from Reconstruction to Expansion*. New York: Scribner, 1903.
Auchampaugh, Philip Gerald. "The Buchanan-Douglas Feud." *Journal of Illinois State History* 25 (Apr. 1932): 5–48.
Badeau, Adam. *Grant in Peace: From Appomattox to Mount McGregor*. Hartford, CT: S. S. Scranton, 1887.
Bailey, Stephen K. "The President and His Political Executives." *Annals of the American Academy of Political and Social Science* 307 (Sept. 1956): 24–36.
Baker, Jean H. *James Buchanan*. New York: Henry Holt, 2004.
Baker, Nancy V. *Conflicting Loyalties: Law and Politics in the Attorney General's Office, 1789–1990*. Lawrence: University Press of Kansas, 1992.
Baker, Ross K. *House and Senate*. 3rd ed. New York: Norton, 2001.
Ball, Terence, ed. *The Federalist*. Cambridge: Cambridge University Press, 2003.
Bancroft, Frederic. *The Life of William H. Seward*. 2 vols. New York: Harper and Brothers, 1900.
Banning, Lance. *The Jeffersonian Persuasion: Evolution of Party Ideology*. Ithaca, NY: Cornell University Press, 1983.
Barker, Charles E. *With President Taft in the White House*. Chicago: A. Kroch, 1947.
Barnard, Harry. *Rutherford B. Hayes*. Indianapolis: Bobbs-Merrill, 1954.
Bartlett, Irving H. *Daniel Webster*. New York: Norton, 1978.

Bassett, John Spencer. *The Life of Andrew Jackson*. New York: Macmillan, 1931.
Bauer, K. Jack. *Zachary Taylor: Soldier, Planter, Statesman of the Old Southwest*. Baton Rouge: Louisiana State University Press, 1985.
Baumgardner, James L. "Abraham Lincoln, Andrew Johnson, and the Federal Patronage: An Attempt to Save Tennessee for the Union?" *East Tennessee Historical Society's Publications* 45 (1973): 51–60.
Beale, H. K. *The Critical Year: A Study of Andrew Jackson and Reconstruction*. New York: Harcourt, Brace, 1930.
Bell, Griffin B. *Taking Care of the Law*. New York: William Morrow, 1982.
Belohlavek, John M. *George Mifflin Dallas: Jacksonian Patrician*. University Park: Pennsylvania State University Press, 1977.
Bemis, Samuel Flagg. *John Quincy Adams and the Union*. Norwalk, CT: Easton Press, 1984.
Bensel, Richard Franklin. *The Political Economy of American Industrialization, 1877–1900*. Cambridge: Cambridge University Press, 2000.
Benton, Thomas Hart. *Abridgment of the Debates of Congress, from 1789 to 1856*. New York: D. Appleton, 1857–1861.
———. *A Thirty Years' View*. 2 vols. London: D. Appleton, 1860.
Berger, Raoul. *Executive Privilege: A Constitutional Myth*. Cambridge, MA: Harvard University Press, 1974.
"Biographical Memoir of the Late Henry A. Muhlenberg." *United States Democratic Review* 16 (Jan. 1845): 67–78.
Bishop, Joseph Bucklin. *Theodore Roosevelt and His Time: Shown In His Own Letters*. 2 vols. New York: Charles Scribner's Sons, 1920.
Blake, John L. *A Biographical Dictionary*. Philadelphia: H. Cowperthwait, 1859.
Blake, Nelson Morehouse. *William Mahone of Virginia*. Richmond, VA: Garrett and Massie, 1935.
Blodgett, Geoffrey. *The Gentle Reformers: Massachusetts Democrats in the Cleveland Era*. Cambridge, MA: Harvard University Press, 1966.
Bonney, Catharina Van Rensselaer. *Legacy of Historical Gleanings*. 2nd ed. 2 vols. Albany, NY: J. Munsell, 1875.
Bornet, Vaughn Davis. *The Presidency of Lyndon B. Johnson*. Lawrence: University Press of Kansas, 1983.
Borrelli, Maryanne, Karen Hult, and Nancy Kassop. "The White House Counsel's Office." *Presidential Studies Quarterly* 31 (Dec. 2001): 561–584.
Boucher, Chauncey Samuel. *The Nullification Controversy in South Carolina*. Chicago: University of Chicago Press, 1916.
Boutwell, George S. *Reminiscences of Sixty Years in Public Affairs*. 2 vols. New York: Greenwood Press, 1968.
Bowers, Claude G. *The Party Battles of the Jackson Period*. New York: Houghton Mifflin, 1922.
Brant, Irving. *James Madison: Commander in Chief, 1812–1836*. New York: Bobbs-Merrill, 1961.
Breen, Matthew P. *Thirty Years of New York Politics*. New York: Arno Press, 1974.
Brinkley, Alan, and Davis Dyer. *American Presidency*. New York: Houghton Mifflin, 2004.
Brodsky, Alyn. *Grover Cleveland: A Study in Character*. New York: St. Martin's Press, 2000.
Brown, Roger G. "Party and Bureaucracy: From Kennedy to Reagan." *Political Science Quarterly* 97 (summer 1982): 279–294.
Brown, Roscoe C. E. *History of the State of New York: Political and Governmental*, ed. Ray B. Smith. 6 vols. Syracuse, NY: Syracuse Press, 1922.
Bruff, Harold H. *Balance of Forces: Separation of Powers Law in the Administrative State*. Durham, NC: Carolina Academic Press, 2006.

Buchanan, James. *The Works of James Buchanan,* ed. John Bassett Moore. 12 vols. Philadelphia: J. B. Lippincott, 1908–1911.

Buck, Solon J. *The Granger Movement.* Lincoln: University of Nebraska Press, 1963.

Burbank, Stephen B. "Politics, Privilege and Power: The Senate's Role in the Appointment of Federal Judges." *Judicature* 86 (July–Aug. 2002): 24–27.

Burke, John P. *The Institutional Presidency: Organizing and Managing the White House from FDR to Clinton.* 2nd ed. Baltimore: Johns Hopkins University Press, 2000.

Burner, David. *Herbert Hoover: A Public Life.* New York: Knopf, 1979.

Burns, James MacGregor. *Roosevelt: The Lion and the Fox.* New York: Harcourt, Brace, 1956.

Butt, Archie. *Taft and Roosevelt: The Intimate Letters of Archie Butt.* 2 vols. New York: Doubleday, Doran, 1930.

Byrdsall, Fitzwilliam. *The History of the Loco-Foco or Equal Rights Party.* New York: B. Franklin, 1967.

Calabresi, Steven G., and Saikrishna B. Prakash. "The President's Power to Execute the Laws." *Yale Law Journal* 104 (Dec. 1994): 541–665.

Calabresi, Steven G., and Kevin H. Rhodes. "The Structural Constitution: Unitary Executive, Plural Judiciary." *Harvard Law Review* 105 (Apr. 1992): 1153–1216.

Calabresi, Steven G., and Christopher S. Yoo. "The Unitary Executive during the First Half-Century." *Case Western Reserve University* 47 (summer 1997): 1451–1561.

———. "The Unitary Executive during the Second Half-Century." *Harvard Journal of Law and Public Policy* 26 (summer 2003): 667–800.

Calhoun, Charles W. *Benjamin Harrison.* New York: Henry Holt, 2005.

Calhoun, John C. *The Papers of John C. Calhoun,* ed. Clyde N. Wilson. 28 vols. Columbia: University of South Carolina Press, 1959–2003.

Candler, Allen D., and Clement A. Evans, eds. *Georgia.* 3 vols. Atlanta: State Historical Association, 1906.

Carman, Harry J., and Reinhard H. Luthin. *Lincoln and the Patronage.* New York: Columbia University Press, 1943.

Carp, E. Wayne. *To Starve the Army at Pleasure: Continental Army Administration and American Political Culture, 1775–1783.* Chapel Hill: University of North Carolina Press, 1984.

Carpenter, William S. "Repeal of the Judiciary Act of 1801." *American Political Science Review* 9 (Aug. 1915): 519–528.

Carter, John Denton. "Abraham Lincoln and the California Patronage." *American Historical Review* 48 (Apr. 1943): 495–506.

Carter, Stephen L. *The Confirmation Mess: Cleaning up the Federal Appointments Process.* New York: Basic Books, 1994.

Cary, Edward. *George William Curtis.* New York: Greenwood Press, 1969.

Chambers, John. *Autobiography of John Chambers.* Iowa City: State Historical Society of Iowa, 1908.

Chambers, William Nisbet. *Old Bullion Benton.* Boston: Little, Brown, 1956.

Channing, Edward. *The Jeffersonian System, 1801–1811.* New York: Greenwood Press, 1969.

Chase, Harold W. *Federal Judges: The Appointing Process.* Minneapolis: University of Minnesota Press, 1972.

Chidsey, Donald Barr. *The Gentleman from New York: A Life of Roscoe Conkling.* New Haven, CT: Yale University Press, 1935.

Childs, Marquis. *Eisenhower: Captive Hero.* New York: Harcourt, Brace, 1958.

Chinard, Gilbert. *Honest John Adams.* Boston: Little, Brown, 1964.

Chitwood, Oliver Perry. *John Tyler: Champion of the Old South.* Newtown, CT: American Political Biography Press, 2000.

Clark, Bennett Champ. *John Quincy Adams: "Old Man Eloquent."* Boston: Little, Brown, 1932.

Clark, Champ. *My Quarter Century of American Politics.* 2 vols. New York: Harper, 1920.

Clay, Henry. *The Papers of Henry Clay,* ed. Robert Seager II, James Hopkins, Mary Hargreaves, Melba Porter Hay, et al. 11 vols. Lexington: University Press of Kentucky, 1959–1992.

———. *The Private Correspondence of Henry Clay,* ed. Calvin Colton. New York: A. S. Barnes, 1856.

Cleaves, Freeman. *Old Tippecanoe: William Henry Harrison and His Times.* New York: Scribner, 1939.

Clemmer, Mary. *Ten Years in Washington: Life and Scenes in the National Capital, as a Woman Sees Them.* Hartford, CT: A. D. Worthington, 1874.

Cleveland, Grover. "The Independence of the Executive, I." *Atlantic Monthly* 85 (June 1900): 721–732.

———. "The Independence of the Executive, II." *Atlantic Monthly* 86 (July 1900): 1–14.

———. *Letters of Grover Cleveland, 1850–1908,* ed. Allan Nevins. New York: Houghton Mifflin, 1933.

Clinton, Bill. *My Life.* New York: Knopf, 2004.

Coffey, Matthew B. "A Death at the White House: The Short Life of the New Patronage." *Public Administration Review* 34 (Sept.–Oct. 1974): 440–444.

Colby, Peter W. *New York State Today: Politics, Government, Public Policy.* Albany, NY: SUNY Press, 1989.

Cole, David B. *Martin Van Buren and the American Political System.* Princeton, NJ: Princeton University Press, 1984.

———. *The Presidency of Andrew Jackson.* Lawrence: University Press of Kansas, 1993.

Conkling, Alfred R. *The Life and Letters of Roscoe Conkling.* New York: Charles L. Webster, 1889.

Coolidge, Calvin. *Autobiography.* New York: Cosmopolitan Book Corporation, 1929.

Cooper, Phillip J. *By Order of the President: The Use and Abuse of Executive Direct Action.* Lawrence: University Press of Kansas, 2002.

Cornog, Evan. *The Birth of Empire: DeWitt Clinton and the American Experience, 1769–1828.* New York: Oxford University Press, 2000.

Corwin, Edward S. *The President: Office and Powers, 1787–1957.* New York: New York University Press, 1957.

Cotter, Cornelius P. "Eisenhower as Party Leader." *Political Science Quarterly* 98 (summer 1983): 255–283.

Cox, Jacob D. "The Civil-Service Reform." *North American Review* 112 (Jan. 1871): 81–113.

Cranston, Ruth. *The Story of Woodrow Wilson.* New York: Simon and Schuster, 1945.

Cresson, W. P. *James Monroe.* Chapel Hill: University of North Carolina Press, 1928.

Crittenden, John J. *The Life of John J. Crittenden, with Selections from His Correspondence and Speeches,* ed. Chapman Coleman. 2 vols. Philadelphia: J. B. Lippincott, 1873.

Crockett, David A. "The Contemporary President: Should the Senate Take a Floor Vote on a Presidential Judicial Nominee?" *Presidential Studies Quarterly* 37 (June 2007): 313–330.

Croly, Herbert. *Marcus Alonzo Hanna: His Life and Work.* New York: Macmillan, 1919.

Cullinan, Gerald. *The Post Office Department.* New York: Praeger, 1968.

Cullom, Shelby M. *Fifty Years in Public Service: Personal Recollections of Shelby M. Cullom.* Chicago: A. C. McClurg, 1911.

Cunningham, Noble E., Jr. *The Jeffersonian Republicans: The Formation of Party Organization, 1789–1801.* Chapel Hill: University of North Carolina Press, 1957.

———. *The Presidency of James Monroe.* Lawrence: University Press of Kansas, 1996.

Curran, M. P. *Life of Patrick A. Collins.* Norwood, MA: Norwood Press, 1906.

Current, Richard Nelson. *Pine Logs and Politics: A Life of Philetus Sawyer, 1816–1900.* Madison: State Historical Society of Wisconsin, 1950.

Currie, David P. *The Constitution in Congress: The Federalist Period 1789–1801.* Chicago: University of Chicago Press, 1997.

Curtis, George T. *Life of James Buchanan.* 2 vols. New York: Harper and Brothers, 1883.

Curtis, George William, and Sherman S. Rogers. "Civil Service Reform." *Atlantic Monthly* 71 (Jan. 1893): 20.

Cushing, Marshall. *The Story of Our Post Office.* Boston: A. M. Thayer, 1893.

Dallek, Robert. *Flawed Giant: Lyndon Johnson and His Times, 1961–1973.* New York: Oxford University Press, 1998.

D'Amato, Al. *Power, Pasta and Politics: The World According to Senator Al D'Amato.* New York: Hyperion, 1995.

Dangerfield, George. *The Era of Good Feelings.* New York: Harcourt, Brace, 1952.

Daniels, Josephus. *The Life of Woodrow Wilson.* N.p.: Will H. Johnston, 1924.

Darling, Arthur B. "Jacksonian Democracy in Massachusetts, 1824–1848." *American Historical Review* 29 (Jan. 1924): 271–287.

Davidson, Roger H., and Walter J. Oleszek. *Congress and Its Members.* Washington, DC: CQ Press, 2000.

Davis, Kenneth S. *FDR: The New Deal Years, 1933–1937.* New York: Random House, 1986.

Davis, Richard. *Electing Justice: Fixing the Supreme Court Nomination Process.* New York: Oxford University Press, 2005.

Dawson, Matthew Q. *Partisanship and the Birth of America's Second Party, 1796–1800.* Westport, CT: Greenwood Press, 2000.

Day, J. Edward. *My Appointed Round: 929 Days as Postmaster General.* New York: Holt, Rinehart, and Winston, 1965.

Decatur, Stephen Jr. *Private Affairs of George Washington: From the Records and Accounts of Tobias Lear, Esquire, His Secretary.* New York: Da Capo Press, 1969.

Depew, Chauncey M. *My Memories of Eighty Years.* New York: Scribner, 1922.

De Santis, Vincent P. "The Republican Party and the Southern Negro." *Journal of Negro History* 45 (Apr. 1960): 71–87.

———. *Republicans Face the Southern Question.* Baltimore: Johns Hopkins Press, 1959.

"Diary of Richard Smith in the Continental Congress, 1775–1776." *American Historical Review* 1 (1896): 291.

Diket, A. L. *Senator John Slidell and the Community He Represented in Washington, 1853–1861.* Washington, DC: University Press of America, 1982.

Dobson, John M. *Politics in the Gilded Age: A New Perspective on Reform.* New York: Praeger, 1972.

Dodd, William E. *The Life of Nathaniel Macon.* Raleigh, NC: Edwards and Broughton, 1903.

Donald, David Herbert. *Charles Sumner and the Rights of Man.* New York: Knopf, 1970.

———. *Lincoln.* New York: Touchstone, 1996.

Donovan, Herbert D. A. *The Barnburners.* New York: New York University Press, 1925.

Donovan, Robert J. *Eisenhower: The Inside Story.* New York: Harper and Brothers, 1956.

Dorman, Lester M. "A Century of Civil Service." *Scribner's Monthly* 15 (Jan. 1878): 395–402.

Doss, Harriet E. Amos. "The Rise and Fall of an Alabama Founding Father, Gabriel Moore." *Alabama Review* 53 (July 2000): 163–177.

Dowding, Keith M. *The Civil Service.* New York: Routledge, 1995.

Dunar, Andrew J. *The Truman Scandals and the Politics of Morality.* Columbia: University of Missouri Press, 1984.

Dunn, Arthur Wallace. *From Harrison to McKinley.* 2 vols. New York: G. P. Putnam, 1922.

Dunn, Susan. *Jefferson's Second Revolution: The Election Crisis of 1800 and the Triumph of Republicanism.* New York: Houghton Mifflin, 2004.

Eaton, Dorman B. *The Spoils System and Civil Service Reform in the Custom-House and Post-Office at New York.* New York: G. P. Putnam, 1881.

———. "Two Years of Civil Service Reform." *North American Review* 141 (July 1885): 15–25.

Eckenrode, H. J. *Rutherford B. Hayes: Statesman of Reunion.* Norwalk, CT: Easton Press, 1988.

Eckert, Ralph Lowell. *John Brown Gordon: Soldier, Southern, American.* Baton Rouge: Louisiana State University Press, 1989.

Edwards, E. J. "Tammany." *McClure's Magazine* 4 (Apr. 1895): 445–454.

Edwards, Jerome E. *Pat McCarran: Political Boss of Nevada.* Reno: University of Nevada Press, 1982.

Eidson, William G. "Who Were the Stalwarts?" *Mid-America* 52 (Oct. 1970): 235–261.

Eisenhower, Dwight D. *The Eisenhower Diaries,* ed. Robert H. Ferrell. New York: Norton, 1981.

———. *Mandate for Change, 1953–1956.* New York: Doubleday, 1963.

Eisenstein, James. *Counsel for the United States: U.S. Attorneys in the Political and Legal Systems.* Baltimore: Johns Hopkins University Press, 1978.

Ellis, Richard. *The Jeffersonian Crisis: Courts and Politics in the Young Republic.* New York: Oxford University Press, 1971.

Eriksson, Erik McKinley. "The Federal Civil Service under President Jackson." *Mississippi Valley Historical Society* 13 (Mar. 1927): 517–540.

Ershkowitz, Herbert. "Samuel L. Southard: A Case Study of Whig Leadership in the Age of Jackson." *New Jersey History* 88 (spring 1970): 5–24.

Eskridge, William N., Jr. "All about Words: Early Understandings of the 'Judicial Power' in Statutory Interpretation, 1776–1806." *Columbia Law Review* 101 (June 2001): 990–1106.

Evans, Rowland, Jr., and Robert D. Novak. *Nixon in the White House: The Frustration of Power.* New York: Random House, 1971.

Farley, James A. *Behind the Ballots: The History of a Politician.* New York: Harcourt, Brace, 1938.

———. *Jim Farley's Story: The Roosevelt Years.* New York: McGraw-Hill, 1948.

Felice, John D., and Herbert F. Weisberg. "The Changing Importance of Ideology, Party, and Region in Confirmation of Supreme Court Nominees, 1953–1988." *Kentucky Law Journal* 77 (1988–1989): 509–530.

Ferguson, E. James. *The Power of the Purse.* Chapel Hill: University of North Carolina Press, 1961.

Ferling, John E. *Adams vs. Jefferson: The Tumultuous Election of 1800.* New York: Oxford University Press, 2004.

———. *John Adams: A Life.* New York: Henry Holt, 1996.

Ferrell, Robert H. *Harry S. Truman.* Washington, DC: CQ Press, 2003.

Fish, Carl Russell. *The Civil Service and the Patronage.* Cambridge, MA: Harvard University Press, 1904.

———. "Lincoln and the Patronage." *American Historical Review* 8 (Oct. 1902): 53–69.

———. "Removal of Officials by the Presidents of the United States." In *American Historical Association Reports,* vol. 2, 65–86. Washington, DC: GPO, 1900.

Fisher, Louis. *Constitutional Conflicts between Congress and the President.* 5th ed. Lawrence: University Press of Kansas, 2007.

———. *Constitutional Dialogues: Interpretation as Political Process.* Princeton, NJ: Princeton University Press, 1988.

———. "The Legislative Veto: Invalidated, It Survives." *Law and Contemporary Problems* 56 (autumn 1993): 273–291.

———. *The Politics of Executive Privilege.* Durham, NC: Carolina Academic Press, 2004.

———. *The Politics of Shared Power: Congress and the Executive.* 4th ed. College Station: Texas A&M University Press, 1998.

———. *President and Congress: Power and Policy.* New York: Free Press, 1972.

———. *Presidential War Power.* 2nd ed. Lawrence: University Press of Kansas, 2004.

Fite, Gilbert C. *Richard B. Russell, Jr., Senator from Georgia.* Chapel Hill: University of North Carolina Press, 1991.

Fitzpatrick, John C. "The Autobiography of Martin Van Buren." In *Annual Report of the American Historical Association for the Year 1918,* vol. 2. Washington, DC: GPO, 1920.

Foner, Eric. *Free Soil, Free Labor, Free Men: The Ideology of the Republican Party before the Civil War.* New York: Oxford University Press, 1970.

———. *Reconstruction: America's Unfinished Revolution, 1863–1877.* New York: Harper and Row, 1988.

Ford, Henry Jones. *The Cleveland Era: A Chronicle of the New Order in Politics.* New Haven, CT: Yale University Press, 1919.

Formisano, Ronald P. "Deferential-Participant Politics: The Early Republic's Political Culture, 1789–1840." *American Political Science Review* 68 (June 1974): 473–487.

Foster, William E. "Sketch of the Life and Services of Theodore Foster." *Collections of the Rhode Island Historical Society* 7 (1885): 111–134.

Foulke, William Dudley. *Fighting the Spoilsmen.* 1919. Reprint, New York: Arno Press, 1974.

———. *Life of Oliver P. Morton.* 2 vols. New York: AMS Press, 1974.

Fowler, Dorothy Ganfield. *The Cabinet Politician: The Postmaster General, 1829–1909.* New York: Columbia University Press, 1943.

———. "Congressional Dictation of Local Appointments." *Journal of Politics* 7 (Feb. 1945): 25–57.

———. *John Coit Spooner: Defender of Presidents.* New York: University Publishers, 1961.

Fowler, W. Gary. "Judicial Selection under Reagan and Carter." *Judicature* 67 (Dec.–Jan. 1984): 265–283.

Franklin, Benjamin. *The Papers of Benjamin Franklin,* ed. William B. Willcox. 37 vols. New Haven, CT: Yale University Press, 1959–2003.

Franklin, John Hope. *Reconstruction after the Civil War.* Chicago: University of Chicago Press, 1994.

Fred, Perry Powers. "The Reform of the Federal Service." *Political Science Quarterly* 3 (June 1888): 247–281.

Freidel, Frank. *Franklin D. Roosevelt: Launching the New Deal.* Boston: Little, Brown, 1973.

———. *Franklin D. Roosevelt: A Rendezvous with Destiny.* Boston: Little, Brown, 1990.

Freyer, Tony, and Timothy Dixon. *Democracy and Judicial Independence: A History of the Federal Courts of Alabama, 1820–1994.* Brooklyn, AL: Carlson Publishing, 1995.

Friedman, Bernard. "William Henry Harrison: The People against the Parties." In *Gentleman from Indiana National Party Candidates: 1836–1940,* ed. Ralph D. Gray, 3–28. Indianapolis: Indiana Historical Bureau, 1977.

Fuller, Wayne E. *The American Mail: Enlarger of the Common Life.* Chicago: University of Chicago Press, 1972.

Gara, Larry. *The Presidency of Franklin Pierce.* Lawrence: University Press of Kansas, 1991.

Garfield, James A. "A Century of Congress," *Atlantic Monthly* 237 (July 1877): 49–65.
———. *The Diary of James A. Garfield*, ed. Harry James Brown and Frederick D. Williams. 4 vols. East Lansing: Michigan State University Press, 1981.
———. *Garfield-Hinsdale Letters: Correspondence between James Abram Garfield and Burke Aaron Hinsdale*, ed. Mary L. Hinsdale. Ann Arbor: University of Michigan Press, 1949.
Garraty, John Arthur. *Silas Wright.* New York: Columbia University Press, 1949.
Geisst, Charles R. *Wall Street.* New York: Oxford University Press, 2004.
George, Tracey E. "Court Fixing." *Arizona Law Review* 43 (spring 2001): 9–62.
Gerhardt, Michael J. *The Federal Appointments Process: A Constitutional and Historical Analysis.* Durham, NC: Duke University Press, 2000.
———. "Norm Theory and the Future of the Federal Appointment Process." *Duke Law Journal* 50 (Apr. 2001): 1687–1715.
Gibbons, Herbert Adams. *John Wanamaker.* New York: Harper, 1926.
Gibbs, George., ed., *Memoirs of the Administrations of Washington and John Adams.* 2 vols. New York: B. Franklin, 1971.
Gibson, Ellen M., and William H. Manz. *New York Research Guide.* Buffalo, NY: William S. Hein, 2004.
Gilbert, Robert E. *The Tormented President: Calvin Coolidge, Death, and Clinical Depression.* Westport, CT: Praeger, 2003.
Gobright, Lawrence Augustus. *Recollections of Men and Things at Washington.* Washington, DC: W. H. and O. H. Morrison, 1869.
Goebel, Dorothy Burne. *William Henry Harrison: A Political Biography.* Philadelphia: Porcupine Press, 1974.
Goebel, Dorothy Burne, and Julius Goebel Jr. *Generals in the White House.* New York: Doubleday, 1945.
Going, Allen Johnston. *Bourbon Democracy in Alabama, 1874–1890.* Tuscaloosa: University of Alabama Press, 1992.
Goldford, Dennis J. *The American Constitution and the Debate over Originalism.* New York: Cambridge University Press, 2005.
Goldman, Sheldon. "The Bush Imprint on the Judiciary." *Judicature* 74 (Apr.–May 1991): 293–306.
———. "Bush's Judicial Legacy: The Final Imprint." *Judicature* 76 (Apr.–May 1993): 282–297.
———. "Carter's Judicial Appointments: A Lasting Legacy." *Judicature* 64 (Mar. 1981): 344–355.
———. "Is There a Crisis in Judicial Selection?" In *Readings in Presidential Politics,* ed. George C. Edwards III. Belmont, CA: Thomson Wadsworth, 2006.
———. "Judicial Selection under Clinton: A Midterm Examination." *Judicature* 78 (May–June 1995): 276–291.
———. *Picking Federal Judges: Lower Court Selection from Roosevelt through Reagan.* New Haven, CT: Yale University Press, 1997.
———. "Reagan's Second Term Judicial Appointments: The Battle at Midway." *Judicature* 70 (Apr.–May 1987): 324–339.
Goldman, Sheldon, and Elliot Slotnick. "Clinton's First Term Judiciary: Many Bridges to Cross." *Judicature* 80 (May–June 1997): 254–273.
Goldman, Sheldon, Elliot Slotnick, Gerald Gryski, and Gary Zuk. "Clinton's Judges: Summing up the Legacy." *Judicature* 84 (Mar.–Apr. 2001): 228–254.
Goldman, Sheldon, Elliot Slotnick, Gerald Gryski, Gary Zuk, and Sara Schiavoni. "W. Bush Remaking the Judiciary: Like Father Like Son?" *Judicature* 86 (May–June 2003): 282–309.
———. "W. Bush's Judiciary: The First Term Record." *Judicature* 88 (May–June 2005): 244–275.

Golway, Terry. *Washington's General: Nathanael Greene and the Triumph of the American Revolution*. New York: Henry Holt, 2005.

Goodwin, Doris Kearns. *Lyndon Johnson and the American Dream*. New York: St. Martin's Press, 1991.

Gordy, John P. *Political History of the United States: With Special Reference to the Growth of Political Parties*. 2 vols. New York: Henry Holt, 1902.

Gosnell, Harold F. "Thomas C. Platt—Political Manager." *Political Science Quarterly* 38 (Sept. 1923): 443–469.

———. *Truman's Crises: A Political Biography of Harry S. Truman*. Westport, CT: Greenwood Press, 1980.

Gottschall, Joan. "Reagan's Appointments to the U.S. Courts of Appeals: The Continuation of a Judicial Revolution." *Judicature* 70 (June–July 1986): 48–54.

Gould, Lewis L. *The Presidency of William McKinley*. Lawrence: University Press of Kansas, 1980.

Graebner, Norman A. "James K. Polk: A Study in Federal Patronage." *Mississippi Valley Historical Review* 38 (Mar. 1952): 624.

Grant, Ulysses S. *The Papers of Ulysses S. Grant*, ed. John Y. Simon. 28 vols. Carbondale: Southern Illinois University Press, 1967–2005.

Graves, Charles O. "How It Was Done in Great Britain." *Scribner's Monthly* 14 (June 1877): 242–247.

Grayson, Benson Lee. *The Unknown President: The Administration of President Millard Fillmore*. Washington, DC: University Press of America, 1981.

Greeley, Horace. *Recollections of a Busy Life*. New York: J. B. Ford, 1869.

Green, James A. *William Henry Harrison: His Life and Times*. Richmond, VA: Garrett and Massie, 1941.

Greene, George W. *The Life of Nathanael Greene*, ed. W. Gilmore Simms. New York: George F. Cooledge and Bro., 1849.

Greene, John Robert. *The Presidency of Gerald R. Ford*. Lawrence: University Press of Kansas, 1995.

Groennings, Sven, and Jonathan P. Hawley, eds. *To Be a Congressman: The Promise and the Power*. Washington, DC: Acropolis Books, 1973.

Grossman, Joel B. *Lawyers and Judges: The ABA and the Politics of Judicial Selection*. New York: John Wiley, 1965.

Guelzo, Allen C. *Abraham Lincoln: Redeemer President*. Grand Rapids, MI: Eerdmans, 1999.

Guliuzza, Frank, III, Daniel J. Reagan, and David M. Barrett. "Character, Competency, and Constitutionalism: Did the Bork Nomination Represent a Fundamental Shift in Confirmation Criteria?" *Marquette Law Review* 75 (winter 1992): 409–437.

———. "The Senate Judiciary Committee and Supreme Court Nominees: Measuring the Dynamics of Confirmation Criteria." *Journal of Politics* 56 (Aug. 1994): 773–787.

Gunderson, Robert Gray. *The Log-Cabin Campaign*. Lexington: University of Kentucky Press, 1957.

———. "A Search for Old Tip Himself." *Register of the Kentucky Historical Society* 86 (autumn 1988): 330–351.

Hahn, Harlan. "President Taft and the Discipline of Patronage." *Journal of Politics* 28 (May 1966): 368–390.

Hall, Kermit L. *American Legal History: Cases and Materials*. New York: Oxford University Press, 1996.

———. *The Politics of Justice: Lower Federal Judicial Selection and the Second Party System, 1829–1861*. Lincoln: University of Nebraska Press, 1979.

Hamilton, Holman. *Zachary Taylor: Soldier in the White House*. 2 vols. Indianapolis: Bobbs-Merrill, 1951.

Hammond, Jabez D. *The History of Political Parties in the State of New York*. 3rd ed. 2 vols. Cooperstown, NY: H. and E. Phinney, 1844.

Hansen, Harry. *The Civil War*. New York: Duell, Sloan, and Pearce, 1962.

Harris, John F. *The Survivor: Bill Clinton in the White House*. New York: Random House, 2005.

Harris, Joseph P. *The Advice and Consent of the Senate*. Berkeley: University of California Press, 1953.

Harrison, Benjamin. *This Country of Ours*. New York: Charles Scribner's Sons, 1897.

Hart, James. *The American Presidency in Action, 1789: A Constitutional History*. New York: Macmillan, 1948.

Hartley, Roger E., and Lisa M. Holmes. "The Increasing Senate Scrutiny of Lower Federal Court Nominees." *Political Science Quarterly* 117 (summer 2002): 259–278.

Hartman, William. "The New York Custom House: Seat of Spoils Politics." *New York History* 34 (Apr. 1953): 149–163.

Harvey, Donald R. *The Civil Service Commission*. New York: Praeger, 1970.

Hatch, Orrin. *Square Peg: Confessions of a Citizen Senator*. New York: Basic Books, 2002.

Hayes, Rutherford B. *Diary and Letters of Rutherford Birchard Hayes*, ed. Charles R. Williams. 5 vols. Columbus: Ohio State Archeological and Historical Society, 1922–1926.

Haynes, George H. *The Senate of the United States: Its History and Practice*. 2 vols. Boston: Houghton Mifflin, 1938.

Hearn, Chester G. *Impeachment of Andrew Johnson*. Jefferson, NC: McFarland, 2000.

Hechler, Kenneth W. *Insurgency: Personalities and Politics of the Taft Era*. New York: Columbia University Press, 1940.

Heckscher, August. *Woodrow Wilson*. New York: Charles Scribner's Sons, 1991.

Heinemann, Ronald L. *Harry Byrd of Virginia*. Charlottesville: University Press of Virginia, 1996.

Heitman, Francis B. *Historical Register of Officers of the Continental Army during the War of the Revolution*. Washington, DC: Rare Book Shop Publishing Co., 1914.

Herrnson, Paul S., and Dilys M. Hill, eds., *The Clinton Presidency: The First Term, 1992–1996*. New York: St. Martin's Press, 1999.

Hesseltine, William B. *Ulysses S. Grant: Politician*. New York: Frederick Ungar, 1957.

Hirshson, Stanley P. *Farewell to the Bloody Shirt*. Bloomington: Indiana University Press, 1962.

Hoar, George F. *Autobiography of Seventy Years*. 2 vols. New York: Scribner, 1905.

Hofstadter, Richard. *Idea of a Party System: The Rise of Legitimate Opposition in the United States, 1780–1840*. Berkeley: University of California Press, 1969.

Hollingsworth, J. Rogers. *The Whirligig of Politics: The Democracy of Cleveland and Bryan*. Chicago: University of Chicago Press, 1963.

Holt, Michael F. *Political Parties and American Political Development: From the Age of Jackson to the Age of Lincoln*. Baton Rouge: Louisiana State University Press, 1992.

———. *The Rise and Fall of the American Whig Party*. New York: Oxford University Press, 1999.

Hoogenboom, Ari. *Outlawing the Spoils: A History of the Civil Service Reform Movement, 1865–1883*. Urbana: University of Illinois Press, 1961.

———. "The Pendleton Act and the Civil Service." *American Historical Review* 64 (Jan. 1959): 301–318.

———. *The Presidency of Rutherford B. Hayes*. Lawrence: University Press of Kansas, 1988.

———. "Thomas A. Jenckes and Civil Service Reform." *Mississippi Valley Historical Review* 47 (Mar. 1961): 636–658.

Hoover, Herbert. *The Memoirs of Herbert Hoover*. New York: Macmillan, 1952.

——. *The State Papers and Other Public Writings of Herbert Hoover,* ed. William Starr Myers. 2 vols. New York: Doubleday, Doran, 1934.

House, Albert V. Jr. "President Hayes' Selection of David M. Key for Postmaster General." *Journal of Southern History* 4 (Feb. 1938): 87–93.

Houston, David F. *Eight Years with Wilson's Cabinet.* 2 vols. New York: Double, Page, 1926.

Howe, Daniel Walker. *The Political Culture of the American Whigs.* Chicago: University of Chicago Press, 1979.

Howe, George Frederick. *Chester A. Arthur: A Quarter-Century of Machine Politics.* New York: Frederick Ungar, 1957.

——. "The New York Custom-House Controversy, 1877–1879." *Mississippi Valley Historical Review* 18 (Dec. 1931): 350–363.

Hoyt, Edwin P. *James A. Garfield.* Chicago: Reilly and Lee, 1964.

Hrebenar, Ronald J., and Matthew J. Burbank. *Political Parties, Interest Groups, and Political Campaigns.* Boulder, CO: Westview Press, 1999.

Hulsey, Byron C. *Everett Dirksen and His Presidents.* Lawrence: University Press of Kansas, 2000.

——. " 'He Is My President': Everett Dirksen, John Kennedy, and the Politics of Consensus." *Journal of Illinois History* 2 (autumn 1999): 183–204.

Hunt, Gaillard. "Office-Seeking during the Administration of John Adams." *American Historical Review* 2 (Jan. 1897): 241–261.

——. "Office-Seeking during Washington's Administration." *American Historical Review* 1 (Jan. 1896): 270–283.

Hyman, Harold. *The Radical Republicans and Reconstruction, 1861–1870.* Indianapolis: Bobbs-Merrill, 1967.

Iredell, James. *Life and Correspondence of James Iredell,* ed. Griffith J. McRee. 2 vols. New York: Peter Smith, 1949.

Jackson, Andrew. *Correspondence of Andrew Jackson,* ed. John Spencer Bassett. 7 vols. Washington, DC: Carnegie Institution of Washington, 1926–1935.

James, Marquis. *The Life of Andrew Jackson.* New York: Bobbs-Merrill, 1938.

Jay, John. "Civil-Service Reform." *North American Review* 127 (Sept.–Oct. 1878): 273–288.

Jefferson, Thomas. *The Writings of Thomas Jefferson,* ed. Andrew A. Lipscomb and Albert E. Bergh. 20 vols. Washington, DC: Thomas Jefferson Memorial Association, 1905.

——. *The Works of Thomas Jefferson,* ed. Paul Leicester Ford. 12 vols. New York: Knickerbocker Press, 1904–1905.

Jenkins, John S. *The Life of Silas Wright.* Rochester, NY: Wanzer, Beardsley, 1852.

Johannsen, Robert Walter. *Stephen A. Douglas.* Urbana: University of Illinois Press, 1997.

John, Richard R. *Spreading the News: The American Postal System from Franklin to Morse.* 2nd ed. Cambridge, MA: Harvard University Press, 1998.

Johnson, Andrew. *The Papers of Andrew Johnson,* ed. Paul H. Bergeron, LeRoy P. Graf, Ralph Haskins, et al. 16 vols. Knoxville: University of Tennessee Press, 1967–2000.

Jones, Charles C. Jr. *The Life and Services of the Honorable Maj. Gen. Samuel Elbert.* Cambridge: Riverside Press, 1887.

Jones, James Pickett. *John A. Logan: Stalwart Republican from Illinois.* Carbondale: Southern Illinois University Press, 2001.

Josephson, Matthew. *The Politicos: 1865–1896.* New York: Harcourt, Brace, 1938.

Karabell, Zachary. *Chester Alan Arthur.* New York: Henry Holt, 2004.

Kehl, James A. *Boss Rule in the Gilded Age: Matt Quay of Pennsylvania.* Pittsburgh: University of Pittsburgh Press, 1981.

Kendall, Amos. *Autobiography,* ed. William Stickney. Boston: Lee and Shepard, 1872.

Kent, Frank R. *The Democratic Party.* New York: Century, 1928.

Ketcham, Ralph. *James Madison: A Biography*. Charlottesville: University Press of Virginia, 1990.

———. *Presidents above Party: The First American Presidency, 1789–1829*. Chapel Hill: University of North Carolina Press, 1984.

Kettl, Donald F., Patricia W. Ingraham, Ronald P. Sanders, and Constance Horner. *Civil Service Reform: Building a Government that Works*. Washington, DC: Brookings Institution Press, 1996.

King, Rufus. *The Life and Correspondence of Rufus King*, ed. Charles King. New York: G. P. Putnam, 1894.

Kirwan, Albert D. *John J. Crittenden: The Struggle for the Union*. Lexington: University of Kentucky Press, 1962.

Klein, Philip S. *President James Buchanan*. University Park: Pennsylvania State University Press, 1962.

Klein, Philip S., and Ari Hoogenboom, *A History of Pennsylvania*. Blacklick, OH: McGraw-Hill, 1973.

Klunder, Willard C. *Lewis Cass and the Politics of Moderation*. Kent, OH: Kent State University Press, 1996.

Koenig, Louis W., ed. *The Truman Administration*. New York: New York University Press, 1956.

Koeniger, A. Cash. "The New Deal and the States: Roosevelt versus the Byrd Organization in Virginia." *Journal of American History* 68 (Mar. 1982): 876–896.

Kohlsaat, H. H. *From McKinley to Harding: Personal Recollections of Our Presidents*. New York: Scribner, 1923.

Korzi, Michael J. *Seat of Popular Leadership: The Presidency, Political Parties, and Democratic Leadership*. Amherst: University of Massachusetts Press, 2004.

Krent, Harold J. *Presidential Powers*. New York: New York University Press, 2005.

Krueger, David W. "The Clay-Tyler Feud, 1841–1842." *Filson Club History Quarterly* 42 (Apr. 1968): 163–177.

Krug, Mark M. *Lyman Trumbull: Conservative Radical*. New York: A. S. Barnes, 1965.

Kruman, Marc W. *Between Authority and Liberty: State Constitution Making in Revolutionary America*. Chapel Hill: University of North Carolina Press, 1999.

Lambert, Oscar Doane. *Presidential Politics in the United States, 1841–1844*. Durham, NC: Duke University Press, 1936.

Leech, Margaret. *In the Days of McKinley*. New York: Harper, 1959.

Leech, Margaret, and Harry J. Brown. *The Garfield Orbit*. New York: Harper and Row, 1978.

Le Fevre, Benjamin. *Campaign of '84*. New York: Baird and Dillon, 1884.

Leibiger, Stuart Eric. *Founding Friendship: George Washington, James Madison, and the Creation of the Republic*. Charlottesville: University Press of Virginia, 2001.

Lewis, James E. Jr. *John Quincy Adams: Policymaker for the Union*. Wilmington, DE: Scholarly Resources, 2001.

Lincoln, Abraham. *The Collected Works of Abraham Lincoln*, ed. Roy P. Basler. New Brunswick, NJ: Rutgers University Press, 1953.

———. *The Living Lincoln*, ed. Paul M. Angle and Earl Schenck Miers. New York: Barnes and Noble Books, 1992.

———. *Uncollected Letters of Abraham Lincoln*, ed. Gilbert A. Tracy. New York: Houghton Mifflin, 1917.

Link, Arthur S. "Woodrow Wilson and the Democratic Party." *Review of Politics* 18 (Apr. 1956): 146–156.

Lisio, Donald J. *Hoover, Blacks, and Lily-Whites*. Chapel Hill: University of North Carolina Press, 1985.

Lodge, Henry Cabot. *A Fighting Frigate and Other Essays and Addresses*. New York: Scribner, 1902.

Lowitt, Richard. *George W. Norris: The Making of a Progressive, 1861–1912*. Westport, CT: Greenwood Press, 1980.

Lyons, Eugene. *Herbert Hoover*. Garden City, NY: Doubleday, 1964.

Mackenzie, G. Calvin. "The Real Invisible Hand: Presidential Appointees in the Administration of George W. Bush." *PS: Political Science and Politics* 35 (Mar. 2002): 27–30.

———, ed. *Innocent until Nominated*. Washington, DC: Brookings Institution Press, 2001.

———. *The Politics of Presidential Appointments*. New York: Free Press, 1981.

Maclay, William. *Journal of William Maclay*, ed. Edgar S. Maclay. New York: D. Appleton, 1890.

MacNeil, Neil. *Dirksen: Portrait of a Public Man*. New York: World, 1970.

Madison, James. *The Papers of James Madison*. Presidential Series, ed. John Rutland. 5 vols. Charlottesville: University Press of Virginia, 1984–2004.

———. *The Papers of James Madison*. Secretary of State Series, ed. Robert J. Brugger et al. 7 vols. Charlottesville: University Press of Virginia, 1986–2005.

———. *The Writings of James Madison*, ed. Gaillard Hunt. 9 vols. New York: Knickerbocker Press, 1900–1910.

Mahon, John K. *The War of 1812*. New York: Da Capo Press, 1991.

Maisel, Louis Sandy. *The Parties Respond: Changes in American Parties and Campaigns*. Boulder, CO: Westview Press, 2002.

Mallam, William D. "Butlerism in Massachusetts." *New England Quarterly* 33 (June 1960): 186–206.

———. "The Grant-Butler Relationship." *Mississippi Valley Historical Review* 41 (Dec. 1954): 259–276.

Malone, Dumas. *Jefferson the President, First Term 1801–1805*. Boston: Little, Brown, 1970.

Mann, Dean E., and Zachary A. Smith. "The Selection of U.S. Cabinet Officers and Other Political Executives." *International Political Science Review* 2 (1981): 211–234.

Marcy, William L. "Diary and Memoranda of William L. Marcy, 1857." *American Historical Review* 24 (July 1919): 641–653.

Marshall, Lynn L. "The Strange Stillbirth of the Whig Party." *American Historical Review* 72 (Jan. 1967): 445–468.

Martin, John M. "The Senatorial Career of Gabriel Moore." *Alabama Historical Quarterly* 26 (summer 1964): 249–281.

Matthews, Marty D. *Forgotten Founder: The Life and Times of Charles Pinckney*. Columbia: University of South Carolina Press, 2004.

Mayer, George H. *The Republican Party, 1854–1964*. New York: Oxford University Press, 1964.

Mayes, Edward. *Lucius Q. C. Lamar: His Life, Times, and Speeches*. Nashville, TN: Publishing House of the Methodist Episcopal Church, 1896.

McAdoo, William G. *Crowded Years*. Boston: Houghton Mifflin, 1931.

McBain, Howard Lee. "DeWitt Clinton and the Origin of the Spoils System in New York." Ph.D. diss., Columbia University, 1907.

McCabe, James Dabney. *History of the Granger Movement or the Farmer's War against Monopolies*. New York: A. M. Kelly, 1969.

McCombs, William F. *Making Woodrow Wilson President*, ed. Louis Jay Lang. New York: Fairview, 1921.

McCormac, Eugene Irving. *James K. Polk: A Political Biography*. Berkeley: University of California Press, 1922.

McCormick, Richard P. *The Second American Party System: Party Formation in the Jacksonian Era*. Chapel Hill: University of North Carolina Press, 1966.

McElroy, Robert. *Grover Cleveland: The Man and the Statesman*. 2 vols. New York: Harper, 1923.

McFarland, Gerald W., ed. *Mugwumps, Morals and Politics, 1884–1920*. Amherst: University of Massachusetts Press, 1975.

McFeely, William S. *Grant*. New York: Norton, 1982.

McKenna, Marian C. *Franklin Roosevelt and the Great Constitutional War: The Court Packing Crisis of 1937*. New York: Fordham University Press, 2002.

McMaster, John Bach. "The Political Depravity of the Fathers." *Atlantic Monthly* 75 (May 1895): 626–633.

Meese Edwin III. *With Reagan: The Inside Story*. Washington, DC: Regnery Gateway, 1992.

Melius, Louis. *The American Postal Service: History of the Postal Service from the Earliest Times*. Washington, DC: National Capitol Press, 1917.

Merrill, Horace Samuel. *Bourbon Democracy in the Middle West, 1865–1896*. Baton Rouge: Louisiana State University Press, 1953.

———. *Bourbon Leader: Grover Cleveland and the Democratic Party*. Boston: Little, Brown, 1957.

———. "Ignatius Donnelly, James J. Hill, and Cleveland Administration Patronage." *Mississippi Valley Historical Review* 39 (Dec. 1952): 505–518.

Michaelsen, William B. *Creating the American Presidency, 1775–1789*. Lanham, MD: University Press of America, 1987.

Milkis, Sidney M. *The President and the Parties: The Transformation of the American Party System since the New Deal*. New York: Oxford University Press, 1993.

Miller, John C. *Alexander Hamilton: Portrait in Paradox*. New York: HarperCollins, 1959.

Miller Center of Public Affairs. *Improving the Process of Appointing Federal Judges: A Report of the Miller Commission on the Selection of Federal Judges*. Charlottesville, VA: Miller Center of Public Affairs, 1996.

———. Interview with A. B. Culvahouse. Ronald Reagan Oral History Project, Apr. 1, 2004. http://webstorage1.mcpa.virginia.edu/library/mc/poh/transcripts/ohp_2004_0401_culvahouse.pdf (accessed Mar. 29, 2007).

———. Interview with Griffin Bell. Carter Presidency Project, Mar. 23, 1988. http://webstorage1.mcpa.virginia.edu/library/mc/poh/transcripts/ohp_1988_0323_bell.pdf (accessed May 1, 2007).

———. *The Lloyd N. Cutler Conference on White House Counsel, November 10–11, 2006*. Charlottesville, VA: Miller Center of Public Affairs, 2007.

Mintz, Max M. "The Political Ideas of Martin Van Buren." *New York History* 30 (Oct. 1949): 422–448.

Miraldi, Robert. *The Pen Is Mightier: The Muckraking Life of Charles Edward Russell*. New York: Palgrave Macmillan, 2003.

Molot, Jonathan T. "Exchange: The Rise and Fall of Textualism." *Columbia Law Review* 106 (Jan. 2006): 1–69.

Monaghan, Henry P. "The Confirmation Process: Law or Politics." *Harvard University Law Review* 101 (Apr. 1988): 1202–1212.

Monroe, James. *The Writings of James Monroe*, ed. Stanislaus Murray Hamilton. 7 vols. New York: Knickerbocker Press, 1898–1903.

Montgomery, David. *Beyond Equality: Labor and the Radical Republicans, 1862–1872*. New York: Knopf, 1981.

Montgomery, H. *The Life of Major-General William H. Harrison*. Philadelphia: Porter and Coates, 1852.

Moraskit, Bryon J., and Charles R. Shipan. "The Politics of Supreme Court Nominations: A Theory of Institutional Constraints and Choices." *American Journal of Political Science* 43 (Oct. 1999): 1069–1095.

Morgan, H. Wayne. *From Hayes to McKinley*. Syracuse, NY: Syracuse University Press, 1969.

———. *William McKinley and His America*. Syracuse, NY: Syracuse University Press, 1964.

Morgan, Robert J. *A Whig Embattled: The Presidency under John Tyler*. Lincoln: University of Nebraska Press, 1954.

Morrel, Martha McBride. *Young Hickory: The Life and Times of President James K. Polk*. New York: E. P. Dutton, 1949.

Morris, Robert. *The Papers of Robert Morris*, ed. E. James Ferguson. 9 vols. Pittsburgh: University of Pittsburgh Press, 1973–1995.

Morse, John T., Jr. *John Quincy Adams*. Boston: Houghton Mifflin, 1882.

Murphy, James B. *L. Q. C. Lamar*. Baton Rouge: Louisiana State University Press, 1973.

Myers, Elisabeth P. *Benjamin Harrison*. Chicago: Reilly and Lee Books, 1969.

Myers, Gustavus. *The History of Tammany Hall*. New York: Boni and Liveright, 1917.

Myers, Walter Starr, and Walter H. Newton. *The Hoover Administration: A Documented Narrative*. New York: Scribner, 1936.

National Civil Service Reform League. *Civil Service Reform in the National Service, 1889–1891*. Boston: Press of Geo. H. Ellis, 1891.

Navasky, Victor S. *Kennedy Justice*. New York: Atheneum, 1971.

Neff, Alan. "Breaking with Tradition: A Study of the U.S. District Judge Nominating Commission." *Judicature* 64 (Dec.–Jan. 1981): 256–278.

Nelson, Caleb. "What Is Textualism?" *Virginia Law Review* 91 (Apr. 2005): 347–418.

Nelson, Henry L. "Some Truths about the Civil Service." *Atlantic Monthly* 51 (Feb. 1883): 231–243.

Nevins, Allan. *Grover Cleveland: A Study in Courage*. New York: Dodd, Mead, 1932.

———. *Hamilton Fish: The Inner History of the Grant Administration*. New York: Dodd, Mead, 1936.

———. *Ordeal of the Union*. 2 vols. New York: Scribner, 1947.

Nichols, Roy Franklin. *The Democratic Machine: 1850–1854*. New York: Columbia University, 1923.

———. *Franklin Pierce: Young Hickory of the Granite Hills*. Philadelphia: University of Pennsylvania Press, 1931.

Niven, John. *Martin Van Buren: The Romantic Age of American Politics*. Newtown, CT: American Political Biography Press, 2000.

Northen, William J., ed. *Men of Mark in Georgia*. 6 vols. Atlanta: A. B. Caldwell, 1907–1912.

Nott, William E. *The Republican Campaign Text Book for 1882*. Washington, DC: Republican Printing and Publishing Co., 1882.

Ogundele, Ayo, and Linda Camp Keith. "Reexamining the Impact of the Bork Nomination to the Supreme Court." *Political Research Quarterly* 52 (June 1999): 403–420.

O'Neill, Johnathan G. *Originalism in American Law and Politics: A Constitutional History*. Baltimore: Johns Hopkins University Press, 2005.

"Origin and Growth of the Spoils System." *Century* 46 (July 1893): 472–474.

Ostrogorski, Moisei. *Democracy and the Organization of Political Parties*. 2 vols. New York: Macmillan, 1922.

Paine, Arthur Elijah. *The Granger Movement in Illinois*. Urbana, IL: University Press, 1904.

Parmet, Herbert S. *George Bush: The Life of a Lone Star Yankee*. New York: Scribner, 1997.

Parton, James. *Life of Andrew Jackson*. 3 vols. New York: Mason Brothers, 1860.

Patterson, James T. *Mr. Republican: A Biography of Robert A. Taft*. Boston: Houghton Mifflin, 1972.

Pearson, Charles Chilton. *Readjustor Movement in Virginia*. New Haven, CT: Yale University Press, 1917.

Peck, Harry Thurston. *Twenty Years of the Republic, 1885–1905*. New York: Dodd, Mead, 1920.

Pepper, George Wharton. *Philadelphia Lawyer: An Autobiography*. Philadelphia: J. B. Lippincott, 1944.

Peskin, Allan. "Who Were the Stalwarts? Who Were Their Rivals? Republican Factions in the Gilded Age." *Political Science Quarterly* 99 (winter 1984–1985): 703–716.

Pessen, Edward. *Jacksonian America: Society, Personality, and Politics*. Urbana: University of Illinois Press, 1985.

Peters, Ronald M. *The Massachusetts Constitution of 1780: A Social Compact*. Amherst: University of Massachusetts Press, 1978.

Peterson, Lorin. *The Day of the Mugwump*. New York: Random House, 1961.

Peterson, Norma Lois. *The Presidencies of William Henry Harrison and John Tyler*. Lawrence: University Press of Kansas, 1989.

Pfiffner, James P. "Establishing the Bush Presidency." *Public Administration Review* 50 (Jan.–Feb. 1990): 64–73.

Platt, Thomas Collier. *The Autobiography of Thomas Collier Platt*, ed. Louis J. Lang. 1910. Reprint, New York: Arno Press, 1974.

Poage, George Rawlings. *Henry Clay and the Whig Party*. Gloucester, MA: Peter Smith, 1965.

Polk, James K. *Correspondence of James K. Polk*, ed. Wayne Cutler et al. 10 vols. Nashville, TN: Vanderbilt University Press; Knoxville: University of Tennessee Press, 1969–2004.

———. *The Diary of James Polk during his Presidency, 1845 to 1849*, ed. Milo M. Quaife. 4 vols. Chicago: A. C. McClurg, 1910.

Polsby, Nelson W. "The Institutionalization of the U.S. House of Representatives." *American Political Science Review* 62 (1968): 146–147.

Poore, Benjamin Perley. *Perley's Reminiscences of Sixty Years in the National Metropolis*. 2 vols. Philadelphia: Hubbard, 1886.

Posner, Eric A. "The Political Economy of the Bankruptcy Reform Act of 1978." *Michigan Law Review* 96 (Oct. 1997): 47–126.

Potter, David M. *The Impending Crisis, 1848–1861*. New York: Harper and Row, 1976.

Prakash, Saikrishna. "Hail to the Chief Administrator: The Framers and the President's Administrative Powers." *Yale Law Journal* 102 (Jan. 1993): 991–1017.

———. "Regulating Presidential Powers." *Cornell Law Review* 91 (Nov. 2005): 215–257.

Prince, Carl E. "The Passing of the Aristocracy: Jefferson's Removal of the Federalists, 1801–1805." *Journal of American History* 57 (Dec. 1970): 563–575.

Proceedings: National Civil Service Reform League, Dec. 8 and 9, 1904. New York: National Civil Service Reform League, 1904.

Proceedings: National Civil Service Reform League, Jan. 12, 1926. New York: National Civil Service Reform League, 1926.

Proceedings of the Republican National Convention, 1876. Concord, NH: Republican Press Association, 1876.

Proceedings of the Republican National Convention, 1880. Chicago: Jno. B. Jeffery Printing House, 1880.

Quincy, Josiah. *Memoir of the Life of John Quincy Adams*. Boston: Phillips, Sampson, 1859.

Quinn, Arthur. *The Rivals: William Gwin, David Broderick, and the Birth of California*. New York: Crown, 1994.

Rakove, Jack N. *Original Meanings: Politics and Ideas in the Making of the Constitution*. New York: Vintage Books, 1996.

"The Rank and File of Democracy: Pennsylvania." *United States Democratic Review* 3 (Dec. 1838): 385–394.

Ray, Perley Orman. *An Introduction to Political Parties and Practical Politics*. New York: Charles Scribner's Sons, 1913.

Rayback, Robert J. *Millard Fillmore*. Norwalk, CT: Easton Press, 1959.

Read, George. *Life and Correspondence of George Read*, ed. William Thompson Read. Philadelphia: J. B. Lippincott, 1870.

"Recollections of an Old Stager." *Harper's Monthly* 45 (Sept. 1872): 600–604.

"Recollections of an Old Stager." *Harper's Monthly* 47 (Oct. 1873): 753–760.

Reedy, George. *The U.S. Senate*. New York: Crown, 1986.

Reeves, Thomas C. *Gentleman Boss: The Life of Chester Alan Arthur*. New York: Knopf, 1975.

Reeves, William D. "PWA and Competition Administration in the New Deal." *Journal of American History* 60 (Sept. 1973): 357–372.

Remini, Robert V. "The Albany Regency." *New York History* 39 (Jan. 1958): 341–355.

———. *Andrew Jackson*. 3 vols. Baltimore: Johns Hopkins University Press, 1998.

———. *Daniel Webster: The Man and His Times*. New York: Norton, 1997.

———. *The Election of Andrew Jackson*. Philadelphia: J. B. Lippincott, 1963.

———. *Henry Clay: Statesman for the Union*. New York: Norton, 1993.

———. *John Quincy Adams*. New York: Times Books, 2002.

———. *Martin Van Buren and the Making of the Democratic Party*. New York: Columbia University Press, 1959.

"Reminiscences of Washington: VI, the Harrison Administration." *Atlantic Monthly* 46 (Sept. 1880): 369–380.

Rich, Wesley Everett. *The History of the United States Post Office to the Year 1829*. Cambridge, MA: Harvard University Press, 1924.

Richardson, Leon Burr. *William E. Chandler: Republican*. New York: Dodd, Mead, 1940.

Ridge, Martin. *Ignatius Donnelly: The Portrait of a Politician*. St. Paul: Minnesota Historical Society Press, 1991.

Rienow, Robert, and Leona Train Rienow. *Of Snuff, Sin and the Senate*. Chicago: Follett, 1965.

Robinson, Edgar Eugene, and Vaughn Davis Bornet. *Herbert Hoover: President of the United States*. Stanford, CA: Hoover Institution Press, 1975.

Roosevelt, Theodore. *The Letters of Theodore Roosevelt*, ed. Elting E. Morison. 8 vols. Cambridge, MA: Harvard University Press, 1951–1954.

Rorabaugh, W. J. *Kennedy and the Promise of the Sixties*. New York: Cambridge University Press, 2002.

Rosenbloom, David H. *Federal Service and the Constitution: The Development of the Public Employment Relationship*. Ithaca, NY: Cornell University Press, 1971.

Rossum, Ralph A. *Antonin Scalia's Jurisprudence: Text and Tradition*. Lawrence: University Press of Kansas, 2006.

Rozell, Mark J. *Executive Privilege: Presidential Power, Secrecy, and Accountability*. 2nd ed. Lawrence: University Press of Kansas, 2002.

Rudman, Warren B. *Combat: Twelve Years in the U.S. Senate*. New York: Random House, 1996.

Rutland, Robert Allen. *The Democrats: From Jefferson to Clinton*. Columbia: University of Missouri Press, 1995.

———. *The Republicans: From Lincoln to Bush*. Columbia: University of Missouri Press, 1996.

Sacher, John M. *Perfect War of Politics: Parties, Politicians, and Democracy in Louisiana, 1824–1861*. Baton Rouge: Louisiana State University Press, 2003.

Sageser, Adelbert Bower. *The First Two Decades of the Pendleton Act: A Study of Civil Service Reform*. Lincoln: University Studies of the University of Nebraska, 1935.

Sanders, Jennings B. *The Presidency of the Continental Congress, 1774–89: A Study in American Institutional History*. Gloucester, MA: Peter Smith, 1971.

Sargent, Nathan. *Public Men and Events*. 2 vols. Philadelphia: J. B. Lippincott, 1875.

Savage, Sean J. *JFK, LBJ, and the Democratic Party*. Albany, NY: SUNY Press, 2004.

———. *Roosevelt: The Party Leader, 1932–1945*. Lexington: University Press of Kentucky, 1991.

Schapsmeier, Edward L., and Frederick H. Schapsmeier. *Dirksen of Illinois: Senatorial Statesman*. Urbana: University of Illinois Press, 1985.

Scherer, Nancy. *Scoring Points: Politicians, Activists, and the Lower Federal Court Appointment Process*. Stanford, CA: Stanford University Press, 2005.

Schlesinger, Arthur M., Jr. *The Age of Jackson*. Boston: Little, Brown, 1948.

———. *Robert Kennedy and His Times*. New York: Houghton Mifflin, 2002.

———. *A Thousand Days*. New York: Fawcett Premier, 1965.

Schmidhauser, John R. *Judges and Justices: The Federal Appellate Judiciary*. Boston: Little, Brown, 1979.

Schott Richard L., and Dagmar S. Hamilton. *People, Positions, and Power: The Political Appointments of Lyndon Johnson*. Chicago: University of Chicago Press, 1983.

Schouler, James. *History of the United States of America: Under the Constitution*. Rev. ed. 7 vols. New York: Dodd, Mead, 1917.

Schwartz, Herman. *Packing the Courts: The Conservative Campaign to Rewrite the Constitution*. New York: Scribner, 1988.

Seager, Robert II. *And Tyler Too*. New York: McGraw-Hill, 1963.

Sears, Louis Martin. *John Slidell*. Durham, NC: Duke University Press, 1925.

Sefton, James E. *Andrew Johnson and the Uses of Constitutional Power*. Boston: Little, Brown, 1980.

Segal, Jeffrey. "Senate Confirmations of Supreme Court Justices: Partisan and Institutional Politics." *Journal of Politics* 29 (1987): 998–1015.

Segal, Jeffrey A., Charles M. Cameron, and Albert D. Cover. "A Spatial Model of Roll Call Voting: Senators, Constituents, Presidents, and Interest Groups in Supreme Court Confirmations." *American Journal of Political Science* 36 (Feb. 1992): 96–121.

Seigenthaler, John. *James K. Polk*. New York: Henry Holt, 2003.

Sellers, Charles. *James K. Polk: Continentalist*. Norwalk, CT: Easton Press, 1966.

Severn, Bill. *Frontier President: James K. Polk*. New York: Ives Washburn, 1965.

Sewell, Richard H. *A House Divided: Sectionalism and Civil War, 1848–1865*. Baltimore: Johns Hopkins University Press, 1988.

Sheldon Charles H., and Linda S. Maule. *Choosing Justice: The Recruitment of State and Federal Judges*. Pullman: Washington State University Press, 1997.

Shepard, Edward M. *Martin Van Buren*. New York: Houghton Mifflin, 1899.

Sherman, John. *Recollections of Forty Years*. New York: Greenwood Press, 1968.

Sievers, Harry J. *Benjamin Harrison: Hoosier President*. Indianapolis: Bobbs-Merrill, 1968.

Simon, Paul. *Advice and Consent: Clarence Thomas, Robert Bork, and the Intriguing History of the Supreme Court's Nomination Battles*. Washington, DC: National Press Books, 1992.

Sinclair, Andrew. *The Available Man: The Life behind the Masks of Warren Gamaliel Harding*. New York: Macmillan, 1965.

Skowronek, Stephen. *Building a New American State: The Expansion of National Administrative Capacities, 1877–1920*. 8th ed. Cambridge: Cambridge University Press, 1997.

Slotnick, Elliot E. "Reforms in Judicial Selection: Will They Affect the Senate's Role? (Part I)." *Judicature* 64 (Aug. 1980): 60–73.

———. "Reforms in Judicial Selection: Will They Affect the Senate's Role? (Part II)." *Judicature* 64 (Sept. 1980): 114–131.

Slotten, Hugh R. *Patronage, Practice and the Culture of American Science: Alexander Dallas Bache and the U.S. Coast Survey*. New York: Cambridge University Press, 1994.

Small, Melvin. *The Presidency of Richard Nixon*. Lawrence: University Press of Kansas, 1999.

Smith, Elbert B. *The Presidencies of Zachary Taylor and Millard Fillmore*. Lawrence: University Press of Kansas, 1988.
———. *The Presidency of James Buchanan*. Lawrence: University Press of Kansas, 1975.
Smith, Page. *John Adams, 1784–1826*. 2 vols. Garden City, NY: Doubleday, 1962.
Smith, Rixey, and Norman Beasley. *Carter Glass*. New York: Da Capo Press, 1972.
Smith, Theodore Clarke. *The Life and Letters of James Abram Garfield*. New Haven, CT: Yale University Press, 1925.
Smith, William French. "The Attorney General's Memorandum on Judicial Selection Procedures." *Judicature* 64 (Apr. 1981): 428.
Sobel, Robert. *Coolidge: An American Enigma*. Washington, DC: Regnery, 1998.
Socolofsky, Homer E., and Allan B. Spetter. *The Presidency of Benjamin Harrison*. Lawrence: University Press of Kansas, 1987.
Sollenberger, Mitchel A. "The History of the Blue Slip in the Senate Committee on the Judiciary (1917–2003)." *Congressional Research Service*, RL32013 (Oct. 22, 2003).
———. "The Law: Must the Senate Take a Floor Vote on a Presidential Judicial Nominee?" *Presidential Studies Quarterly* 34 (June 2004): 420–436.
Sollenberger, Mitch, Jack Rossotti, and Mark J. Rozell. "Reagan and the Courts." In *The Reagan Presidency*, ed. Paul Kengor. Lanham, MD: Rowman and Littlefield, 2005.
Soloman, Rayman L. "The Politics of Appointments and the Federal Courts' Role in Regulating America: U.S. Courts of Appeals Judgeships." *American Bar Foundation Research Journal* 2 (1984): 285–343.
Spencer, Ivor Debenham. *The Victor and the Spoils: A Life of William L. Marcy*. Providence: Brown University Press, 1959.
Spielman, William Carl. *William McKinley: Stalwart Republican*. New York: Exposition Press, 1954.
Sproat, John G. *"The Best Men": Liberal Reformers in the Gilded Age*. New York: Oxford University Press, 1968.
Stahr, Walter. *John Jay: Founding Father*. New York: Hambledon and London, 2005.
Steele, Henry J. "Life and Public Services of Governor George Wolf." *Pennsylvania German Society* 39 (Oct. 12, 1928): 5–25.
Stewart, Frank M. *The National Civil Service Reform League*. Austin: University of Texas Press, 1929.
Stewart, William M. *Reminiscences of Senator William M. Stewart of Nevada*. New York: Neale, 1908.
Stid, Daniel D. *The President as Statesman: Woodrow Wilson and the Constitution*. Lawrence: University Press of Kansas, 1998.
Stoddard, Henry L. *As I Knew Them*. New York: Harper and Brothers, 1927.
Storey, Moorfield, and Edward W. Emerson. *Ebenezer Rockwood Hoar: A Memoir*. Boston: Houghton Mifflin, 1911.
Straus, Oscar Solomon. *Under Four Administrations: From Cleveland to Taft*. Boston: Houghton Mifflin, 1922.
"Suggestions of the Past: John Tyler's Administration." *Galaxy* 13 (Feb. 1872): 202–212.
"Suggestions from the Past: John Tyler's Administration." *Galaxy* 13 (Mar. 1872): 347–359.
Summers, Mark Wahlgren. *Rum, Romanism and Rebellion: The Making of a President, 1884*. Chapel Hill: University of North Carolina Press, 2000.
Taft, William Howard. *Our Chief Magistrate and His Powers*. New York: Columbia University Press, 1925.
Tarr, G. Alan. *Understanding State Constitutions*. Princeton, NJ: Princeton University Press, 2000.
Tarr, Joel Arthur. *A Study in Boss Politics: William Lorimer of Chicago*. Urbana: University of Illinois Press, 1971.

Task Forces of Citizens for Independent Courts. *Uncertain Justice: Politics and America's Courts.* New York: Century Foundation Press, 2000.

Thomas, Lately. *Between Two Empires: The Life Story of California's First Senator William McKendree Gwin.* Boston: Houghton Mifflin, 1969.

Tolchin, Martin, and Susan Tolchin, *To the Victor . . . Political Patronage from the Clubhouse to the White House.* New York: Random House, 1971.

"Topics of the Time: Pubic Service and Private Business." *Century* 23 (Feb. 1882): 616–617.

Totenberg, Nina. "Will Judges Be Chosen Rationally?" *Judicature* 60 (Aug.–Sept. 1976): 92–99.

Trani, Eugene P., and David L. Wilson. *The Presidency of Warren G. Harding.* Lawrence: University Press of Kansas, 1977.

Trefousse, Hans L. *Andrew Johnson.* New York: Norton, 1997.

———. *The Radical Republicans: Lincoln's Vanguard for Racial Justice.* New York: Knopf, 1969.

———. *Rutherford B. Hayes.* New York: Times Books, 2002.

———. *Thaddeus Stevens: Nineteenth-Century Egalitarian.* Mechanicsburg, PA: Stackpole Books, 2001.

Tribe, Laurence H. *God Save This Honorable Court: How the Choice of Supreme Court Justices Shapes Our History.* New York: Random House, 1985.

Trimble, William. "Diverging Tendencies in New York Democracy in the Period of the Locofocos." *American Historical Review* 24 (Apr. 1919): 396–421.

Turner, Henry A. "Woodrow Wilson: Exponent of Executive Leadership." *Western Political Quarterly* 4 (Mar. 1951): 97–115.

Turner, Kathryn. "Federalist Policy and the Judiciary Act of 1801." *William and Mary Quarterly* 22 (Jan. 1965): 3–32.

Tutorow, Norman E. *James Gillespie Blaine and the Presidency.* New York: Peter Lang, 1989.

Van Deusen, Glyndon G. *The Jacksonian Era, 1828–1848.* New York: Harper and Row, 1959.

———. *William Henry Seward.* New York: Oxford University Press, 1967.

Van Riper, Paul P. *History of the United States Civil Service.* Evanston, IL: Row, Peterson, 1958.

Ver Steeg, Clarence L. *Robert Morris: Revolutionary Financier.* New York: Octagon Books, 1972.

Wallner, Peter A. *Franklin Pierce: New Hampshire's Favorite Son.* Concord, NH: Plaidswede Publishing, 2004.

Warshaw, Shirley Anne. "The Implementation of Cabinet Government during the Nixon Administration." In *Richard M. Nixon: Politician, President, Administrator,* ed. Leon Friedman and William F. Levantrosser. New York: Greenwood Press, 1991.

Washburne, E. B., ed. *The Edwards Papers.* 3 vols. Chicago: Fergus Printing Co., 1884.

Washington, Booker T. *The Booker T. Washington Papers,* ed. Louis R. Harlan and Raymond W. Smock. 14 vols. Urbana: University of Illinois Press, 1972–1989.

Washington, George. *The Papers of George Washington.* Presidential Series, ed. W. W. Abbot. 12 vols. Charlottesville: University Press of Virginia, 1987–2005.

———. *The Writings of George Washington,* ed. John C. Fitzpatrick. 39 vols. Washington, DC: GPO, 1931–1944.

———. *The Writings of George Washington,* ed. Worthington C. Ford. 14 vols. New York: Knickerbocker Press, 1889–1893.

Watson, George L., and John A. Stookey. *Shaping America: The Politics of Supreme Court Appointments.* New York: HarperCollins, 1995.

Watson, W. Marvin. *Chief of Staff: Lyndon Johnson and His Presidency.* New York: St. Martin's Press, 2004.

Webb, Samuel Blachley. *Correspondence and Journals of Samuel Blachley Webb, 1783–1806,* ed. Worthington C. Ford. 3 vols. Lancaster, PA: Wickersham Press, 1893.

Webster, Daniel. *The Works of Daniel Webster,* ed. Edward Everett. 11th ed. 6 vols. Boston: Little, Brown, 1858.

Welch, Richard E., Jr. *George Frisbie Hoar and the Half-Breed Republicans.* Cambridge, MA: Harvard University Press, 1971.

———. *The Presidencies of Grover Cleveland.* Lawrence: University Press of Kansas, 1988.

Welles, Gideon. *Diary of Gideon Welles, Secretary of Navy under Lincoln and Johnson.* 3 vols. Introduction by John T. Morse Jr. Boston: Houghton Mifflin, 1911.

———. *Lincoln and Seward.* New York: Sheldon, 1874.

Werner, M. R. *Tammany Hall.* Garden City, NY: Garden City Publishing Company, 1932.

Whichard, Willis P. *Justice James Iredell.* Durham, NC: Carolina Academic Press, 2000.

White, George. *Historical Collections of Georgia.* 3rd ed. New York: Pudney and Russell, 1855.

White, Leonard D. *The Federalists: A Study in Administrative History, 1789–1801.* New York: Macmillan, 1948.

———. *The Jacksonians: A Study in Administrative History, 1829–1861.* New York: Macmillan, 1954.

———. *The Jeffersonians: A Study in Administrative History, 1801–1829.* New York: Macmillan, 1951.

———. *The Republican Era: A Study in Administrative History, 1869–1901.* New York: Macmillan, 1958.

White, William Allen. *A Puritan in Babylon.* Norwalk, CT: Easton Press, 1986.

White, William S. *Citadel: The Story of the U.S. Senate.* 2nd ed. New York: Harper, 1957.

———. *The Taft Story.* New York: Harper, 1954.

Williams, Charles R. *The Life of Rutherford Birchard Hayes.* 2 vols. New York: Da Capo Press, 1971.

Williams, David A. *David C. Broderick: A Political Portrait.* San Marino, CA: Huntington Library, 1969.

Williamson, Hugh P. "Correspondence of Senator Francis Marion Cockrell: December 23, 1885– March 24, 1888." *Bulletin of the Missouri Historical Society* 28 (July 1969): 296–305.

Wilson, Major L. *The Presidency of Martin Van Buren.* Lawrence: University Press of Kansas, 1984.

Wilson, Woodrow. *The Papers of Woodrow Wilson,* ed. Arthur S. Link et al. 69 vols. Princeton, NJ: Princeton University Press, 1966–1994.

Wise, Henry A. *Seven Decades of the Union: A Memoir of John Tyler.* Philadelphia: J. B. Lippincott, 1872.

Wolfe, Christopher. "The Senate's Power to Give 'Advice and Consent' in Judicial Appointments." *Marquette Law Review* 82 (winter 1999): 355–379.

Wolfe, Harold. *Herbert Hoover: Public Servant and Leader of the Loyal Opposition.* New York: Exposition Press, 1956.

Wood, Gordon S. *Creation of the American Republic, 1776–1787.* Chapel Hill: University of North Carolina Press, 1998.

Woolfolk, Sarah Van V. "George E. Spencer: A Carpetbagger in Alabama." *Alabama Review* 19 (Jan. 1966): 41–52.

Wormuth, Francis D., and Edwin B. Firmage. *To Chain the Dog of War: The War Power of Congress in History and Law.* 2nd ed. Urbana: University of Illinois Press, 1989.

Yoo, Christopher S., Steven G. Calabresi, and Anthony J. Colangelo. "The Unitary Executive in the Modern Era, 1945–2004." *Iowa Law Review* 90 (Jan. 2005): 601–731.

Yoo, Christopher S., Steven G. Calabresi, and Laurence D. Nee. "The Unitary Executive during the Third Half-Century, 1889–1945." *University of Notre Dame* 80 (Nov. 2004): 1–109.

Yoo, John C. "The New Sovereignty and the Old Constitution: The Chemical Weapons Convention and the Appointments Clause." *Constitutional Commentary* 15 (spring 1998): 87–130.

Young, John Russell. *Around the World with General Grant*. 2 vols. New York: American News Company, 1879.

Zelizer, Julian E. *The Reader's Companion to the United States Congress: The Building of Democracy*. New York: Houghton Mifflin, 2004.

Public Documents

Elliott, Jonathan, ed. *The Debates in the Several State Conventions of the Adoption of the Federal Constitution*. 2nd ed. 5 vols. Washington, DC: J. B. Lippincott; Washington, Taylor and Maury, 1836–1859.

Farrand, Max, ed. *Records of the Federal Convention of 1787*. Rev. ed. 4 vols. New Haven, CT: Yale University Press, 1966.

Ford, Worthington C., ed. *Journals of the Continental Congress*. 34 vols. Washington, DC: GPO, 1904–1937.

Mosher, Robert Brent. *Executive Register of the United States, 1789–1902*. Washington, DC: GPO, 1905.

Richardson, James D., ed. *A Compilation of the Messages and Papers of the Presidents*. 11 vols. New York: Bureau of National Literature, 1911. Supplement ed., 1925.

Smith, Paul H., ed. *Letters of Delegates to Congress*. 26 vols. Washington, DC: Library of Congress, 1976–2000.

Sparks, Jared, ed. *The Diplomatic Correspondence of the American Revolution*. 12 vols. Boston: Nathan Hale and Gray and Bowen, 1829–1830.

Swanstrom, Roy. *A Dissertation on the Fourteen Years of the Upper Legislative Body*. S. Doc. 99-19, 99th Cong., 1st sess. Washington, DC: GPO, 1985.

Thorpe, Francis Newton. *The Federal and State Constitutions, Colonial Charters, and Other Organic Laws of the States, Territories, and Colonies Now or Heretofore Forming the United States of America*. 7 vols. Washington, DC: GPO, 1909.

U.S. Civil Service Commission. *A Brief History of the United States Civil Service*. Washington, DC: GPO, 1929.

———. *Eleventh Report*. Washington, DC: GPO, 1895.

———. *Thirty-fourth Annual Report*. Washington, DC: GPO, 1917.

———. *Thirty-fifth Annual Report*. Washington, DC: GPO, 1918.

———. *Thirty-sixth Annual Report*. Washington, DC: GPO, 1919.

———. *Thirty-seventh Annual Report*. Washington, DC: GPO, 1920.

———. *Thirty-ninth Annual Report*. Washington, DC: GPO, 1922.

———. *Fortieth Annual Report*. Washington, DC: GPO, 1923.

———. *Forty-first Annual Report*. Washington, DC: GPO, 1924.

———. *Report to the President, April 15, 1874*. Washington, DC: GPO, 1874.

U.S. Congress. *Annals of Congress*. 42 vols. Washington, DC: Gales and Seaton, 1834–1856.

———. *Congressional Globe*. 44 vols. Washington, DC: Blair and Rives, 1834–1873.

U.S. Department of Justice. *Official Opinions of the Attorneys General*.

U.S. House of Representatives. *Journal of the House of Representatives*.

———, Commissions to Examine Certain Custom-Houses of the United States. *First Report of the Commission on the New York Custom-House, and Instructions Related Thereto*. Ex. Doc. No. 8., 45th Cong., 1st sess. (May 24 and Oct. 19, 1877).

———, Committee on the Civil Service. *Investigation of Civilian Employment: Hearings before the Committee on the Civil Service*. Part 1, 78th Cong., 1st sess. (Mar. 10, 1943).

————, Committee on Post Office and Civil Service. *Taking Politics out of Postmaster and Other Appointments and Promotions in the Postal Service.* 90th Cong., 2nd sess. (Feb. 6, 7, 8; Mar. 26, 28, 1968).

U.S. Post Office Department. *List of Post-Offices in the United States.* Washington, DC: Way and Gideon, 1828.

U.S. Senate. *Journal of the Executive Proceedings of the Senate.* 145 vols. Washington, DC: Duff Green (vols. 1–3); GPO (vols. 4–145), 1789–2003.

————. *Journal of the Senate.*

————, Committee on Civil Service. *Methods and Procedure of Civil Service Examining Division.* 67th Cong., 2nd sess. (1922).

————, Committee on the Judiciary. *Confirmation Hearing on the Nominations of Larry D. Thompson to Be Deputy Attorney General and Theodore B. Olson to Be Solicitor General of the United States.* 107th Cong., 1st sess. (2001).

————, Subcommittee on the Constitution. *Judicial Nominations, Filibusters, and the Constitution: When a Majority Is Denied Its Right to Consent.* 108th Cong., 1st sess. (May 6, 2003).

Weekly Compilation of Presidential Documents.

Index

ABA. *See* American Bar Association
Abraham, Henry J., 6
Abraham, Spencer, 159
Acheson, Eleanor, 156–157, 172
Adams, Henry, 35
Adams, John
   administration, 33–35
   cabinet, 33, 200n63
   consultation with Congress, 34, 184
   late-term appointments, 35, 201n71
   pre-nomination process, 34–35, 184
   Sherman's correspondence with,
      20–21, 187
Adams, John Quincy
   administration, 43–45, 54
   pre-nomination process, 43–44, 45,
      48
   re-election bid, 47
   removal of officeholders, 43
   as secretary of state in Monroe
      administration, 40, 41, 42,
      204n119
   view of executive leadership, 48
Adams, Samuel, 34
advice-and-consent role of Senate
   constitutional authority, 2, 170
   discussion at state ratification
      conventions, 17–19
   Hamilton on, 19–20, 169
   importance, 189
   Jackson's interpretation, 52–53
   senators' interpretations, 166
   See also Appointments Clause,
      Constitution; pre-nomination
      process, congressional role;
      senatorial courtesy
African Americans
   members of Congress, 98, 127

   Republicans, 98, 127, 129–130,
      228n90
   Taft's refusal to nominate, 129–130,
      242n42
Akerman, Amos T., 107–108, 179
Albany Regency, 40, 56, 58, 59, 203n111,
   211n94
Aldrich, Nelson W., 126–127, 172
Alito, Samuel A., Jr., 167
Allen, William, 68
Amalgamators, 57–58, 210n72
American Bar Association (ABA), 140,
   160, 175, 248n146
Anderson, John, 142
appeals courts. *See* circuit court judges
appointment process
   of Continental Congress, 9–12, 21
   development in Washington
      administration, 27–29
   executive power, 38–39, 115–116
   lack of details in Constitution, 8, 16
   Senate approval, 14, 15
   shared power, 2, 14, 15, 16, 18, 125
   in states, 12–13, 21
   See also blocked appointments; pre-
      nomination process
Appointments Clause, Constitution
   advice-and-consent role of Senate, 2,
      16, 17–20, 52–53, 166, 170, 189
   development, 13–16
   discretion of appointing power, 108
   discussion at state ratification
      conventions, 16–19, 21
   historical background, 8–12
   implementation, 5, 22, 167–168, 181,
      189
   intentions of framers, 185, 186–187,
      189

interpretations, 3, 4, 22–23, 167–168,
169, 170, 185
Jackson's interpretation, 52–53
lack of consensus among Founders,
21
Pendleton Act and, 107–108
text, 8
views of unitary executive school,
183
Archer, William S., 65
Armstrong, William H., 93
Arthur, Chester A.
administration, 105–111
Civil Service Commission members
appointed, 108
as New York collector, 99, 100,
229n112
Pendleton Act and, 106–109
pre-nomination process, 109–111,
162
relationship with Conkling, 99,
109–110
removal of officeholders, 110
as Stalwart Republican, 104, 233n34
support of civil service reform,
105–106
as vice president, 101, 104
Articles of Confederation, 10–12, 13
attorneys. *See* district attorneys; U.S.
attorneys
attorneys general
conflicts with Senate, 114–115
qualifications, 177–178

Babbitt, Bruce, 158, 256n118
Baker, Edward D., 80
Baker, Howard H., Jr., 150
Baker, Ross K., 176
Bancroft, George, 57
Bank of the United States, 51, 53
Bankruptcy Amendments and Federal
Judgeship Act, 153
bankruptcy court judges, 153
Banning, Lance, 36
Barber, Isaac, 126
Barker, James N., 58
Barnard, Daniel D., 73
Barnburners, 69, 75, 216n19
Barrow, Alexander, 65
Barry, William, 54
Bassett, John Spencer, 48
Beard, Alanson, 110
Bedford, Gunning, Jr., 14–15

Bell, Griffin, 147
Benton, Thomas Hart, 25, 70
Bentsen, Lloyd M., 148
Berrien, John, 26, 73, 198n17
Biden, Joseph, 155, 157, 172, 256n118
Bigler, John, 77
Bingaman, Jeff, 157
Birney, James, 82
Blaine, James G., 88, 95–96, 111–112,
227n58, 234n54
blocked appointments
Bush I nominees, 155
circuit court judges, 165
Ford nominees, 145
Grant nominees, 87
Hayes nominees, 99–100
A. Johnson nominees, 81–82,
83, 84
Monroe nominees, 42
Polk nominees, 69
Reagan nominees, 153, 156, 174
F. D. Roosevelt nominees,
245nn88, 96
Senate procedures, 153, 164–165,
174, 175–176
Supreme Court nominees, 124, 141,
156
Truman nominees, 137, 246n109
Tyler nominees, 65–66,
215nn153–154
See also filibusters; senatorial
courtesy
Blount, William, 11–12
Blount, Winton, 143–144
blue slips, 158, 159, 164–165, 175, 176,
261n182
Boardman, Michelle E., 5
Board of Referees, 127, 129–130
Bond, Christopher, 154
Booth, Newton, 100
Borden, Nathaniel Briggs, 56
Bork, Robert, 156
Boston collectors, 57, 88, 98, 110,
117–118
Bourbon faction, 117, 236n93
Boutwell, George, 88, 110
Boxer, Barbara, 163
Brady, Nicholas, 152
Brandeis, Louis, 178
Breese, Sidney, 68
Brennan, William J., 156
Breyer, Stephen G., 149, 158
Broderick David C., 77

Brodsky, Alyn, 116, 123
Brooke, Hunter, 82
Brower, John M., 122
Brown, Jeremiah, 61
Brown, Michael D., 180
Brown, Orlando, 62
Bruce, Blanche K., 98, 127
Bruff, Harold H., 170
Buchanan, James
    administration, 76–78
    Amalgamators and, 210n72
    appointments sought for others, 50,
        57–58, 210n76
    pre-nomination process, 77–78
    removals policy, 76–77
    rivals, 57, 74
    as secretary of state, 69
Buckley, James, 145
Bunning, Jim, 160
Burchard, Samuel D., 112
Burleson, Albert S., 131
Burnett, John D., 114–115
Burt, C. K., 101
Burt, Silas W., 100, 101, 229n114
Bush, George H. W. (Bush I)
    administration, 153–156
    pre-nomination process, 153–156,
        172
    relations with Congress, 154–155,
        174
Bush, George W. (Bush II)
    administration, 160–167
    consultation with lawmakers,
        160–167, 181
    FEMA administrator, 180
    judicial nominations, 2, 160–167,
        173, 175
    pre-nomination process, 160–167,
        173
    recess appointments, 166
    relations with Congress, 5, 160,
        162–163, 165, 181
    signing statements, 179, 265n55
Bush, Jeb, 161, 173
Butler, Benjamin F., 88, 98, 173,
    203n111
Butler, Pierce, 30, 32
Byrd, Harry F., 139–140, 171, 245n96

Cabell, Edward Carrington, 73
cabinet members
    congressional roles in appointments
        of, 95–96, 133

controversial nominees, 180–181
    roles in pre-nomination process, 60,
        63, 71–72, 74, 95–96
    Tenure of Office Act and, 83
Calabresi, Steven G., 183, 184, 185
Calhoun, John C., 51, 58, 69, 208n31,
    210n72
California
    Democratic factions, 77
    district court selection committee,
        163
    Republicans, 80
Cameron, J. Don, 95, 101, 110
Cameron, Simon, 69, 83, 88, 95, 101
Campbell, Thomas Jefferson, 61
Cannon, Joseph, 129, 173
Cantwell, Maria, 164
Capper, Arthur, 134
Carcieri, Donald, 161
Carney, Thomas, 80
Carroll, Charles, 27
Carter, Jimmy
    administration, 147–150
    merit selection of judges, 147–148,
        149–150, 182
    pre-nomination process, 147–150,
        172
    removal of officeholders, 148–149
Cass, Lewis, 70, 71, 74, 219n63
Census Bureau, 177
Chafee, Lincoln, 161
Chambers, John, 62, 213n126
Chambliss, Saxby, 160
Chandler, William E., 110
Chandler, Zachariah, 81, 82, 88
Chase, Clifford, 145
Chase, Harold, 23–24, 140
Chase, Salmon P., 79
checks and balances, 2, 169, 170, 186,
    187–188
Chiles, Lawton, 145
Chivalry faction, 77
circuit court judges
    blocked or delayed nominations,
        165
    congressional influence on
        appointments, 152–153, 154, 157,
        159, 161, 163, 164
    efforts to limit congressional
        influence, 133–134, 149–150
    merit selection commissions, 147,
        148, 150, 154
    new positions, 87, 149–150

circuit court judges, *continued*
  pre-nomination process, 151–152
  See also judicial appointments
civil service
  classification system, 106, 232n12
  expansion, 89, 109, 113, 118, 123, 129,
    136
  offices included, 106, 107, 109, 138
  rules circumvention, 109
  temporary appointments, 109
  See also civil service reforms
Civil Service Act of 1871, 89–93, 94, 107
Civil Service Commission
  Cleveland's support, 123
  constitutionality, 107–108
  establishment, 5, 106, 108
  implementation of Pendleton Act,
    107, 108–109, 232n13
  New Deal agencies and, 137
  T. Roosevelt as member, 118
Civil Service Commission (established
    by Grant, 1871), 93, 101, 108
civil service examinations
  examinations bill of 1853, 74
  exemptions, 232n30
  in Hayes administration, 96–97, 101
  postal appointments, 101, 132–133
  repealed, 109, 132–133, 136
  rule of three, 107, 108, 132–133, 136,
    179, 232n20
  See also Pendleton Act
civil service reforms
  circumvention of, 109
  classification system, 106, 232n12
  in Cleveland administrations,
    112–113, 123
  effects on pre-nomination process,
    181–182
  examinations bill of 1853, 74
  examinations introduced, 96–97, 101
  in Garfield administration, 102–104
  goals, 188
  in Grant administration, 89–93, 94,
    107
  in Hayes administration, 95, 96–97,
    99, 100–101
  limited effects, 125
  merit systems, 74, 97, 181, 182
  obstacles, 94
  public support, 105
  supporters, 181–183, 229n94, 234n57
  Truman's proposals, 138
  See also Pendleton Act

Civil War, 78, 89
Clark, John C., 58
Clark, Ramsey, 141
Clay, Henry, 44, 45, 61–62, 72, 184
Cleveland, Grover
  administrations, 111–118, 122–125
  civil service reforms, 112–113, 123
  conflict with Senate, 113–116
  political use of appointments, 172
  pre-nomination process, 116–118,
    123–125
  removals policy, 112, 113–116
  use of patronage, 124–125
Clinton, De Witt, 40, 44, 202n103
Clinton, George, 31
Clinton, William J.
  administration, 156–159
  consultation with lawmakers,
    156–157, 158, 172, 256n118
  pre-nomination process, 156–159,
    173
  relations with Congress, 5, 159,
    161–162, 165
Cockrell, Francis M., 116–117
Coffee, John, 53
collector positions
  Boston, 57, 88, 98, 110, 117–118
  Chicago, 78
  congressional endorsements, 39
  New Orleans, 75
  Philadelphia, 58, 64, 69, 81
  San Francisco, 77, 100
  Van Buren appointments, 57, 58
  See also New York collectors
Collins, Patrick, 117–118
Colorado, judicial selection
    commission, 173
Congress
  African American members, 98,
    127
  conflicts over removals of
    officeholders, 51–52
  Reconstruction policy, 80–81, 83, 84,
    223n142
  roles in officeholder removals,
    51–52, 54, 113–116
  See also House of Representatives;
    legislative branch; pre-
    nomination process,
    congressional role; Senate
Conkling, Alfred, 44
Conkling, Roscoe
  conflict with Garfield, 102–104

conflict with Hayes, 98, 99–100, 105,
    184, 229n112
influence on appointments, 87–88,
    95, 110
presidential candidacy, 95
relationship with Arthur, 99, 105,
    109–110
Constitution
    ambiguous provisions, 1, 186
    express and implied powers, 1, 4
    judicial interpretations, 4
    originalist interpretations, 4, 185,
        186–189, 192n8
    republican principles, 1, 186
    shared powers, 2, 183, 187, 189–190
    state ratification conventions, 16–19,
        21
    textualist interpretations, 4, 185, 186,
        188–189, 192n8
    See also Appointments Clause,
        Constitution
Constitutional Convention, 8, 13–16
constitutions, state. See state
    constitutions
Continental Congress
    appointment process, 9–12, 21
    duties, 8–9
Cook, Isaac, 78
Coolidge, Calvin
    cabinet, 133
    pre-nomination process, 133
    respect for tradition, 243n63
Cornell, Alonzo B., 99, 100, 103
corruption
    in post office, 54
    prevention, 181, 182
Corwin, Edward S., 178
Couzens, James, 133
Cox, Christopher, 163
Cox, Jacob D., 74
Craig, Larry, 158
Crane, Winthrop, 172
Cranston, Alan, 143
Crawford, Andrew J., 53
Crawford, William, 41, 204n132, 210n72
Crittenden, John J., 48, 62, 72
Crockett, David A., 185, 186, 187–188
Crotty, Paul A., 163
Cullom, Shelby, 119
Curtis, Charles, 133
Curtis, Edward, 61, 64, 213n121
Curtis, George William, 93
Cushing, Caleb, 65, 215n153

Cushing, Marshall, 121
customhouses. See collector positions
Customs Bureau, 138

Daily National Intelligencer, 26
Dallas, George M., 57, 210n72
D'Amato, Alfonse M., 152, 153, 154,
    164
Danforth, John, 154
Dawes, Henry L., 110, 226n42
Day, J. Edward, 140
Dayton, Mark, 164
Decatur, Stephen, Jr., 26–27
DeGette, Diana, 173
Del Tufo, Robert J., 148–149
Democratic Party
    Albany Regency, 40, 56, 58, 59,
        203n111, 211n94
    Jackson supporters, 43
    rise of, 47–48
    in South, 98, 230n126
    supporters of civil service reform,
        112–113
    Tammany Hall, 50, 58–59, 77, 111,
        207n23, 211n89
Democratic Party, factions
    in California, 77–78
    divisions over slavery, 73–74, 77–78
    in 1850s, 73–74, 77–78, 85, 219n63
    in Louisiana, 75
    in Minnesota, 117, 236n93
    in New York, 58–59, 69, 75, 77,
        216n19, 219–220n77
    in Pennsylvania, 57–58, 69, 210n72
    Polk and, 69
    progressives, 131
    Van Buren and, 56–59
Deneen, Charles S., 133
Denton, Jeremiah, 152
Department of Homeland Security
        Appropriation Act of 2007, 179
Dickerson, Mahlon, 56
Dickerson, Philemon, 56
Dickinson, Daniel S., 70, 72, 75
Dickman, Murray, 155
DiFrancesco, Donald T, 161
Dionne, E. J., Jr., 162
Dirksen, Everett, 141, 142, 172
district attorneys, 114–115, 124, 133–134
district court judges
    congressional influence on
        appointments, 151–152, 154, 157,
        158, 160–161

district court judges, *continued*
  merit selection commissions, 148,
    163, 252n45
  new positions, 149–150
  pre-nomination process, 149,
    151–152
Dix, John, 75, 203n111
Dodd, Thomas J., 140
Dodge, Augustus, 75
Dodge, Henry, 75
Domenici, Pete, 161
Donnelly, Ignatius, 117
Donovan, Raymond J., 152
Doolittle, James R., 81, 222n137
Doran, Michael, 117
Doty, David, 174
Douglas, Stephen, 75, 76, 78, 221n107
Downs, Solomon W., 75
Driggs, John F., 82
Driver, William J., 142
Duane, William J., 51–52, 53
Dubois, Jesse K., 79
Dudley, Charles E., 50
Durbin, Richard J., 164–165
Durenberger, David F., 152, 174
Durkin, John, 150
Duskin, George M., 114–115
Dwyer, William, 152

Eagleton, Thomas, 150
Eastland, James O., 140, 147, 148, 171,
  175
Eaton, Dorman B., 108
Edwards, John, 159, 162, 165
Edwards, Ninian, 41
Egan, Michael J., 148, 149, 150
Eggleston, Benjamin, 82
Eilberg, Joshua, 149
Eisenhower, Dwight D.
  administration, 138–139
  cabinet, 138, 180, 246n115
  judicial nominations, 141
  pre-nomination process, 138–139,
    141
Ellsworth, Oliver, 15
era of good feelings, 39–40, 46
Ervin, Sam J., Jr., 149
Estrada, Miguel, 165, 175
Evarts, William M., 96–97
Ewing, Thomas, 63
examinations. *See* civil service
  examinations
executive branch
  under Articles of Confederation,
    10–12, 13, 21
  Hamilton on, 19–20
  independence, 38–39, 115–116
  legitimacy, 170
  relations with legislative branch, 1,
    2, 143
  shared appointment power, 14, 15,
    16, 18, 125, 169
  shared powers, 2, 183, 187,
    189–190
  See also presidents; unitary executive
    school

factions, of Jeffersonian Republicans,
    41, 43, 44, 203n111, 204n125. *See
    also* Democratic Party, factions;
    Republican Party, factions
family faction, Democrats, 57–58,
    210n72
Farley, James T., 100, 135, 137
Federal Emergency Management
    Agency (FEMA), 179, 180
federal employment, expansion, 89,
    136–137. *See also* civil service
Federalist Papers, 2, 19–20, 185, 186
  No. 10, 176
  No. 66, 19
  No. 76, 187
  No. 77, 12
Federalist Party
  decline, 35
  formation, 34
  members in J. Adams
    administration, 33, 35
  members in J. Q. Adams
    administration, 44
  midnight appointments by
    J. Adams, 35
  Monroe nominees, 42
  removals by Jefferson, 36
Feingold, Russ, 163, 164
Feinstein, Dianne, 163, 164
FEMA. *See* Federal Emergency
    Management Agency
Fenton, Reuben, 87
Ferry, Orris Sanford, 90
Few, William, 25, 26, 27
filibusters
  cloture motions, 261n186
  efforts to limit, 166, 175
  of judicial nominations, 165–166,
    261n188

minority rights and, 175–176
"nuclear option," 166
Fillmore, Millard
  administration, 72–73
  compromise policy, 72–73
  political use of appointments, 172
  rejection of Taylor appointments,
    72–73
  removal of officeholders, 72, 73,
    218n57
  as vice president, 72
Finance Department, 10–12, 21
Findlay, William, 42
Fish, Carl Russell, 78–79, 83–84
Fishbourn, Benjamin, 24–27, 198n19
Fisher, Louis, 10
Fitzgerald, Peter, 160
Flanigan, Timothy, 162
Flemming, Arthur S., 179
Flynn, Edward J., 135
Ford, Gerald R., pre-nomination
    process, 145
Ford, Wendell, 152, 157
Fortas, Abe, 141
Foster, John W., 94
Foster, Theodore, 37
Four Years Act. *See* Tenure of Office Act
Fowler, Dorothy Ganfield, 6, 43, 54, 71,
    130
Frankfurter, Felix, 4
Franklin, Benjamin, 10, 13–14
Fred, Perry Powers, 93
Free-Soil Democrats, 77, 78, 216n19
Frémont, John C., 76, 220n87
Frist, Bill, 166, 175
Frye, William Pierce, 95–96

Gage, Lyman J., 126–127
Gallatin, Albert, 38, 39
Gang of Fourteen, 166, 167, 261n193
Garfield, James A.
  administration, 101–104
  civil service reforms, 102–104
  conflict with Conkling, 102–104
  consultation with lawmakers, 102
  pre-nomination process, 102–104,
    111
  on Tenure of Office Act, 84–85
George, Walter F., 138
Gerhardt, Michael J., 22–23
Giles, Warren, 38
Gilpin, Henry D., 58
Ginsberg, Ruth Bader, 158

Goldman, Sheldon, 6, 137, 145, 150, 158,
    162
Goldstein, Jonathan, 148
Goldwater, Barry, 142–143
Gonzalez, Alberto, 163
Goodell, Charles E., 143
Goodhue, Benjamin, 3, 23, 170
Gorham, Nathaniel, 12, 14, 15
governors, roles in federal
    appointments, 31, 145, 151, 154,
    157, 161, 173
Graebner, Norman, 70–71
Granger, Francis, 63
Granger, Gideon, 36, 39, 202n103
Grangers faction, 117, 236n93
Grant, Ulysses S.
  administration, 86–94
  civil service commission, 93, 101,
    108
  civil service reforms, 89–93, 94, 107
  nominees rejected by Senate, 87
  opposition to Tenure of Office Act,
    86–87, 224n4
  pre-nomination process, 87–92,
    93–94, 103, 173
  removal of officeholders, 87
  as secretary of war ad interim, 84
  support for nomination for third
    term, 101, 102
Grassley, Charles, 161
Greeley, Horace, 79
Greene, Nathanael, 26
Gregory, John M., 108
Grundy, Joseph R., 134
Guiteau, Charles J., 104
Gunn, James, 25–26, 27, 198n19
Gwin, William K., 77

Habersham, John, 26, 198n17
Hagel, Chuck, 164
Half-Breed Republicans
  conflict with Arthur, 110
  conflict with Hayes, 96
  demise, 234n52
  influence on appointments, 97–98,
    173
  leaders, 88
  public view of factional conflict, 105
  See also Garfield, James A.
Hall, Nathan, 72–73
Hamilton, Alexander
  on advice-and-consent role of
    Senate, 19–20, 169

Hamilton, Alexander, *continued*
    at Constitutional Convention, 14
    Federalist Papers, 12, 19–20, 185, 186,
        187
Hancock, Winfield Scott, 102
Hand, Judith, 164
Hanna, Marcus, 126
Hannegan, Edward, 73
Harding, Warren G., pre-nomination
        process, 132–133, 199n31,
        242n55
Hardshells, 75, 77, 219–220n77
Harmon, Judson, 124
Harris, Ira, 80
Harris, Joseph P., 6, 115–116, 132
Harrison, Benjamin
    administration, 118–122
    demeanor with officeseekers, 119
    pre-nomination process, 119–122,
        173
    relations with other Republicans,
        119, 180, 237n116
    removal of officeholders, 118
    support of civil service reform,
        118–119
Harrison, Robert H., 30
Harrison, William Henry
    administration, 59–62
    appointments, 61–62, 213nn119–121
    cabinet, 60, 62, 63
    pre-nomination process, 60–62, 63,
        184
    reform efforts, 59–60
    removal of officeholders, 59, 60,
        214n145
    view of executive power, 211n95
Hart, Gary, 181
Harvey, Donald R., 137
Hastings, Daniel Oren, 134
Hatch, Orrin, 158, 164, 165, 172
Hatfield, Mark, 154
Hawkins, Benjamin, 30
Hawkins, Paula, 152
Hayes, Rutherford B.
    administration, 94–101
    cabinet, 95–96
    civil service reforms, 95, 96–97, 99,
        100–101
    conflict with Conkling, 98, 99–100,
        105, 184, 229n112
    consultation with Congress, 97
    criticisms of appointments, 97–99
    as member of Congress, 82

nominees rejected by Senate, 99–100
    pre-nomination process, 95–96,
        97–100
    removals policy, 95
Haynes, George H., 6, 25, 93
Hazard, Ebenezer, 10
Hazelton, Gerry W., 94
Heflin, Howell, 152
Helms, Jesse, 159, 165
Henderson, John, 61
Henn, Bernhart, 75
Henry, John, 32
Henshaw, David, 57
Hill, David, 124
Hill, James J., 117
Hines, William Henry, 124
Hitchcock, Frank H., 130
Hoar, Ebenezer Rockwood, 87
Hoar, George F., 80, 97–98, 110, 116, 124,
        224n8, 228n77
Holt, Michael F., 72
Hoogenboom, Ari, 89, 97, 101
Hoover, Herbert
    pre-nomination process, 133–135
    as secretary of commerce, 133
Hoover Commission, 136
Hornblower, William B., 124
House, Edward M., 131
House Judiciary Committee, 148–149
House of Representatives, involvement
        in pre-nomination process
    appointments within district, 3, 91,
        116–118, 121, 133, 138–139, 173
    consultation with members, 32–33,
        37, 50, 157, 173
    greater influence than senators, 88
    influence on appointments outside
        district, 121, 122
    judicial nominations, 154, 161
    postal appointments, 173
    postmasters, 54–55, 79, 82, 131, 133,
        138–139, 140
    See also Congress; pre-nomination
        process, congressional role
Howard, Jacob M., 82
Howe, Timothy O., 94
Howell, David, 11
Hoyt, Jesse, 58–59
Huger, Daniel, 70
Hughes, Charles Evans, 3–4
Humphrey, George, 138
Hunkers, 69, 216n19, 219n77
Hurricane Katrina, 180

INS v. Chadha, 4
Iredell, James, 17, 18, 30, 32
Irvin, Thomas, 50
Irwin, William W., 65, 215n153
Izard, Ralph, 27, 32

Jackson, Andrew
    administration, 47–55
    Bank of the United States
        controversy, 51, 53
    cabinet, 45, 50, 51–52, 53
    conflicts with Congress, 51–53
    consultation with Congress, 50–51,
        53, 55, 184
    divisions in Democratic party, 210n72
    inaugural address, 48
    "Outline of Principles," 49
    pre-nomination process, 48, 49–51,
        52–53, 54–55, 184
    reform policies, 48, 49, 54, 55
    removal of officeholders, 48–49, 51–
        52, 53, 55, 206–207n10, 207nn11, 15
    selection of nominees supporting
        policies, 33, 51, 55
    supporters, 43, 45, 205n153
    understanding of Appointments
        Clause, 52–53
    Van Rensselaer and, 209n60
Jackson, James, 2, 170
Jackson, Robert H., 189–190
James, Francis, 61
Javits, Jacob K., 141–142, 143, 145
Jay, John, 99
Jefferson, Thomas
    administration, 35–37
    on Four Years Act, 42–43
    judicial appointments, 37
    postal appointments, 36–37
    pre-nomination process, 36–37
    removal of officeholders, 33, 36
    as secretary of state, 33
    selection of nominees supporting
        policies, 33, 36
    view of Senate power in pre-
        nomination process, 43
Jeffersonian Republicans. *See*
        Republican Party, Jeffersonian
Jeffords, James, 152, 155–156, 165, 172,
        174
Jenckes, Thomas A., 89
Johnson, Andrew
    administration, 80–85
    cabinet, 83, 84

conflicts over Reconstruction, 80–81,
        83, 84
    impeachment, 84
    nominees rejected by Senate, 81–82,
        83, 84
    personal supporters, 83
    political use of appointments, 172
    pre-nomination process, 81–85
    relations with Congress, 67, 80–81,
        82–85
    removal of officeholders, 81, 83
Johnson, Lyndon B.
    administration, 140–142
    pre-nomination process, 140–142,
        162, 172
Johnson, Thomas, 31
Johnson, William, 32
Johnston, Samuel, 32
Jones, George, 75
Josephson, Matthew, 87, 88, 94
Judgeship Act of 1961, 141
judicial appointments
    by J. Adams, 35
    by J. Q. Adams, 44
    bankruptcy courts, 153
    bipartisan, 141–142, 143, 248n146
    blocked or delayed, 128, 145, 153,
        155, 159, 164–166, 174, 261n188
    by Bush I, 154–155, 172, 174
    by Bush II, 2, 160–167, 175, 261n189
    by Carter, 147–148, 149–150
    by Clinton, 156–159, 161–162, 165
    congressional involvement, 147–148,
        149, 154, 155–156, 157, 160–167,
        181
    by Eisenhower, 141
    family members of lawmakers,
        160
    floor vote controversy, 2, 166
    by Ford, 145
    by Grant, 87
    by Hoover, 133–134
    by Jackson, 50
    by Jefferson, 37
    by L. Johnson, 140–142
    by Kennedy, 140, 141
    by Nixon, 143
    political considerations, 141, 144,
        149–150, 152, 153, 182
    qualifications, 177
    by Reagan, 150–153, 174
    by T. Roosevelt, 128
    three-name rule, 152, 154–155, 161

judicial appointments, *continued*
    See also Senate Judiciary Committee;
        Supreme Court justice nominees
judicial branch
    constitutional interpretation, 4
    exclusion from pre-nomination
        process, 4
    lack of guidance on appointments
        process, 22
    supremacy, 3–4, 191n5
judicial selection commissions
    Carter administration, 147–148,
        149–150, 182
    circuit court judges, 147, 148, 150, 154
    district court judges, 148, 163,
        252n45
    impact, 182
    of senators, 148, 159, 163–164, 173
    state, 158, 159, 161, 173
Judiciary Act of 1789, 177
Judiciary Act of 1801, 35, 36
Judiciary Act of 1869, 87
Justice Department. *See* attorneys
    general; U.S. attorneys

Kellogg, William P., 97
Kelly, Patrick H., 117
Kempthorne, Dirk, 158
Kendall, Amos, 213n119
Kennedy, Edward, 149, 154
Kennedy, John F.
    administration, 139–140
    consultation with senators, 139–140,
        162, 171, 172
    judicial nominations, 140, 141
    pre-nomination process, 139–140,
        162
Kennedy, Robert, 139, 181
Kerry, John, 154
Ketcham, Ralph, 45, 48
Key, David M., 96, 97, 227nn67, 74
King, Horatio, 77
King, Preston, 75, 80
King, Rufus, 27, 40, 44, 203n106,
    204n117
King, William Rufus, 50, 53
Kohl, Herb, 163, 164

Lamar, Lucius Q. C., 98
Lane, James Henry, 80
Lane, Joseph, 75–76
LaRocco, Larry, 158
Lawrence, Alexander, 141

Lawrence, Cornelius Van Wyck, 69,
    217n20
Lawrence, Joseph, 61
Leahy, Patrick, 157, 159, 165, 167
Lear, Benjamin Lincoln, 26–27, 198n23
Lear, Tobias, 26
Lecompton constitution, 78, 221n107
Lee, Henry, 31
Lee, Richard Henry, 32
legislative branch
    constitutional functions, 144
    majority rule, 2
    minority rights, 2, 175–176
    relations with executive branch, 1, 2,
        143
    representative role, 170, 182
    shared appointment power, 14, 15,
        16, 18, 125, 169
    shared powers, 2, 183, 187, 189–190
    views of unitary executive school,
        182–183
    See also Congress; pre-nomination
        process, congressional role;
        Senate
Leib, Michael, 38, 39
Leitch, David, 161
Leonard, David, 37
Levin, Carl, 165
Lincoln, Abraham
    administration, 78–80
    consultation with Congress, 67,
        78–80
    pre-nomination process, 67, 78–80
    removal of officeholders, 79
Lingle, Linda, 161
Locofocos, 58–59, 211n89
Lodge, Henry Cabot, 172
Logan, James, 96, 101
Logan, John A., 88, 110
Louisiana, Democratic factions, 75
Lowrie, Walter, 42

Mack, Connie, 154
Mackenzie, G. Calvin, 139
Maclay, William, 32
Macon, Nathaniel, 37
Madden, Martin B., 133
Madison, James
    administration, 37–39
    advice to Washington as House
        member, 32–33
    on appointments process, 3, 5, 23,
        171

cabinet, 38, 39
at Constitutional Convention, 14, 15
on majority power, 176
pre-nomination process, 38–39
removal of officeholders, 38, 39
Mahone, William, 111, 162
Malone, Dumas, 36
Manion, Daniel A., 152, 174
Marcy, William L., 49, 59, 69, 74, 75,
203n111
Marine Hospital Service, 177
Marshall, John, 35, 191n5
Marston, David W., 149
Martin, John, 124
Martin, Luther, 14
Martinez, Mel, 161
Mason, Samson, 61
Massachusetts
congressional influence on
appointments, 56–57, 88, 98, 110,
117–118
Republican factions, 88, 173
state constitution, 13
Mathias, Charles, 142
McConnell, Mitch, 152, 154
McDuffie, George, 215n154
McHenry, James, 31
McIntyre, Thomas, 150
McKinley, John, 50, 51, 208n31
McKinley, William, pre-nomination
process, 126–127
McLean, John
as Postmaster General, 45, 54,
205n153
as Supreme Court justice, 45, 56
Meigs, Jonathan, Jr., 39, 40
"Memorandum of Understanding on
Judicial Nominations," 166
Merit selection commissions. See
Judicial selection commission
merit systems
in Hayes administration, 96–97
in Pierce administration, 74
supporters, 181, 182
See also civil service examinations;
civil service reforms; Pendleton
Act
Merrick, William D., 65
Merrill, Horace Samuel, 113
Merritt, Edwin A., 100, 101, 229n114
Michaelsen, William B., 12
Michel, Robert, 154, 173
Miers, Harriet E., 167

military appointments, 30, 34
Minnesota, Democratic factions, 117,
236n93
Mississippi, black Republicans, 98, 127,
129–130, 228n90
Mitchell, John I., 110
Monroe, James
administration, 39–43
cabinet, 40, 41, 204n119
fusion policy, 40
pre-nomination process, 40–43
Moore, Arch, 145
Moore, Gabriel, 50–51, 53, 208n31
Morgan, John Tyler, 106–107
Morgan, Robert, 149
Morris, Gouverneur, 15, 16
Morris, Robert, 10–12, 26, 32
Morton, John M., 100
Morton, Marcus, 57
Morton, Oliver P., 88, 91, 92, 94, 95,
100
Moynihan, Daniel Patrick, 154, 157, 164
Mugwumps, 111, 112, 117–118, 229n94,
234n53
Muhlenberg, Henry A., 58, 210n79
Murphy, James B., 98
Murphy, Thomas, 87–88
Murray, Patty, 157, 164
Myers, Elisabeth P., 118
Myers v. United States, 178

national banks, 51, 53, 65
National Civil Service Reform League,
112, 234n57
Nelson, Ben, 164, 167, 261n193
Nelson, Knute, 128
Nevins, Allan, 71
New Deal, 136–137
New York
Albany Regency, 40, 56, 58, 59,
203n111, 211n94
civil service reform efforts, 101
constitutional ratification
convention, 17
Council of Appointments, 12–13, 17,
195n40
Democratic factions, 58–59, 69, 75,
77, 216n19, 219–220n77
Jeffersonian Republican factions, 44,
203n111
judicial nominations, 163
patronage appointments, 55, 87–88
patronage conflicts, 99–100, 102–104

New York, *continued*
  state constitution, 12–13
  Whig Party, 58, 60, 61
New York City
  customhouse, 88, 99–101, 105,
    229n112, 233n34
  Tammany Hall, 50, 58–59, 77, 111,
    207n23, 211n89
New York collectors
  Arthur as, 99, 100, 229n112
  conflicts over appointments, 58–59,
    99
  congressional influence on
    appointments, 50
  Conkling's influence on
    appointments, 87, 110
  examination requirements, 101
  W. H. Harrison appointment, 61–62
  Hayes appointment, 100, 101
  Jackson appointment, 50, 58
  Pierce appointment, 75
  Tyler appointment, 64
  Van Buren appointment, 58–59
New York Times, 143
Niven, John, 57
Nixon, Richard M.
  administration, 142–144, 145
  cabinet, 142
  civil service protection for Post
    Office, 143–144, 182
  pre-nomination process, 142–144
nominations. *See* appointment process;
    judicial appointments; postal
    appointments; pre-nomination
    process
Norris, George W., 173
North Carolina, constitutional
    ratification convention, 17–18
"nuclear option," 166
nullifiers, 51, 208n33

O'Connor, Sandra Day, 166
officeholders. *See* removal of
    officeholders
Office of Personnel Management. *See*
    Civil Service Commission
officeseekers
  in J. Q. Adams administration, 44
  increased number, 69–70,
    206–207n10
  in Washington administration, 32
  Whigs, 60

Olsen, Arthur J., 142–143
originalism, 4, 185, 186–189, 192n8

Packwood, Robert, 154
Parker, Fred I., 155
Parks, Gorham, 56
Parmenter, William, 56–57
Parsky, Gerald, 163
parties. *See* political parties
party leaders, consultation with, 3, 134,
    136, 138–139, 154, 161
Pataki, George, 163
Paterson, William, 14, 32
patronage
  conflicts, 99–100, 102–104,
    229n112
  negative views of, 182
  postal appointments, 36–37, 45,
    205n153
  of senators, 130, 131
  use by presidents, 124–125
  See also collector positions
Patterson, Josiah, 124
Patton, Paul, 157
Pendleton, George H., 106
Pendleton Act
  amendment to limit congressional
    involvement, 106–107, 109
  constitutional questions, 107–108
  drafts, 231n5
  effects, 105, 125
  implementation, 107, 108–109, 123,
    232n13
  objectives, 105, 106, 107
  passage, 106
  scope, 106, 107, 113, 118, 123,
    231n8
Penn, Alexander G., 75
Pennsylvania
  constitutional ratification
    convention, 17
  Democratic factions, 57–58, 69,
    210n72
  judicial selection commission, 159
  representation in Van Buren cabinet,
    57–58
  Whig Party, 61
Peterson, Norma Lois, 60
Pierce, Franklin
  administration, 73–76
  cabinet, 74
  pre-nomination process, 67, 74–76

relations with Congress, 220n85
removals policy, 74
Pigott, James P., 124
Pinckney, Charles, 15, 16, 37
Platt, Thomas C., 95, 103, 104, 119, 127,
    180, 237n120
Poindexter, George, 53
political parties
    disregarded by presidents, 40, 42,
        43, 45
    first two-party system, 34–35, 47
    importance in pre-nomination
        process, 56, 66
    second two-party system, 43, 45,
        47–48, 206n9, 211n95
    state leaders, 134, 136, 138, 139, 154,
        161
    third two-party system, 67
    See also removal of officeholders; *and
    specific parties*
Polk, James K.
    administration, 68–71
    appointments, 69, 217n20
    cabinet, 69
    nominees rejected by Senate, 69
    pre-nomination process, 68–71
    removal of officeholders, 68,
        216nn6–9
Pomeroy, Samuel C., 82, 90
postal appointments
    civil service reform proposals, 138,
        143–144
    controversies, 40–41
    examination requirements, 101,
        132–133
    partisan appointments and
        removals, 36–37, 118, 131,
        143–144, 205n153
    as patronage, 36–37, 45, 205n153
    presidential involvement, 36–37, 39,
        53–54, 63, 72–73
    presidential powers, 41, 54
    referee system, 173
    removals, 71, 116, 118, 143–144,
        209n60
    in Revolutionary period, 9–10, 21
    rule of three, 132–133, 136
    rural letter carriers, 140
    terms, 136
postal appointments, congressional
        involvement
    end to, 143–144

House member influence, 110,
    173
House members and postmaster
    selection, 54–55, 79, 116, 131, 133,
    138–139, 140
partisan appointments and
    removals, 132–133
referee system, 121–122
senators' roles, 54, 82, 110, 131
Postal Reorganization and Salary
    Adjustment Act of 1970, 144,
    182
postmasters. *See* postal appointments
postmasters general
    appointment powers, 9–10, 31,
        36–37, 40–41, 53–54, 97, 184
    appointments, 96
    cabinet-level status, 54
    political use of patronage, 45,
        205n153
Post Office Department
    circulars sent to representatives,
        109
    civil service positions, 129, 133, 136,
        138, 143–144
    corruption, 54
    establishment, 9
    as government corporation, 143–144
    reform efforts, 140
Post Office Reorganization Act of 1836,
    54
Prakash, Saikrishna, 177–178, 180,
    185
Pratt, Daniel D., 94
pre-nomination process
    adaptability, 146, 147, 167
    cabinet member roles, 60, 63, 71–72,
        74, 95–96
    existing research on, 5–6
    informal limits on presidential
        powers, 132, 180–181
    institutional and political influences,
        171–173
    lack of details in Constitution,
        8, 16
    participants, 173–174
    presidential domination, 5, 38–39,
        138–140, 142, 169
    qualifications for office, 108,
        176–180, 265n55
    steps, 3
    See also specific presidents

pre-nomination process, congressional
    role
  attempts to influence appointments
    in other states, 62, 184
  benefits for members, 37
  checks and balances rationale, 169,
    170, 186, 187–188
  collaboration among lawmakers,
    122, 154, 161, 163, 164, 173
  constitutional authority, 2, 3, 144,
    179, 185–186, 189–190
  consultation with home-state
    senators, 3, 131–133, 145,
    149–150, 157, 160
  consultation with political
    opponents in same party,
    139–140, 171
  of Continental Congress, 10, 11–12
  criticism of, 43, 155–156, 167–168,
    182–183, 185
  defenders of, 91, 92
  development in Washington
    administration, 27–29
  dominance, 69–71, 77, 85, 89–91,
    93–94, 132, 140, 181
  in early twentieth century, 126–130
  endorsements, 32, 39, 74
  evolution, 3, 41, 167–168, 169
  formal recognition, 130
  Founders' discussions of, 14–21
  importance, 184–185
  influence of members of other party,
    82–83, 141–142, 145, 152, 158–159,
    162–164, 172
  interpretations of Appointments
    Clause, 3, 22–23, 52–53
  involvement seen as right, 60, 70, 77
  knowledge of candidates as
    advantage, 20–21, 32, 120,
    121–122, 171, 186, 187
  lessened influence, 138–140
  Madison's understanding, 38–39
  military appointments, 30, 34
  modifications, 134, 136
  "nuclear option," 166
  partisanship, 161–162
  persistence of custom, 146, 147
  political opponents not consulted by
    presidents, 70, 82, 143, 173–174
  practical political reasons, 113,
    128–129, 171
  presidents' acceptance, 37, 184,
    185–186

presidents' failures to consult, 67,
    128, 138–139, 169, 174–176
  pressure on presidents, 60–62, 67, 94,
    107, 110, 143
  qualifications for office, 176–180,
    265n55
  reforms aimed at limiting, 89–92, 95,
    96–97, 100–101, 105, 106–107,
    133–135
  representation of state interests, 30
  states with split-party
    representation, 121, 154, 157, 160
  timing of consultation, 27
  See also House of Representatives,
    involvement in pre-nomination
    process; judicial appointments;
    postal appointments,
    congressional involvement;
    senatorial courtesy
presidential signing statements, 5,
    178–179, 265n55
presidents
  appointment powers, 38–39, 115–116
  domination of pre-nomination
    process, 5, 38–39, 138–140, 142,
    169
  efforts to be nonpartisan, 40, 42, 43,
    45, 48
  informal limits on appointment
    powers, 132, 180–181
  nomination power, 38–39, 132, 169
  objections to limits on appointment
    power, 178–179, 265n55
  political use of appointments, 64–66,
    135, 172–173
  selection of nominees supporting
    policies, 33, 47, 48, 51, 68, 97
  See also executive branch; and specific
    presidents
Preston, William C., 65
Prince, L. Bradford, 99–100
Proffit, George H., 65, 215n153
Pryor, Mark, 165, 167, 261n193
Public Works Administration (PWA),
    137
Pugh, James Lawrence, 115
PWA. See Public Works Administration

Quay, Matthew, 119, 127, 180

Radical Republicans, 81, 83, 223n142
Ramsey, Alexander, 82, 90
Ramspect-O'Mahoney Act of 1938, 136

Ramstad, Jim, 161
Randolph, Edmund, 13, 15, 31
Readjuster Party, 111, 162, 233–234n46
Reagan, Ronald
   administration, 150–153
   as California governor, 145
   pre-nomination process, 150–153,
      174
   removal of officeholders, 151
Reconstruction, 80–81, 83, 84, 223n142
Redfield, Herman J., 75
Reed, David, 134
Reed, Thomas, 119
Reedy, George, 175
referee system, postal appointments,
    121–122, 173
Rehnquist, William, 167
Reid, Harry, 167
Rell, Jodi, 161
Remini, Robert V., 45, 51–52, 54
removal of officeholders
   by J. Adams, 33–34
   by J. Q. Adams, 43
   by Arthur, 110
   by Buchanan, 76–77
   by Bush II, 160
   by Carter, 148–149
   during Civil War, 89
   by Cleveland, 112, 113–116
   conflicts with Congress, 51–52
   congressional concurrence, 51–52
   congressional influence, 54, 113–116
   criticisms of, 56, 85
   development of custom, 33,
      206–207n10
   by Fillmore, 72, 73, 218n57
   by Grant, 87
   by B. Harrison, 118
   by W. H. Harrison, 59, 60, 214n145
   by Hayes, 95
   by Jackson, 48–49, 51–52, 53, 55,
      206–207n10, 207nn11, 15
   by Jefferson, 33, 36
   by A. Johnson, 81, 83
   limited number by presidents of
      same party as predecessor, 37, 38,
      40
   by Lincoln, 79
   by Madison, 38, 39
   party power changes and, 36, 55–56,
      59, 60, 68, 79, 113–116, 118
   of political opponents, 48–49,
      76–77

   in Post Office, 71, 116, 118, 143–144,
      209n60
   presidential powers, 51–52
   by Reagan, 151, 154
   by Taylor, 71
   by Tyler, 63–64, 214n145
   by Van Buren, 55–56, 209n59
   See also Tenure of Office Act
Republican National Committee,
    138–139
Republican Party
   African Americans, 98, 127, 129–130,
      228n90
   control of Congress after 1994, 158
   dominance of executive branch, 86,
      104
   former Whigs, 73
   "lily-white" movement, 130
   rise of, 67, 73, 76, 78
   in South, 98, 111, 127, 129–130,
      228nn81, 90
   unity during Civil War, 78–79
Republican Party, factions
   in Hayes administration, 98–99
   in Massachusetts, 88, 173
   Mugwumps, 111, 112, 117–118,
      229n94, 234n53
   Radicals, 81, 83, 223n142
   See also Half-Breed Republicans;
      Stalwart Republicans
Republican Party, Jeffersonian
   dominance, 37, 39–40, 46, 47
   factions, 41, 43, 44, 203n111, 204n125
   formation of party, 34
   Jefferson's appointments of
      members, 36
   members of Congress, 37, 38
   rise of, 35
republican principles
   checks and balances, 2, 169, 170, 186,
      187–188
   in Constitution, 1, 186
   legislative role as representatives of
      people, 170, 182
   majority rule, 2, 176
   minority rights, 2, 175–176
   shared power, 183, 187
Republicans, National, 43, 44, 47
Richards, Ann, 157
Riegle, Donald W., Jr., 148
Roberts, John G., 167
Roberts, Jonathan, 64
Robertson, William H., 102–103, 110

Robinson, James K., 148
Rodino, Peter W., Jr., 148–149
Rogers, William P., 142–143
Romer, Roy, 173
Romney, Mitt, 161
Roosevelt, Franklin D.
    administration, 135–137
    appointments rejected by Senate,
        135, 245nn88, 96
    New Deal agencies, 136–137
    political use of appointments, 135
    pre-nomination process, 135–137,
        244n87, 245n88
    relations with Congress, 135
    supporters, 244n86
Roosevelt, Theodore
    administration, 127–128
    as civil service commissioner, 118
    pre-nomination process, 127–128,
        185–186
Roosevelt, Theodore, Sr., 99–100,
    229n109
Rose, Jonathan, 152, 153
rotation of officeholders, 47, 48, 49,
    55–56, 85, 207n11. See also
    removal of officeholders
Rudman, Warren, 156
    rule of three (highest examination
        scores), 107, 108, 132–133, 136,
        179, 232n20
Russell, Richard, 141
Rutland, Robert Allen, 37–38, 40
Rutledge, John, 13

Sageser, Adelbert Bower, 74
Saltonstall, Leverett, 118
Sanford, Nathan, 50
Santorum, Rick, 159
Sarbanes, Paul, 148, 149
Sargent, John G., 133
Sawyer, Philetus, 110, 121
Schlesinger, Arthur, Jr., 65
Schmults, Edward C., 150
Schofield, John M., 84
Schumer, Charles, 162, 163, 164, 166
Schurz, Carl, 94, 96–97
Scott, William L., 145
Scott, Winfield, 61, 74, 219n65
Seagrove, James, 25–26
Semple, James, 68
Senate
    advice-and-consent role, 2, 16,
        17–20, 52–53, 166, 169, 170, 189

changing party control, 165, 166
Commerce Committee, 99, 100
filibusters, 165–166, 175–176,
    261nn186, 188
Finance Committee, 171
floor votes on judicial nominations
    controversy, 2, 166
Gang of Fourteen, 166, 167, 261n193
mechanisms for delaying
    nominations, 153, 155, 164–165,
    174, 175–176
minority power, 175–176
"nuclear option," 166
public misunderstandings of
    appointment power, 32
roles, 187–188
See also pre-nomination process,
    congressional role
Senate Judiciary Committee
    adverse reports on Supreme Court
        nominees, 87
    blocked or delayed nominations,
        128, 145
    blue slip procedures, 158, 159,
        164–165, 175, 176, 261n182
    chairmen, 140, 147, 152–153, 155,
        158, 165, 171, 172
    civil service reform bills, 89, 90
    inquiries into removals, 114–115
    See also judicial appointments
senatorial courtesy
    in Cleveland administration, 124
    early examples, 24–27, 30
    effects of ignoring, 169, 172, 237n120
    establishment of custom, 18, 27
    extended to House members, 82
    in Ford administration, 145
    in Hayes administration, 100
    ignored by presidents, 128, 169,
        174–176
    in A. Johnson administration, 81–82
    in L. Johnson administration,
        140–142
    judicial nominations, 140–142, 145,
        149–150, 157, 159, 160–161, 165,
        181
    in Lincoln administration, 79, 80
    as mechanism to force consultation,
        23
    military appointments and, 30
    origins of custom, 23–24
    postal appointments, 82, 110
    presidents' views, 120

role of home-state senators, 30–31,
    131–132, 133, 157, 169
Supreme Court nominees, 124
in Taft administration, 172
senators
    holds on nominations, 153, 155, 174,
        176, 263–264n30
    merit selection commissions, 148,
        159
    patronage, 130, 131
    presence for confirmation votes on
        supported nominees, 82
Sensenbrenner, James, 163
separation of powers, 13, 91, 108, 170,
    183
Seward, William H., 61, 72, 73, 80,
    221n110
Seymour, Horatio, 86, 224n1
Shaw, Clay, 161, 173
Shepard, Edward M., 55
Sherman, John, 82, 91, 94, 97, 104, 110,
    121
Sherman, Roger, 14, 15, 20–21, 186–187
Sherman Silver Purchase Act of 1890,
    124–125, 239n153
Shields, James, 76
signing statements. See presidential
    signing statements
Simmons, William A., 88
Skaggs, David, 173
slavery, 76, 77–78, 221n107
Slidell, John, 75, 77, 220n94
Slotnick, Elliot, 158
Smith, John Speed, 48
Smith, Nathan, 48
Smith, Robert, 38
Smith, Samuel, 38
Smith, Theodore Clarke, 104
Smith, Truman, 72
Smith, William French, 150–151
Snow, George C., 82
Socolofsky, Homer E., 119
Softshells, 75, 77, 219–220n77
Soule, Pierre, 75
Souter, David H., 156
southern states
    carpetbag governments, 98, 127,
        228n90
    Reconstruction, 80–81, 83, 84,
        223n142
    Republican Party, 98, 111, 127,
        129–130, 228nn81, 90
Specter, Arlen, 159, 161–162

Spencer, George E., 97, 228n81
Spencer, John C., 64
Spencer, Samuel, 17–18
Spetter, Allan B., 119
spoils system
    apogee, 67
    development in Jackson
        administration, 47–55
    efforts to eliminate, 106–107, 182
    New Deal era, 136–137
    survival, 113
    See also civil service reforms;
        patronage; removal of
        officeholders; rotation of
        officeholders
Spooner, John C., 110, 121
Sprague, William, 79–80
Sproat, John G., 181
Stabenow, Debbie, 165
Stalwart Republicans
    conflict with Hayes, 96, 99
    demise, 234n52
    Garfield and, 102
    influence on appointments, 88–89,
        94, 98, 173, 233n34
    power in Congress, 94
    public view of factional conflict, 105
    support of third term for Grant, 101
    See also Arthur, Chester A.
Stanbery, Henry, 84
Stanford, Leland, 121
Stanton, Edwin M., 83, 84
state constitutions, appointment
    powers, 12–13, 21
State Department
    nominees for secretary, 38, 96
    officeholders, 74, 142–143
state ratification conventions, 16–19, 21
states
    governors, 31, 145, 151, 154, 157,
        161, 173
    judicial selection commissions, 158,
        159, 161, 173
    party leaders, 134, 136, 138, 139, 154,
        161
    representation in Senate, 30
Stennis, John C., 149, 172
Stevens, Ted, 145
Stevens, Thaddeus, 83
Stewart, William M., 119
Stokes, John W., 81
Stone, Richard, 145
Summit, Stuart, 153

Sumner, Charles, 81, 88, 173, 224n4
Supreme Court
    on bankruptcy law, 153
    chief justices, 35, 167
    INS v. Chadha, 4
    Myers v. United States, 178
Supreme Court justice nominees
    of Bush I, 156
    of Bush II, 166–167
    of Cleveland, 124
    of Clinton, 158
    of Grant, 87
    of Jackson, 45
    of Lyndon Johnson, 141
    of Polk, 68
    of Reagan, 156
    rejected by Senate, 124, 141, 156
    senatorial courtesy and, 30
    of Washington, 30, 32
Swanstrom, Robert, 32
Swartwout, Samuel, 50, 58
Swayne, Noah, 208n27

Taft, Robert A., 138, 180, 246n115
Taft, William Howard
    administration, 128–130
    blacks excluded from office,
        129–130, 242n42
    pre-nomination process, 128–130,
        162, 172, 173–174
Tait, John, 158
Tallmadge, James, 44
Tallmadge, Nathaniel P., 58, 60, 65
Tammany Hall, 50, 58–59, 77, 111,
    207n23, 211n89
Taney, Roger B., 51
Taylor, James, 17, 18
Taylor, Zachary
    administration, 71–72
    appointments rejected by Fillmore,
        72–73
    cabinet, 71–72
    nonpartisan policy, 71
    personality, 217–218n38
    pre-nomination process, 67, 73
    removal of officeholders, 71
Teague, Olin, 142
Teller, Henry M., 121
Tenure of Office Act of 1820 (Four Years
    Act), 42–43
Tenure of Office Act of 1867, 83–85,
    86–87, 113, 114, 116, 224nn4–5
textualism, 4, 185, 186, 188–189, 192n8

Thoman, Leroy D., 108
Thomas, Francis, 54
Thomas, Jesse Burgess, 41
Thomas, Lorenzo, 84
Thornberry, Homer, 141
Thornburgh, Dick, 155–156
three-name rule, 152, 154–155, 161
Thurmond, Strom, 150, 152–153, 160,
    161
Tilden, Samuel J., 95
Tompkins, Daniel D., 40, 44
Townsend, E. D., 84
Townsend, John Gillis, Jr., 134
Treasury Department
    clerks removed, 97
    secretaries removed, 51–52, 53
    See also collector positions
Trefousse, Hans L., 81, 84
Truman, Harry S
    administration, 137–138
    appointments rejected by Senate,
        137, 246n109
    civil service reform proposals, 138
    pre-nomination process, 137
Trumbull, Lyman, 89–90, 91–93, 94, 106,
    181
Tunney, John, 143
Tweed, William, 87
two-party systems. *See* political parties
Tyler, John
    administration, 62–66
    cabinet, 63, 64, 214n136
    consultation with Congress, 62–63,
        65–66
    efforts to form third party through
        appointments, 64–66, 172
    lack of party affiliation, 62–63, 64,
        65, 214n128
    nominations of Harrison nominees,
        64, 213nn119, 121, 126
    nominees rejected by Senate, 65–66,
        215n153
    pre-nomination process, 62–63,
        64–66
    removal of officeholders, 63–64,
        214n145
    as vice president, 62, 214n128

unitary executive school, 5, 182–185, 188
U.S. attorneys
    Bush II early replacements, 160
    Carter appointments and removals,
        148–149

congressional influence on
appointments, 122, 153–154, 157,
160, 164
political considerations in
appointments, 154, 182
qualifications, 177–178
Reagan appointments and removals,
151, 154
U.S. marshals
congressional influence on
appointments, 122, 133–134
proposed civil service protection, 138
U.S. Patent and Trademark Office, 177

Van Buren, Martin
administration, 55–59
Albany Regency and, 40, 56, 58, 59,
203n111, 211n94
cabinet, 57–58
consultation with congressmen,
56–59
leadership of faction, 69
on Monroe's fusion policy, 40
pre-nomination process, 56–59
re-election defeat, 59
removal of officeholders, 55–56,
209n59
as secretary of state, 50
Van Buren, Smith, 69
Van Rensselaer, Solomon, 40, 41, 55–56,
61, 204n117, 209n60, 213nn116,
118–19
Van Riper, Paul P., 108, 113, 125
Vest, George G., 116
Vilas, William F., 116
Virginia, Readjuster Party, 111, 162,
233–234n46
Voorhees, Daniel W., 125

Wade, Benjamin F., 82
Wall, Marvin, 147
Wanamaker, John, 121
War Department, 83, 84
Warner, John, 152, 160, 261n193
War of 1812, 61, 209n60
Washington, Benjamin F., 77
Washington, Booker T., 242n42
Washington, George
administration, 31–33
cabinet, 33
negotiations with Senate, 27–29
nominations, 24–27, 30, 31
on postal appointments, 31

pre-nomination process, 27–29,
31–33, 183–184
recommended military
appointments for Adams, 34
selection of nominees supporting
policies, 33, 35
unitary executive and, 183–184
written communications with
Congress, 27–29
Washington Post, 143, 149, 167
Wayne, Anthony, 25–26
Webster, Daniel
as secretary of state, 59–60, 61, 62,
63, 213n121, 214n136
as senator, 72
Weed, Thurlow, 44, 61, 79
Welch, Richard E., Jr., 110, 123
Weld, William, 154
Welles, Gideon, 79, 87
Wells, Daniel, Jr., 75
Wellstone, Paul, 157
Wetmore, Robert C., 61
Whichard, Willis R., 30
Whig Party
demise, 67, 73
distrust of Tyler, 64
divisions, 72, 73
former Democrats, 58, 62, 64
as national party, 211n95
in New York, 58, 60, 61
officeholders removed, 68
officeseekers, 60
presidential candidates, 59, 61, 71, 74
senators, 72
view of shared powers, 211n95
White, Alexander, 170
White, Leonard D., 34, 50
Wilkinson, Reuben, 25, 26
Williams, George, 90–91
Williams, Harrison A., Jr., 148–149
Williamson, Hugh, 33
Wilson, James, 13, 14, 16, 17
Wilson, Pete, 152, 154
Wilson, Woodrow
administration, 131–132
pre-nomination process, 131–132,
162, 242n53, 243n59
Winberry, Charles, 149
Wingate, Paine, 32
Wirt, William, 41, 92
Wise, Henry A., 54, 65, 215n153
Wofford, Harris, 157, 159
Wolcott, Edward O., 121

Wolf, George, 58, 210n79
Worthington, Roland, 110
Wright, Silas, Jr., 58, 59, 65, 69–70,
    203n111, 217n20
Wyden, Ron, 263–264n30
Wythe, George, 31

Yates, Richard, 90
Yoo, Christopher S., 183, 184
Yoo, John C., 183
Young, C. W. Bill, 161, 173

Zelizer, Julian E., 9